FLASHBACKS

By John A. Williams

FLASHBACKS

A Twenty-Year Diary
of Article Writing

John A. Williams

ANCHOR PRESS/DOUBLEDAY

Garden City, New York

1973

PS
3573
I4495
F5
1973

Portions of the general introduction first appeared as "Author vs. Editor" in the February/March 1972 issue of the Authors Guild Bulletin.

"The New York State Fair" first appeared in the Syracuse *Post-Standard* in 1953.

"Sex in Black and White" first appeared in the September 1963 issue of *Cavalier*.

"This Is My Country Too," Parts I and II, first appeared in the August and September 1964 issues of *Holiday*.

"Three Negro Families" first appeared as "The Negro: Three Families" in the March 1967 issue of *Holiday*.

"The Great White Whore" first appeared in *Nickel Review* in 1969.

"An Afro-American Looks at South Africa" first appeared in *Vista* in 1969.

"Subject: Charles Parker" and "Dick Gregory: Desegregated Comic" first appeared in *Swank* in 1961.

"Smalls Paradise" first appeared in the November 1963 issue of *Cavalier*.

"Never Before or Since" first appeared in the April 25, 1965 issue of *New York*, the Sunday *Herald Tribune* magazine.

"My Man Himes: An Interview with Chester Himes" first appeared in AMISTAD I, edited by John A. Williams and Charles F. Harris, Random House (New York, 1970), pp. 25–91.

"We Regret to Inform You That" first appeared in the December 1962 issue of *Nugget*.

"Black Man in Europe" first appeared in the January 1967 issue of *Holiday*.

"This Is My Country Too: A Pessimistic Postscript" first appeared in the June 1967 issue of *Holiday*.

"Time and Tide: The Roots of Black Awareness" first appeared in Jack Agueros, et al., edited by Thomas Wheeler, *The Immigrant Experience: The Anguish of Becoming an American*, The Dial Press (New York, 1971).

"Their Country Too" first appeared in the *Yardbird Reader*, Vol. I, published in 1972, Copyright © 1972 by Yardbird Publishing Company.

ISBN: 0-385-09452-3
Library of Congress Catalog Card Number 72-84954
Copyright © 1972, 1973 by John A. Williams
All Rights Reserved
Printed in the United States of America
First Edition

This book is dedicated to *E. J. Jones, Dennis Lynds, George* and *Vivian Patterson, Wendell J. Roye, Gene Williams* and *Mrs. Lee Esther Williams* for sharing other days past, but not forgotten.

CONTENTS

SECTION III: PERSONALS

FLASHBACKS

GENERAL INTRODUCTION

I

J. Luther Sylvan!

A thin man with a voice in the middle registers, Mr. Sylvan looked a little like a dusky young John Barrymore. He wore his felt hats brim down at the side; beneath them his hair was long—for the time and place—and tightly waved. We all wished we had waves in our hair like Mr. Sylvan. His Van Dyke beard seemed to go well with his face; it was a part of him, like his hats, like his soft voice.

Mr. Sylvan was editor and publisher of the *Progressive Herald*, a black weekly newspaper in Syracuse that served other black communities throughout central New York state. J. Luther Sylvan lived in a large red brick building on East Fayette Street at the time I became aware of him, his paper, and felt some strange stirrings within myself about words and writing; he'd probably lived elsewhere when I was younger. The large black and gold sign on the side of the East Fayette Street building told you that this was also the office of the *Progressive Herald*, and if you knew anything about Syracuse you knew that Mr. Sylvan, a Democrat, and therefore a lamb back then, was in a den of vicious Republican lions; Onondaga County has always been so and impossibly conservative as well, but then the two always seem to go together.

Like *Jet* magazine today, everyone sneered at the *PH*—but they bought it. Its tabloid format, varying from four to six and on rare occasions eight pages, contained local news as it affected Syracuse Negroes, general black news culled from the large black weeklies, a society section, run by Mrs. Sylvan, and a gossip column called at one time "The Periscope." This last was written by a former high school track star, Emmanuel Henderson, fondly known by nearly everyone as Emo. Many of the people who sneered at the *PH* could be seen plying Emo with drinks on weekends in Little Harlem, Whitey's, Claude's, The Club, Homer's and Hank's.

Most papers of this kind are often badly smudged or underinked from letter press printing. And there was the widespread assumption that Mr. Sylvan was not a rich man, no matter how Barrymoreishly he dressed. On the other hand, he could not be a poor man—no one, no matter how mean his publication—could be. We thought.

One day, I think it was shortly after I'd been discharged from the Navy, I called on Mr. Sylvan to ask if I could write for his paper. The office was a part of his flat. Piles of *PH*s rose from floor to ceiling and the place reeked of newsprint and stale paper. Also like most papers of that genre, the need for people to hustle ads to place in the paper far exceeded the need for writers. I don't remember what happened at that meeting, but somehow I did come to write for the paper, covering visiting black bands or white bands with black members and the annual Syracuse Civic Lenten Services, when black clergymen like Shelby Rooks came to deliver sermons.

At about the same time on a trip to Chicago I'd met Enoch Waters; Waters, a former World War II correspondent, was editor of the Chicago *Defender*. I persuaded him to take me on as a stringer in Syracuse. Baseball had opened up to blacks then, Jackie Robinson being the lone black flash in the International League, playing for the Montreal Royals. The Syracuse Chiefs were in the same league, so Robinson came to town often enough, followed soon by Vic Power and Elston Howard. I also sent in nonsports pieces.

The Associated Negro Press Association, run by the late Claude Barnett, was also located in Chicago, and from time to time I wrote pieces for him which were then used by black papers.

The *Progressive Herald*, Chicago *Defender* and the National Negro Press Association had two things in common. The first was that they didn't pay, although Messrs. Sylvan, Waters and

Barnett talked vaguely of a "space rate" basis. The second was that they were not terribly critical in the sense that they merely edited your copy, but didn't tell you why or how to improve the quality and content of your pieces. Naturally, they ran my stories without byline.

In the winter of 1951, when I was trying desperately to find some place to land when I came out of the Graduate School at Syracuse University, I turned to *Ebony*. Black students didn't have to be told that they were *not* going to wind up on white radio stations or white newspapers. John H. Johnson, the publisher asked me to do an article on the relationship between the university and the Negroes in the city, as a kind of a test. I was fired up; there was little doubt in my mind that I was going to give him a socko piece. My attitude did much to shore up the sagging confidence that my wife had in me and writing. I didn't much blame her; we had a son going on three and she was three months pregnant with what turned out to be another boy. For five years it'd been classes and part-time jobs, summer jobs; the GI bill and the 52–20 club. She was sick of it and so was I.

I probed through every facet of the university and the community and found a great deal of interesting material; I badgered the Chancellor half to death for his views. I interviewed old Syracusans and newcomers, one of them being the first black man on the SU faculty in the department of sociology, Charles V. Willie, now Dr. Willie and vice-president in charge of student affairs.

I sent the article together with pictures to Johnson. Silence, long silence. Another letter, slightly more desperate in tone, and another. Silence. Finally, I put together what little money we had, borrowed twenty dollars and took a Greyhound bus to Chicago where I knew I could stay with relatives. I called Johnson and managed to get an appointment, and then I called Dr. Ellsworth Hasbrouck about whom I've written more elsewhere. (He figured prominently in the article I did for Johnson, having been booted out of the SU medical school by its director, Herman G. Weiskotten, for no other reason than being black.) I told Hasbrouck why I was there and he offered to intercede for me, since he knew Johnson and had examined many of his policyholders when Johnson was an insurance man. For the record I can only say that then I didn't know how things worked, and I refused his help. In retrospect, I can also say I'm glad I did.

But when I emerged from Johnson's office, after a five-minute conference, I wasn't so sure. Johnson told me that he'd decided to give me the five minutes because I'd come from so far away. As far as the article was concerned, he didn't like the writing; I should write like Dan Burley, he said, whose work I'd read in the columns of the *Amsterdam News*. That was that. Before me lay the ride back on the cold bus, a wife with a bellyful of child and an I-told-you-so look, and a place back coremaking at the foundry where I'd worked summers. I wasn't so sure about the writing, but I knew I was damned good at my job in the foundry, one of the best coremakers to come down the pike. That knowledge, however comforting those summers when I knew that September would find me back in class, this time out seemed hollow.

II

It was a long time from the foundry to this autumn day. Gray hairs pepper my head and people always comment on how gray my beard is getting. My older sons toss off their martinis with the super-cool of their generation, and one day my daughter-in-law will blossom in her belly and I'll be a grandfather. I've written all that time and if I've ever come to one single, positive conclusion it is that writing articles is no sane way for a man to make his living. Article Writing Highway is littered with wrecks, maimed and dead.

Article writing is a craft or a profession that brings the writer into direct confrontation with his editor; this is more true in this genre of writing than it could ever be in writing books, novels or nonfiction. Book editors are the repositories of power; their judgments are made out of their own understanding of the writer they may be working with and their own experiences. Magazine editors, with a few exceptions, are filters. They are judges, too, but their function mainly is to filter. During the days of gladiatorial combat in Rome, the judges were the people who, after glancing at the emperor for the cue, gave the sign that told the crowds whether a fallen gladiator should live or die; thumbs down and he'd had it.

The magazine editor carries out the wishes of his emperor. Who's the emperor? The readers of his magazine. The editor stands between the writer and the reader; he decides what is good for the reader and that, of course, must be good for the magazine. He has been hired to do exactly that job, and if he fails, he might find himself confined to Editors' Purgatory, which is where former editors try to write articles. The number of former editors who've survived this particular corner of purgatory is almost nonexistent. It is far wiser and perhaps even easier to move on to edit another magazine.

From many angles magazine editors seem pretty much like other people; a few are. But most are a breed apart. To be sure many are good drinkers, and love their wives and hate their bosses. However, once behind his desk he becomes the filterer, the protector; he knows what his readers want, and he demands, sometimes subtly, sometimes not, that you provide them with what they've always found palatable. If the taste is to be changed, it is to be changed in very slight degree, and *he* must be the carpenter who measures how great that degree shall be. He couldn't afford to slip even a millimeter.

Generally there are two ways in which the popular magazines obtain their material. The first is by devising a story idea within the magazine itself. The editors then select a writer to do the article. The second method for gathering material is to call in writers they know, or some the editors wish to know better, and ask them for ideas that can be worked up into pieces. There is a third way, but it is seldom used, and it is utilizing material that's come in unsolicited, or, as they say, "over the transom."

Caskie Stinnett, editor of *Travel & Leisure* and formerly travel editor and editor in chief of *Holiday*, whom I'll discuss later on, echoes magazine editors everywhere when he says: "I have long since learned to expect nothing from the mails and very little in the random submissions from agents." When a magazine editor finds a writer who is good for his magazine and good for its readers, the writer can count on an association of several months and even years.

These writers are white; and at the top of the heap they command big fees and expenses. Some earn every penny; others don't. The white article writer's range is practically unlimited. He writes about white people, brown, black, yellow people; space shots, presidents. Everything. There are no barriers and, in fact, a number of white writers have become specialists in writing about people who are not white—to the growing anger of a rapidly increasing number of nonwhite writers. There are two reasons for that anger, the first being at the arrogance of most white writers to in the first place undertake to delineate what they know so little of. And, second, there is both a subconscious and a calculated effrontery in dismissing, if even considering, the possibility that a nonwhite writer might be able to turn in a better piece on the subject.

The very best of the white writers move in a rarefied atmosphere, writing about those close to the fulcrum of power, or the most popular entertainers of the day; sometimes the two are one and the same. Often such journalistic associations lead to certain tenuous friendships. For some writers I've known, becoming friends with the mighty far outranked producing the article that got them together in the first place. There is a poison in such relationships.

When a writer's considerations are primarily based on going, being and doing first class, his creative effort necessarily becomes a secondary thing. I've seen it happen to more than one white writer. Never to a black writer who doesn't get the opportunity—or rarely—to become tainted or blunted or ineffective. Magazine editors simply do not conceive of black writers as even being in the same ballpark with white writers.

There exists a few magazine editors who try to move out ahead of current history. But most allow themselves to be overtaken by tidal waves of current problems and action and reaction to them. Twenty years ago there were few editors who considered what we call the black experience. Today the editors sluggishly seek out black writers on the rare occasions when they're willing to publish their work, only to give their readers a peek at black life. They've never wanted the gut view of black America; they still don't. There is not a single black article writer living today who has the stature or reputation of Aubrey Menon, Richard Gehman, Steve Birmingham, Paul Good or Thomas B. Morgan. It is ridiculous to assume this is so because black writers are without talent or perception.

Julius Lester writes on occasion for *Evergreen Review*, Alex Haley produces regularly for *Reader's Digest;* James Alan McPherson does his thing for *Atlantic Monthly*. Ishmael Reed, Claude Brown and others often come up with one-shot assignments for the mass circulation magazines, but almost invariably their articles are never published. Even should they publish their articles black writers will have written "black"; they will not have written, for example, articles on the President; and rarely articles on sports where there are so many black participants. They are as confined in their subject matter as inmates in Attica.

III

I've written about the editor being a filter, a protector, between the writer and the reader. The editor also is a molder of opinion. Therefore, he protects the reader from ideas that do not coincide with his own or those of his publisher for whom he works. His ideas or his publisher's are what's passed on to the public, which, just as it wordlessly and spinelessly accepts the glittering junk from Detroit, accepts what the editor has caused to be delivered to his door or placed on the newsstand nearest his home.

I know few magazine editors and fewer magazine publishers who are genuinely concerned with eliminating racism in all its myriad forms from the American way of life. I don't have to run down the record, because it speaks for itself, and everyone in the field of article writing knows it. In fact, they would be shocked beyond belief if this were not the case.

Clearly, in this role the magazine editor has far more influence than the book editor, who's lucky if his author's work reaches 15,000 people; the magazine editor is dealing with hundreds of thousands of readers. And since nonwhites and poor whites are considered hardly more than vermin on the American scene, editors treat their writer representatives like the dirt from which they believe the vermin spring.

I suppose Messrs. Sylvan, Waters and Barnett could have told me all this long ago if they'd had the least suspicion that I'd somehow continue writing. For black folks know many things they don't talk about or, if forced to, talk around. For example, black writers are uneasily aware of the large numbers of white editors from the South who run the mass circulation magazines in New York. Many are style-setters. If one of their publications runs a feature by a black writer, then other magazines might. Magazines are like fashion designers; if a style works, it's copied; if a style is boycotted by a style-setter, then everybody boycotts. I don't wish to give transplanted southern editors an undue amount of power here. I've known a couple who were fine men and good editors. The fact is, editors from the South run just about neck and neck with guys who've never been south of Central Park.

The economics of the magazine publishing business promises us that things will not become better for black writers. There were more publications ten years ago than there are today, and chances are that with the prohibitive costs of mailing being socked to the magazines, there may be ten fewer next year. As I write this introduction, for example, there are still repercussions from the announcement that *Look* has folded. (Most *Look* articles were done by members of its staff, not free-lance people. There were two black editors on the staff; one had been there seventeen years.)

In short, the easygoing racism so pervasive in the magazine

publishing industry, plus the crushing weight of economic considerations, has severely limited the opportunity for a nonwhite writer to break into the field. There have been clues, on the other hand, that white magazine publishers see some sign of survival in the black communities. At least one was discovered behind the scenes trying to manipulate and gain control of a black woman's publication. And one or two "black" magazines are steady making money for white owners.

IV

This collection of twenty-four articles is about being a black writer in the U.S. The headnote to each supplies some of the backstage action which should give platform to the articles themselves. Some of them went unpublished and the headnotes will give my version of why. Two or three white writers for mass circulation magazines suggested me to their editors for possible assignments. In every case where this happened, the editors and I reached an impasse—none of my ideas were any good, they said, and they couldn't come up with any.

The articles here cover a period from the early 1950s to 1971. They helped, when I was paid for them, to keep the wolf from the door. More than that, researching and writing them gave me ideas and material which in some form or other went into my novels. Even if cheaply purchased by some magazines, things were rather balanced out in novels by the utilization of magazine ideas.

One agent I had protested that swinging back and forth between fiction and articles was dangerous, but I like the change of pace; working in one field gives you good moves for another, not to mention the material and ideas available just by being *out there*, rather than staying shut up in your novelist's nook.

Six articles included here are about myself, so I should explain why. Editors, when handling black writers, generally have insisted on the personal approach, the "I" piece. Of course other writers have employed this approach as well, the difference be-

ing that they were not required to examine *themselves* in varying situations. For black writers the approach has been, as
though suggested by editors, "Bleed for me, baby." Like other
black writers, I've done my share of articles like this. There'll be
no more. They all turn out to be the same, or sounding the same.
From the beginning I've had an aversion to bleeding or hurting
in public, but I did it because I wanted to eat and care for my
family. That's not an apology, just a statement. There were many
other things I didn't do, hunger and family be damned.

Undoubtedly bitternesses will be found in many of the articles.
I don't apologize for that either, for learning what one *must*
learn to survive in a journalist's-novelist's world is an embittering
process of which even white writers speak with anger.

There were times when I swore I'd never write another article, but then, later, I've accepted commissions. There are magazines I'd never write for again, even if they paid a million dollars a word; even if the editors promised not to touch a line. But
if they were willing to pay a million dollars a word, they'd
surely be paying white writers *two* million dollars per word.
I've had many an article rejected after being commissioned to
do it.

A couple of years ago while visiting Syracuse to give a talk,
I looked out and saw Mr. J. Luther and Mrs. Sylvan in the
audience. I was moved by their presence, their tender claim on
my past. I don't know what's happened to Enoch Waters. Claude
Barnett is dead; lingering long with a stroke, he finally went, but
not before I saw him in his hospital bed unable to talk, staring
out of his prison of illness with eyes only slightly clouded.

I'd like to think that this collection will do for other youngsters
what they were trying to do for me, although they were incom-
plete. They did listen. They did give me purpose and some opportunity. If they didn't know specifically what a young black
writer would face working as a free-lance for white publications,
they knew generally. The specifics, as I've set them down, only
pick up where Messrs. Sylvan, Waters and Barnett left off;
there is a continuity.

SECTION I

Topicalities

THE NEW YORK STATE FAIR

I WROTE *this article which appeared in the Syracuse* Post-Stand-*ard Sunday, September 13, 1953, while I was a part-time copy-writer with Doug Johnson Associates, a public relations firm. DJA had the New York State Fair account. This piece is one of my oldest I could resurrect; Doug Johnson cleaned out his files to get it for me.*

Other pieces, including those I wrote for Sylvan, Waters and Barnett, were in a scrapbook that I threw away on one of the numerous occasions when I decided to give up writing and wanted nothing around to remind me of how much I'd already done.

The fair continues, although I don't know who handles the account. Doug Johnson is now associated with an advertising firm—Barlow-Johnson—and is still in Syracuse, where I've seen him on infrequent visits. There's nothing I can say about the piece; it is what it is. Of more interest perhaps, is how I came to be associated with DJA.

I was working full-time with the Onondaga County Depart-ment of Public Welfare, first as a caseworker, and then as a children's worker in Children's Protective Service. I was moon-lighting, "driving" an elevator in the Loew Building in down-town Syracuse at night. Radio station WAGE was located there, and Doug was an official of it. The offices of the Syracuse Com-munity Chest were also there. Doug and another man, Wink Berman, now dead (tennis) were frequent passengers. I'd taken a sequence in radio writing in college, and so, one night I put it to Wink who was more approachable than Doug, that I'd like to do some part-time writing for WAGE. He said he'd speak to Doug.

About four days later I reported to Hank Rosso, the big man at DJA, and I had myself a part-time job as a copywriter. The offices then were on East Fayette Street, half a block from the Post-Standard, but we moved soon after to the top floor of the Syracuse Hotel. I worked for over a year with DJA on The March of Dimes, Civilian Defense, New York State Fair and other accounts I no longer remember.

Hank Rosso, I hear, is now located in San Francisco; Pete Johnson, Doug's younger brother, died suddenly; another guy, a quiet intellectual, now owns a country music station in Syracuse.

Doug Johnson spoiled me. His was the only white firm I ever approached and was employed by without the usual racist non-sense. I asked for a job, walked in and got it, all without fanfare or condescension; that doesn't happen often, not even today. As for WAGE, DJA was doing work for it, too, so it didn't matter that I wound up doing PR instead of radio writing.

T HE 107th New York State Fair, which closed last night, has a history as dramatic as that of the little town that changed its name three times before adopting its present name—Syracuse.

The imposing and pillared structures at the fairgrounds, the gaudy midway with its flashing lights and feverish music; the exhibitions themselves all have roots as far back as 1819 when the state legislature appropriated $20,000 for distribution among agricultural societies. Onondaga County was eligible for $300.

Fairs came to America by way of Europe where they were first held as early as 1777. Fairs were originally neutral territories where bartering took place between warring nations in the pre-Christian era.

The Europeans placed emphasis on agriculture and that stamp is still obvious in most county and state fairs. Introduced in the United States in 1804, three fairs were held near Washington, D.C. The Columbian Exposition ran a series of five fairs in 1810.

After the 1838 reorganization of the Onondaga County Agricultural Society, which had disbanded during the years, the state legislature granted $180 to the organization, if it raised an equal amount. The society had been the sponsor of many fairs held in the district and was first created in 1819.

After a few years of jockeying, the first New York State Fair opened up in what is now Cortland Avenue in 1841. The main features were placed in the courthouse which had just recently been moved from Onondaga Hill. The area was conspicuously placed midway between the communities of Syracuse, which had been incorporated in 1828 as a city, and its rival, Salina.

In the Townsend Street area more than twenty-five freight carloads of cattle were placed which had been shipped in from the Hudson River Valley.

The stage was set. The news had gone around and the opening day arrived as hundreds of people came on foot, by horse and buggy over the corduroy roads running throughout the state. When the fair opened September 29, it was raining. The next day, the last day of the fair, it was damp, but when the final tally was made, more than 12,000 people had attended the first state fair. The biggest attraction? A plowing contest held in Onondaga Valley.

When the fair left Syracuse in 1841, it visited no less than ten cities, returning here in 1849 and 1858. A chart of the state fair itinerary, a jaunt that lasted forty-nine years, is listed below:

Albany—1842, 1850, 1859, 1871, 1873, 1876, 1880, 1885

Rochester—1843, 1851, 1862, 1864, 1868, 1874, 1877, 1883, 1887, 1889

Poughkeepsie—1844

Utica—1845, 1852, 1863, 1865, 1870, 1879, 1882, 1886

Auburn—1846

Saratoga—1847, 1853, 1866

Buffalo—1848, 1857, 1867

Syracuse—1841, 1849, 1858

New York City—1854

Elmira—1855, 1860, 1869, 1872, 1875, 1878, 1881, 1884, 1888
Watertown—1856, 1861

Returning to Syracuse in 1849 for three days, September 11,
12 and 13, the fair was held on the Wilkinson grounds in James
Street. This return marked many new features, among them, the
Ferris wheel which was designed and operated by two Syracusans for the first time.

Distinguished visitors were Horace Greeley and Henry Clay.
Yank Sullivan and Tom Hyer engaged in a boxing bout.

Imposing new structures were ready for the '49 fair. Daisy
Hall, a women's building, had been erected for female displays;
Flora's Temple, a replica of the Greek Pantheon, and Mechanics'
and Machinery Hall. Attendance figures were placed at about
15,000. The fair of 1858 opened in the Cortland Avenue site in
Syracuse. By this time most enmity between Syracuse and Salina
had disappeared and the citizens of both places united in an
effort to make the fair one of the best ever.

The newspapers, then as now, gave a full measure of support
to the exhibition, particularly the livestock competitions.

Not to be outdone, the Syracuse, Binghamton and New York
railroads announced that they would run excursions to the very
gates of the fair. Boats and more trains ran from the western
sector of the state into Syracuse.

To further entice the citizens of the state into coming to the
fair, city papers announced lodgings at low rates with free
lunches included. This custom is still very much alive, though
without the free lunches. The papers of today mark lodgings for
fairgoers with a star.

On the thirty-one-acre fair site, 300 stalls were erected for
cattle, 250 for horses and more than 200 for sheep and swine.
Floral Hall, Daisy Hall and Mechanics' Hall were dusted off and
the new Dairy and Vegetable Hall had just been completed.

The doors opened Tuesday, October 5, with big attractions
scheduled for the fairgoers. A steam plow, a bright new inven-
tion built by a man from Troy was exhibited. A "corn-husker"
from Connecticut showed Central New Yorkers how to shuck
corn with a minimum of effort.

J. G. K. Truair, proprietor of the Syracuse *Daily Journal,* and Joseph R. Williams, president of the Michigan State Agricultural College, were outstanding speakers.

Among the other notable attractions were the parade by the spick-and-span Utica Hook and Ladder company, with its demonstration of the bucket-brigade technique; the daily afternoon trotting on the pavilion course, the Indian dances each day in Mechanics' Hall and a daily minstrel show.

When the fair closed, it was estimated that more than 20,000 persons had helped surpass the total gate receipts of the previous year of the fair at Buffalo.

During the era of Lincoln and the Civil War, the fair was in full swing, jumping from one city to another and returning to Syracuse in 1858, two years before the outbreak of the war.

Perhaps the post-war feeling of consolidation invaded the state legislature. Perhaps even the members of the fair commission were weary of traveling from one extreme of the state to another for the annual event—anyway the New York State Fair began to undergo close scrutiny for the next thirty-two years.

Many questions were being raised and answered as the fair ran footloose and fancy free. What about the profits derived from horse racing? Where shall the fair be located?

The first question to be answered was about the racing profits. In 1887, the state legislature passed an act stating that funds derived from horse racing were to be turned over to the state fair commission to be used as premiums for livestock awards. By 1891 this figure had reached the proportion of $30,373.70.

As to the fixed position of the fair, by 1889 serious consideration had been given to the problem. Since Syracuse was the city most easily accessible from other parts of the state, lands were purchased by the farm commission to the northwest of the city in a move which decided that the fair should be permanently located at Syracuse.

Besides the $75,000 appropriated for the New York State Agricultural Society to erect the buildings, the funds from racing profits were also added for the development of the fairgrounds.

The decision to settle the fair at Syracuse caused some mixed feeling. The following was taken from the Syracuse Sunday *Herald*, October 9 of that year.

"The advent of the state fair was not enthusiastically welcomed by the citizens who missed the neighboring breezy Onondaga county fair with its generous management, hospitality and revenue. . . . The present year has seen the beginnings of an income to Syracuse. In this, mainly the hotels and boarding houses have gained, and year by year the older residents recall the delightful days of the old Onondaga fair with pleasure and regret at its demise."

Briefly, the first fairs held on the present fair site did not "go" too well, and maybe one of the reasons lay in such declarations.

However, there may have been other reasons. Arrangements had been made meanwhile for the Solvay Process Co. to fill in stipulated areas within a certain time. Buildings had to be constructed from many designs—buildings which would present a pleasing appearance down through the years.

By way of competition, the Chicago World's Fair of 1893 and the Columbian Exposition in 1904 were drawing an untabulated number of people whose fair interests had been first created by the New York State Fair.

Architects too attended these fairs and garnered ideas on buildings and grounds for the state fair, and thus from 1890 for about twenty years, the New York State Fair consolidated itself, explored ideas.

Typical of the ideas that poured into the fair commission was the practicability of harness racing which was submitted by Edward A. Powell, a W. Genesee Street resident who had toured the 1904 Columbian Exposition in St. Louis.

He reported that the fair excelled in all classes of horse racing except the harness. It is ironic that the New York State Fair which has been instrumental in raising harness racing to high levels has this year decided to abandon them.

The World's Fair along with the Columbian Exposition at St. Louis and fairs held in Buffalo influenced architects to lay out the classical style of the Empire Court on the fair site, another example of ideas put into use here.

Grand Circuit racing at the fair took place prior to 1901 and gained such popularity that by 1904 the Legislature appropriated $10,000 for it and said, ". . . an adequate scheme of development of the State Fair grounds and buildings."

By 1906, $51,000 was placed at the disposal of the fair commission for a new grandstand and $20,000 for additional real estate.

Racing in all forms had proved by far to be the strongest attraction and these appropriations seemed to prove the point. The first automobile race was held September 12, 1903. Special cars and professional drivers participated.

Harness racing, Grand Circuit racing and auto racing were the three attractions largely responsible for the growth of the fair during the period of consolidation.

Prices during these times were way down compared to the figures of today. Train fare was three cents a mile; lunches twenty-five cents and room and board for $1 a day.

Most unusual is the comparative admission price for the 1911 fair against this year's fair. Then admission was ninety-one cents—the fifty cents admission on advance tickets still stand for this year's fair.

As the fair grew in size and number of exhibits, it was clear that classifications would have to be set up. They were originally set up as follows:

Class I—Cattle.

Class II—Horses.

Class III—Sheep, Swine, Poultry.

Class IV—Plowing Implements.

Class V—Grain, Seed, etc.

Class VI—Domestic Manufactures.

Class VII—Paintings, Silverware, Stoves, Leather.

Class VIII—Flowers, Plants, Designs.

Although these classifications were set up during the early period when the fair was moved to Syracuse, they still stand. A few have been added, but mostly only subdivision has been needed.

The main building program of the fair which began in 1906

with the reconstruction of the grandstand, originally set up in
1901, and two comfort stations, gained momentum in 1909.

In that year the Dairy Building, the racing stables and the
State Institutions Building were built. The Liberal Arts Building
had been constructed the year before. From 1912 through 1919
the cattle, poultry and horse exhibit buildings were erected at a
total cost of $480,763.02.

The next decade saw the horse show stables, sheep and swine
buildings, the Coliseum and the Museum go up on the fair site
and during the '30s no less than 15 buildings went up. Among
them were Horticultural, Pure Foods, Farm Machinery, Boys'
and Girls' Livestock.

The Conservation annex to the State Institution Building was
the sole construction effort just before war broke out in 1941.
Two other buildings were constructed from 1942 through the
war's end; one was a blacksmith's shop, the other an electrical
repair shop, both put into operation by the Army Air Force which
moved onto the fairgrounds during the war.

The lesser building program involving smaller buildings, land-
scaping, troopers' barracks, road construction and lighting began
in 1900 and cost about $1,000,000.

Since 1900 the present fair site represents a capital invest-
ment of more than $5,000,000. Proof that building has not yet
reached an end is the new administration building, which costs
$222,000.

The Air Force moved into the fair grounds in March 1942 and
terminated its lease in September 1946. During this time no
fairs were held, and 1948 saw the first post-war fair, a limited
exposition.

The history of the New York State Fair is one that matches
the history of the city and state in agricultural and social development.

Like the city, the fair is still growing and glittering. Crowds
swarm through the buildings, around the midway each summer
beneath the Ferris wheel. They listen to the jazzy noises, buy
the candied apples and take the fair pretty much for granted—
the way most of us do.

SEX IN BLACK AND WHITE

In the fall of 1963, Cavalier *magazine billed itself as "the new magazine for the new man," but in reality it was the same old magazine for the same old man. Which is to say, that it was a girlie magazine for men who like to look at pictures of nude women.*

My agent got me together with George Dickerson, who was managing the magazine. George and I sat down to see if we could come up with an idea for a piece that would be suitable for this new image of Cavalier, *and as I remember I came up with the idea of "Sex in Black and White." At the time I was living in the Village and had been there for three or four years. I could see some changes taking place having to do with sex in black and white. I was disturbed by some of them, and I wanted to write about them.*

Lately we have come to see that one of the most conservative groups, one of the most anti-Negro groups in this nation is the Italian-American bloc. And of course Greenwich Village, just south of Washington Square Park, is heavily Italian. The Village has always been a shelter for mixed couples, and I saw them every day, especially on weekends on Eighth Street or the side streets, in the cafes. And I took a great deal of pleasure in knowing that New York did afford some kind of refuge for couples like this. But slowly and subtly the atmosphere began to change.

I was sitting in Washington Square Park one day when 3 young Italians walked up. One had a baseball bat, and he hit a black youth sitting with a white girl, without a word of warning, smack in the back of the head, and they walked off. On weekends there would be young white toughs hanging around, trying to incite blacks to battle, which they often did. Then the situation passed out of the hands of the young whites and into the hands of the older whites of the area. They began complaining of the folk-singing in Washington Square Park and how it was seeping down through the streets, and how they were sick and tired of it. But it was not the guitars or the folk-singing that they were upset about; it was the mixed couples.

And so I sat down and did this piece for George Dickerson. I don't recall that we messed around with it too much, and it remains one of the pieces that I most like.

Now the production of this piece is an example of what an agent often does. He'll get his client together with a magazine editor, and then the editor and the writer will sit around, hash up ideas, and out of that will come a story.

On this piece there was no editorial pressure and no censorship involved.

Two summers ago, citizens, rich and poor, who lived near Washington Square Park in New York's Greenwich Village, complained vigorously that the folk singers who gathered near the fountain to play guitars and sing were bawdy and disturbed the weekend peace. In the ensuing meetings with city officials, it became apparent that what was opposed was not so much folk singing as the increasing presence of mixed couples in the area, mostly Negro men and white women. This occurred near election time, and city officials reacted quite sharply to the odiousness of racial prejudice; they allowed the folk singers to continue their impromptu performances on a limited basis.

Thus, openly hostile opposition to mixed couples in New York was officially discouraged. Unofficially, however, despite the increased and increasing presence of the interracial couple, great hostility remains and with it, very often, violence. In the South, death, no longer as insanely rendered as it was during the first 40 years of the century, is the penalty for the black man foolish enough to be a partner in the affair. Sometimes, as in the case of 15-year-old Emmett Till, to merely whistle at a white woman is to invite death.

Regardless of Mississippians, other Southerners, and Northerners, the barriers between black and white, man and woman, continue to fall. We know that the black-and-white affair has been with us for a long, long time, and, therefore, more of us may be Negro (on the basis of that proverbial "one drop" of black blood) than we know. Reliable estimates actually state that perhaps 20,000,000 white Americans have at least one Negro ancestor. The late Walter White, who was head of the NAACP, once wrote that nearly every Negro in America knows of, and remains quiet about, another Negro who is "passing"—being fair enough to be taken for white.

At the outbreak of the Civil War, whose centennial we are reluctantly celebrating, there were more than a half million mulattoes among fewer than four and a half million Negroes, the result of the sexual union of white men and black women. Having created this caste group, the white men returned to it again, preferring as sexual objects the lighter-skinned Negroes. Quadroons and octaroons flourished and were given certain status. With time, they merged quietly into the protective anonymity of the Caucasian race.

Especially in Dixie, there seems to have been more fornicating than farming, and, with the lines and strains crossing in myriad directions, who knows but that this is a land so steeped in incest that it cannot bear itself nor bear to be reminded by the presence of the Negro of its sordid past. This may be the dilemma of Dixie.

But the dilemma is contagious; the entire land falls prey to it. The sight of a black man and a white woman incites to anger and blind rage. The gentle, the indifferent, the liberal quiver with fury. A recent example of this occurred when the brilliant, self-styled liberal, Norman Podhoretz, writing in *Commentary* (February 1963) gave a highly subjective view of the "Negro problem" in which he said: "The hatred I still feel for Negroes is the hardest of all the old feelings to face or admit . . . it is the most hidden and the most overlorded by the conscious attitudes into which I have succeeded in willing myself. . . . It no longer has . . . any cause or justification. . . . How, then, do I know that this hatred has never entirely disappeared? . . . I know it from the disgusting prurience that can stir in me at the sight of a mixed couple. . . ."

The black man-white woman combination carries us far beyond prurience; it carries us to anger. Although not socially approved, we see little danger in the white man-black woman duo. The white man may be accorded an extra portion of masculinity when seen with a black woman; he may be given sly smiles; male passers-by may wink at one another. "He's gone native," one might say, and the other might reply, "He likes dark meat."

What is operating here, of course, is the myth of the fantastic sexuality of the Negro woman. Somewhat altered, the myth assigns to the Jewish female more sensuality than to the Gentile. The white man who has "gone native" may lose friends and occasionally a job. But on the whole he is acting out his history as the conqueror to whom go all the spoils. Because he is wrapped in this subliminal history, he is not even remotely as vulnerable as the black male.

For the white man who is truly in love, the black-and-white affair is not easy. He must help his mate strike that precarious balance between aggression many black women feel (because they've had to be go-getters in a society that has psychologically castrated their "proper" mates) and the ostracism she may also secretly feel, since in the situation she is likely to be considered at best "sick" or, at the very worst, a whore or concubine by people outside her milieu (and often within it), black as well as white.

In relating to a white mate, the Negro female can be more "female." The white man's economic mobility is precisely what the black man doesn't have or finds difficult to attain. A young Negro female underlined this when she said, "White men are more considerate. They aren't disturbed by things that break in on them every day. In fact, because they have money or access to it, they are immune to things which cripple a black man."

Consideration and money are important to this young woman. They are two of the important factors which have brought the black woman and the white man together. The rest of the answer may lie in this passage from Kardiner and Ovesey's *Mark of Oppression*, a book which is, incidentally, despised by great numbers of Negroes:

". . . a Negro female loses respect for her spouse whose economic condition prevents him from acting according to white ideals or prototypes. The unhappy economic plight of the Negro male does not only contribute to the economic dominance of the Negro female, but also makes her psychologically dominant. . . . The [Negro] female now has some of the social value attributes of the male and those of the female. The . . . Negro female cannot be 'feminine' nor the male 'masculine.' Their roles are reversed. . . . The male fears and hates the female; the female mistrusts and has contempt for the male because he cannot validate his nominal masculinity in practice."

When the black man, more often than not a visible symbol of the bottom income group, walks the streets with the white woman, the whole complex structure of economic, sociological, and psychological barriers is threatened. Those barriers permitted the white man the mobility inherent in the resulting double standard. Now, the white man may no longer choose—without danger of retaliation—a black woman as well as a white one, while denying the black man the same right through legal or extra-legal means.

Within certain classes, admittedly, there is at least a superficial tolerance of the black man-white woman combination. Because of the relationship, the white woman may take on, in the eyes of the casual observer, a certain aura of overt sexuality, even though she may be considered basically an outcast. The Negro man may be considered "sick" or, like Othello in Brabatio's eyes, a "mountebank," a dispenser of spells and medicines. He may be amateurishly psychoanalyzed as being filled with self-hate because of his relationship. And the remarks in the streets will not necessarily be whispered; indeed, they may not be remarks at all, but insults.

In times not long enough past, the reaction against the mixed couple, especially in the South, was one of raging, depraved insanity. Note these reports, the first from the Washington *Eagle* for July 16, 1921, of a lynching in Moultrie, Georgia, and the second from the Baltimore *Afro-American* for March 16, 1935, of a lynching in Florida:

"They tore the Negro's clothing off before he was placed in a waiting automobile. . . . The Negro was unsexed and made to eat a portion of his anatomy which had been cut away."

"In the case of Claude Neal, a mob . . . dismembered his genitals and stuffed them into his mouth to compel him to eat his own flesh."

Violence does not always work. The white man then instituted another extra-legal means, that of frightening white women out of the desire to have sexual contact with the black man. In varying guises, the most important of these deliberately contrived myths tells of the wild sexual abandon of the Negro, abandon fortified by the immense sexual organ of the Negro male. But this is by no means the scientific truth. Kardiner and Ovesey write:

"Contrary to expectation, the sexual drive of the adult Negro is relatively in abeyance. We saw no evidence of the sex-craved and abandoned Negro."

But, apparently, no amount of authoritative comment can offset the propaganda. Many white females buy completely the genitalia myth. In Greenwich Village there is known to exist a certain group of white women who will sleep—to use a euphemism—only with Negroes who, in the middle of the act (it has been related often enough to give some basis for truth), have been put out to hear themselves addressed as "black prince" or, at the extreme end of the range of racial epithets, "dirty, black nigger."

Whether there are organized groups like this in other cities, I cannot say. Certainly, today more white women know intimately more Negro men than was possible a quarter of a century ago when Dr. Helena Deutsch wrote to John Dollard:

"The fact that white men believe so readily the hysterical and masochistic fantasies and lies of the white women who claim they have been assaulted and raped by Negroes is related to the fact that they (the men) sense the unconscious wishes of the women, the psychic reality of those declarations, and react emotionally to them as if they were real."

It remains that, despite the overwhelming scientific conclusions drawn up against the genital myth, the truth has not been accepted. Mythology is more intriguing, especially if, among vast numbers of people, it can still function. In his *The White Negro*, for example, Norman Mailer, after offering many acute observations about the life of the Negro in America, expects him to lead "a new breed of adventurers, urban adventurers," in a search for "action with a black man's code to fit their facts."

This, according to Mailer, is the black man's code:

"Knowing in the cells of his existence that life was war, nothing but war, the Negro (all exceptions admitted) could rarely afford the sophisticated inhibitions of civilization, and so he kept for his survival the art of the primitive. He lived in the enormous present; he subsisted for his Saturday night kicks, relinquishing the pleasures of the mind for the more obligatory pleasures of the body, and in his music he gave voice to the character and quality of his existence, to his rage and the infinite variations of joy, lust, languor, growl, cramp, pinch, scream, and despair of his orgasm."

Sadly, this wishful mythology, past and current, has had a kickback upon many a black man. We have seen this man who has come to believe that he is the greatest thing in bed since duck feathers. We have seen him in the more permissive sections of cities across the land, stalking the streets, blaring his blackness, his thick mop of hair, his skintight clothing, his genitals grouped before him like heavy artillery. He is forever ready to act out a role he thinks he has created. It is sad, or, rather, *he* is. But in this society, which places so much stress upon sex and, in underground quarters, on the ability to have or make one have an orgasm, his arrogance has sick excuse. We have demanded in our films, our magazines, our visual media, sex to be seriously considered as a part of our American Way of Life, as though, in the past, it had not been, at least not as completely as we now seem to want it.

Twenty-five years ago, few white women in America would have openly dared to express even a liking for a Negro matinee idol, had one existed. Today the names of Harry Belafonte, Johnny Mathis, and Sidney Poitier, to name but a few, gush from the lips of black as well as white females. This may indicate that the psychic reality of which Dr. Deutsch wrote does not—cannot —anger white men today as much as it did in the past. It cannot because women have a thousand times more independence than 100 or even 25 years ago. And that independence has encouraged them to express likes and dislikes, black or white. This is not at all strange because America is essentially a female-dominated society.

There is a relationship between the new freedom of women and the extension of the American grapevine which communicates news of the most delicate kind. Just as, long ago, word spread mysteriously and improbably from one slave quarter to another, now a new rumor, reinforced in certain circles by personal experiences (a Negro male said he had never met another Negro who hadn't slept with a white woman), has also spread. The most tantalizing rumor along the grapevine is the increasing impotence of the white man.

Predictably, the black man seizing upon this information develops an even deeper contempt than he already possesses for the white man. Impotence cannot be pitied in this society where, it is suggested by the white man himself, potency is the very essence of manhood. Bardot, Loren, the hundreds of models with which we are bombarded have become unconsciously the objects upon which we wish to demonstrate that potency.

According to Dr. Paul Niehans, from 1911 to 1928 more than sixteen reputable doctors successfully transplanted sex glands from one variety of animal to another as a first step in transplantation from animal to man. In 1918, Voronoff, who had previously worked with old rams, grafted monkey testicles on old men with considerable success.

The search for the Fountain of Youth, as we know, took Ponce de León to his death.

However frantic the search for potency may have been in the past, we have no proof today of widespread impotence among white men.

Rather, the current panic surrounding the "population explosion" in America suggests otherwise. The rumor is still (and may be for sometime) kicked around by black men. Why? The answer is that the myths of Negro sexuality persist, however false they have been proved, and if the truth will not be accepted by whites, there is no reason under the sun why it should be accepted by blacks. The notion that, after nearly four hundred years of demonstrating his potency with black women, the white man is now impotent serves as a highly delectable counter-myth. The propagation of this myth is also caused by the fear of the white man.

It is this fear which has resulted in the imbalance of interracial marriages. Black woman-white man relationships end more often in marriage than do white woman-black man combinations. On the public roster, we see Pearl Bailey and Louis Bellson, Diahann Carroll and Monte Kay, Lena Horne and Lennie Hayton, Nina Simone and Don Ross, Lorraine Hansberry and Bob Nemiroff, Eartha Kitt and Bill McDonald. Only Harry Belafonte and Julie Robinson, and Sammy Davis, Jr. and Mai Britt are notable opposites. Both Belafonte and Davis were previously married to Negro women. (Figures on interracial marriages are hard to come by. In the South, there are none or, at least, none that are recorded. In most other states, in the interests of maintaining a democratic society, statistics of this kind are not kept.)

Because marriages of the former type are more successful than the latter, and because of the multiplying incidence of mixed affairs, the black woman has come to look upon the white woman as a serious and persistent competitor. Ten years ago, she may have thought about the inroads white women were making, but she did not dare to complain aloud. Today, she speaks out with sharp, feminine bitchiness. According to the late E. Franklin Frazier, a shrewd sociologist who viewed his black brothers with unscaled eyes: Negro women, in rationalizing the success of white women, claim that the black male is immediately relegated to an inferior position. The white woman herself, they used to say, had to be a tramp. Other black women are somewhat resigned.

"Hell, you expect it," a single Negro school teacher said. "I guess what we want is the kind of black man who approaches the white-man mold—and there aren't enough to go around. To fit a mold like that, a man goes to a certain kind of school, he's been around. He doesn't try to fit the mold on purpose; he just comes out like that. You expect this man to marry a white woman. She is more of a woman, he thinks, and she has that little, terribly important feminine edge. Don't ask me to explain it."

The school teacher felt that white women do a lot more "sleeping around" than black women, another rationalization and, more important, an indication of the "middle-class" mores of a vast number of Negro women. Recent studies indicate that the black woman has a tendency to strain so hard to attain white standards (like the black man, for what else is there?) that she often overshoots the mark and becomes rigidly fixed in neo-Puritan concepts, particularly about sex. Frigidity is the frequent result.

And why not? We have seen the dilemma of the Negro woman. She wants the same good life her white counterpart seems to have. She wants to be loved and cared for by the book of white concepts. She wants independence. Instead, she has found herself a matriarch and a breadwinner, a decision-maker, a doer. Emerging from a background like this to become involved with a white male, she may feel the same need for revenge the Negro male may often feel in his relationship with the white woman. After all, it is the whites who have caused the situation, the misery, the pain, the shattered generations. . . .

While revenge (against self, parents, or friends) may be a
factor in many interracial affairs, to say that they are all so
motivated would be, again, mythology. Certainly revenge, cruelty, masochism, and sadism are present in white-white and
black-black relations. To observe them as a cause or result of
interracial liaisons is to fall far short of reason. But, sadly, we
have all heard of cases in which a black man can achieve satisfaction only with a white woman, and cases in which a white
woman can only gain climax with a Negro. In our world, with
its emphasis on color, people motivated in this wise are to be
pitied rather than condemned; the background of our society
has caught up with them.

Dollard suggests that, in terms of social advancement and
mobility, there may be, particularly for the black man, more
American ingredients present in the interracial affair than we
dare admit.

In our large urban centers, where there exists a degree of
sophistication about the mixed couple, it is the psychogeography
—proximity and state of mind—that will make for continuing
and increasing affairs, if not marriages, in black and white.

Essayist Seymour Krim has noted: ". . . Negroes are increasingly your neighbors, friends, lovers, wife, husband, landlord—
Christ, your goddamn analyst!"

Further, improvements in birth-control techniques have virtually banished the fear of pregnancy and the resulting ostracism for those mixed lovers who do not contemplate marriage.

The mark of "mixture" is stamped upon the face of every
"race" in the world. The Russian (and many another Eastern
European) bears the Mongolian fold and high cheekbones of
Tamerlane's raiders; the East African often carries the features
of sailors from ancient China; the Sicilian, Spaniard, Portuguese,
and southern Frenchman carry in their skins the burnt sun of
the African deserts and sing the songs of those arid lands. But
nowhere has the mixture been as potent as in America, much of
it for the wrong reasons. But that is our heritage. The traffic between peoples is both inexorable and inevitable. However much

progress America makes in accepting the mixed couple, the people involved—that is, the man and the woman—must be resilient, strong, and alert. And to withstand the outside, they'd better be very much in love.

THIS IS MY COUNTRY TOO

As FAR *as novels were concerned, 1963 began as a disastrous year for me. My novel* Sissie *came out during that long newspaper strike in New York. From other places in the country the reviews of the book were good, but if you don't get the reviews locally, in the* Times, *forget it. However, I didn't spend too much time worrying about the novel; I had articles to write, half a dozen. And I was getting restless; I wanted to get to Africa. Also, another book of mine, this one for young people,* Africa: Her History, Lands and People, *was published early in 1963.*

Summer came and went and I felt that I'd been especially productive—if not in books, in magazine articles. In September my agent called to say that Harry Sions, editorial director of Holiday, *wanted to get together with me to discuss my writing an article for his magazine. I was interested, but I didn't want any article to upset my travel plans, which were beginning to jell. On the other hand, I'd never written for a magazine of* Holiday's *stature, and I wanted to take a crack at it. My magazine-writing experience had been with publications like* Dude, Gent, Cavalier *and* Swank—*all girlie books. The articles I'd done for publications like* The New Leader *and* Saturday Review *never gave me stretching room and their commissions ran to small pieces and small payments.*

It was at Holiday *that I met Al Farnsworth, but the project under discussion was Harry Sions' baby. Sions had been the man behind* In Quest of America, *articles by John Steinbeck. His pieces ran in* Holiday *in 1961 and 1962, and were published in book form in 1962 with the title,* Travels with Charley. Charley *was Steinbeck's dog, a big poodle.*

I was asked to travel around the country, rather like Stein-

beck, to see what was going on. I was to Travel with Mr.
Charlie. This was to be, what they call in the business, a major
piece, and I had to weigh what it would do for me in terms of
career and what would happen if I said no, picked up my bags
and took off. I was between marriages, and to a certain extent
my time was my own.

Furthermore, Holiday was one of the best, if not the best
magazine in the country at that time. The prestige of writing for
it was not to be easily dismissed. The commission would pay
well, both in terms of the fee and expenses. I could move from
the minor league in article writing directly to the major league.
The men at Holiday then had a respect for writers that I've
never found at any other magazine. They insisted that their
writers come to know good food, rest well, not in luxury, but
well. The entire staff is at the writer's disposal when he's on
assignment.

Even so, I accepted the commission with some misgivings.
I'd traveled across the country and back before; it wasn't
pleasurable. I knew pretty much what was out there and had a
great reluctance to go up against it again.

My agent was arranging for me to get the loan of a car from
the Ford Motor Company in exchange for an article I'd write
for them. In the middle of negotiations, he suddenly vanished,
saying nothing, and I didn't know if I had a car or not. His
mother, who runs the agency, stepped in one morning and by
noon called me to tell me my car was ready in Detroit. I'd
already done New England in a rented car.

I came off the plane in Detroit carrying a typewriter, shotgun
and high-powered rifle. I'd planned to do some hunting on the
trip; Steinbeck had done some hunting. The man from Ford
looked at the guns just a little too long and I wondered if I was
going to have problems with him. As it happened, I did. He
called me later that evening at my hotel and said that if I insisted on taking the guns South, where I was heading on the
next leg of the trip, I couldn't have the car. He knew as I knew
that those guns would be used for more than hunting animals if
the situation came up, and the Ford Motor Company was

perfectly willing to see me lose in that situation, and you have to lose if you don't have the guns. Ford didn't want to be involved in any incidents. I delivered the guns to the Ford man and went South empty-handed.

I returned to New York late in December, the people from Holiday—anxious to get their hands on the article, which was to run 30,000 words. It was to run in two parts of 15,000 words each, but I hadn't had a chance to do anymore than take notes. Now I had to write it. I'd sublet my apartment in the Village. I made arrangements to live in East Hampton, on the outside of the village, in a cinderblock garage part of the time, and in the home of friend when she wasn't there.

My only heat in the garage came from a pot-bellied wood stove, and my only light from a propane gas lantern. The house, when I could use it, was of course a vast improvement. Anyway, having rebooked passage to Europe, the Middle East and Africa, I sat in East Hampton and wrote the first draft. I handed it in a few days before I was to leave, fully intending to do a second draft. I hadn't told the people at Holiday that, though.

Soon after, I was called into a conference at Holiday and surrounded by glum-looking people: Harry Sions, Al Farnsworth, and the blue-pencil man, copy editor par excellence, Harry Nickles. More work was required on the article, they said; it hadn't measured up to what they'd expected. I agreed. In first draft, nothing looks very good, and I assured them that I'd be working on a second.

But, they said, we understand you're about to go off on a trip. Correct, I said. Sions wondered if I was running out on the assignment, which was a silly presumption, because that Holiday bread looked like a million and I wasn't about to leave it up there. I convinced them that even as I traveled I'd be working, and they relaxed.

So I took off, typewriter and notes and carbon of the first draft in hand. I worked in London, Paris, Rome, Athens, Tel Aviv, Haifa, Cyprus, Cairo and finished the piece in Addis Ababa. Actually, on the advice of Harry Nickles, I'd been work-

ing on an entire book*; Holiday *could then select the parts it wanted to publish. In addition to working on the book, I'd been sending copy back to New York to* Newsweek, *but the* Newsweek *story comes a little later in this collection.*

By the time I arrived in Kano, Nigeria, I had a cable from Harry Sions, saying that the book was okay. I finished my African jaunt, flew back to Europe and then home. When I got to New York, Holiday *had selected two hunks of the book and they were published the summer of 1964. I didn't select the title; I couldn't think of one, so Sions settled on* This Is My Country Too, *which I thought then, and still do, was pretty atrocious. I wrote for* Holiday *until 1967.*

A final note to This Is My Country Too: *my agent took full credit for this advance in my career by getting me together with* Holiday. *I was disillusioned when I later learned this was not true. Harry Sions had sought me out to do the pieces—and proved it.*

LATE last September I set out in search of an old dream, one that had faded, come back into focus and faded again. The search was for my America. Some of my boyish concepts of it remained, altered by time and experience. Between these, resting like day-old cornbread, hard and gritty, was what I had learned of America as a black American.

I knew that concepts change day by day, second by second, impulse by impulse, and that 1963 was a year of change so great that it has yet to be measured. And I felt this far behind the news headlines. I wanted to know how America was picking its way through a transition that was inevitable even if it was being resisted on almost every side.

I learned my America in Syracuse, New York, a city that came

* The book was published a year later, in 1965.

into existence because of the great salt beds beneath its foundations. I knew boys named Katzman and Halpern, Carrigan and
Finnegan, Popoff and Demetriades, Schalk and Migdai, Storto
and Grandinetti. I learned, as children do, that they were good
students or poor, good athletes or awkward ones. I don't know
what they were told at home about me or the other colored boys
with whom they played tin-can soccer in the schoolyard or football under the principal's window. In my own home, on frequent
bad days, my parents snarled about "crackers" or "peckerwoods,"
a vague race of mean people—white, to be sure, but not my
friends.

I grew up in a time when the Boy Scouts were still fashionable; I became a Life Scout. In contrast, one of my sons, Greg,
dropped out before reaching the Second Class rank, and the
other, Dennis, never did get full wear from his Cub Scout uniform. I do not fault them for lack of interest in the Scouts; rather,
I am disturbed that they seem to know so much more about
America than I did. And I am also very glad that they know.
In my boyhood, the Third Reich emphasis on physical fitness
had penetrated America, and there were mass demonstrations of
Indian-club swinging and gymnastics on the horses, rings and
parallel bars. Recesses were for deep, deep breathing. We sa-
luted the flag, said prayers and ducked the heavy rulers (do-
nated by the bankers of the city) swung by impatient teachers.
Looking up at the summer skies, we never expected a plane to
emerge from a bank of clouds—and hardly believed it when
one did. The Goodyear blimp, which sent scores into the streets
as it passed overhead, was for us the most fantastic creation of
our time. During the Depression, we, the black people of Syracuse, did not feel in a complete sense that we were the victims
of any special set of circumstances; since there were more
white people than black, there had to be, logically, more white
people out of work and poor. The fact is that we were poor
before the Depression and would be poor after it.

For me, Syracuse was my home and I knew it as such; its hills
and creeks; its lakes, its alleys, its parks. I knew what the roads
felt like after a hot day—soft, so soft you could sink into the

asphalt deeper than the sole of your shoe. I knew the winters, when snow came for days on end and rose so high that you had to stand on the porch to see across the street. Church picnics and near drownings I remember, and scooters made from two-by-fours, roller skates and crates, and rubber guns triggered with clothespins, and homes with kitchens as large as the living room I now have. I remember my father playing touch football in the roadway when work was slow, and the slap of the men's shoes as they raced down the street grunting and shouting for a pass: "I'm in the clear. Stosh!" Black men and white men, little men and big men.

Only when I became a teen-ager did the dream of America begin to taste sour in my mouth. I was not a good student, nor was I a bad one. There was a period when I would be in school for a time, then out of it to help out. I was the first-born of four. At a time when the white boys I knew were still going to school, I was riding the sanitation-department trucks, emptying steel barrels filled with ashes. Even some of my black friends had not left school. I spent my evenings dripping bitterness and trying to take extra classes at night to catch up.

Because I liked Glenn Miller's music, I began to smoke Chesterfields. I also began to drink, and to go through the process of seeming drunk when I was not—an obvious attempt to call attention to my plight. But somehow I would be back in school in time for the football season, the basketball season, the track season; there is little sense of competition in hauling ashes. And when I returned to classes my fellow students would seem so young, so out of touch with things as I had known them during my brief sojourns away from learning. I had heard truck drivers and older men discuss their women; I had sat in joints I used to shun as "sporting places" (my mother's words). I had sat atop garbage and burning papers and unnamable other objects listening to the other men's rhythms of bitterness, the cadence of their despair. I had seen wild battles among the dump heaps, had seen knives flash, had walked to a doctor with a man who had a knife in his back.

By the time the war came, I was exhausted by the fight to

keep my original dream of America alive; war seemed to be a welcome change. My condition by that time was directly related to my color. I could not have made this statement then. It would have killed me; I would have had to reject all that I had.

But the war. First there was the segregated naval base at Great Lakes, Camp Robert Smalls, then the segregated units. I was warm and secure in the bosom of the Super Chief hustling out of Chicago. Like most raw boys of that age, I was fearful that, with the aid of a Japanese bullet, I really would be "going west," as the men of World War I used to say. On the other hand, I had a growing hunch that, since war was a heroic thing, more white men than black would be allowed to die in it.

My biggest battles, however, were not against the Japanese but against the United States Navy and many of my white comrades. I had more fire then. I raised some little hell. I spent three hitches in the brig, one of them a Marine brig. I was usually charged with breaking some Navy regulation, but I was fighting for my rights as a sailor who was also a human, black or not. I saw white Marines and black sailors line up for a race riot on Guam. A Chamorro girl told me she had been warned to stay away from black men because they had tails. My parents wrote asking what was being cut out of my letters; I had endless conferences with the censors and refused to stop writing home and saying that the Navy was rotten. I have a pitted face from the dry shaves I got in the Marine brig. I traveled up and down the islands of the Pacific because black hospital corpsmen were not wanted aboard ship, and I wound up with a land force. A white Texan on a dark night in the New Hebrides was a minute away from shooting me. A white Mississippian who had been there and who had dissuaded the Texan told me, "Williams, you ain't like them other niggers." When I told him he was wrong, he laughed. "*You* crazy," he said. "They ain't."

At the end of the war, while the white servicemen were screaming their triumph over the Krauts and the Gooks (in the Pacific the war had been fought along racial lines), I had concluded sadly that America had become a stranger to my earliest dreams. My experiences in the Navy and earlier had had a curious impact: my wariness, or as some of my white friends put it, my paranoia, grew. But hope, forever crouched on the starting line, filled the rear of my mind. It was there each of the four times I crossed the country, my stomach knotted with nervousness, with eagerness to gain those islands of safety, the cities mentioned by railroad porters and waiters and itinerant musicians as being "all right." As I packed to begin my trip in 1963, I had memories of being refused service in Arizona, of being passed a miserable sandwich through the window of a restaurant in Jefferson City, Missouri (the window was for Negroes). And I recall now my helpless, suicidal anger when I had to beg for milk for Greg's breakfast when he was four and we were on a trip through Hammond, Indiana; and I remember being shouted at in a crowded Wichita, Kansas, restaurant for having the nerve to ask for service.

But there was hope, tensed on the line, ready as always to go. In my thirty-eight years so much had happened—so quickly. From dirigibles to rockets, from heavy, lumbering styles in machinery and in life itself, we had come to a lightness, an almost automated way of living. From a depression-idled population we had progressed to one of great leisure. Negroes were no longer being hunted down and lynched except upon occasion, and then the lynchings were not done in the classic manner, with rope and gasoline, with men and women ready to sever genitals as souvenirs. No, things had changed, were changing still. America was stirring as it had never stirred before. It was indeed a time in which to live, and a time to go.

I left on a warm September morning. There had been shopping for camp gear, for clothing tough enough to stand long hours of sitting or walking through brush, for drip-dry shirts (an utter failure). Lists of names and places had been compiled. The guns had been cleaned, for there was the possibility of hunting bird and game, shells had been bought, and the car checked—a borrowed car, since mine was not yet ready. Then, finally, it was time to begin the search.

I drove north and west, of course, for a search begins at the point where the hunter was believed lost. For me, it was Syracuse.

What did I lose first? Religion, perhaps, for cleaning the pastor's porch one afternoon, I found a number of empty whisky bottles under a box—a find I confided to no one, not even when, at a very early age, I stopped taking the Methodist communion. As a result, the first Sunday of every month brought on a crisis between my parents and me, and I had not the courage nor the words to tell them what I knew. They could drink, but the preacher could not.

The second thing I lost in those days, when there were still blacksmiths and troughs for horses, was the feeling that I was *just like* Larry Katzman or Hecky Alpert or Vasco Finnegan or Chuckie Sullivan. The awakening came one afternoon while we were reading that children's classic, *Little Black Sambo*. I remember the giggles in the class, the swelling that grew in me until I closed my eyes, hoping to open them and find the kinky-headed pickaninny with the great toothy smile gone. When I opened my eyes, he was still there.

That was the day when Larry, Hecky, Vasco and Chuckie *also* discovered that I was different, not like them, but coal black and with liver lips and nappy hair. And it didn't matter any longer if I could beat them at running or fighting, or play touch football or soccer better than they.

I saw Hecky Alpert in Syracuse, in a restaurant, and my impulse was to cry across the room, "Hecky!" but I didn't. I kept watching him, hoping to draw his eye, hoping that a sudden gleam of recognition would come and *he* would cry across the room, "Johnny!" No gleam came, and thus no cry. It was not that he was avoiding me. He no longer knew me. Why was it, then, that I knew him? Why did I remember that his hair was tight and curled, that his teeth were crooked, that he was a whiz in arithmetic, that he fought only when there was no other solution, and that he fought wildly, with annihilation in mind, as do many meek people?

But other things concerned me in Syracuse—Greg, who was

fifteen, and Dennis, twelve, and a loss of another sort. For more than a year my boys have been talking about the time when they will enter the service, and I don't know how to answer them when they ask for advice. They have books on what each branch offers, how they can finish college before they get into uniform, or how they can do both at the same time. It is distasteful to me, the matter-of-fact way in which they discuss what must be. I take no joy in listening to them, for I recall my own bad days in the Jim Crow service and worry that they, too, may be visited with the same trouble. I suppose it is in the nature of a father to refuse to believe that his children can be, or will be, tougher than he was. In any case, I was relieved to postpone a discussion of the armed services until after my trip.

My sense of loss was complicated by the civil-rights demonstrations that had besieged Syracuse that summer—Syracuse, which had a Negro population before 1769 and had been a stop on the Underground Railroad. Greg and Dennis agreed that the demonstrations would be helpful, but beyond that they did not discuss the matter. Their minds were filled with books, whose essence had little to do with what was taking place in the streets. Besides, they have a very special mother and, I am sometimes rash enough to think, they also have a special father, despite the divorce. Such a belief, whether true or false, tends to immunize them against outside events; they have yet to learn that true immunization does not exist. And yet, at the core of their beings I sensed a cynicism so great that I feared to measure it, so that on this theme, too, our conversations meandered.

Greg seems to me a large boy; he is taller than I am. And he is quiet, demanding through this quietness that attention be paid to him. Dennis, on the other hand, is outgoing and trigger-quick with a quip. When we spoke of my trip, he asked me, with just the right shade of indifference, "So how come you're not going to Africa?"

"I thought I'd better do this first."

"Will you send us a card from every city?" Greg asked, his

eyes a bit aslant; for this boy, every request opens him up more than he likes.

"Yes." I had good intentions when I said it.

Our world is bigger than I have indicated here. The important fact is that we have one and move through our paces accordingly.

Soon, with a sweep of upstate New York and the Adirondacks behind me, I was on my way to New England. It was another golden day, and I was not even irritated that my new car hadn't yet come. The urge to *go* must have been born in me, and I never feel as good as when pointing myself away from where I've *been*. (More often now, however, I am glad to return.)

And it was my good fortune to be going to Vermont. I have never met a person who has been to Vermont and not loved it. It is a land of physical grace. The roads slant upward softly, every curve unfolds a new exciting vista. It was aptly named; the hills are green and wounded with daggers of basalt and ancient granite. There are no crowds crawling underfoot.

I was going to spend a few days with John Engels and his family. I had met John a few summers earlier, at the Breadloaf Writer's Conference. He lives in Hinesburg, a very small town, in a red-brick colonial trimmed with white. A great green lawn sets off the house, and the green flats reach up into a series of low hills in the distance.

John and I waste little time on courtesies. Some men like each other for their acts, their looks, their intelligence. John and I became friends at first, I think, because we liked athletics and played touch football at Breadloaf. He is a poet but doesn't look the way we conceive them; he is six-one and was a lineman at Notre Dame. Like most former athletes, he is always talking about getting back into shape. To me, he is a rare man because he is honest, incapable of deceiving anyone. More than that, he seems to me a man whose religion is his philosophy—not the other way around. I think I was the first Negro he ever met man to man, intellect to intellect, and he hurt me sometimes, piercing through the anesthesia a black man must build up if he is to survive.

It didn't hurt so much this time, sitting on his front lawn that first evening and talking about my trip.

"Will this be about civil rights?" he asked. He has a direct and disarming way of asking questions.

"Whatever's there."

"You've mellowed," he said. "You once said you didn't think an honest white man existed, and I concluded that you couldn't see beyond the civil rights issue."

"I told you that?" I was thinking of his thinning blond hair, his blue eyes and pale skin. I hadn't thought about his features until then.

I probably did say it, only I'd forgotten. Has any Negro ever confessed that civil rights can be a boring issue? Necessary, yes, but boring as well because it is war, and only the sick can like war. A man wants and needs peace from travail; that is why civil rights can sometimes be as lifeless as a rock. I do not mean that the boredom lasts forever, only that all the attitudes and arguments, the patterns, the rationalizations are, for most Negroes, old. I should think, for example, that most Americans would get bored with the annual autumn ritual of the opening of schools in the South.

When I made that remark to John, my anger must have been keen. Perhaps I had mellowed, for the moment, at least. John is a man with whom I feel comfortable; I don't have to pull my punches or keep my guard up. There are few people, black or white, who give me such a feeling.

It was a good time to be with the Engels family: the thermometer climbed into the 80's, the forest floors were golden with billions of small yellow flowers. We lunched on trout taken right from the freezer, where John had put them after a summer of fishing, and homemade French bread and cold beer. Afternoons we walked the hills, looking to the west at the Adirondacks and to the east at the Green Mountains. I was overwhelmed by a sense of peacefulness.

The feeling was shaken one day as we sat around the kitchen

table. John's little son David climbed into my lap. "Why are you so chocolaty?" he asked. He pushed his hand firmly against my face and glanced at his palm.

I looked at John, who said urgently, "Tell him, John. Now's your chance to explain that you're a Negro and that there are a lot of different people in the world. Go ahead. *Go ahead!*"

My first thought was that it was not my job but John's. Then I started slowly. "You know Indians?" Only yesterday the kids next door had asked if I were Chinese or Indian.

"Yes," he said.

"Well," I said, groping. I wondered how *does* one explain oneself? "He's different. I mean he's not white like you, is he, an Indian?"

But David was scrambling down to go play with the other kids in the yard. "Damn it, John, you flubbed it; you've lost him," John said, and I had. But perhaps not forever.

I did not buy my maple syrup in Vermont, I bought it in New Hampshire, where I was beginning to see the hosts of rusty, joyless New England towns that sat on the curves of roads, dying, their mills gone south. Buses provide their only access to other towns or cities because the trains, too, have left.

At one point I pulled off the road and went into a lunchroom attached to a motel. A man at the front counter looked questioningly at me as I came through the door. I paused when I saw no one in the dining room. Bad time of day, I thought; that had to be the reason it was empty. I moved forward.

"Can I help you?" the man asked. Suddenly it occurred to me that he thought I was going to ask for a room—and he didn't know how to handle the situation.

"I'd like to eat," I said, not really stopping, but not moving either.

Pure, undisguised relief flooded his face. In a fraction of a second he was transformed from a cipher to a charming person. "Oh, I *am* sorry," he said. "The lunchroom's closed right now. I guess you missed the sign at the side of the door."

I had. I walked to the car, musing. How much of this would

I run into? I had told myself, of course, that there would be a lot of it, a hell of a lot of it, but I believed myself tough enough to take it. Now I wasn't so sure. It isn't like war, in which every soldier feels sure that someone else will get it; every Negro *expects* to be rebuffed, whether he will admit it or not. This does not mean that he *likes* it, or will accept it passively. Too many people still make that mistake. A white man will never know, could never know, what has happened to the Negro to whom he has just delivered an insult. A white man ought to assume that, if the Negro before him is twenty-five years old, he has had twenty if not twenty-five years of insults and rebuffs, and that the Negro may have had quite enough. A white man ought to assume this, and if he had any sense he would.

After the encounter at the motel lunchroom, I found myself picking out places to stop—or rather, letting them pick me out. It works like this. You begin to drive more slowly. The eye drifts over this motel or that seeking some instinctive assurance that you will not have to put your life on the line by asking for a single for the night; that is what it amounts to in many places in these United States. Twenty-nine states have definite laws prohibiting the turning away of anyone seeking public accommodations. Kentucky had an executive order, but as of this writing it has expired. Florida and Virginia innkeepers may not advertise that they discriminate. Louisiana and Tennessee have anti-bias laws on the books, but these were passed during the Reconstruction period and have not been enforced since then. (I have reference to the continental states. Alaska has anti-bias legislation. Hawaii prohibits discrimination only in the payment of wages.) Yet in each of the states in which discrimination in public places is forbidden, discrimination in public places exists. There are no exceptions, not even in big cities—not in New York, San Francisco, Chicago, Boston. There are none.

"Yes, Mr. Williams, your new car is ready, but you'll have to come to Detroit to pick it up unless you want further delays."

To Detroit! By this time I was ready to go to Vladivostok for that car. Detroit? *Yes!* On the next plane, overweight and all!

I had pictured myself behind the wheel a thousand times. How enticing is the prospect of owning that which one has never owned before. Used cars I have had, yes, but a new one, stinking of fresh paint and leather, with the clock and radio working perfectly—a vehicle seemingly with the will of a woman, requiring a nudge here, a touch there, a prayer in this city and a curse in another—never.

I found Detroit a great, ugly city, except for the new structures in Cadillac Square—and one that always looks back to 1943, the year of its big race riot. No city that has had a race riot or a pogrom can forget it. A root goes down, and unless it is dug out it will sprout again and bear fruit. Well and good, but there was the car, a nine-passenger station wagon with more than four hundred horses hidden under the new white hood. Red upholstery, white walls, automatic. A gas-eater? Perhaps, but it promised comfort and power.

I drove into the city and checked into a downtown hotel, carrying typewriter and bag, rifle and shotgun, a road atlas and a copy of *Travelguide*, which lists places in America where Negroes can stay without being embarrassed, insulted or worse.

I saw by a newspaper that in Detroit, as in Syracuse, civil rights was the major topic, so I sought out my boyhood friend John Clair, a sociologist. He could tell me what was going on in the city, tell me what I could smell but could not see. The single most important thing I remember about John Clair is that once, when we were kids in a Scout camp, he whipped another boy half to death for chopping up a milk snake with an axe. He is now a Community Organizer Supervisor. He is very tall and very dark, and you are surprised to see that he has great, brown eyes instead of black ones.

Over barbecue and beer, we talked; it came out. "The Negroes feel that their bloc of votes put Mayor Cavanagh in office. Now they want some benefits. They'll agitate until they get some. White people move to the suburbs to get away from us but they leave the voting power in our hands."

What would it be tonight—Leonard Pennario with the Detroit Symphony at Ford Auditorium, or jazz? Perhaps because of our

conversation, neither of us wanted to spend that evening among
white people. It was a thing left unsaid but easily understood.
So we began at the Driftwood Lounge, where we looked out at
table upon table crowded with men and women who were
black, brown, beige, plum, yellow or white. On stage, with
great flash and soul, was Chuck Jackson, a rock 'n' roll singer.
Opposite him, in a shimmering dress, was another singer, Yvonne
Fair, who took the magic of the spotlight and made it her own.
There was a looseness in the air, as there is in almost any Negro
night club, that you can't find in a white one, American or not.
Negroes really listen to the music in a night spot, and for many
of them such a place is a relief from a high-rent flat in a ghetto.

Later Clair and I prowled the Negro section. The night was
filled with voices raised in call, with the sound of car doors
slamming, of people going and coming. In one place we visited
—it had no music and it was bare, unrelieved in its shabbiness—
a scowling young man looked up at Clair. "Hey, ain't you Mr.
Clair?" The scowl split and a smile came. They talked while I
stood by, feeling awkward, unrelated. At length Clair finished
and guided me outside. "I helped him when he got in some
trouble," he said.

As Clair drove me home, out of the ghetto and semi-ghetto, he
said, "Man, this town is ready all over again. Guys have been
buying guns. Jobs getting tight. Young guys, like the one I talked
to, got nothing to do. Any kind of trouble comes as a diversion.
And if they can tie that in with striking a blow for freedom, it fits
even better."

"There's only one thing to do if it breaks," I said.

"Run like hell," he said. And he had said it.

On another night we dined at a good restaurant—Clair, his
wife Lily and I. I was disconcerted, for an instant only, to see
that the maître d'hôtel and the waiters were Negro. There
they were, sharp in their dinner jackets, crisp in movement, and
I thought, with the barest suggestion of contempt in their
demeanor when they leaned over a white patron to suggest an
entree or a wine. (Do it, brother!) After we ordered, the moment

came to select a wine—and the maître and I went into battle. His eyes reflected the feeling that we had no business there, among all those whites. He suggested one wine, I insisted on another. The dispute went on until finally, with a brief glint of approval in his eyes, he brought the wine of our choice. Perhaps he didn't want us there, but he sure knew we had *been* there.

So did many of the diners. We were really looked at. We had a well-placed table and our color made us conspicuous. Of course, a Negro does not know why white people glance at him in public places. Perhaps some are thinking, "It's about time." Others, "Who is he?" And still others, "My God! Here too!" It is hard to know, for no one tells.

Now it was time to move southward. Cold air and blue skies greeted me the morning I waited outside the hotel for the car to come—for my white beauty with smooth lines, the quiet flash, the concealed power. A man who was also waiting—for what I do not know—struck up a conversation. At first it had to do with kids, teen-agers. We saw a few of them skylarking across the street, reluctant to go to school. He wondered why they were so destructive these days, why their parents let them get out of hand. I always listen with half an ear to such talk. It takes more than physical parental strength to bring up kids; it takes intelligence and a great deal of luck.

In his day, the stranger continued in a faraway voice, his folks really lit into him if he showed the slightest inclination to go astray.

Yes, I said, so did mine.

The sun was full on the stranger now. He was slight, and this made his frame seem youthful, but his face was old and wrinkled. Dirt specks showed on his nose. When he spoke, he stared intensely at me, as though to pull agreement out of me.

Kids stole cars or broke their windows, he went on. They stole when they didn't have to; they were insolent and aimless and always sought the world without wanting to pay for it.

Where is the car, I wondered.

He had warmed up to his subject. Suddenly he was speaking more easily, more rapidly and with an accent I couldn't place: Northern rural? Southern urban?

In his day he had walked miles to school, he said.

Where's the car, damn it, where's the car?

He had eaten tons of fatback and grits.

I looked around for the car.

Suddenly: "What do you think of the Black Muslim crowd?"

So—white man and black man, getting down to cases.

But now, floating around the corner, the driver languid behind the wheel, *my* wheel, came the car. *Deus ex machina.* So long. Bye-bye.

My sleeping bag was stacked under a seat. My typewriter rested on the carpeted floor, and my suitcase, packed to bulging, was squeezed between the seats. I wanted no clothes displayed on hangers, which might give the people of the South the impression that I was on a leisurely jaunt through their region; the "foreign" license plates on the car would do enough to suggest that. In the rear was a five-gallon can for gas for emergencies. Left behind, at the insistence of friends, were my rifle and shotgun; they would be sent on to Chicago. "They're tough on Northern *whites* going down there," I had been told, "even without guns. If they stop you with them, you've got trouble, licenses or no. They may even accuse you of transporting arms." I had to agree.

A sense of helplessness crept over me, but it soon passed.

After a good night's rest in Cincinnati, I picked up my first cop on the way to Louisville. I also saw an all-Negro telephone line crew in Kentucky. I had never before seen a Negro lineman. When I saw these fellows I nearly ran the car off the road. They waved. I stuck my hand out of the window and called, "Hi, you-all." It was said with admiration but the rushing wind took my words and lost them.

The sun was bright and the weather warm. I felt I could have made up a cornball song about the Kentucky River that day.

I curled around the mountains at a good pace and looked into the deep valleys falling away from the roadside. I rumbled over an old metal bridge, a work of no beauty, a work of yesteryear, a shame to the river that moved quietly beneath it.

Then, passing a turnout, I saw a state trooper's car. I drove on with the soft flow of traffic, and forgot about him. I thought I was watching my mirrors closely, but when next I looked up, there he was, sitting very officially in his car, very sure of himself. All at once I was conscious of the big, spanking, brand-new station wagon with its chrome trim winking in the sunlight. He stayed with me for about seven miles. Waiting for an infraction? Radioing and waiting for a reply on my license number?

I was surprised by my own actions. I had felt that, as soon as something of this kind happened, I would panic. Instead, I flagged him down and pulled over to the side. He slowed and passed, looking at me very carefully. He stopped ahead of me and came out of his car. He was a tall, lean young man, handsome, with a bluish cast to the areas of his face where he shaved. His uniform looked as though he had put it on just a second before. The wide brim of his hat was perfectly straight. On the front of his sharply creased shirt a name plate glittered.

"Officer," I said when he came up, "I'm having some trouble with a bump in my right front tire." It was true: a bump had developed. "Do you know of a good garage in or near Louisville?"

"Well, let's get to a wider shoulder," he said. He did not look at me.

We drove down the road and stopped again. Together we crouched and looked at the tire while traffic whistled past. "It's bumpy, huh?" His manner of speaking was crisp, fast. Once he looked at me with his deep-blue eyes, then looked away. "Where you stayin' in Louisville?"

"Sheraton."

He told me of a garage nearby, and then, studying my plates once more, got into his car and drove away. So if I were a car thief, a murderer, a narcotics peddler or an FBI Most Wanted, he had the number and the hotel, plus a good description. He no longer had to follow me.

A newsman has described Louisville as a "Midwest city with a Southern exposure." As I passed through the lobby of my hotel, Southern accents began to assail me. Gentlemen sat in the stuffed chairs wearing wide-brimmed hats and smoking cigars. I expected to see a Negro roll out a cart loaded with mint juleps. But the courtesy at the desk stunned me. I was given rooms I was glad to have.

The bellman came over to pick up my things—an elderly Negro, thin and very dry. I let him struggle to the elevator with the bag while I carried the typewriter. When he rang I picked up the bag and handed him the typewriter.

"You take this," I said, "and look out for your health."

I could see him hauling bags up and down long corridors, going through the motions of opening draperies and raising windows until someone said, "Here, boy," and gave him his tip. I could not stand the thought; he should have been sitting on a sunny porch watching his great-grandchildren. He reached out with his bony claw and took the bag. "Son," he said, "let's just do this first-class now."

The elevator came. I was fuming when we got on. I feared he might drop dead carrying my bag, but all he could think of was to do his job "first-class." I was a guest, and he was a bellman. Beyond that, he undoubtedly refused to believe that he was too old to do the work. I trailed behind him down the hall. My bag slapped against his leg; he walked unsteadily, his breath coming hard. The rooms were superb—old but well appointed, quiet, soothing.

At the garage it turned out that the station wagon's tires were slightly out of balance hence the bumping sound. All the mechanics were white, and I felt a certain coolness from them, but otherwise there was an air in Louisville that seemed to say, "By God, this is going to work!" In places of public accommodation I found no hesitation, none of the scanning looks to see if I was the "right kind" of Negro. People looked you right in the eye. And I liked that.

Later I had a telephone conversation with a high-placed politician, who said, "Louisville's a bit different than the rest of the state. More cosmopolitan. When you get to the smaller towns, and down near the Southern-border areas, you'll find that they think just like white Mississippians. A lot of people still feel that Negroes are not ready as a race, however fast they're growing up. Northerners don't understand the problem, and they're pretty two-faced anyway. Take New England. Why, there are families up there still living off the profits of the slave trade." I felt too good about Louisville to be depressed by his words.

Besides, I had a date. You know how it goes. The fellow from New York comes to town, bringing with him the romance and flair of Harlem, the jumbled intellect people believe still exists in Greenwich Village, intimate knowledge of and gossip about the current idols. The New Yorker may be treated cautiously outside his city, but no New Yorker is believed to be without a certain glamour, real or false. He is, no matter what his business, a throwback to the drummer of the last century; he is the salesman who, even if he has no goods, has himself to sell.

I did not know my date except that she was a schoolteacher and had been described as a "swinger." Her name, let us say, was Mary, and she came to the hotel. I was watching the news on television when I heard the swish-swish of fabrics and the soft thumps that high heels make on carpeted floors. The sounds stopped at my door and the knock came. Good-by, Huntley-Brinkley; adieu, Walter Cronkite.

I opened the door and she came in. Sometimes I think a man should spend all his time on the road. Yes, there are those times, and this was one of them. Mary had flaming red hair, natural hair, and her color was a rich beige. Her superb figure was set off by a black dress short enough to reveal nice legs.

She had just returned to Louisville after living in Cleveland twelve years. Did I detect some nervousness on her part?

Perhaps so. If I did, it only made me more determined that the evening should go well. It would never do for both of us to be on edge.

After a couple of drinks, we breezed through the lobby of the Sheraton, through the middle, sensing the turning heads. The Negro porters and bellmen watched us warily. We passed into the street and walked the few blocks through the warm night to the restaurant. There the service—the little courtesies that make dining out a pleasure—left Mary numb. She had been too busy with family matters and classroom routine to notice the integration of Louisville. When she talked about her friends, I had the impression that they were all stunned by it and were finding it hard to break the patterns they had been forced to live with. It couldn't be true that Louisville was now an open city. It had to be an illusion.

This is what many whites will have to face when the barriers come down. You cannot dispense distrust and cruelty and inequity for four centuries and then expect your victims to be suddenly filled with love; expect them to jump at the new life which may be (past experience tells us) but another hoax. No, the patience and wisdom American Negroes have so long exhibited will now have to be required of whites until belief sets in. Mary, I think, would be one of those who would not believe for a long time.

How wonderful a dinner can be when the company is pleasant, and it was. We had only one bad moment, when she said, "You know what all this had brought on? Colored men and white women. Oh, they've always been ducking and slipping around, but now they've brought their affairs into the open." She was not speaking from a Negro point of view but from an entirely feminine one, which is growing daily in black America. On this basis she offered her judgment of integration in Louisville: "It won't work."

Ominously, the way to Nashville lay via the Dixie Highway. Where did it end, the Dixie Highway—in a cotton patch surmounted by a Confederate flag and an *a cappella* choir of White Citizens Council members singing *Dixie?*

The very roads seemed downhill going out of Louisville. For the first time I wished the car were smaller and of another color; I wished it were less conspicuous. I watched the speed signs and obeyed them to the letter, and rolled gently through the smaller towns, where, tucked in alleys off the main streets, manned police cars sat waiting for the unknowing. I felt something close in around me and wished I had not come. This land is death to me; the lovely scenery a mocking camouflage for crime.

Along the roads were tattered open-front shops which displayed quilts and cheap vases, souvenirs of the region, all for sale, all proof that one had indeed been South. Down went the roads, down, then up, sweeping around mountains and great masses of pines stumbling up the hills. That morning I felt a certain stillness in the air, a waiting. It is me, I thought; it must be me. Somewhere between Louisville and Nashville, I lost the sense of ownership that seven generations of my people in this land had brought me. At the moment I did not feel fear. I was just uneasy; acutely aware of the possibility that I might run into trouble and not be able to emerge from it without great difficulty.

No man knowingly gives up his life for a reason over which he has no control. Yet heading South I was placing myself in greater danger than I have ever faced in the North—so far. I have never been tortured, so I do not know how much physical pain I can bear, but I do have a fuzzy idea of how much psychological punishment I can stand. What I am saying is this: I was prepared not to return from the South or anywhere else in America if it were put to me that I was less than a man, less than an American with more right than most to be here. I am descended from the one black in every ten who survived the slave raids, the Middle Passage and slavery. Yes, there are times when I am frightened; I have been frightened and will be frightened again; but I do come from that surviving tenth and I have pride enough not to want to disgrace the line, ever.

Now I watched the rear-view mirrors relentlessly. And now I toyed with the idea of stopping at a gas station, meeting a Southerner on his home ground. Soon enough, I thought, soon enough, and I continued on to Nashville, where traffic blazed along the superroads and poured into the heart of the city. I became lost several times and pulled into gas stations and shouted, "Hey, where's Buchanan Street?" Invariably the answer would be, "*Buck*anan? Hmm." It was in the Negro section, of course. I drove down the narrow street, past the gas stations, liquor, food and dry-goods stores, and wondered if they were owned by Negroes. Later I learned that they were not.

It was very hot, and the sight of the swimming pool at my motel cheered me immensely. I swung into the parking lot with a flourish: the drummer from New York was here. At first my reservation was checked at ten dollars a day, but when I questioned the price and was questioned in turn about my profession, the figure was lowered. The desk clerk, a young girl, was slow. Even her face was slow. I could see her boss ordering her to charge all salesmen ten because they made money and were on fantastic expense accounts. I, being a writer, got a cheaper rate for the same room. Ah, Negro business! Perhaps we are not ready.

The temperature was in the 80's and I was eager to get into the pool. Did they have trunks? No. Where could I get some? Down the street at the dry-goods store. The girl's accent was Southern, but altogether different from the accent of white Southerners. What would Shakespeare sound like with an all-Southern cast, backwoods Southern?

My room faced an open field. On the edge of it stood a hen house. Beyond was countryside, for the motel was at the very edge of town. I drove to the store for trunks. It was filled with the smell of mothballs. There were a few white women trying on house dresses, and they all seemed alike: middle-aged, worn, with dull brown hair.

"Mr. Solomon," one of the women said, "he wants a pair of trunks." Mr. Solomon, I thought, are you anti-Negro while Negroes around here are anti-Semitic because of you? Shades of Harlem, Manhattan, New York City! I asked for my size. These were my size, he said, keeping his hand on them. Back at the motel I discovered they were two sizes too big, but they were elastic and stayed on. But, Mr. Solomon, you knew better. How many others have you dealt with in this manner, knowing that clothes tried on at home by a Negro are not returnable?

I swam until I was tired, then went to my room and slept for a while.

That evening I had a date with a very dear person whom I shall call Martha. At the first moment of our meeting I forgot all about the South, but when we sought a place to eat, when she underlined the words, "You must remember where you are," I recalled that I was in the South, and how much this can narrow one's life. We found a place that had no liquor license, so that did away with the drinks. But as if to compensate, it did have a jukebox turned up as loudly as it could go. It vibrated the fried chicken, fried potatoes and dried peas all the way down.

Early next morning I drove to Tennessee State University. The sun was breaking, spattering gold on the brown dirt reaches of the campus. Here and there were patches of green, but mostly I saw acres and acres of leached-out soil on which stood worn Quonset huts. The important buildings were obvious for their brick, for the walks that surrounded them. There were hundreds of dust-covered cars. So many for a school supported by the state? Yet there they were, parked inches apart, leaning at dangerous angles on hillsides, rows of them curving around the buildings.

The students streamed by, some obviously from the city, to judge by their dress—the tight, cuffless trousers, sometimes ankle high, the shirt colors bold, the haircuts neat, studied for the current fashion. These quipped loudly and hiply to one another as they passed from building to building, walking on grass wherever they could find it, to avoid getting their Italian shoes dusty. Other youths were quiet, almost sullen, and un-caring of styles or dust as they plodded along. Suddenly I knew why. College was not a ball for them, as it was for the others. These were burdened with the task of breaking their families' pattern of living. The fathers were of the soil, but the sons were advancing toward a new world of books, of ideas. Most of them would leave the land, or go back to it changed. The girls were the same, some stylish, some not; and like the male students, the chic ones walked together.

"The biggest, most attractive building on the campus will be the physical-education building," I had been told, and so it was. After all, Tennessee State University produced Olympic track champions Wilma Rudolph and Ralph Boston. Its basketball teams annually clobber the best white teams allowed to play against its sharpshooters. Its football seasons are generally successful.

The man I was looking for, Earl Clanton, was lifting weights. There were a couple of uneasy seconds, seconds of study. Then I mentioned the magic name of the person who suggested I see him, and Clanton lowered his weights. I waited for him to shower and dress. Fittingly, he came rushing out of the dressing room and set a murderous pace about the campus. Former athletes seem to run the school, coaches and assistant coaches, men whose names are legendary in Negro collegiate football. They were big, hearty men, quick with their big hands, rumbling with their laughter. Doctors of Physical Education? I could only guess. I shared lunch with them; not once was there a moment of true levity. Bantering, mock threats of violence, pretended interest in me, and once more the polite hand-shakes. Gone.

Besides Tennessee State, Nashville has the college complex of Fisk University and Meharry Medical College. Trees and grass and a stone wall mark the boundary of Fisk, a symbol of the "kind of school" to which Negro parents once wished to send their children. Just across the street lies Meharry, which had to produce fine Negro doctors because white medical schools rarely accept them. Meharry spills downhill beneath groves of trees; walks radiate from building to building.

At Meharry I heard unfunny jokes about "the Jew." This is the mythical man the students believe they will have to compete against if they set up offices in the large cities of the North. Already they discuss how to hold their patients, how to keep them from giving money to Jewish doctors. Little if any of these student conversations dealt with being better doctors than the Jews. Their attitude was, quite simply, that of anti-Semitism.

I left Nashville for Atlanta on a Sunday morning, long before the churches began ringing their bells. Beside me on the seat, wrapped in waxed paper, was a small pile of Southern fried chicken. The big new car and the supply of chicken didn't go together. Stories are still current about Negroes who now live in the North and plan to return home in the South; they debate whether they should drive their Cadillacs. Some wear chauffeur hats or carry them on the seat alongside; others pretend that they are just delivering the car. The stories seem to come less often now, but on this trip the daughter of a Midwest Negro district attorney told me that, when her father travels South, he will not leave his car for any reason until he is safe in a Negro neighborhood.

Thinking such thoughts, I pulled into Bill and Joyce Eure's driveway, in Atlanta. Bill and I had grown up together. At one time his family lived upstairs above us. We called him "Dirty Bill," only because, in our sports-minded circle, he was a tough competitor. Pick the sport. Bill Eure starred. And to this day he swears by athletics; he believes they saved most of us from long periods in jail.

I was most curious about one thing: how Bill, having been raised in the North, in Syracuse, could find a life in the South.

Bill is very chunky, about five-ten or eleven; he shrugged and said, "I don't know. I came down, played ball, got a good job while I was in school, made a little change, finished, got married, and here I am, teaching."

Like most of their neighbors, Bill and Joyce live in a moderately expensive house and have two cars. Most of their friends are teachers or professional people. Atlanta Negro society ranks high, and it seemed to me that life there must be largely cannibalistic with the competition for status so keen—status being based on material objects. The fact that so many people are so well educated cancels out any intellectual achievement. Ph.D.'s are a dime a dozen. Indeed among American cities, Atlanta, with Atlanta University, Morris Brown College, Clark College, Morehouse College (the Negro's Harvard), Spelman College, plus a couple of divinity schools, produces—and keeps—the highest number of educated Negroes.

Atlanta is the home of "M.L."—Martin Luther King. There was much talk of how he grew up and how successful he had come to be. But black Atlantans told me they required a city leader: "M.L." was so busy being a national Negro leader that his time for leading at home was always little, and his work, excluding the March on Washington, was not very effective in long-range gains.

Out of the search for a new leader may come Jesse Hill, Jr., editor of a Negro weekly, the Atlanta *Enquirer*. Young Mr. Hill and I didn't get on too well. At first he seemed to doubt my sincerity; then he indicated that I, coming from the North, was as far removed from the problem as a white man. Subdued heat flashed back and forth. His impatience was obvious. He did say that a summit meeting representing eight organizations was being called to find a new leader for Atlanta.

Dr. Albert Davis, a man with a sense of humor (Hill showed none) and a vision that surmounts the horizon, could also become a prime candidate. He is bitter because so few professional men like himself are deeply committed to action. "Atlanta politics are pretty much like politics anywhere," Davis said. "Joining the Old Guard"—conservative Negroes—"which acts out of a sense of personal belief, mostly, are the Negroes who accept payoffs and who find later, when it's time to make demands, that they cannot."

Davis is a slender man who slides easily between the vernacular of the street Negro and the precise grammar of the medical profession. He leaned back in his chair and went on: "Our big problem is resegregation—the closing up of places we've already opened. We don't have the follow-up. The first-class places are usually the ones that open first, but who can afford to take dinner out two or three times a week? They see that we aren't coming back right away and without fanfare reinstitute the old regime. We've got to organize our people so that they will, by turns, keep the pressure on those places, get them used to seeing us in them." He looked very weary when he stood to go.

One of the people I most wanted to meet and talk with in the South was Ralph McGill, publisher of the Atlanta *Constitution* and winner of a number of awards for journalism. I had enjoyed much of his writing and appreciated the importance of the time in which he wrote. It was surprisingly easy to arrange the appointment.

He was not as tall as I had imagined from his pictures, but just as sturdy, just as ruddy. He seemed glad to see me, although he didn't know me. He would be glad, I imagined, to see a Negro walk through the door of his office on assignment for *Holiday*, and later he implied as much. We sat in his office, a room made all the more cozy because of the hundreds of books in it. They gave off the smell of freshly printed pages still to be opened, and combined with this was the comfortable odor of ink and newsprint from the presses downstairs. My eyes kept sweeping back to the books. The man was inundated with them. I imagined a hundred publicity people in publishing houses checking off his name and saying. "McGill *must* get a copy of this one!"

I found him very deliberate, most cordial and warm. As we edged our way into conversation, he was leaning back in his chair, his hands folded over his head. Downstairs, on Forsyth Street, a part of the business district of Atlanta, the city hummed on its way.

Was there a possibility of a political civil war between Democrats of the North and South?

McGill did not think so. He expressed the hope that change would be more rapid after the Old Guard—white, in this case—passed. He stared at the ceiling and, as if receiving an idea from it, said, "We're now in a time of change and examination. It goes slowly. An idea gets going, stops, starts, takes form, becomes alive, becomes real."

Atlanta had changed in the past decade or so, I observed. He smiled a little. Yes, it had. "New businesses which require trained people, black and white. We need a crash program." He came forward in his chair, its spring catapulting him toward a stack of newspapers. He thumbed through one and ripped out an ad placed by a vocational school which offered courses in data processing, computer programing, computer analysis.

"They'd hire a nigra just as quickly as a white man if he had these courses under his belt. We have a constant influx of rednecks who don't have the training in human existence, let alone formal schooling."

Nigra? I thought.

I asked if he believed that college education had been over-sold among Negroes. Negro families were bending all their efforts toward getting their children into college and keeping them there. Negro communities were being glutted with academicians. Should there not be a return, not to the fundamental Booker T. Washington formulas of working with the hands, of being one with the soil and separate and apart from whites, but to blue-collar work attuned to automation, whose demands were daily growing greater?

"No, college hasn't been oversold," he said. "We'll always need college-educated people."

And now a wall began to grow between us. He was not aware of it, and it was not a wall as such but a great difference of opinion. I had been meeting social workers, teachers, college instructors, doctors, nurses, insurance managers and the like. Only in a barbershop had I met the people of the street, loud with their arguments, unmindful of passers-by, plain, vigorous, kinetic. Between the Negroes of the street and the Negroes of the professions there existed very little contact.

To what extent had resegregation hampered desegregation efforts?

In his view, the places which had opened to Negroes (he said this time) were still open to them. And others would follow suit. I wondered what would happen if Doctor Davis and Mr. McGill ever sat down together to compare notes. McGill is white. He doesn't have to go out to dinner when he doesn't want to or can't afford to, just to see if a place will let him in, merely to keep a foot in the door.

Was he aware of police harassment of Negroes?

"Rednecks. Country people who are always difficult."

I suppose when a man is very famous and very good in his field, a great many people beat a path to his door, and after a time there are no new questions he can be asked. All the answers are at his fingertips. And I am sure he had reason to be pleased with the changes in the city, changes for which he was partly responsible.

I sat there irritated with myself because I could not find within myself that stunning question to ask, a question that would catapult him forward once more, that would even explode the warm cordiality in which we sat. We had reached, I felt, a kind of impasse. I liked him very much, but knew him well, instinctively. His words, "We are a part of all we've met," told me that, in a way, he knew me too. He rose, stretched his hand across a pile of books and said, "Just remember—change. Ten years ago you would not have been here as you are, not even three or two, for *Holiday*."

I think he saw me, in that moment, as a product of his work.

It was morning. Bill Eure stood beside the car. Last-minute instructions. "Remember, stop for your gas in the large cities, don't mess around with the small places. As soon as you see a speed zone, *slow up*. Don't wait for another sign. Even if you don't see a sign but there are houses, slow down. Some of these places don't post the speed limits until you're on the far side of town, and by then you've had it. They'll pull you back to appear before the judge, but the judge won't be there. They'll tell you that you have to post a bond of fifty dollars, seventy-five or a hundred. They'll tell you when to come back and appear before the judge. You never come back; who in the hell wants to come back to Georgia? And they *know* that all you want is to get away. Watch your step, keep your tongue inside your head, and *remember where you are.*"

A fine goddamn send-off. I clutched my sandwiches and looked longingly toward the north, but got in the car and drove on south toward Alabama.

I had crossed the border and was driving through a small town when I almost missed seeing a red light. I rammed down hard on the brakes and would have hit the windshield had it not been for the seat belt. The squeal of my tires attracted the attention of passers-by, and I cringed in the seat. A youthful daydream came flooding back into my mind. After every reported lynching I saw myself in a specially made car, with perhaps Bill Eure and about four other friends, heading South. Built into the front of the car were three machine guns, two .30-caliber and one .50. The two .30's could track 90 degrees on each side. The car, of course, was bullet-proof, and the engine was supercharged; nothing on the road could catch us.

The light changed and I continued on through Alabama.

One morning, as I neared the town of Tuskegee, I stopped to pick up five Negro children hiking patiently along the road, tattered notebooks under their arms. I asked the obvious question: "Going to school?"

"Yes, sir," said the boy who seemed to be the leader. His head was long, and behind his long, curled lashes, his big eyes were bold.

"How far do you have to walk?"

"Three mile." The other kids were looking at and feeling the red upholstery, giggling and sneaking glances at me.

"That's a long way to go," I said. They kept turning, picking out, I supposed, landmarks they would not yet have reached on foot.

I let them out at a narrow path. "Where's the school?"

"It back there," the leader said, pointing. I looked. Far beyond the roadside sat a gray, leaning building. It looked like a disused barn.

"What kind of school is that? Don't you go to a public school?" The boy shrugged.

"Is that a church school?"

"Yes, sir," he said. "I guess."

The others, already running into the woods, shouted, "Thank y', mister." Hurrying to tell about the man with the beard and the big car with the strange license plates. Hurry on, then.

I had late breakfast in Tuskegee and then headed for Montgomery, the cradle of the Confederacy. Its streets and buildings seemed to me shabby. There was a listless, to-hell-with-it air about the city. I didn't like it; I don't like it now.

I checked in at the only hotel for Negroes. It was a miserable two-story hovel with a restaurant. The clerk asked me if I wanted to pay in advance.

"Only if you insist," I said.

"Them's the rules," he said.

"I don't think much of them rules," I said, but I paid and left a deposit on the key.

This was the town that started the struggle in 1955, when the Negroes boycotted the buses with M.L. leading. As a direct result, I was told, the attitudes have hardened since then. "Nothing much going on here," an elderly man said. "After all we been through, it looks like it was for nothing. Maybe the buses changed, but not much else. Town's as tight as a drum."

I drove to Alabama State College, which looked, as so many do in the South, like a high school. A group of students gathered around the car. "You from the North, mister?"

"Yes, from New York."

"Where you going when you leave here?"

"Mobile."

"Mobile? Got a gun or *some*thing? They pretty bad down there."

"I got something," I said, thinking of my skinning knife at the bottom of a duffle bag under a seat.

"You better have. They tough down there, mister."

Wouldn't anyone give me a good word along the way, something cheerful?

I looked for a chap whose name had been given to me, but learned he had had the good sense to leave. As a substitute, I was offered a professor of sociology. I won't name him. I am sure that if Governor Wallace wants to give him a medal, he can be found. For myself his name is a four-letter word—and I wish I could think of something worse. I introduced myself, but the words were hardly out of my mouth when he said, "Governor Wallace pays my salary; I have nothing to say to you. Excuse me, I have a class to get to."

And he went in his finely cut suit; he went out to teach young people the mechanics of getting along with one another. I stomped down the stairs, my stomach suddenly kicking up, and crept back to my hovel of a hotel. I lay in the sagging bed and thought of all those people who had walked all those miles for the right to sit anywhere on a bus, and here was a man of position, of some intellect, who in his own quiet way was working just as hard as the segregationists to maintain the status quo. And what was he teaching those kids on Governor Wallace's pay check? I shudder to think.

I had no trouble in Mobile; I wasn't there long. Then I was cruising along the Gulf, looking out toward the sea. Without a perceptible change in the palm trees, I was in Mississippi, driving through Biloxi and Gulfport. The land now was flat and sandy, sparse, as it is in the Hamptons on Long Island, but the sea was bluer and warm air wafting in brought with it a hint of salt. Way out there were Cuba, Haiti, Puerto Rico, the Virgin Islands. I thought of lazy days in St. Thomas and Puerto Rico, of good swimming, good food and good drinks. Ah, perhaps New Orleans would be like that. Perhaps, perhaps.

With the map of New Orleans on the seat beside me, I managed to find the way to Mason's Motel on Melpomene Street. As

I rounded a curve, gay colors leaped over the gray houses. Mason's Motel! After the dump in Montgomery, the road *had* to lead up.

Mason was a tall, thin man, graying beneath his wide-brimmed hat. His grin was broad and his eyes danced. I had the feeling I had met him before. He gave me the M. L. King suite for half the going rate. But before I could get to it, he took me to the bar and introduced me to a group of market specialists, those people who go about convincing businessmen and Madison Avenue how many millions of dollars are spent in the Negro market. I knew the types. Bourbon all around. "Drink up, Williams. Drink up." I drank. They were going to show me a big night. Where was I from? New York? Yeah—and veils began to drop over their eyes.

A fresh member of the group showed up with a new iridescent suit and tried it on to cries of, "Man, that's tough!" "It flashes, Billy." The new man described what he would wear to a dance that night. The eyes of the others around the table glittered.

They asked me more about myself and the veils dropped further. Even so, they urged me to get some rest for the big time ahead that night. We'd have a ball.

I went upstairs to the M. L. King suite and dropped off to sleep. When I woke it was past the hour for our balling, and there had been no calls.

"The boys taking you out tonight?" Louis Mason asked with a grin.

"Supposed to," I said.

They never showed. I spent the evening talking with people in the bar and eating red beans and rice with Louis.

I don't know why I thought New Orleans would be different from other cities in the South. My dreams, I guess. I went to the motel's roof-top patio and almost did fall in love with the city. A slight breeze blew over the roofs. I listened to the music coming up from below and wondered what it was about me that had put the hucksters off. From the next block came the organ and tambourine sounds of a revival meeting. There seemed to be a lot going on.

The next day I called a restaurant to make a reservation for dinner, saying that I was from *Holiday*. The reservation was quickly confirmed, so quickly and effusively I felt as though my hand were being kissed from the other end of the wire.

"Wait a minute," I said. "I'm Negro."

There was a long pause, as if the poor man were trying to catch up with the world and had become breathless from the effort. "Oh, we can arrange to send you something."

"Forget it."

I went downstairs and out to the old section, the French Quarter, thinking how strange it was that a city as cosmopolitan as New Orleans should be part of the old order. Its appearance, its layout, its people all seem to belie its Deep South character. I walked the streets of the Quarter and stopped in amazement at the Mammy dummies. They were full-sized, big-bosomed, black and dressed in loud colors. They stood outside the gift shops. Were the white shopkeepers merely making fun of Negro femininity or making fun of their own fear of it? I shopped the Quarter and found only trash, and therefore bought nothing. The clerks hustled, of course, as they do in Greenwich Village; if they didn't have what I wanted, they tried to sell me something else.

I returned to the motel and got directions to the colored restaurant that last night's red beans and rice had come from. "Soul food," Louis said. "Good."

I walked around the corner and got lost. I looked up the street and down, but saw only one restaurant, Nick and Tony's. At the time it didn't even bother me that the name sounded wrong. I crossed the street and went in. The place was rather dark. Several men, all white, were standing at the bar. I walked up, placed my elbows on the bar and looked around. The bartender came running toward me.

"Outside. I'll take your order from the window." He pointed. Ah, yes, the Nigger Window.

"I only want information," I said.

"All right, let's talk outside," the bartender said. He was a big man, going to pot, with a full head of hair and the kind of face that you forget one second after you've seen it.

We moved outside, and as we did, several of the men at the bar followed us out. I told the bartender, without glancing at the others, that I was looking for a colored restaurant. He said he didn't know any and waved in some obscure direction. I left them, never having felt, if indeed I was supposed to, any threat. But the threat was there. I just could not, even refused to, cope with the thought of violence snowballing over nothing. But that is the South, and the North and the East and the West. And the moment I entered Nick and Tony's I had committed the unforgivable sin: I had not kept my mind on danger. I had dropped my guard—and had walked away without a lump. Lucky.

The restaurant that served the soul food was not a place to eat soul food in, and I brought it back to the motel with me. Relating my adventure at Nick and Tony's to the regulars in the bar, I received only quiet smiles; no laughter. Had I jeopardized the peace and tranquillity of custom, and therefore brought danger to them?

Next door to the restaurant stood an old theater. In the street was a large van which advertised that Gene Ewing, a revivalist, was bringing a "Living Christ to a Dying World." I saw elderly Negro women, late for the meeting, hurrying to it, sweat spotting their hastily powdered faces. Ewing was white. He sold Christ and he sold books; and I heard somebody complain that, if Negroes would give as much to the movement as they did to that cracker Ewing, we'd get things done.

When I saw Ewing on the stage, he looked to me as though he could drive one of his two cars across town and join a rock 'n' roll band without a change of pace. Perhaps he had hit a gold mine with Negro audiences—he a white man, preaching to people who couldn't get into the white churches in their city. He had moved into a Negro neighborhood (at least to conduct the revival) with his giant van with all kinds of leaflets in it, and his organ. . . . Rock, Gene, *rock!*

One night an acquaintance drove me in his own car to a good

restaurant. On the way back to the motel, we were stopped by
two policemen. We had been traveling rather fast, but I had
assumed that my host understood the risk. He had a gun in his
car, a .32 automatic. The cops found it and began hitching up
their pants and puffing their chests preparatory to taking us in.
My host got out and took them aside. I sat wondering what a
New Orleans jail would be like. He returned to the car and
drove away, the cops following. We went to his place of business,
and while I waited and the cops waited, he unlocked the door.
A light went on. A couple of minutes passed and my host returned, went directly to the cops, leaned inside the lowered
window, then came back to me.

"How much did they want?" I asked.

"Twenty. Ten each. Gave them twenty-five. They don't make
no money. You can generally buy 'em off." He looked at me and
grinned. "Scared?"

I had been badly scared. I had had visions of people saying,
"Gee, the last we heard of John, he was in New Orleans."

Jackson, Mississippi. That name, on my mind when I awoke
next morning, depressed me. Who was I kidding? Hell, I didn't
want to go to Jackson. Then, turning over in M.L.'s bed—in
which he had slept once—I remembered that I had already come
through a part of Mississippi, driving along carefully, looking at
the sea and palm trees. Besides, think of all those colored people
who've *always* lived there. That's *their* problem, I thought in the
shower.

Jackson is my mother's birthplace, and was her home for a
time. I was born there. My parents were married and made their
home in Syracuse, where I was conceived (I refuse to give all
my heritage to Mississippi), but they returned to Jackson for the
birth of their first child, according to the custom of that time.
Thus, in my family, a line of "free" Negroes on my father's side,
and one of former "slave" Negroes on my mother's side, were
merged.

Some years ago, my boys asked me, "Dad, where do we come
from?" Although I had started thinking what to tell them years

before, I was startled. Quickly I mentioned Jackson, but I was in panic. A man *ought* to be able to tell his children where they come from. I envied those Italians who return to Italy to visit their homes, the Polish and Hungarian Jews who return to see their relatives, the Irish who make the hop to Shannon and go off in search of old homes and friends. But the boys and I, seeking our lineage before Mississippi, moved to the map of Africa on the wall. We looked at the West African coast, and with falling voices and embarrassed eyes concluded that we could have come from anywhere along the 3,000-mile coast and up to 1,500 miles inland. Then to books with photographs of Africans. Did we resemble any of the people shown? Around the eyes? The cheekbones? The mouth? Which were our brothers? Another check: which peoples were brought to Mississippi? Ah, how can you tell, when they arrived in coffles from other states, already mixed with a hundred different peoples? Mandingo? No, most certainly not. Kru? What, then—Baule?

"Dad, where do we come from?" Up to great-grandfather, some trace; beyond him, fog. We came out of fog. We did not perish in it. We are here.

But Jackson lay north; at least the direction was right. I had tired of down-home Southern cooking, soul food. Let them sing about it. Now I know the dark, greasy gravy, the greens cooked to the consistency of wet tissue paper, the grits, the red-eye gravy, the thick, starchy rice. I ate my breakfast, one of soul food, and drove out of New Orleans on the Pontchartrain Causeway. The twenty-four-mile ride over the soft blue water was hypnotizing, as if the end of the ride over that stretch of steel, concrete and asphalt had to be a plunge into the lake. At first, up ahead, there was only the suggestion of land, a silvery haze rimmed in a darkness; only that and the causeway, with few cars going and coming on it. But presently the land at the northern end of the lake became solid, took on color, green and brown. Then the lake lay behind me, its clean, small morning waves dancing now for other drivers.

I was still in Louisiana, but in "stomp-down cracker" land, and I had to start watching my step more carefully. I stopped for gas, and again the ritual of the South was trotted out; a Negro attendant came to wait on me. The white attendants, in the stations that can afford this silly double standard, take care of white customers. Before long I had threaded my way across the border and into Mississippi. The land along the way was flat. Although I watched the speedometer, the car sometimes seemed to have a mind of its own, like a colt: it would leap forward, and it would be seconds before I could get the motor to simmer down and keep me out of jail. "I'm gonna let you run, baby," I promised it. "Later."

My *Travelguide* had given me the name of a hotel in Jackson, and I came upon the city cautiously, looking for the street. From the south, the city sweeps from a plain to a modest hill, but the aspect is one of flatness and of rigidly dull buildings. Used-car lots filled one side of the street, small hardware stores the other. As I drove up the gentle hill, the stores improved in quality and in merchandise. Following directions, I drove off the main street, went two blocks—and suddenly the streets were filled with Negroes. I had arrived in the Negro section; it seemed boxed in. Almost at once I saw two colored cops; they were employed after the summer demonstrations and they seemed, in their new uniforms, as proud as kids in new drum-corps suits.

The hotel was very much like the one in Montgomery, even to the key deposit. But why run a place in this manner simply because transient Negroes have no other place to stay? Segregation has made many of us lazy and many of us rich without trying. No competition—therefore, take it or leave it, and you have to take it. The slovenly restaurant keeper, the uncaring hotel man, the parasites of segregation need only provide the superficial services of their business. I had coffee in the dingy little dining room and rushed out, overwhelmed by the place, which not only accepted the code of Mississippi but enforced it to the hilt.

I fled to Jackson State College, but even there I found small comfort. Somewhere this must end, I thought, walking around the campus. Tennessee State, Alabama State, Jackson State, a pattern. Brick buildings like high schools, surplus prefabs, some grass, some dirt. Here, you colored people, take this! But had I been brainwashed, perhaps? I have seen many campuses rolling among soft hills or edging up the sides of valleys, overhung with chestnut and maple and cedar. I have seen domes and columns, and baroque and Gothic structures, cushioned lecture seats and marble walls inscribed with gold; I was spoiled.

I wrestled with these thoughts and finally knew them to be valid, however brainwashed. No great ideas of the past stalked these halls or sandy stretches of walk. When the state legislatures of the South created the Southern Negro college, they thought they knew what they were doing. Books and teachers and space. Build what you will. But the white schools had grass, and baroque and Gothic structures, and great ideas sometimes trod those halls, even if unminded.

I talked with a faculty member at Jackson State, one who, like Bill Eure, had been raised in the North. I asked the inevitable question. He sighed heavily and answered, "I've been in the South a long time now. We have this house. I have my doctorate. I make good money and I'm in a position to maneuver for more. I've got security"—and he reached over and pushed my knee. "Up there—you know how we lived in my town—we had nothing and couldn't *do* anything, couldn't go places. Here, I keep my nose clean. I don't look at white women. I have my contacts. Hell, everyone in this business has his contacts, better have them. My wife has her car, I have mine. I ask you, what in the hell would I have had up there?"

I nodded, too depressed to continue. The elite among the Southern Negroes, the teachers and professional people, were as estranged from the masses of Negroes as the whites were. If New Orleans is any example, the people I met there were not of the professions, and they seemed totally without leadership, but at least they talked about the movement. In Mississippi, few did.

What can instructors so far removed from life give their students?

"We give them a cycle of ignorance," another Jackson man, not a teacher, said to me bitterly. "Many of our instructors are ill prepared to teach, because Southern legislatures don't care about their ability as long as they make the shoddy mark set up for them. They in turn pass on a haphazard education to their students, many of whom become teachers themselves. From last year's class, for example, seventy-six students became teachers; only eight went on to graduate or professional schools; two became secretaries, and so on. Seventy-six teachers. They will pass on what their instructors gave them, and so down the line. Yes, some go to the big schools in the North for advanced degrees, but not because they're interested in the course. More money."

True, some of what the Southern Negro teacher learns in the North (what it is capable of teaching) may filter down to his students. But if the motive isn't pure, can the method be?

And yet, out of the wastelands that whites and Negroes together call colleges, there has come the rebirth of America's greatest idea, that a man is a man and is free under the sky and over the earth. From brick buildings so new that they still sparkle red, from dingy prefabs, from re-used floors, from out of the desert, and despite many of their teachers—from here have come sit-ins, Freedom Walks, kneel-ins.

I drove out to Tougaloo, where Ola, my mother, went to school. Much more beautiful than Jackson State, Tougaloo Southern Christian College is set among grass-covered mounds, within touch of partly timbered land and with a forest in the background. I tried to picture young Ola walking about in this setting. When she was here, the school trained domestics; young Negro girls were taught that their mission was to serve white people, unless they could find other work and the chance of that was small. Ola has spent better than half her life in other people's kitchens and bedrooms and bathrooms. She knows more about white people than they can ever know about her. I hoped the campus had been as nice in her day as it was during my visit.

At the moment, however, the place was buzzing. White men had been riding past the campus at night and firing blindly into it. The co-eds were unsettled, and male students stood guard at night. My mother would call the gunmen "night riders," and every Southern Negro who has ever lived in an outlying section knows what the term means. A woman or a girl found outdoors alone at night was subject to mass rape; a lone Negro male walking home was subject to a beating. By whites. It was for these reasons that my grandfather, who had five daughters to worry about, kept a loaded rifle slung over the door—and he knew how to use it. Here at Tougaloo, however, the male students shot at everything that moved, sometimes even at instructors returning from Jackson. Perhaps they knew what they were doing.

I drove back to my hotel feeling disassociated. I had not found the family roots in Jackson, and felt as though we had sprung out of air. When I checked out the next morning, the boarders in the dining room were talking about drilling for oil and the chance of striking it on property they had. They would be rich because, as one said guffawing into his coffee, "All the scared niggers done left Mississippi and ain't got no more claim on anything." General laughter, in time for my exit.

There are two reasons why Greenville, Mississippi, is unlike Jackson. One is that the city is a river port and thus a place exposed to ideas and people from outside the state. The second is that the Hodding Carter family lives there and publishes the *Delta-Democrat Times,* a "liberal" newspaper.

I went to Greenville to see Hodding Carter, Jr., who has taken over the paper from his eminent father. I thought, as I drove carefully through the neat, quiet streets, this is a place where a man ought to be able to relax. Yet I was cautious even in asking directions to the paper. I should have been more relaxed; I had been in the South long enough to learn that whites and blacks weren't continually at each other's throats; that their back yards touched and that they sometimes chatted across the back fences. In the shops—in Atlanta, in Nashville, even in Jackson—I had heard cashiers say "Thank you" to Negro customers and had seen clerks waiting on Negroes go rushing off to the storeroom for

items not on the shelves. There was not the cleared space, the
No Man's Land, the demilitarized zone. No, lives dovetailed.

Carter's office was a dark, leathern kind of place, comfortable;
there was something solid here, I felt. I knew something about
him—not much, to be sure, but something. I knew that even
though he was away from home, someone was guarding his family with a loaded firearm. I knew that he had learned to live
with threats on his life. This was the price for holding a view
unpopular in his city and state—that a law existed, a federal
law, and should be obeyed. The Carters were not for Negroes
but for law, and because they were, in the minds of the white
masses they were "nigger-lovers."

Of all the newspaper people I had talked to about civil rights,
only Carter said, "It's going to get worse before it gets better."
Surely the others must have been aware of the steady approach
of violence, but they avoided the problem as if to wish it away.
For Carter, there was not even the hope that matters would improve with the passing of the Old Guard. The throb of violence
was too near, and only a miracle could avert it.

It had become almost a macabre game, by now, asking questions and having them answered. I found myself looking for
some new nuance. No. The questions we asked, the answers we
gave bounded from one corner of a closed box to another, like
Mexican jumping beans.

I felt a sudden, billowing tiredness. I tried to conceal it, but
Carter saw it. "What's the matter?"

"Tired," I said, not at all surprised that I would admit it to this
stranger, who, in a larger way, was not a stranger. "Tense," I
added.

"I'll bet you are," he said, and he grinned. "First time South?"

"Since 1946, but I was born in Hinds County."

His nod was an understanding one.

As we parted he gave me directions through a less trouble-
some part of the state. But driving away, heading for Tennessee
and points north, I knew I had to take the other route, the one
where possible trouble lay, in order to live with myself and in

order to overcome the shame I suddenly felt at confessing my tiredness, my tension to this white man. Drive the cliff edge.

The land was flat, the earth powder. Trees rimmed the distance, so far from the fields that I could not tell what they were. Cotton fields with Negroes in them, pulling long gunnysacks. I thought of Ola and her sisters and brothers and wondered what it had been like for them to pad between the bushes snatching off the cotton and dumping it into the bag in one motion, for speed meant money, money meant survival. There were fields filled with peas and corn. How level the land was, empty almost, as if even the great Mississippi had fled it in terror.

Above, the sky held blue. It was colder now. I wanted to make southern Illinois before I stopped. I edged through the dangerous towns, tired but somehow hyperalert, at times seeing what wasn't there and hearing what had no sound. Clarksdale. Ah, there was a town that Carter had warned me about, but I was through it and on the open road again. Tunica, Hollywood and the land continued flat, but the timber was growing taller. Now the fields began to tilt upward, the timber thickening. Eudora off to the right and then, right on the Mississippi-Tennessee border, Walls! Coffee now, a ham sandwich and a rest.

Now through western Tennessee, through Kentucky, threading along mountains in the falling night. They turned from green to gray, from blue to black. The night became my ally, shielding me from the police in the small towns. I know many Negroes who travel in the South only at night. Now I knew how fugitives felt when they crossed these borders, waiting joyously for starlight.

The drone of the car was making me sleepy and I lowered the rear window. Cold air came snapping into the car, whipped at my ears, numbed my nose. I should stop now, I told myself, for I was driving with my left foot on the gas pedal; my right knee had almost locked, and I had it stretched out toward the right-hand door. There was no place along my route where I could stop in safety. And the rule among Negroes who travel in the South is: don't sleep in your car. Now the high beams of oncoming cars and the lights of towns were blinding me for a second, and I knew that soon I'd have to stop. Where was I? Tennessee, Tennessee, *Kentucky*. Kentucky, Kentucky, *Illinois*.

Let it have changed in this section, let it have changed.

It had. After fourteen hours, I was in a warm room and a warm bed, after hot food and a bath to soak my knee.

I arrived in Chicago about noon, scuttling along the Dan Ryan Expressway or, as the natives call it, the Dyin' Ryan or the Damn Ryan, because of the high accident rate. Driving along, I was remembering the imitation whisky during the war, the jitneys hustling up and down South Parkway, Lindy-hopping at the Parkway Ballroom; and remembering my great-aunt, who used to wait up for me, when I was on liberty, and try to hustle me off to church if the next day was Sunday; remembering Tiny Bradshaw and Charlie Parker at the Savoy, the boxing ring next door, the smell of fried chicken and fish that permeated 47th Street; remembering girls, and one New Year's Eve on Calumet Avenue when people were opening windows and shooting pistols into the street; remembering Chicago hippies in wide-brimmed hats, draped coats and wildly pegged trousers and knobbed shoes.

There were times when I did not love Chicago at all, but at this moment, like an old love you've never forgotten, it insisted itself on me. Of course much of this had to do with the sense of freedom I felt, after experiencing restriction at every turn in the South. Even an illusion can be infinitely more satisfying than the stark reality of nothing at all.

Lunch with Bob Johnson and Hoyt Fuller. Bob is managing editor of *Jet* magazine, a Negro news weekly. He is a small man, dark, electric, demanding of himself, his family and his staff. Hoyt, the editor of *Negro Digest,* is a tall, sharp-faced, unruffled man. With them I felt myself loosening, laughing at everything, relishing my Martinis, emerging from mild shock. The dark fears of the South were behind me. The thought of the legislated anarchy that exists down there, and of my only answer to it, which was to slap it down if it slapped at me, slid to repose in the back of my mind.

There followed breakfasts in restaurants overlooking Lake Michigan, dinners in quiet places, and aimless rides to nowhere but the heart of the senses. There were parties and late hours and more dinners in exotic places with exciting foods. And women. How wonderful Chicago was with them, all sizes and colors and shapes. It was like New York, a potpourri, an invigorating blend, stylish, with the gestures a big city forces people to make. In Chicago the drummer from New York had nothing to sell. New York—isn't that a little place somewhere in the East?

I had started to feel human again. Actually, it did not take long—a few days at the most, and I was able to file the South on a shelf. The white people I met in Chicago, and there were not many, I met without ill will. There had been times in the South when my mind in its desperate cage had envisioned for me a life of no contact with whites. Stupid, but the idea held me together, and its purpose was not hate but survival. Chicago changed that. It was a blessed, tipsy island washed by a great amount of intelligence.

Just as I was at the zenith of normality, I appeared on a local radio show, one which accepted phone calls from listeners. My interviewer talked mostly about civil rights. The line was lighting up. And after a few calls, *the* call.

"Mr. Williams?" He had a young, white-boy voice.

"Yes."

"Have you ever been to Africa, Mr. Williams?"

"No."

"Then why don't you go?"

Loud laughter, fading, and then a click as I was saying heatedly, "Because the average Negro in America has six or seven generations of ancestors here, probably more than you, and has more right—"

"He's gone," my interviewer said. "He's gone."

Part II

It felt good to be on the open road again. I had found the drivers in Chicago most selfish but they were behind me now, scrambling through the Loop, zipping around Lake Shore Drive, killing one another on the Dan Ryan Expressway. Some forty miles north of the city, I let the car out and it jumped ahead, moving cleanly and easily, and the joy of having so much power at toe tip filled me completely. Here it was, the ground-level height of Everyman's automated existence. Get in, turn the key, set the gear and mash down. Beneath the hood, currents surged like flashes of lightning and hundreds of horses snorted, kicked and began to gallop. Two and a half tons of metal, resting on rubber hoofs, bucked for one second, then soared ahead.

As I had had the feeling of going downhill en route to the South, so I now felt that I was going uphill as I moved through northern Illinois, Wisconsin and Minnesota. The Illinois plain was but a memory now; the roads wound through hills and mountains, through thick coniferous forests, past dead and dying little towns with sturdily built homes, some a century old; and there were glimmering lakes and rivers and ducks floating close to the shore. Occasionally a pheasant speared up, catching the sunlight, his flight swift, beautiful and short, and vanished on the opposite side of the road.

In visiting various places in these states, I was either ignored or paid too much attention, and I don't know which disturbed me most. I think I prefer anonymity. One evening in Duluth, a city that climbs the side of a hill and overlooks Lake Superior with its ore-laden freighters easing in and out of the harbor, I dined at a restaurant on the lake's edge. I sat alone, clear across the room from the bandstand, but I noticed that the leader, who doubled on violin and trumpet, kept staring at me. He spoke to the rest of the musicians, and from time to time they all looked my way. I wanted so much to shout to them, "It's all right, fellows. I'm not a musician, and I'm not really concerned that your music is lousy—a jazz violin always is. Go ahead, knock yourselves out."

But then I'm always being mistaken for a musician. Perhaps it is my beard and color. In almost any night spot, no matter the city, a musician comes over and says to me, "Hey, I know you. Good to see you. I'm sorry, what's your name again?" Along with this go hearty handshakes and back-slapping. Then I tell them my name.

"Piano—you blow the piano?" (There is a fine pianist-composer named Johnny Williams.)

"No."

"Trumpet?"

"No."

"No. What do you blow then?"

"A typewriter."

I think those musicians in Duluth were relieved when I left the restaurant. They were, all things considered, pretty bad.

There is not much to do in the cities and towns of the northern plains. Night comes with a thudding finality, and the restaurants and bars are usually quiet places where a man can reflect on his day or escape reflection completely. I passed places where snow had fallen, but all I had was rain, or the threat of it. For days the sky was overcast. Mornings were never pleasant now, and the driving became monotonous, with flat black earth spread all around and only an occasional dun-colored hillock to break the monotony. My beautiful new car was spattered with dirt; its value was now purely utilitarian, for there was no sun to bring out its beauty. Except for a few other cars on the road and the occasional town, and one passenger train I saw rounding a great curve outside Duluth, the earth seemed uninhabited. I took a side road and it was worse. By the time I arrived in the outskirts of Grand Forks, North Dakota, I was mentally beat and hoping for some pleasant experience to lift my spirits.

It was in 1960 that I had heard some ugly stories about racial prejudice in Grand Forks and the nearby Strategic Air Force base—the kind of stories that were so commonplace during World War II that after a while they stopped being news. I wanted to see the town and talk to some Air Force people.

I found the town small and misshapen, gray in the rain, seeming to sit upon the plain apologetically. I checked into a motel that paid tribute to the old West. It had a corral, hitching posts, and of course a bunkhouse which held the rooms. I lunched quickly, asked directions to the air base and got behind my horses again.

At the gate of the base, the guard looked at my authorization very carefully. He was from Virginia, I judged, and had a heavy accent. When he called the Public Information Officer, he probably wanted to say, "There's a colored fella out here." But he looked at me once—I was standing close to the phone— and made the call straight.

At the Public Information Office a sergeant asked me to wait because the lieutenant was out. I noticed a Negro airman, second class, at a desk across the room. He was trying to stifle a smile. He winked at me a couple of times. I made a note to talk to him. I wanted to know what it was like for a Negro airman out there. I wanted to know for my sons, Greg and Dennis, who lean toward the Air Force, and because I am concerned that this world could be blown up by some madman. I am concerned whether that nut is black or white. I wouldn't be at all happy to know that a Negro, driven mad by prejudice, crazed by discrimination, decided to take out his hurts on everyone else, but we are well within the realm of that possibility.

Presently the Negro airman struck up a conversation with me. "Where you from?" he asked.

"New York."

"Manhattan?"

"Yes."

"I'm from Brooklyn." He smiled and winked once more. Surely he had something to tell me.

"Where you staying?"

"Motel about eighteen miles back toward town."

"I know that one. How long you going to be around?"

"Until tomorrow."

"Like wrinkled steaks?"

"Wrinkled what?"

"Chitlins."

"Chitlins? In North Dakota? Yes."

"My wife and I are having them for dinner. Come on over."

There was the nice thing I had wanted to happen. Even after the lieutenant came in and we sat talking in his office, I was conscious of this young Negro and his secret smile. Did no one else see it?

At first the lieutenant and I discussed such matters as "offensive posture," the missiles at this base, how long it took to get the bombers off (fifteen minutes), and so on.

"Being ready to go seems just as important as living normally," I observed. "Doesn't this create some mental conflict among the crewmen?"

"The crew are watched every minute on their four-day alerts," the lieutenant assured me.

"How many psychiatric cases do you have in, say, a year?"

"Don't know offhand, but those people don't get up. Every man in the crew watches the other men. Each one is carefully and routinely checked out."

I changed the subject. "You had a severe housing and racial problem here a couple of years ago. How's it going now?"

Without pausing he said, "We have 300 new base houses. They take care of 1,700 family units. We don't have any racial problems here. The town's wide open. Our boys get along all right."

We'll see, I thought while he was issuing a pass for me. He assigned the Negro airman to take me around. We went downstairs and got into my car. He drove. As we went down the road he turned to me and smiled. "You shook 'em up in there."

"How do you mean?"

"The lieutenant didn't know what to make of it all. When the call came in that there was a guy out there from *Holiday*, we expected—you know, a white guy. Then you came in." He started to laugh. He was in his early twenties, a nice-looking kid. He went on, "I don't know why the lieutenant sent you out with me. He wasn't using his head, you shook him up so much. There's a lot going on here."

"Like what?"

"It's a bitch here." We passed through gate after gate, pausing to show my pass to the guards. "I'll let you talk to some of the guys. Don't use my name though. I'm getting out in January. After that, I just don't give a damn, but they might take it out on some of my friends who still have time to pull."

I will call the airman Tim—just in case his tour of duty has been extended; just in case his friends are still there. And I hope the P.I.O. by now has changed post.

We cruised down the flight line and I stared at the silver birds squatting there, heavy-winged with fuel. Hound Dog missiles nestled in their metal armpits. We stopped at the Guidance Control Center, a cement-and-steel building rather like a vault, a mortuary, with most of the space given over to banks of computers, long, dark, formidable-looking objects. I could not absorb or comprehend all that these machines could do. The readiness of it all stunned me.

Finally my guide led me outside, my head swimming. With him was another Negro airman. He didn't wait for introductions. He said, "Can you help us?"

I thought, No, not twenty years later, still. But I fenced, I fished for my illusion. "What is it?"

He saw through my stupid question and did not embarrass me. I thought suddenly of Greg and Dennis. Can I help? What could I do, no matter how exciting the prospect of tackling the entire Air Force? The second airman flushed livid. He was dark, and now his skin took on an ugly purple color. He began ticking off his fingers: "We get passed over for promotions. We get the lousiest houses in town. We can only be served in two or three restaurants. Our officers, mostly from the South, don't back us up; they don't even care."

"What about your Negro officers?" I asked.

"Nearly all of them are on the crews and they stick to themselves. Once in a while some cracker gets drunk in the officers' club and calls them 'niggers'; everybody laughs for a week."

Tim spoke now: "We get the stiffest sentences, bar none, for minor infractions. And don't let something happen with the cops in town. The white guys really get upset when we have dances and some of the colored guys bring white girls from Winnipeg. We've had one or two rumbles already. They hush those up right quick. There are no colored women here, except the wives and daughters of the personnel. The single guys go all the way up to Winnipeg whenever they have time off rather than hang around this Jim Crow town."

"Your congressman?" I asked. The second airman was also from New York and lived in Adam Clayton Powell's district. He turned his face up to the skies in disgust and shifted his feet. "We wrote to Powell and he checked around and some brass told him it wasn't so and that was that." He spread his legs and placed his hands on his hips. "Look. You can use my name, that's how much I don't give a damn any more."

I felt fatherly when I said, "No, you don't want to do that." But I knew the feeling from my own days in the Navy. God, how I knew the feeling.

"I don't give a damn," the second airman repeated, with the air of one who is prepared to take matters in his own hands.

"I'll do what I can," I said, shaking his hand, and feeling useless as hell. What do I tell my sons now?

The chitlins were good that night, but the rooms that Tim and his wife shared were matchboxes with buckling walls. The place came furnished, but the furniture must have been brought from England at the height of the Victorian period; there was hardly room to pass between the chair and couch in the living room. Dinner was served on a card table. "So we can fold it up and make believe that there's more room than we actually have," the young wife said. She was a nurse in town, and hated it. "I've been here for months, but they still treat me like I'm some kind of freak."

Just as we finished, four Negro airmen in civilian clothes came in.

"Where you guys going?" Tim asked.

"To a movie," one of them said. "We've never been to one before in this town. We don't even know if they'll let us in, but we're going to try. Safety in numbers, you know." They all grinned. As they filed out the door, he turned and said, "Sure hope you can do something, Mr. Williams."

"Man, he's already started," my host said with a laugh. "He called *Jet* magazine two hours ago." I had phoned the editor, Bob Johnson, in Chicago.

"Yeah?"

"Yeah!"

So much faith in *Jet?* I don't know. They went out smiling; they hadn't come in that way.

Later Tim took me around the town, pointing out places whose windows ordinarily carried signs that read: *Indians and Colored not allowed.* But it was dark; the signs were small, and I didn't see them. Only the places where I was told they were. As we walked, we came upon a pinch-faced woman pushing a baby in a stroller. She slowed, as if demanding that we move off the sidewalk. When we didn't, she drew up her skinny frame and came straight ahead, looking neither right nor left. The stroller struck my ankle as she passed. I thought, You little bitch!

We passed beneath the Christmas lights strung along two or three short blocks in the center of Grand Forks. Merry Christmas.

The rains had come by morning, when I set out for Montana. By now I was becoming aware of people turning in their cars to look at me as I went by. I had noticed this ever since I left Duluth, but it hadn't mattered, not even when they pointed. Now I found myself suddenly tired of it all, the grins, the double takes. One man, his car filled with children, turned to grin and point at me. His car spurted dust as it veered off the narrow road and into the deep, rocky trench beside it. I watched him in the rear-view mirror as he skidded back onto the highway, and I felt nothing for him or the kids, not hate, not joy.

Now the land began to slant; the car hummed as it moved steadily up the hills, which were becoming mountains. The rain stopped and the entire sky became blue and unimaginably vast. It *was* the land of the big sky. After the plains, I exulted in the climb, the curves, the massive shifting panorama. Coming through one pass, with the sun burning fiercely high in the blue sky, I had the feeling that the car was aimed directly toward it. I went up and up and up, and as I topped the crest, I had the wild, joyous feeling that I could reach up and touch the sun, bring it down and fondle it in my lap.

I was still in some kind of secret, bubbling elation when I pulled into a gas station in a half-mile-long town named Wolf Point. The attendant buoyed up my mood with a big smile and the way he moved to check the car.

When he was finished he asked, still smiling, "Playing in town tonight?"

"I'm afraid I don't understand," I said, feeling that his question and my presence, put together, amounted to something terribly Negro.

He hastened to say, "I thought you were with the Harlem Globetrotters. I read they would be in town tonight. I'm sorry."

So he knew that he had goofed. The conclusion he had jumped to was based on color; had to be, for I stand only five feet eight inches tall. But I suppose it is a mark of progress to be mistaken for an athlete rather than an entertainer or a musician.

But my day was not complete. Later I walked into a motel. A teen-aged girl came out of a rear room and stopped dead still when she saw me. I asked for a room as if I hadn't noticed. She hesitated, still on the balls of her feet, and then said, "All right."

I pushed the matter, asking if my room were downstairs or up, and when she said up, I asked for one down. I didn't feel like lugging my gear all the way up and then down again the next morning.

The man I assumed to be her father wouldn't talk to me the

next morning. When I asked questions, he rattled his paper, reddened at the back of his neck, and continued reading. It was a good thing his daughter had been at the desk the night before.

Late in the afternoon, after turning south and coming through Great Falls and Missoula, where I had seen a group of Shriners riding the streets in Go-Karts, I found a camp site in the Bitterroot Range. I had crossed the Continental Divide at Rogers Pass, and there had been snow. There was even more snow in Lolo Pass, more than 5,000 feet up. But the air was clean and pure, and there were no people except a few deer hunters, and they were all on the way in. I dug out my cold-weather gear and dressed, then got a few dry twigs and some wood—and the instant soup and coffee were on, next to a can of sausages. Afterward I spread out the sleeping bag inside the station wagon. Now for a cognac. Peace, damn it, no people.

In 15,000 miles of travel on this trip, I was refused accommodations only once, and then not outright. It happened in Lewiston, Idaho. I had come through the mountains with night falling fast. The road had been tricky enough and ice and snow had tripled the hazards. And as I came into town, exhausted and with all defenses gone, I had a nagging feeling that this was going to be my night.

The woman at the motel told me that there were no singles left. She was dressed in black, with jewelry, as though she was ready to go to a dance or a party.

"Then a double or a family unit," I said, I had to get to bed. I wasn't even hungry.

She retreated to the back room, where she addressed a man out of sight in a voice so low that I was unable to hear her words. Another customer came in at that moment, a white man, and he stood with all the assurance in the world. There would be a room for him anywhere, any time. Then the woman raised her voice suddenly and sharply, and I heard her say, "Well, tell me. Do you want him or don't you?"

He didn't want me. The woman came out of the room walking very fast, her face set. "I'm sorry, but we have no more vacancies." I had been studying the racks where the registration cards are kept; there were only four slips in them. I took a deep breath to block the words that wanted to come out. Once they began, I knew, they would pull me along and I would not have been satisfied until I had torn the whole place apart. And yet, for all my anger, there was room in me for something else: pity for the woman who was the tool. Now she dropped her head and turned to the newcomer. He would have a reservation—at least in my presence.

For an instant, striding toward the car, I felt as though I were plunging helplessly down through space, with nothing to grab hold of. I raced the car around on screeching tires, fully intending to try every hotel and motel in town. I sped across the street to another motel, jammed on the brakes and bounded out, belligerent as hell.

And do you know what happened?

The clerk couldn't sign me in fast enough.

I sat in a parking lot in Walla Walla, Washington, and basked in the sunshine. I was waiting for Bill Gulick, a writer whom I had never met. I sat feeling devilish. Did he know that I was Negro? What would be his reaction? Over the phone he had invited me to sleep at his home. Would he suddenly find some excuse now? Well, Bill Gulick pulled into the lot and looked over at my car, the only one there. He got out and walked over. And didn't bat an eyelash over his wise blue eyes.

Bill and Jeanie Gulick have a small place outside town. They don't like cities, having lived in many of them from the Atlantic to the Pacific. From their yard I could see an occasional house, but mostly miles and miles of green fields backed by the brown, soft folds of the mountains.

In the afternoon we went on a trip around town, and to Ice Harbor Dam, where I peered down into the locks and saw, for the first time in my life, salmon swimming upstream. Perhaps it was the company of Bill and Jeanie, but I took a child's delight in watching the fish.

Later, over drinks, Bill and I discussed many topics. One I

asked about was the Abominable Snowman of northern California. Bill laughed. "People used the legend of a huge Indian to scare their children into behaving. But the kids got wise. Sometimes they went out and made a pair of big feet and tracked them through the mud and snow, scaring the hell out of their parents. To my knowledge, no one has ever actually seen the creature."

Then we ran down some of the giants in legend—Goliath, the one Jack killed, the ones lurking in *Beowulf*, and so on. Not once did we discuss civil rights. Bill Gulick did not demean me by assuming I could not be interested in any other subject; to him I was another guy, another writer.

I slept in the room where Bill works. The small brown desk with the office model typewriter sat ready. Behind, on the wall, were his working tools, and over the bed, his bookshelves. The place where I work is foolishly sacred to me. I get nervous when my boys sit at any desk and peck on the typewriter. If any visitor goes near my desk or starts peering at my papers, I automatically say, "Here! What are you doing?" But there I was in Bill's room, his work space, manuscript in progress and all. I felt very special.

I did not see much more of the great beauty of the Northwest because of the rain. I paused in Seattle and Portland long enough to have dinner and a talk with friends, and then started south to San Francisco, and thence to Los Angeles, where Ola, my mother, lives.

The rain followed me down the Oregon coast and into California, where I took the Redwood Highway for the sheer grandeur of it. The road twists and turns and sometimes doubles back upon itself, so that one moment I was in sight of the Pacific Ocean as it clambers in a wild white froth up the shoreline, and the next I was cast back thousands of years by the gigantic Sequoias which stood so tall and thick that they blocked out what was left of the gray daylight. The feeling they gave me was at once eerie, exultant and goose-pimpling. I reflected on *time*, time past and time passing. What was the earth like when those trees first took root? How I envied them; centuries and centuries old, they lived still, monuments to themselves.

It was Sunday, November 17, when I arrived finally in the driveway of my mother's home in Los Angeles. The lights were on, and Ola and my stepfather, Albert, stepped onto the porch. We went through the formal things, the handshakes, the embraces. "Thought you'd never get here," Ola said. "Waited dinner for you and then had to eat. Got hungry. But I did fix a few little ol' chitlins."

I am very fond of chitlins, and she knows it, yet she added, "But you don't like chitlins, do you?" She pinched me. "Does you, boy?" She believes my tastes have changed since I began to write, or at least she always tests to see if they have.

It has been a long road for Ola, accepting my desire to write. When I was young, she made one of her rare concessions—after all, I would surely change my mind about writing in a few years. She gave me a copy of Keats' poems bound in leather. Only my younger brother, Joe, had encouraged me—"Well, man, you know. Go ahead"—and today he actually doesn't mind that I have killed him off in two novels. But Ola in her letters to me invariably expressed, with little subtlety, the hope that things were going well—and she did not mean writing. Sometimes she would enclose a five- or a ten-dollar bill. At least she never asked me, as some of my other relatives have, "Are you *still* messing around with that writing?"

I feel many things when I visit Ola. A great pride that she is my mother, old hen that she is sometimes, and a sense of guilt. We have always sweated for our money in my family, and bent our backs, and often held our tongues because we had to eat, and to feed those younger than ourselves. When dawn breaks, I may be turning over in my bed. But I know that my mother and stepfather are up, warming the car, exchanging their first sleep-touched words before getting off to work. Joe may already be at work, since he heads up three departments for a manufacturer of lighting fixtures; I feel the same guilt whenever I shake his hand, because his is so big and hard, and mine, once also hard and callused, is soft except for the two fingers I use for typing. My sisters, too, are up and at work. And there I lie. It doesn't matter that I may have been writing until two in the morning. You cannot see a brain work; it doesn't smell of sweat and it doesn't wear out as quickly as a biceps. My body no longer is an instrument; my mind is. I am not saying that they do not use their minds on their jobs. I am saying that their *bodily* presence, more than their minds, is required where they work.

At times I think Ola understands my feelings better than I do myself. For example, the den had been cleared out for me to work in, and a heater hooked up to offset the chill of the Los Angeles mornings. It was her way of telling me that it was all right, my divorce from their way of earning a living.

I wanted to rest the next day, but I couldn't. I was up early—shortly after Ola and Albert had left for work—and out strolling the lawn, looking up and down the block for any change that had occurred since my last visit. There had been changes. My parents had been the first colored people to buy in the block. But by 1961, only four years after they had moved in, there were only three or four white families still there. Now they, too, were gone.

I spent the day browsing and doing nothing except getting bored with myself. And remembering how much I disliked Los Angeles in the short time I lived there. This brought to mind the house on Beverly Drive where I once worked as a butler. It had been huge, with two wings, a great dining room and cork floors. My own room and private bath were the epitome of luxurious living. I wore a serving jacket (white) at the table and a house jacket (gray) for dusting and cleaning. There were three children, two of them snots whom I had to drive to Beverly Hills High School each morning. I hated that job even before I began it. I could find nothing else. I had been unemployed in California for an astronomical number of days.

The day I started, the cook looked at me and said, "You ain't never buttled before, have you?"

"Oh, yes I have," I told him. I *needed* that job, which made me despise it the more.

"No you ain't," he said with a knowing smile.

"Aw, man, later for you," I answered.

Ola had given me a few quick courses on setting the table, serving and picking up. But as the day wore on and my hatred grew, the lessons were forgotten, and by dinner time I panicked.

"Man, help me with this goddamn table—please."

"I knowed it," he said. He laughed, how he laughed; but if it hadn't been for him I would have lost my job that night.

On this visit I looked up some friends in the next few days, and made a point of seeing Ola's doctor because she had complained of a couple of heart attacks.

"To my knowledge," the doctor said, "your mother hasn't had a single coronary. She has hypertension."

"She worries too much about all of us, and all the time," I said, suddenly amused. That old faker! What Negro in America doesn't have hypertension? And on top of that, Ola does worry —but unless she reads this, she will never know that I knew she wasn't as ill as she said she was. Perhaps we just need to let her know more clearly that we love her. Ours is not a very demonstrative family; you could be away ten years and return home, and one of us would say, "So what's new?"

Back at the house, Ola wasn't behaving like someone with a bad heart; she was planning a family dinner, a pre-Thanksgiving affair, since I would be on the road that day. I could hear her speaking on the phone to relatives and friends. Her lines were always the same: "I want you to come to dinner Sunday. Johnny's here. My boy Johnny, the writer. Yes. He's doing a little writing for"—and here she would pause for emphasis— "*the Holiday* magazine. Yes, uh-huh. All right, we'll look for you then."

John F. Kennedy was murdered in Dallas as I was shopping with my niece on Olivera Street. She tuned in her transistor radio, an instrument she is never without. Sobbing and broken voices rushed out of it: facts were helter-skelter and being altered every ten seconds. Customers gathered near us, stood shoulder to shoulder. One woman burst into tears on the spot.

A Negro man was reported to have fled the scene. A Negro boy was reported to have seen two people struggling on an overpass along the President's route. "Negro" kept running through the reports like some lesser theme in a wild symphony, a theme which seemed destined to become dominant at the finale.

We rushed back to the car, drove home and turned on the television set. There, calmly holding his earphone was baggy-eyed Walter Cronkite, a man who often irritates me, but who was a superb newsman that morning. On another channel, Frank McGee held forth, as calm but more solemn. Both were a relief from the sobbing, hysterical radio reporters.

Before long we watched a man-in-the-street show and heard an interviewee say, "Some nigger did it." And later in the afternoon, my sister called to say that they had announced in her school, over the public-address system in the cafeteria, that the assassin was a Negro. "Johnny, *we* would never do a thing like *that!* We're not crazy like *they* are."

The reports of a Negro assassin seemed to prove how fearful the white public is, at least in Los Angeles, of an outbreak of racial violence. They expect it. When Lee Harvey Oswald was taken in, a sense of relief seemed to descend over the city, which had probably come closer to a race riot than it dared dream. (I learned later that only two or three other cities had been bombarded with such racially slanted news.)

My mother kept rising from her deep well of depression to express her disgust ("They just haven't got any sense") and grief ("That poor boy riding with his wife on such a pretty day"), only to sink into it again. My niece wandered around sobbing. That day I watched my family reach across generations of poverty and persecution and extend to the Kennedys a deep and sincere sympathy. But a heavy air of irony remained, as if they had known all along that disaster, sickness and hate had to reach out and encompass even the mightiest.

That Sunday our pre-Thanksgiving dinner was a quiet affair, with nearly everyone watching television. Lincoln had gone to his burial by train, I thought, and Kennedy by jet; only the way they travel varies. In this land of the free, since the Revolution, Americans have averaged one murdered President every forty-four and a quarter years.

Then my car was idling in the driveway, with my gear loaded. The flag Ola had ordered flown at half-mast on the lawn was limp. There had been hints in our final words of time, what it gives and what it takes away. Ola and Albert are not young and have worked hard, and knowing that they must go one day is not an easy thing for me to accept, with so much distance between us.

Las Vegas was quiet that Monday after the murder, quiet and seedy, but outside the town the land has a harsh, rugged beauty. Farther east, nestled among the configurations of an ancient and terrible diastrophism, was Lake Mead, created by the tons of concrete that gave rise to Hoover Dam. Here the land is terribly warped, rising up from the ground to twist and spear toward the sky. In the center of that frozen violence is the dam, and never before had I seen the hand of modern man so beautifully and precisely merged with the hand of nature. I stopped at the rim and gazed down. The top of my groin ached with the primeval instinct to hurl myself into space, through the cleanliness of the scene, far down into the slowly churning blue-green water.

I had forgotten how strikingly lovely is northern Arizona. Massive snow-capped mountains, their shoulders spreading far across the land, rose thousands of feet into the sky. Now, passing through the towns, I saw life-sized figures of Indians, all males. Were these the counterparts of the Mammy dummies I had seen in New Orleans? And fittingly, I stopped in Williams, Arizona, to eat. I did so with trepidation, for I had been through Arizona four times before and had always been refused service. I do know Negroes who have had no trouble eating in that state, so perhaps I always picked the bad spots.

I was part way through my meal when a cowboy came in. He smiled and said hello. I did not think he was speaking to me, but turning around, I saw that I was the only other customer in the place. He asked if I'd heard Lyndon Johnson's address and I said I hadn't. He said it had been good. I was eating rapidly now, suspecting that he was buttering me up for a lift; I like to choose my passengers. I nearly choked from eating so fast in order to get out of there before him. But he beat me anyway and hopped off his stool, saying, "See you, buddy." He piled into a spanking-new car and drove away. My apologies, cowboy. My excuse is that I was wary; I had never before been served in a restaurant in your state.

I came to Denver from the south, through New Mexico. The way lies through Raton Pass and you drive through it with sun-rays bouncing off the snow-covered slopes. Because there was snow, the thousands of acres of timber seemed unbelievably green. Slush and ice lay on the road. In the most isolated places, you come around a curve and see a sturdy frame house tucked behind a grove of spruce, with smoke coming lazily out of its chimney.

The Colorado Plateau is a fantastic geophysical formation. For miles and miles, more than 5,000 feet up, it is flat, as flat as southern Ohio or Illinois. From every side you see the Rockies at mid-height. The air was clean and brisk; you can smell the snow on the peaks and sense the direct, enticing, suggestive flirtation of nature: come, make love to me; know me. But this love faded the closer I came to Denver and became involved in traffic, speedways and the choking odor, so prominent after the mountains, of gas and oil and hot metal.

In this "Mile High City" a wonderful thing happened to me—again. I made new friends. In a way, I think, this happened all over America, for doors were opened to me and people talked with me about many things, but mostly about themselves, as people are prone to do. There were the first few minutes of or-nate politeness, of stiffness, until, at last, the easy smile, the crossed leg—as if inner gears had just been shifted from low to high. I sat easily in the home of Bob and Marilyn Hackworth, who are white; I sat at dinner, talked without strain to kids. In the probing there had come a relationship, and I was no longer black and they were no longer white, my hosts and their other guests. It is so goddamn good just to be people, with hosts who until two hours earlier had never laid eyes on you, and who are whipping up the meal in the kitchen. Eating together, I think, is the basic expression of friendship.

I went with the Hackworths to the mountains, 5,000 feet farther up. We left on a clear, cold afternoon and at once began curving upward until we reached a ski resort. There, climbing out of the car, I became drunk and giddy with the altitude. What a marvelous explosion of space! We were in a kind of pit, and all around us the mountains rose powerfully, their narrowing necks collared with cedars and snow, except where the ski trails slashed through them. Bob and Marilyn may have been used to the view, but I was transfixed and hated to leave.

On the way down I remarked to Bob that I expected constantly to see an Indian in full headgear, his knees dug into the sides of his pony, atop one of the bluffs.

"Do you?" he said, his tone surprised and glad.

"OK, I feel foolish."

"Oh, no," he said. "*I* always feel that way, but I've never told anybody. Now I don't feel so silly."

It was something subjective, that shared feeling about Indians, and I guess friendships are built on such things.

We came to the old mining town of Central City just after dusk. It is small, with the present homes built atop old mining digs. The streets go up at a thirty-degree angle along the walls. The street lights are tiny, just barely glowing, and behind the counters of stores I could see silhouettes of people moving like ghosts. It is difficult to say what makes a man like a place. Half an hour at dusk, and *wham*—Love.

We took the back roads returning to Denver. Night had come, and the shapes of the mountains were bold and raw; they seemed ready to open caves and let loose dark secrets from the bottom of the world. I half expected to see, formed against the dark-blue sky, the shape of some monster never conceived in the mind of man. But nothing happened until we rounded a curve and Bob came to an abrupt halt. The headlights picked out a buck with a full head of antlers. His white tail flattened out behind him and quivered. He stared at the car and then, regally, turned to look into the darkness. This from the heart of nature, at night. No monster but a beautiful creature.

Then the buck turned back toward the car, lowered his head and began to paw the road. I have read and heard of bucks who will charge a hunter, but until that night I had never seen it happen. Still pawing, he lowered his head until his points became menacing. And then, with a scrape of his hoofs on the roadway, he started toward us.

Bob forgot all about the car horn. He, born of the near woods, with almost the physiognomy of an Indian and nearly as brown as one, forgot about the horn, the instrument of automated man. He flung open the door of the car, leaped out with his hair flying, and shouted, "*Boo!*" stamping his foot at the same time. The buck recoiled in the middle of his charge and scampered up the slope. Only then did we see the doe; she had been waiting in the shadows.

Denver lay below us. The moon was up fat and orange, and as we rushed downhill it was below us; we would, it seemed, rendezvous with it at some point down among the passes that led to the city. We drove in silence, each with his own thoughts of the night. We arrived in the city, the silence continuing. What, after all, was there to say?

We were having dinner with other friends, Irene Daugherty and her daughter, Patti Cutler. But other people were there, and the occasion was stiff for a while—until dessert, when Irene, her gray hair shimmering in the candlelight, her cheeks redder than usual, came out of the kitchen with a candlelit creamed pumpkin pie, and the entire table began to sing *Happy Birthday*. To me, a stranger wandering about the country. I did not know how they knew that my birthday was practically upon me, but there they were, friends and strangers alike, singing at the tops of their voices. I took the candle and placed it in an envelope, and I have it still to remember, when I look at my bookshelves where it is now placed how I went to Denver a stranger and came away enriched by friendships.

For a Negro, the face of the enemy is varied—all sizes and shapes and colors, even black. Often there is no face at all, but an attitude, one which I began to encounter after I had gone north through Cheyenne. East of the Warren, Wyoming, missile site, the land becomes a long, silent plain with tall, dull green grasses bending in the wind like waves of the sea. The towns along the way are small and filled with a chill. It was in this region that, whenever I presented my credit card at motels and gas stations, I began to encounter suspicion and deep distrust. The expressions changed; I no longer was an anonymous black. The attendants' eyes came up and saw me for the first time. Often they fingered the precious bit of plastic and gave themselves time to trigger all the ugly hidden machinery that told them, by everything they knew, that I should not have it in my possession.

One attendant, his face falling as I handed him the card, rushed into his office. I followed him and watched while he peered at the list of cards that had been lost, stolen or canceled.

"You won't find my name there," I said.

"I'm supposed to look anyway," he said, and while this was perhaps true, I knew and he knew that he didn't make it a practice unless he thought he had a sure thing. In many places the attitude persists that a Negro isn't supposed to have anything; that if he has, he is a thief. Still, clerks and attendants who hold this attitude expect a Negro to have a bundle of cash to pay his bills on a cross-country trip. Paradox.

The middle of America is a lonely place; oases of life are few and far between, and usually small and cautious of strangers. I felt no response to me, except a coldness, all through Nebraska and Kansas until I came to Kansas City, Missouri, and there I found worse than coldness, at least for the moment. While I was waiting to register at my hotel, one old maid clerk nudged another and, looking straight at me, said, "Something stinks." The other turned and shook her head grimly. I ignored them both. By now I was weary of being the catalyst by which white people make fools of themselves.

But my sense of rejection did not, could not persist with Thorpe Menn in town. He is the book editor of the Kansas City *Star*, and a man with whom I had become friends after three brief meetings in New York and a few hours spent in listening to jazz. He met me at my hotel and went into action at once, calling and gathering people for me to talk with, not as a traveler but as a writer. Thorpe believes I have something important to say and will not believe me when I tell him I haven't.

The beautiful thing about ugly Kansas City was the people I met through Thorpe. Of course, they formed a kind of closed circle, and what held them together was an organization called the Panel of Americans—a group of Negro, white and Oriental women whose religion could be Catholic, Protestant, Jewish, Bahai or almost anything else. Panel members journey to the hinterlands with their message of a united America, and more than that, they seem to live by their own message.

They gathered one night, with their husbands and children, at a party at which I was the guest of honor. The hosts were Paul and Esther Brown, a white couple. Talk ran the length and breadth of the room for a couple of hours. Then Thorpe called them together to listen to what I had to say. They gathered near my chair, some crouching down on the floor. I panicked. I prefer to leave the talking to those who enjoy it, and I evaded my audience as politely as I could.

But wasn't it something to see them all there? The house must have been bulging. The white neighbors of the Browns must have thought them nuts to have so many strange people coming to their home. The women around me, however, promised that, when I left, I would take some home-cooked ham and cake and other goodies with me—and wouldn't I eat some more right now?

I had known few people when I was in Kansas City ten years earlier, and had been uneasy there in the middle of a blistering summer. Now the weather was cold, but wherever I turned there was warmth. It goes without saying, except humbly and boastfully at the same time, that I felt good being in Kansas City.

Even so, I moved on eastward to St. Louis with an increasing depression. I had had a bad experience checking into my hotel in Kansas City. It had been even worse when I checked out. Besides, traveling in some parts of Missouri is like traveling in the South. The good people I met in Kansas City had told me that I must pick my spots for stopping; there were places the Panel of Americans had not yet visited.

I had last been in St. Louis ten years earlier, and had had to drive around and around looking for the colored YMCA. Now I drove directly to a bold, multicolored structure and up a sleek ramp and thence made my way to a room knee-deep in luxury —without a single sour look and only curious glances from the Negro parking attendants.

It was my birthday, and the occasion would have been sorrowful had I not spent the evening with two lovely young white women over *coq au vin* and candlelight. I had wearied by now of news of pickets and demonstrations, of charges that CORE's white members were too militant, that police had clubbed so many people. I no longer gave much of a damn about the presence of the John Birch Society in town. Enough was enough.

My hostesses talked about men, affairs, divorces. One of them came from the Deep South but had been away so long that she had no accent. The other was from a nearby town but had worked in New York where I had met her. Two lovely young brunettes sitting in the middle of a St. Louis night, the fog dripping heavily outside, talking about what seemed to them elusive. I looked at the flickering candles and thought of the women in New York, the roommates who also served *coq au vin* by candlelight, who also talked about the arts, superficially about civil rights—and men.

The candles burned lower; the wine was gone. At evening's end, after a nightcap of Scotch, Peggy walked to the door with me and out to the landing. She was the one who had fled New York; I do not know why. Down on the street, I could see a man waiting for a bus. His pale face glowed through the

dark and fog. I did not know if Peggy saw him. We embraced
and kissed, as we had done when I arrived, a friendly kiss
recalling a couple of dinners in New York and an evening
of listening to Ornette Coleman with his new sound when it was
new.

The face of the man in the street had frozen in our direction.
This was Missouri, and I have been set upon in New York for
less. I went down the steps and crossed the street to where
he stood. I passed in front of him, expectantly. A sick kind of
joy welled up in me. Parts of a hundred scattered dreams came
together in a completed puzzle. Only when I had passed him
did I realize that my right arm was tense, my fist drawn so
hard that the knuckles ached. No wonder, I thought, getting
into the car, my right armpit perspired more than my left; it
had been that way since New England, where my trip began.

I didn't linger long in Indianapolis, nor in Chicago, which was
now held fast in the grip of a bitter lakeside winter. Then I
was cutting across Ohio, driving dully, the seat belt tight against
my waist. In midafternoon I saw a patrol car coming up behind
me. I checked my speedometer and it read seventy, the limit.
I held steady at this speed, expecting the trooper to pass me,
but when I glanced around I found him keeping pace with me.
Then he signaled me to pull over.

After Kentucky, I had been followed by police or troopers in
Georgia, Tennessee, Mississippi; I had been pulled over in Illinois and California. Followed, pulled over and made to know
that I was a lone black man in a big car, and vulnerable as hell.
I had had enough. I snatched off the seat belt and rolled down
the window. It didn't give me room enough, so I practically
kicked the door open.

"What's the matter?" I shouted at the trooper. He didn't
answer as he walked to the car. And then I decided to commit it
all—my body, too, if he wanted it—for I would not take any
more harassment.

"Let's see your license."

"I asked you what the trouble was." That was not what he

wanted. The ritual said that I should hand my license over to him without a word.

"I want to see your license."

I gave it to him, smelling the odor of a man about to exercise the "insolence of office." It was the old game: "You black, me white, and I'm a cop besides."

He fingered the license and then, leaning casually in the window, said, "John, what's your occupation?"

I laughed. What does occupation have to do with an alleged traffic violation? Was the nature of my work supposed to tell him that I had money enough to pay him off? Was it to let him know that I was the "right kind" of Negro, one with political connections that could make it hot for him? Was I supposed to be jobless and transporting drugs, a corpse or young girls across the state line? Police and troopers of America, come a slow day, you can always find a Negro or two wandering through your state. Brighten up that day by making like exactly what you are.

"My name," I shouted, "is Mr. Williams." I'm sure that cops and troopers use the familiar address with many people who are white, but this one I smelled out. "John" was synonymous with "boy." He snatched his arm from the window. I flung my authorization for the trip at him. I watched him as he read it, and thought, not only am I not the "right kind" of Negro, not only will I not pay you off, but I am about five seconds away from total commitment—which means five seconds from beating your head.

He glanced over the top of the sheet. "Mr. Williams, you were doing eighty coming down the road. When I caught up with you, you were doing eighty-two."

"You're a liar. I was doing seventy. Eighty? Take me in and prove it."

"Mr. Williams—"

"Tired of taking all this crap from you guys."

"Mr. Williams—"

"You're going to run this nonsense *and* yourselves right into the ground."

Cars were slowing as they passed us. The trooper's face took on an anxious look. Yes, I was rambling in my anger, but I was ready to go. What is more, for the insults I delivered, he would have taken me in *had he been right*. Instead, he returned to his car and I drove on—at seventy miles an hour.

The explosion of anger, pent up for so many weeks, left me more exhausted than ever. But I kept thinking about the direct and indirect insults I had received from clerks, bellboys, attendants, cops, strangers in passing cars. I believe the white friends I made on this trip would have been just as incensed as I was, but they were far from me and I was completely vulnerable to attacks against my black person. A physical attack might have been better; one never knows just how effective words are, or even if they are understood.

Christmas was but a few days away by now, and I had promised to return to Syracuse to spend it with my boys. I made it, though driving through snowstorms, on roads iced over for long distances, is a most nerve-racking experience. It is a paradox that the snow, coming down gently, blowing gleefully in a high wind, all the while lays down a treacherous carpet, freezing the windows, blocking the driver's view. The horses, the powerful electrical systems, the deep-tread tires all go for nothing. One minute the road feels firm, and the next you are sliding over it in a panic, wondering what the heavy trailer trucks behind you are going to do.

I arrived in Syracuse in a muddy-brown dark. There were traffic snarls from one end of the city to the other. It was quitting time, and those who had left the factories and the offices were Christmas-shopping. I crept and slid cross-town in gray-brown snow, pulled up in the driveway and leaped out. The snow was knee-deep.

"Well, look who's here," Greg said. "It's the old man."

"Hi, old man," Dennis said. We shook hands all around. We don't kiss anymore, not even on the cheek. Then we sat looking at each other.

"A glass," I said. They exchanged smiles. I've taught them to mix pretty good Martinis for me. Their mother, my former wife, came in and presently we sat down to dinner. Afterward she and I had a brandy. There was not much else that evening. My return had been quiet; there had been no questions. All the warm feelings had been cloaked.

"We waited until you got here to help put up the tree."

"You look tired. Have another drink, Dad."

"How long are you here for this time?"

I left and drove to my aunt's home, where I stay on my visits to Syracuse. She was out of town, so I let myself in and unloaded the car. Her son Moon, my cousin, lives upstairs with his family. I went up to congratulate him on his brand-new political career; he had been elected Supervisor of the 15th Ward, the first black Republican to gain the post. In 195 years of black existence in Syracuse.

I was very tired when I came down again. I showered, fixed up my bed and got in it, but sleep wouldn't come. A shaft of light lanced downward past the window, and I could see snow falling silently, thickly. I had gone through hundreds of cities and towns, had traversed six mountain ranges while living out of a suitcase. I should have fallen right off to sleep but did not for a long while.

Morning. The snow had piled up again, sending every citizen back into his private little shell. I heard my cousin come pounding down the stairs on his way to work. His car racked and coughed and finally started. Now the busloads of students began to move up toward the university. Trucks and more cars. The city was awake and in motion.

Like someone in a daze, I went out and began making the rounds of friends. In the next few days I drank and talked and visited some more. I went Christmas-shopping with the boys and lunched and dined with them. We plodded through snowdrifts to this place, to that. The tree was up and stacks of presents glittered beneath it. Everywhere there was food and drink, carols, songs and decorations. And in me, a certain emptiness.

One night I crept back to my aunt's house and sat alone listening to *The Messiah*, drinking brandy and feeling lonely in a house that I had known practically all my life. It was as much a stranger now as the city and the people I had known. My friends, people I had gone to school with, are somehow self-conscious when I am in Syracuse. I reflected that all I had done was to move away. Why should that have raised walls so thick they blocked out the past?

Even so, I did at last get into the swing of Christmas Eve. The most stolid people begin to come alive in the late afternoon of Christmas Eve, when the sense of the season comes rushing up to be drowned in toasts and gifts. I was no exception.

The boys walked around the tree counting their presents. Which would they open before going to bed?

"Not a single one," Greg said vehemently. "I'm waiting until morning."

"I am too," Dennis said.

On the spot I concocted, through a swirl of Scotches, a new verse for *Hark! the Herald Angels Sing*, and while Dennis blew on his trumpet, I sang:

> *Hark! the drunken angels sing,*
> *Bring more wine and everything;*
> *Bourbon, Scotch and cognac too,*
> *Apple cobbler and turkey stew.*

Greg refused to join in such sacrilege. He covered his ears. My ex-wife, a tolerant soul, put up with us. Her mother shook her head; she knew all along that I was an irreligious nut. Fittingly, there was more snow blotting out the Christmas lights that adorned the houses along the street.

And so, Christmas came. It was a quiet day, with all the polite things said upon the opening of the gifts. There were few surprises; the boys got just what they wanted. There were visitors who came by briefly, remembering the old days but overlaying them with laughter, jokes, a galloping heartiness. Then Christmas night came and we parted; the next morning I would continue on to Washington. My trip was not yet finished.

From New York City I took the train to Washington; a heavy snowstorm had ruled out driving. The pace seemed slow and easy, irritatingly slow, the landscape drifting backward at a snail's pace. At lunchtime I sat in the diner, next to the window, and lazily watched the aged, bumbling waiters moving through the jammed aisle. I had not gone to Washington by train since 1946, and in those days, before a Negro could be served in the diner, he had to wait until almost all the white people were finished. Then, with great courtesy, he was shown to the Jim Crow corner and the thick green curtain was pulled, closing him off from view, since seeing him might have distressed the whites. There was no green curtain now, but you don't forget the past just because it is the past.

Baltimore and memories of Billie Holiday, and then Washington, where the minions of government huddled outside the station, furiously hailing cabs. I remembered that spot, too, for I had arrived there with my cousin Moon at night, and the lights had been shining on the Capitol dome. An elderly Negro woman had been waiting for a cab so long that she finally became angry and began shouting at the taxi starter. Cabs had not been integrated in 1946; nothing in Washington had been. The woman became so loud and furious, silhouetted in the light of the dome, that we were afraid the starter might hit her. If he had, we would have stepped in; there was no other choice. We listened and watched and sweated. When the crisis reached the point of no return, a Negro cab driver drove up and took her away—to our immeasurable relief.

But Washington this time struck me as having no little amount of charm. In a few days I was to call at the White House, but before that, I was invited to a gathering at the house of columnist and essayist Marquis Childs. The company was stellar; there was even a tuxedo or two, and an ambassador with his wife. It seemed like a special session of a special club, for here were people close to everything, who were deluged hour after hour by rumor and fact and had to separate the two; the people who knew Presidents and would-be Presidents and who could help make or break them. An easy sense of power was there, and the grace with which the powerful often move.

That evening and the others sped by. Washington had a soft look because of the snow, and there was even something exciting about trying to catch a cab late at night, or listening to the merry clinking of car chains. There were dinners in quiet, plush restaurants in which sleek diplomats sat talking in corners, twirling cognac in great snifters. The Goldwater signs were up; one of the largest hung on the front of the Duryea Building on Connecticut Avenue, and it showed the Senator with all the crags and crevices touched out; he looked very benign.

I could have enjoyed Washington night life even more, from what I saw of it, except that in many places I felt that it was now the rule to be nicer than possible to Negroes; it was a nagging, uneasy feeling. I could never forget what Washington used to be, that my family, on their way up from Mississippi, had paused here briefly and moved on, for it was still pure South. I would be the first to admit that the city is losing that posture, but then it had better lose it.

An hour before my appointment with an official at the White House, I took a cab to the Washington Monument and had the cabby drive very slowly around the grounds. I was remembering the March on Washington, which had taken place in August, 1963. The sun was out but the grounds were still and cold, sterile, and it was hard to recall the sight of those multitudes who had gathered there as the English barons had done at Runnymede, but not to petition for a new Magna Charta of guaranteed rights, only to call for the reinstitution of the old ones.

I took part in that great March. I left New York as a passenger in one of two cars filled with black people and white people. Our lunches were packed, and sleep had been set aside. When we emerged from the Holland Tunnel and gained the New Jersey Turnpike, we saw hundreds of other cars and buses hurtling southward, signs snapping in the midnight wind: FREEDOM, or FREEDOM Now. When we stopped in a parking lot to eat, we knew that everyone there was going to Washington. Greetings rolled into the night, and black hands and white hands together slammed car doors and proceeded toward the capital. In some cars we heard babies crying.

The great caravan sped on. We waved as we passed other cars

and the people in them waved to us. Snatches of song were strung along the highway. On they came, the cars and buses. Sleep was impossible. The spirit soared at the sight of so many people, and the spine tingled with a primeval, instinctive knowledge that something great and electric was moving at last in the nation.

By dawn the buses were already prowling toward their appointed places in the city. By ten, the folk singers were at work. Their voices drifted down from speakers set high atop the Washington Monument, now gleaming like a golden bar in the sunlight. Contingents hoisted their signs for everyone to see. Newsmen dashed through the crowds or mounted platforms. Still they came. Planes bringing more Marchers droned overhead. How many thousands—25,000, 50,000, 1,000,000? They were everywhere. Odetta sang, Joan Baez, the Chad Mitchell Trio. From all sides they came; many arrived by rail, others disembarked from their buses and walked down Connecticut Avenue, banners and posters held high. One man skated in. Finally they spilled down over the Mall, a slowly spreading river.

And suddenly it was time for the March, and more than a quarter of a million people, black and white, moved down the roads toward the Lincoln Memorial. They were so tightly massed that it was impossible to cross between the ranks. Overhead, mottled with the shadows of millions of leaves on the great trees that lined the streets, the television cameras swung back and forth, peered down into the crowds. The armies shuffled along singing, arm in arm, hand in hand, strangers no more. It hurt to look into some of the faces: the power of the sun at full shine. Some of the Marchers were so old they had to be wheeled, and some were so young they had to be carried, and some so sightless they had to be led. Some people wept as they moved along, and unable to extricate their hands from those of their new-found friends, let the tears roll freely. Some people smiled, but they all moved with the grace of those endowed with a powerful purpose. The Marchers pinched in from two roads, spilled onto the Mall, back, back, back, until the grass around the Reflecting Pool was entirely covered with humanity. And still they came.

I sat on the steps of the Lincoln Memorial with Bob Johnson, editor of *Jet*, and comedian Dick Gregory. We weren't supposed to have liquor but we had, and we spiced our Cokes with it. At one point, Gregory looked up at the airplanes constantly passing overhead and said, "How do I know that isn't the Mississippi Air National Guard?"

Then Martin Luther King, Jr., came up to speak.

"I have a dream!" M.L. said.

"Tell 'em, Martin!" Bob shouted.

"I have a dream!" M.L. said again and again, and behind us a man screamed, "To hell with that dream, Martin! Now, goddammit, *now!*"

It had been a day of which America could be proud. There had been no occasion like it before in history, and there would be none like it again. One could feel the intense desire to surmount the rage of the times. Now, several months later, as I passed the Lincoln Memorial in a line of traffic, only the tingle of my spine assured me it had been real.

I leaned forward and said to the cabby, "You'd never believe the March took place, would you?"

"Wasn't that somethin'?" he said, turning to look at me. "Were you here?"

"Wouldn't have missed it."

"Wasn't that somethin', an' all the white folks too."

I had found a man to help me recreate that day. Wherever I had gone in the country, and when people talked about the March, I dropped in the information that I had taken part in it. Taken part in history.

We have been in this land for seven generations and are descended from the one African in every ten who outlived death, disease, displacement and degradation. And we, in the person of myself, stood outside the East Gate of the White House. I was not to see the President, but that didn't matter. I, John Alfred Williams, the son of a son of a son of a son of a slave, himself the son of free Africans, was going into the home of the Presidents.

There were Negro workmen outside, and as I got out of the cab, they stopped to look at me. Who was I?

I knew who I was, and knew how far we had come, and knew we were capable of going the necessary distance. Yes, it was rough; yes, people were stupid and bitter and mean and bigoted and murderous—some of them, many of them, too many of them. But striding up the walk I thought, Oh, God—Ola and John, look at your goddamn boy!

THREE NEGRO FAMILIES

THIS ARTICLE *was written before* The Negro Middle Class, *in 1966, and was published in* Holiday *in March 1967. Lori and I had been back from Europe not quite a month and hadn't really settled into our small apartment in Chelsea, because we were looking for a larger place. Long trips seem to shrink the home town, the apartment. I was at loose ends; between apartments and chunks of money. And Greg, my oldest boy, had started his second year of college.*

So I was both glad and grateful when Don Gold, managing editor of Holiday, called and asked if I wanted to go to Chicago and do a piece on some families. An upcoming issue of the magazine would be devoted entirely to the Second City.

Two days later, feeling very much the journalist on the move—back from Europe one day, flying out to Chicago the next—I took the plane. Moving like that helped me to get back into America quickly; moving back to New York from London, Amsterdam, Rome or Paris, is not moving back to the United States. America is west of the Hudson, south of the Narrows and north of Riverdale.

Don and I'd agreed that I would interview three black families. One was to be wealthy, another middle-class and the third, poor. The rich family was easy and the middle-class family not difficult either. The problem was finding a poor family. Amazingly, poor families are well protected by the agencies; you simply cannot walk into an agency and announce that you're a writer and want to do an article on one of its families.

For about two days I drove up and down the West Side of Chicago, trying to pick a family at random. Picture it: you drive up in a rented car, jacket off but tie on, asking about families in

corner stores, buttonholing dudes in the street. I was lucky I
didn't get my head bashed in, stranger as I was, and everyone
uptight about plainclothes cops. I gave up that gig pretty
quickly and turned to a friend, Bob Cromie, then working on
the Chicago Tribune, who in turn got me next to a young beat
reporter, Joe Boyce, who came up with a family on Springfield
Boulevard. Worth a passing comment is the fact that either none
of my contacts on the black press knew of or they were unable to
set me up with a poor black family.

I started with Mrs. Merkson and her family, went on to Dan
Caldwell and his and finally to Mr. and Mrs. Earl B. Dickerson.
The middle-class family, the Caldwells, were the most sterile. I
think that was because they were on the way up; more than
strivers, they were chewing up the road, trying to get to the top
of the hill. The wealthy Dickersons were quite loose, easy to
talk with, ready with answers.

But they all sounded alike when discussing black aspirations.
Black people have had as many differences between groups as
other people; but now they sounded alike, and it was refreshing.
Dr. Martin Luther King's campaign earlier that year in Chicago,
which was not an overwhelming success, perhaps had a great
deal to do with the similarity of viewpoint.

When I left Chicago, I stopped in Syracuse to visit my sons
and take in a football game, then I returned to New York. Two
weeks later I turned in the article. No rewrites were asked for.

This really is the kind of article I think I write best. Mainly,
it's me talking about the people who are the subject of the article.
Their quotes tend to round out my observations, not the other
way around, where the fat quote tends to guide you like a broken
field runner around things that're smacking you in the face.
My view is that if a magazine editor is good, he hires you to
bring him back some whole people who are trying to function in
a given situation. If it's fat quotes he wants, then most subjects
can write their own stories. In short, if an editor's willing to
pay you good money to do your thing—and that supposedly
is why he hired you in the first place—then he ought to have
sense enough to let you do it.

I N 1772, four years before the American Revolution, a trader built a trading post on the ground now occupied by the Wrigley Building in Chicago. He was Jean Baptiste Pointe DuSable, a man mostly Negro as we measure differences in genes, and he has been honored as one of the fathers of the city to which have come one million of his brothers. Some seem to be faring very well; others are trying to make it, and some appear to be trapped in the ghetto that lies some distance from the spot where DuSable built his cabin on the Chicago River, within sight of Lake Michigan.

Late in the afternoon, the sun slants in from the southwest, lays its rays in a tired, golden ripple over the battered buildings of Chicago's West Side, and pokes tentative fingers inside the dim apartment of Mrs. Laverne Merkson. She lives on Springfield Avenue, two blocks from where the 1966 riots had their epicenter.

Mrs. Merkson's building is of brick—a brick dark and worn, filled with the grime of industry and time, and perhaps in its last ten years of use. Like so many other buildings that stretch for mile upon dull, lifeless mile, hers is inhabited by Negroes. This is the new Negro ghetto; the other, the old South Side ghetto, is being phased out. Hospitals and universities have bought land there and cleared it; splendid new buildings for the middle-class Negro, such as the Lake Meadows and Prairie Shores, soar far above streets that had made up the worst of the South Side slums. Now the worst slums are on the West Side; these are the newer slums, with newer victims.

Mrs. Merkson stands about five feet eight inches tall and must weigh close to 170 pounds. Not much of it is fat. She has an unbelievably unblemished complexion and a full, strong face.

Her teeth are irregular but powerful-looking; her legs are heavy. She is thirty-three years old, and is cast almost in the mold of the classic Negro matriarch.

It is a few moments before Springfield Avenue explodes with the sound of children laughing and running home from school past the broken whiskey and wine bottles. Mrs. Merkson sits in her five-room apartment, which is clean and orderly and somehow surprising in view of its location; somehow surprising, considering the smells that linger in the shabby lobby downstairs. Plain curtains and shades hang at the windows. Beside Mrs. Merkson, on a small end table, lies a short leather strap. The living room is rugless. Inexpensive furniture stands backed against the often-painted walls. The couch and the chairs are all angled toward the twenty-one-inch television set, which stands beside a high-fidelity phonograph. It is clear that only Mrs. Merkson's soap, water and elbow grease are retarding the decay that lingers in the building.

Laverne Merkson is a Democrat and a Baptist, but she doesn't attend church regularly. She came from near Forest City, Arkansas, in her early twenties. She thought she would be able to get an education in Chicago. However, her "sponsors" to the city, a brother and his wife, insisted that she keep house for them while they both worked. Being obligated to them for food, shelter and clothing, she did, and she could not break out of the trap until she married. That in itself proved a trap, for the children started to come. Then, almost predictably, she was deserted by her husband. By attending classes at night, Mrs. Merkson did manage to secure a tenth-grade education. This took her until 1964. She also managed to study for and secure a license as a hairdresser, but she cannot practice because she receives public assistance; were she to begin employment, assistance to herself and the children would be either halted or adjusted. In either case the Merksons would be extremely hard pressed to survive in Chicago. It would cost at least $100 a month to rent a salon—exactly what she pays for her apartment with its rooms of bunk beds. The thirty dollars a week she spends for food, a figure already inadequate, would be cut to less than a third. Then there would be the utilities to pay, both at home and at the salon, plus clothing costs. Mrs. Merkson might rent a booth in someone else's salon, but that would cost her fifteen dollars a day and she would have to bring in her own clientele—which she does not have. In addition, someone would have to keep the children, and that person would have to be paid.

If she could see daylight, Mrs. Merkson would tackle these problems, hard as they might be, but she doesn't know where the break is coming from.

It is four o'clock. The children have started to come home from school. Anthony, eleven, comes in with Caesar, seven, Alexander, six, and Juan, five. Like Mrs. Merkson, all are quite brown, their colors ranging from a deep cocoa to tanned cowhide. Alexander brings word that Drucilla, twelve, and Eunice, ten, who are bringing home the twins, Renita and Benita, four, have been jumped on by some boys in the yard of Marcy Center, a nearby church-sponsored community center and nursery. Kenneth, nine, brings in further word that Eunice, who is nicknamed Princess, was struck in the mouth and that her lip is bleeding. The mother, children milling all about her, picks up the phone and calls Marcy Center for details. She tells Anthony to put on his jacket and prepare to return to the center. The other children are told to remove their school clothes. Satisfied with the information she has received, Mrs. Merkson hangs up. Now through the door come Princess, Drucilla and the twins, accompanied by a woman who has seen them home. Her name is Mrs. Aikens. Princess does indeed have a swollen and somewhat bloodied lip.

Mrs. Merkson has grasped her strap; she stands up and lectures the children on playing in schoolyards when they should be home. Silence descends on the brood. Mrs. Aikens listens just as attentively as the children do; in her eyes is reluctant approval of Mrs. Merkson's handling of the situation. This collides head on with the attitude of sympathy for the children. When Mrs. Merkson finishes her lecture—the strap in her hand waving in slow, aimless circles, the children's eyes watching it every turn—Mrs. Aikens remarks that she has to go, and Mrs. Merkson with the greatest courtesy thanks her for seeing the children home. The poor know they must look after each other. The often florid courtesies they exchange help reinforce their self-respect.

When the flurry dies down, the children vanish into the rooms, change clothes and return to the living room. Their after-school clothes are just as neat as those they wore to school. Most of the kids crouch in front of the television. Juan carefully inspects a sheet of paper with a drawing done by a friend of his named Perry. Mrs. Merkson resumes her seat, the strap set aside, and soon the smaller children edge across the room and into her ample lap. They seem to be having a contest: who can show the most affection for mother. For Laverne Merkson, the heaviest part of the day has begun.

Each day begins at six, and they are all gray, sun or no sun. "I wash and dress, 'n' then goes upstairs to visit my other brother and his wife for coffee—I don't keep coffee down here. Then I comes back down, wakes the kids, washes them that can't wash themselves too good. Oh, the big ones help out. They wash the dishes and help pick up the house and carry out the garbage, and watch out for my babies when they're in the street." The twins are Mrs. Merkson's babies.

When the older children have gone to school, Mrs. Merkson turns to the housework—making the beds, washing, cleaning and sewing. "I makes most of their little dresses." When the older children return for lunch, the mother has readied the younger three for their afternoon in the nursery; they will be left there by Drucilla and Princess. Now Mrs. Merkson can spend about two hours shopping at the local supermarket and at Sears. Somehow, during those two hours she has every day, she finds time to do volunteer work in the community. In 1964 she was cited in the Chicago press for having been one of the

most active volunteers in the city; she ranked seventeenth in a
list of hundreds.

There is little recreation for Laverne Merkson. "Well, you got
to watch your kids. I don't like to leave them alone." The constant
surveillance of her brood, who, like ghetto children the world
over, can be drawn quickly away from the stabilizing influence
of the family and into trouble, takes most of her time. She
considers her membership in the Ladies Auxiliary of Marcy
Center to be part recreation. "Sometimes I listens to doo-ap
music—that's a combination of blues and rock 'n' roll—and I
visit some of my other relatives who live in the city or they
come here, and I takes myself a drink now and again. I don't
get into downtown too much. Once I went to a musical, a church
musical in McCormick Place, and it was so—so lovely I cried."

Mrs. Merkson has put her hands to her eyes as she describes
the musical; when she takes them away, they are wet with
tears. It is hard to say whether Mrs. Merkson has a great
deal of faith or a wide streak of naïveté. Whichever, it has
given her a certain softness. No bitterness seems to have touched
her, yet traditionally, bitterness was one of the ingredients that
went into the make-up of the Negro matriarch. She came to
Chicago with a vision of self-improvement. She has made some
progress, but she has very far to go, not for herself now so much
as for her children. She wants them to have the education she
did not receive; she wants them to finish high school, at least,
and if possible go on to college.

Of Chicago she says, "I like Chicago. I don't think it's all bad,
just some of the people. If I had a chance to go to another city,
though, where I could do better, I'd pack up and go, but not
down South, you know."

Her day ends fifteen hours after it began. She prepares the
children for bed, washing them as they eat their last snacks
and take their last peeks at television.

"By nine o'clock I'm the only one up, and I lay down on the
couch and watch television." She laughs. "I generally falls asleep

and wakes up in the middle of the night and have to get up and go to bed."

Then it is only a few hours until morning, only a short time before the start of another identical day.

When he was growing up in a small city 900 miles from Chicago, Daniel Wesley Caldwell planned to become a doctor. Today, at forty-two, he is one of two assistant principals at Carver High School, which is at the very edge of the Chicago city limits on West 130th Street.

Caldwell lives with his wife Melba, thirty-two, and their son Danny, seven, in East Hyde Park Boulevard, the extension of West 51st Street. It has been said by Chicago Negroes that the change in the street's name was designed to show where the Negro neighborhood left off and the white neighborhood began. East Hyde Park Boulevard is well planted with trees, many of them tall, graceful poplars. The homes and apartments are set back at gracious distances from the front lawns. The area has the look of substance. Drexel Boulevard, near where the change in street names occurs, and a half block from where the Caldwells live, once marked (with two or three exceptions) the farthest eastward expansion of the restless Black Belt until after World War II. Now the area is to be integrated with people from different ethnic and economic backgrounds: it ranges from middle to upper class. This is the location of the ever-shrinking "white island," with the University of Chicago at its core. It is only five minutes by auto to the land of the very rich who have remained along Chicago Beach Drive.

The Caldwells live on the third floor of a sturdy brick apartment building: their eight rooms, floor through, rent for $160 a month. The front sun parlor overlooks the Boulevard, and the rear sun parlor the neat back yards and garages. In between there is wall-to-wall carpeting and contemporary furniture in nearly every room. Sunday is the one day that the Caldwells, together, can enjoy life in their sun-filled apartment, because they both work long hours in different professions and in different parts of the city.

After thirteen years of teaching zoology, Caldwell was recently promoted to assistant principal. The Melba Caldwell Booking Agency, specializing in supper-club entertainment, is just becoming well known. Melba Caldwell is the only Negro woman in this field to have an office in the Loop, on West Randolph Street.

Melba Vitale Caldwell comes from Saint Louis, where her mother owned a restaurant. Her soft voice is filled with the inflections of Border State Speech. She is five feet eight inches tall and weighs 135 pounds; she has curled black hair and is fair-skinned like her husband.

Caldwell is six feet tall and was a high-school and college athlete in Syracuse, New York. His voice is crisp and unaccented; he is a Northerner. He dresses in dark suits and ties and favors white or light-colored shirts. Mrs. Caldwell looks chic at home in slacks and blouse, and in her office in dresses that come just above the knee and are designed to show her small waist. In speech and manner Caldwell appears at all times serious; his levity is labored. Melba Caldwell, perhaps because of her work and her past as a nursery-school supervisor, is brisk and jovial. The couple complement each other well.

A day in their home is already in high gear at 7:30 A.M., when Caldwell drives off in his 1966 Chevrolet Impala toward his school, forty-five minutes away on the Dan Ryan Expressway. An hour later, Mrs. Caldwell takes her young son to Saint Thomas the Apostle, a private parochial school two blocks from home. Mrs. Caldwell is a member of the board of this school, which is considered one of the most "progressive" in the city. Two to three hours later, she gets into her car, a 1962 Chevrolet Biscayne, and drives to her four-room office. Her day may end after midnight, what with trips around and outside the city to check on the talent she has placed in various clubs. Sometimes, in connection with her work, she may have to fly to New York as well.

Caldwell is in charge of programming and teacher supervision at Carver. His small office is so plain that it could not be mistaken for anything but the office of a public-school official. He has a picture of his wife and son on his desk. And he has a private washroom. Carver is a part of a complex that includes a grade school, a junior high and a public-housing project. Once the area housed the predominantly white workers who made tanks for the Pullman Company during the War. After the War, the whites began to drift away and more and more Negroes came in, so that now the section is solidly black. There is one white student in Caldwell's school, and most of the teachers are Negro.

When Caldwell eats in the school cafeteria, it is with department heads. Usually he takes his meals at a nearby restaurant. He does not go to the teachers' lounge after lunch because he doesn't smoke, and he can pass up the bridge game. Most of the administrative staff do not fraternize in the lounge with the teaching staff. On a good day Caldwell may be finished at the school by four o'clock, at which time he usually picks up his son. (Sometimes he leaves that chore to his mother-in-law, who lives with them.) He heads for the YMCA, where he may play basketball, swim, or take a steam bath to retard the signs of middle age that are appearing at his midriff and jowl. Returning home, he has dinner with his son and then prepares for his three-nights-a-week teaching job at Dunbar, a gigantic public-school educational plant established near the Lake Meadows development on South Parkway.

Daniel and Melba Caldwell seldom have time to talk together. At the infrequent parties and other social functions they attend, people complain that they spend too much time with each other. Many of the functions the Caldwells attend are dances.

The Caldwells go to church infrequently. "I go there with Danny and Melba on occasion," says Caldwell; he is Episcopalian, his wife and son are Catholic. "But not too often." Between them the Caldwells earn, Caldwell says, "much less than $25,000 a year." They would be earning even less if they were living in Saint Louis or Syracuse and doing comparable work—which for Mrs. Caldwell would be very unlikely.

Syracuse lost Caldwell half by design and half by accident.

He says he placed second on a list of teacher appointments in the early 1950's, but that the appointments were repeatedly frozen. At last the only position he was offered even tentatively was in a school that was predominantly Negro and having severe disciplinary problems. Discouraged, he went to Chicago to visit friends and see a football game. For the hell of it, he filed an application with the Chicago Board of Education. Then he returned to Syracuse and went back to his old job as a redcap at the New York Central Railroad, another of his many marking-time employments. Within a few weeks Caldwell received a wire that requested him to report for work in Chicago, which he did; that was thirteen years ago.

Syracuse, he says, was not ready then for Negro teachers in the public schools. He feels, however, that if he had stayed there, things would have been different. "I could have gotten the same opportunities if I had stayed in Syracuse," he says, "but they would have been another six or seven years in coming." Two years after Caldwell moved to Chicago, he says, Syracuse hired its first Negro public-school teacher. He has no regrets about moving to Chicago; he finds it, as he says, "an exciting and important city with a great deal to offer to America, particularly to Negroes. And with the Negro population now over a million and increasing, the city's role would be most important. In the matter of civil rights it has to be a major factor, a pivotal factor because of its location; it's north and by the same token it's also the center. What happens in Chicago would have a great effect on what happens in the nation."

Pure recreation comes hard for the Caldwells. Mrs. Caldwell manages to combine work and recreation to some degree, depending on the talent she is working with. She rarely drinks while talking business in the nightclubs, and this attitude has carried over into her purely social meetings. Caldwell is an inactive member of Alpha Phi Alpha fraternity and an active member of the Frogs, a social club of professional and business men who, among their other activities, organize a large dance every year. Like Caldwell the majority are Democrats. Caldwell says he spends his Saturdays, "generally doing the weekly chores, shopping and so forth, and I try to take in a sporting event, baseball during baseball season, football during football season, and I usually make it to the Y, sometimes take Danny swimming."

Young Danny is a quiet, introspective kid who is used to being cared for by his grandmother, but who looks forward to the sight-seeing excursions, the swimming and the other weekend and holiday adventures he shares with his father. During the week, he watches television when his homework is done. His father averages four to five hours of television a week, mostly sports.

Caldwell reads many educational publications; his wife reads show-business material. Beyond that they read the weekly news magazines, *Ebony* and *Jet* and the Book-of-the-Month Club selections. Caldwell looks forward to becoming a principal and then a district superintendent. Mrs. Caldwell expects her agency to expand in the near future. "I can't stand to be inactive," she says. "I'd continue the agency even if we lost a little money. I like the work and the excitement of the openings for the new acts coming up."

There is little doubt that the glittering, soaring 4800 Building, which rises up from the plains along Chicago Beach Drive—the southern end of Lake Shore Drive—is one of the most exclusive residences in the city. From the twenty-first floor, where Earl and Kathryn Dickerson live in a large, handsomely furnished five-room apartment, the view is stunning. Beneath them Lake Shore Drive twists and curves past the beaches and parks northward into the Loop; to the northwest stand the monumental apartment buildings of the Lake Meadows and Prairie Shores developments, together with Michael Reese Hospital. To the near west are the housing projects and that wide band of brick and gray-limestone houses that for generations have made up Chicago's South Side. Farther west, near the horizon, loom the factories whose stacks spew long, writhing columns of smoke over the West Side ghetto. To the east, the blue water of Lake Michigan seems to press hard upon the Dickersons' windows.

This is a view the Dickersons might have hoped for, but did not expect to have when, separately and long ago, they left Mississippi and South Carolina. The apartment lies hushed in soft, light-gray carpeting. A uniformed Negro maid moves soundlessly from room to room. The apartment is furnished with period pieces that have a comfortable, lived-in look; a teakwood table and chair, the most striking, are Mrs. Dickerson's favorites. A chandelier over the dining-room table traps the light of the lake and sky and sends a thousand tiny reflections about the room. This, along with other fixtures, such as the large, flamboyant brass doorknobs, was brought from the Dickersons' showplace home on Drexel Square, which they have sold. "It was quite some place," Dickerson says. He is seventy-five years old, and this apartment, small compared to the house they had, is all he needs now.

He has been called a millionaire, one of a half dozen such Negroes who live in Chicago. "Anyone with a grain of sense," he says "would realize that a man like myself, who has worked all his life as a Negro attorney for people who didn't have any money, couldn't be a millionaire." This is a moot point and Dickerson is said to have considerable wealth; he is as well known to the white power structure as he is in the Negro community. He has been far more than a "Negro attorney"; he has been a crusader for Negro rights since he first went before the Chicago bar in 1921. He is president of the Supreme Life Insurance Company of America, a legal-reserve company with home offices in Chicago and branches in twelve states and the District of Columbia. The company's clients are mostly Negro. Dickerson joined Supreme Life in 1943 as company attorney and vice president.

Sitting at the curved, glass-topped, eight-foot-long desk in his office, Dickerson can look through the window down at the corner of South Parkway and 35th Street. "I used to hang around this corner like a little urchin when I first came to Chicago and was going to Wendell Phillips High School."

Dickerson is six feet one inch tall and has fair skin, black-gray hair and river-green eyes set shrewdly in his rough-hewn face. He wears glasses with dark frames, and he does not show his age. He weighs a trim 185 pounds, close to what he weighed when he played football at Evanston Academy.

He starts his day in the library of his home; it is a room filled with mementos of his many trips abroad. There are rows of books by the English Romantic writers and a sizable collection of works by or about Negroes. Dickerson works there about four hours, and arrives at his office about noon, where he continues working until eight. The day consists of meetings with department heads, on-the-spot conferences about matters he may have just thought about, or breaks to attend board meetings of other organizations. He is a member of five boards of directors, two of which are banking institutions, two medical and one educational. He is also a member of the American Academy of Political and Social Sciences, and of the American Sociological Association. In his prime his membership in such organizations was twice as extensive.

For example, he was elected to the City Council in 1939 and served four years; he has been an Assistant Corporation Counsel for the city, Assistant Attorney General for the state, and a member of the Fair Employment Practices Committee. He has argued before the Supreme Courts of the United States and Illinois, and has been as highly active in politics. He is a Democrat who has been listed erroneously as a Republican, and he says, "Considering the philosophy of the two parties, there's nothing that gives me any love for the Republican Party. Although I may vote now and then for a Republican, never would I in *these* times change my allegiance from the Democratic Party."

He went into politics after World War I, in which he served in France as a lieutenant with the 365th Infantry. He is one of the founders of the American Legion, an organization he soon came to detest. Mayor Anton Cermak, who was killed in an attempt on President-elect Roosevelt's life in 1933, was one of the many politicians in Chicago who helped to guide Dickerson.

Earl Burrus Dickerson was born in Canton, Mississippi, where he lived until he was sixteen years old. The Illinois Central, running from Chicago to New Orleans, changed crews and engines in his home town. "I was intrigued by the snow I sometimes saw on top of the trains," he remembers. "I knew they'd come from Chicago. I learned all about this city without ever leaving Canton, just by hanging around the station." Following the shooting of his brother by the local chief of police, and after the killing of a friend by whites, Dickerson was sent north by his mother, a washer-woman, before his temper got him into trouble, too. "The accumulation of all those experiences put me in an angry frame of mind," he explains. "So they got me out of there." A railroad porter concealed him in a closet of a coach until the train reached Centralia, Illinois. His family had money enough only for that leg of his journey. Once in Chicago, ironically, it was a wealthy white woman from the South who arranged for him to get a scholarship at Evanston Academy, where he learned Latin, which he can still read, and French, which he still speaks. Scholarships helped him through Northwestern and the University of Chicago Law School. In the process, he met the woman he was to marry.

Kathryn Dickerson is a small, energetic, fair-skinned woman with brown eyes and brown hair whose family moved from South Carolina, first to New York and then to Chicago, when she was three months old. She met her husband at a Kappa Alpha Psi fraternity party, but they were not married until much later, in 1930. Dickerson holds an honored position in the Kappas, a Negro fraternity. The couple have a daughter, Mrs. Diane Dickerson Cohen, who was educated at Mills College in Oakland, California. Mrs. Cohen has three children.

Mrs. Dickerson, who often wears slacks and blouses at home, spends as much time as possible with her grandchildren, but that isn't much. She, too, serves on several boards, notably the Urban League Women's Council, the Women's Board of the University of Chicago and the Women's Board of the Negro College Fund, Chicago. She has been listed several times as one of the best-dressed Negro women in the United States by the National As-

sociation of Fashion and Accessory Designers. Her love of striking, well-designed clothes is one she shares with her husband.
He, too, dresses tastefully; his suits, tending toward the dark
side, are beautifully tailored, and a silk handkerchief leans jaun-
tily from his jacket pocket. Dickerson's sartorial excellence may
be a reaction from his student days, when he considered himself lucky to have a single suit to wear.

Dickerson likes to recall those days, and does so with gusto,
looking backward down the long, wide road of his life. Like
many people of his age, he is a natural raconteur. One does not
converse with Dickerson; one tags along, listening intently while
Dickerson's fingers (one on his right hand carries a handsome
cameo ring) play with a bright-red pack of Du Maurier cigarettes, waiting for the intake of breath that never seems to come.
Although his voice is a little blurred or fuzzed, he speaks rapidly. His wife, on the other hand, is a deliberate speaker; she
chooses and utters her words very carefully. Her daughter is
quite spontaneous, her humor large.

The Dickersons have known Chicago from their youth; they
have grown with it. Some of their friends believe Chicago was a
better city for Negroes before so many of them, crowding the
coaches of the Illinois Central, swarmed in. Kathryn Dickerson
does not agree. "The more Negroes came to Chicago, the more
they brought out the presence of discrimination and segregation,
that so many old-timers had learned to shut their eyes to. Of
course Chicago is having trouble. There's a lot of tension, but I
think Chicago's moving forward." For both husband and wife,
working for interracial harmony has been an important part of
their lives. "We've both had an incurable lust for freedom,"
Dickerson says. Kathryn Dickerson claims that she works for the
Urban League for recreation. She serves regularly as chairman or
co-chairman for a variety of fund-raising affairs sponsored by the
organizations she belongs to.

Once a year they fly to New York for the new season on
Broadway; they think little of Chicago theater. And the "obses-
sion for education" that possessed Dickerson as a young man re-

mains unabated. He has been around the world. With his wife he has traveled to Europe seven or eight times. "I am crazy about Spain," Mrs. Dickerson says. In 1965 Dickerson visited Russia; in 1966 Mrs. Dickerson flew to Dakar for the World Festival of Negro Arts. They have seen out-of-the-way places—Tahiti, Bali, Kashmir. They feel that the only vacations they can enjoy must be those outside the city. But their key interests always bring them back to Chicago and its problems. Dickerson says, "There's no power on earth that can keep the Negro from full citizenship in this country; he'll either get it or there will be a holocaust. Chicago's got to master the new challenges as it mastered the old ones. I'm confident it can succeed."

While the lives of the people in these three families appear to go in different directions, they already have meshed or may yet mesh. Dickerson's insurance company, because its clients are predominantly Negro, may one day insure the Merksons. As Caldwell moves up, he may find himself on the administrative staffs of all-Negro or predominantly Negro schools attended by one or more of the Merkson children. One October night last year Melba Caldwell obtained some talent for an Urban League benefit affair; Kathryn Dickerson was a co-chairman. Thus, within Chicago there is another community, the Black Metropolis, and the color of skin and not the size of the pocketbook dictates many of the movements of the people within it.

THE NEGRO MIDDLE CLASS

EVERY TIME *I read through this article the old anger comes back. This one took much out of me, physically, and it required a great deal of time, work and traveling. When all that was done and the piece written, rewritten and rejected, I decided to quit writing magazine articles. "The Negro Middle Class" was not submitted to other magazines, for I did not feel that it would be properly evaluated.*

I've indicated earlier that from time to time I've given thought to quit writing articles. This time when the thought came, early in 1968, I meant it. I was burned badly by this one and didn't intend to be burned again.

My agent got me together with Tom Congdon, an editor for the Saturday Evening Post. *A literary agent often functions in this fashion, getting client and editor together on a project. After all, if it works the agent is in for his usual 10 per cent. Even if it doesn't, he comes in for 10 per cent of the guarantee or "kill money" which is a small percentage of the amount you would have received with the acceptance of a given article. Say a five-thousand-dollar article that's rejected gives you 10 per cent kill money; five hundred bucks. The amount of the guarantee varies from magazine to magazine, of course.*

The editor, my agent and I met early in 1967. The meeting left me somewhat unfulfilled because the editor had to catch a train. I could tell that he wasn't too sure about my doing the piece. Perhaps I was letting things show, for I was a little lukewarm about the project, which was a big piece on the black middle class. Rather, it wasn't the piece that disturbed me so

much as the Post *wanting it done. I'd had some previous contact with the magazine and they'd been kind of spongy, evasive,
jive.*

I assumed that the Post *wanted to do a major piece on black
America simply because it might help to re-establish them as a
front-running publication. It was no secret that the* Saturday
Evening Post *was in trouble financially.*

*It helps if you like an editor the first time you meet him. I did
not like this one when the three of us met; he looked me over
pleasantly, but from a certain personal perspective. Not unlike
the way a cop looks at you if for no other reason than he has
the license to do so. He had the license; he was the editor. If I
felt all this, why did I agree to go ahead with the article?
The answer's simple: I needed the money. Most writers always
need money. With the exception of one, every other black writer
I ever knew or read about always needed money.*

*I outlined my ideas for Congdon and prepared to make a trip
across country and back to interview people in the black middle
class. The expense money was kind of pinchpenny. The fee for the
article itself—I've now forgotten what it was—would increase
with the length if it ran over the agreed upon ten thousand
words.*

*It was summer 1967 when I started out, the Newark and
Detroit rebellions just over. I went to Syracuse, Chicago, Kansas
City, Los Angeles, Boston, Washington and, of course, New
York. I was to find out about this black middle class, how it felt,
lived and thought; whether it was similar to the white middle
class in its constancy and conservativism or edging toward a
kind of sullen radicalism. It took a little over three months to
complete the traveling, interviewing and blocking out of the
article. And you don't get paid until the article is written and
accepted. During the trip if I'd not been lucky enough to stay
with friends or family in different cities,* Saturday Evening
Post's *expense money never would've covered what Congdon
and I agreed had to be covered—the people and the places.*

Another question—why didn't my agent see to it that I got what I needed for expenses? The answer is complicated. Perhaps the money wasn't there. Perhaps he wasn't tough enough. Perhaps he really didn't care.

I finished the article with the approach of winter; it was 13,300 words long or close to forty pages in length. The editor sent it back, requesting a rewrite. There are some magazines that trust a writer's perception; its editors are willing to see through the writer's eyes. In fact, sometimes that is why they've hired him. There are other magazines, like the Post, where the demand was for the fat quote from the people you're interviewing. The fat quote is everything and the writer's perceptions very much secondary. For me that fat quote piece is superficial because the way in which a person speaks is often more meaningful than his spoken word. From the editor's multitudinous notations I knew the rewrite would be a lost cause, yet I tackled it, bouncing in big, fat, sullen black quotes. He didn't like the symbolism of Bill Chiles teeing off on the white golf ball, which appears in this, the rewritten version.

Of course I sat down to rewrite the article; I'd invested far too much time and energy not to. This time it came out longer, over 15,000 words. This version, too, was rejected and is published here for the first time.

I protested his reasons for the rejection by letter and phone, but no good. The Saturday Evening Post paid me $500 kill money, not even bothering to increase it because the article had grown longer. My agent was about as helpless as my grandmother (who's dead) in trying to get more money; in fact, I'm not even sure he tried. Agents are not known for going around biting hands that feed them and their other clients.

Altogether then, about five months work went in this article. That's about $100 a month, $25 a week, $5.00 a day for five working days, less than $1.00 an hour. No wonder I wanted to quit writing.

Frankly, I don't know if this is a good piece or not; I don't know what is good according to individual editors. I've heard of

articles and books being called "flawed" which is a put-down of
sorts; but then there's the phrase, "brilliantly flawed," which is
genius in progress or some such rot.

My rewrite was better than the first version; it cut deeper because I wanted to sock it to him, convey to him all the anger
the people I interviewed felt, plus my own. In the first version,
sensing rather than knowing, I served up a lukewarm dish which
I believed suited the Post's philosophy. In the second I just
brought it on down front. I indicated earlier that from the editor's
notes I knew I was going to have the piece rejected. There was
not a single one of the thirty-eight pages of the first version that
was not marked with questions, suggestions, comments, etc. I'm
no Robert Graves, but I also know that of 13,000 words 10,000
of them were not going to require what the editor thought they
did. In short, I felt all that scribbling on the first draft was the
questioning of a man completely unknowing of his writer or his
writer's subject.

By letter and phone we raged at each other, or rather, I raged.
He was cool because he could afford to be. He hadn't been
running around the country working for less than a dollar an
hour. He tried to be the soother; he was used to attacks from
writers. He suggested that the good reviews for The Man Who
Cried I Am, published while I was working on the article, gave
me a big head. Funny. I thought the reviews weren't on the
whole at all good.

The novel that followed that one, Sons of Darkness, Sons of
Light, was filled with ideas and attitudes and characters who
came out of the research for this article. The theme of the novel
was that any black revolution that comes would have to be
sparked by black people in the middle class.

I left my agent shortly after this business with the Post;
there wasn't much point in paying a guy to be in your corner
when you couldn't ever find him when a fight started. I really
and truly, honestly and genuinely vowed to give up article writing. I didn't want to run into another editor like this one—oh,
Lord, no.

Well, as it happened, in about a year I was back writing articles. As Chester Himes puts it, "A fighter fights and a writer writes."

*Yeh.**

F ROM the window of the trophy room in his $80,000 home in the Baldwin Hills section of Los Angeles, Dr. George Fossett Thomas stared across the street. There was a FOR SALE sign on the lawn; it was plunged into the carefully tended grass at a rakish, angry angle. He motioned toward the sign and said, "I'm a pretty friendly fellow, but I wouldn't court their friendship."

George Thomas is a middle-class Negro. His neighborhood is mostly white. I met Thomas four years ago when I took a long trip around the United States to study firsthand the early stages of the "Negro Revolution," and to find out how black Americans were participating in it.

This summer I went back on the road to see what happened since; to see if the civil disorders pleased or displeased them; to see if integration was working as well as they'd hoped it would back in 1963, and if not why not. Back then Black Power was known only as the title of a book written by the late Richard Wright, but by 1967 it had become a philosophy that was being hotly debated throughout the nation, by whites and blacks alike. I wanted to know how they felt about it, for the black middle class has become one of the most articulate groups in the nation.

The black middle class is not new. The late sociologist, E. Franklin Frazier in tracing the development of what he called "the Black Bourgeoisie," said, "Some recognition had to be given the individual qualities of the slaves, and it was most often

* Much has changed since the summer of 1967. Bob Johnson, for example, no longer is sure how he feels about the things we discussed then. Joan and Bob Waite have left New York City for New Jersey. And the editor at the *Post* has left magazine publishing for book publishing.

among the house servants. . . . Skilled mechanics, who constituted a large section of the artisans in the South, formed with the house servants a sort of privileged class in the slave community." Free Negroes, many of them of mixed black and white blood, were a major part of the black middle class of the antebellum days and Frazier noted that "The family heritage consisted of traditions of civilized behavior . . . The members' light skin-color was indicative not only of their white ancestry, but of their descent from the Negroes who were free before the Civil War." Then as now the black middle class worked at skilled occupations, but there were teachers, doctors, small-business men and educators among them as well. At that time the majority of Negroes lived in the rural areas of the South. Today, just over half the 21.5 million Negroes remain there but decreasingly are connected with farming. The other half have moved to northern and western cities. Only 4 per cent of the blacks in the United States live in the suburbs.

On my trip last summer I found that education still remains high in the list of Negro goals. The black middle class is well educated and may even be overeducated, if there is such a thing. It is rare to find a member of this group without at least one college degree, and two are now as common as it was years ago to have had a single one. Years ago black women regularly got more education than black men, but this trend has now been reversed. In the past six years the percentage of black men completing high school has about doubled. The reason for this tremendous drive to get an education is because Negroes have always been taught that they had to be twice as good, twice as prepared as whites just to stay even with them in a society that is segregated.

The gains of *all* Negroes are measured by the 2,150,000 whose incomes are in five figures. (Nearly 52,000,000 whites are in this category.) But, in order to make $10,000 a year for the black family, three out of four middle-class Negro wives must work along with their husbands. Even so, their earnings are less than those of white families with only the husband employed. Since 1963 blacks have been moving into better-paying jobs, but, they make up less than 6 per cent of the nations professional workers, less than 3 per cent of the managers and proprietors, and less than 6 per cent of the craftsmen.

Much of the middle class is blue-collar; the Negro holds only 5 per cent of the white-collar jobs in the country's ten largest cities. He is, however, overrepresented in the blue-collar area. In making this trip, I decided to stick to the white-collar Negro in the main. The black middle-class member belongs to a church —most likely Episcopal, Congregational or Catholic; he seldom belongs to the church of his childhood which may have been Baptist or Methodist. A middle-class Negro may be one of the professional athletes seen on television. He does not tend to be light-skinned any more. Many Negroes believe, indeed, are convinced, that a Negro with light skin has a better chance of making it in integrated society than a man with dark coloring and the same qualifications. Once the automobile was the most important status symbol of this class, but today it is the home, and "life styles," or the way they live.

George Thomas likes to live well. A burly six-footer with brown hair and green eyes, he looks like a well-tanned white man. Somehow you are not surprised to learn that he is a big-game hunter. On his first trip in 1961 he bagged a polar bear in Alaska; it is now a rug in his trophy room. While American cities were exploding with civil disorder last summer, Dr. Thomas was off hunting in Angola, where, he says, "I ran into half the Portuguese Army out hunting Angolan guerrillas." For the past six years he has gone on safari, mostly in Africa.

Thomas backed away from the window and bounded about the room; he moves like he talks, restlessly. He is not a listener; he is a talker. "That's a Cape Buffalo," he said, swinging about the room. "That's an impala." He gestured toward a pair of elephant tusks. "You know what those are." A lion skin was draped over one couch and a leopard skin over another. "That leopard was a record, John. It's the third largest ever shot—a hundred and forty-six pounds." Underfoot were two zebra skins.

Los Angeles is famous for this sort of conspicuous consumption. Thomas calls it elegance, but whichever it is, he does have

a flair for it. It is everywhere about him. In the medical office
building he owns, the floors are carpeted and his office furniture
is teak with brass trim. The avocado couch has an imitation tiger
skin pillow on it. One section of the floor is covered with still
another zebra skin. On his desk stands a pair of beautiful pink
quartz sea horses. Almost as if he felt guilty about his taste,
Thomas explains, "I've worked hard for ten years, a minimum of
fourteen hours a day, since coming out of the Navy in 1956."
Born in Macon, Georgia, he traveled to Lincoln University in
Pennsylvania, Howard University in Washington and did his
internship at Philadelphia General. He met his wife, Toni, while
at Howard.

"We had this house built two years ago," Thomas said. A little
smile played on his face. "As soon as it became known that
Negroes lived here, people started driving by, throwing things
on the lawn. One night they burned a cross out there. I called
the sheriff and told him I was a big-game hunter and would fire
on them if they didn't get off my property. A few minutes later a
sheriff's car drove up and *every*body got the hell off my lawn
and I mean in a *hurry!*"

Thomas says he doesn't mind that his neighbors don't speak to
the members of his family. "I can't worry about the Chinese,
they're so busy getting white, and you know there's nothing
more conservative than a middle-class Caucasian doctor. A lot of
those fellows behave like they belong to the John Birch Society."
There are many white doctors in Baldwin Hills.

A senior staff member at California Lutheran Hospital,
Thomas starts his day there at 7:30 in the morning in surgery.
By ten he is in his office on Vernon Avenue. While the neighborhood is predominantly Negro, it is not as Watts, completely
black. "As you can see," Thomas said, "most of my patients are
Negro. A few are Mexican-Americans and two or three, maybe
four, are white."

While there are a considerable number of doctors in Watts,
many of Thomas' patients travel some distance from there to get
to his office, which seems to be a compliment to the man and his
abilities. "Many of my patients are Black Muslims from Watts.

I'm impressed by them; they pay their bills promptly and they don't grumble if I happen to be late coming in from the hospital. The riots? Oh, the Muslims and others agree that they didn't impress white people one way or another. Today, it's just like they hadn't happened.

"I'll tell you, John, they *did* make an impression on the black middle class here. I believe that to a man we disapproved of them. And then I've heard that the next time there's a riot, the Negroes in Watts are first going after middle-class Negroes."

(A few days later while I was visiting white friends in Santa Monica, my host got a phone call. It was a request from a long-time friend of his for cash donations to be used in Watts. For what particular purpose my host wanted to know, and the caller replied, "To keep them from rioting this summer.")

A Life Member of the NAACP, Thomas believes that an individual must advance himself through education, training programs and the courts. Life Memberships cost $500 each for adults, $100 for children; the Thomases have three. In the spring of 1967 the NAACP reported that memberships of this type had increased in number 72 per cent since 1963.

I returned to the Thomas home the next day and talked to Mrs. Thomas while waiting for the doctor to come home. She is thirty-six, three years younger than her husband. She has a rich brown complexion, is sharply attractive and a non-stop talker. "Toni will talk you to death," Thomas had told me. Mrs. Thomas, who is a professional librarian, has done volunteer work in Watts. I asked how the people there felt about her obvious life of comfort, her frequent trips to Europe, the very attitude of well-being and assurance she exudes.

She said, "They like me. Maybe it's a personal thing, I don't know. I've heard, and maybe it's a political thing, that these people are resentful of my group, shall we say. I don't buy this. I had a baby-sitter who came from Watts and had eleven brothers and sisters. I did very little, but I did do something to help her. I helped her to get a scholarship. I don't really find the young people this way. She was not resentful of anything I did for her. I gave her advice that she could not get hold of. In my own little way I tried to take her into the family."

We were in the sitting room, and as she talked I studied it. It was filled with antiques—Louis XIV, XV and XVI. A Meissen clock decorated the mantle of the fireplace that seemed never to have been used. Aubusson tapestries and floor-to-ceiling gold-leaf mirrors lent an uncommonly un-Los Angeles atmosphere to the room. In a conspicuous place on the wall hung a painting, *Nymphs at Fontainbleau,* by Diaz de La Peña, said to be a minor masterpiece. From another part of the house came the sound of Bettina's piano practice; she is eleven and a student at UCLA's experimental school.

We left the sitting room, passed through the main room with its portrait of Bettina and her sister, Theresa, six, and its glittering chandelier. We went up the carpeted circular stairway and into the doctor's trophy room, where we were joined by three-year-old George, and Theresa and Bettina, now finished with her lesson.

The phone rang. It was Thomas calling to tell us that he was being delayed because he had to perform emergency surgery. At the bar in the trophy room, a cold beer in my hand and above the voices of the children, I asked Mrs. Thomas what she thought made her middle-class. This was her answer: "The way we live, the kind of house we live in, our family life—we insist on being together—the way we spend our money, the way we use our leisure time, and our attitude toward education."

It seemed to me that Toni Thomas was talking about more than a "life style." For example, "family life" meant the presence of the father in the home and functioning as the head of the household. This is in direct contradiction to the theory that most Negro males are not in the home at all. Getting a good education is a theme that runs through all classes of Negro life. But Mrs. Thomas does not feel that a college education automatically removes you from contact with the people in the ghetto; she was less inclined to believe that than her husband. "I know at least fifteen doctors' wives who are teaching in Watts or Compton—by choice. If I ever returned to teaching, I'd go there, too."

Thomas arrived and apologized for being late. Mrs. Thomas took the children to the back garden; it does not have a swimming pool. It has a collard green patch that the doctor attends carefully. The afternoon wore on. Downstairs and across the street, the FOR SALE sign remained in full view of Thomas' windows.

"Listen, John," he was saying as he cooled off with a rum drink, "I believe in integration and education—the education of the white man. But I think the problems today are of class, not race."

Thomas is proud of what he owns, what he has made of himself and his family, even if he achieved these white symbols of success through a black clientele. But I sensed that even with his showplace home, office building, ranch in Ventura, Mercedes Benz SL 230 coupe, his annual safaris, he was disappointed that he has not been accepted by the community at large; most of his friends are Negroes. He is a social animal and a loner as well and perhaps he is the latter because he can't be the elegant social person he wants to be. He is unsatisfied, and what's more, he's an apprehensive man.

We were now standing before his gun collection. In one Georgia-accented sentence, and for all the opulence that surrounded him, he reverted back beyond his own rationalizations to what many Negroes have come to feel is the only reality for them. He gestured to the rack filled with handsome, expensive guns and said, "Well, I guess I'm ready for the white man if things got out of hand, wouldn't you say so, John? Man, I could arm half a company!"

Via the Harbor Freeway, it is a short drive from Baldwin Hills to the Watts section of Los Angeles where Jeremiah and Clara Washington live on E. 108th Street. They don't like guns, although, as Mr. Washington says, "There're plenty of them around because it's easy to get them. Or at least it was before the riots."

They are sixty-seven, and both came from South Carolina. They met in Philadelphia, carried there on the crest of the wave of black immigration from South to North during and shortly after World War I. They labored at menial jobs through the Depression and World War II while raising one son; three others died in infancy. When work slacked off after the war, they decided to pull up stakes and move West. "Things were closing down, all the war plants, so we had to make another new start," Mr. Washington said. Their son, Stanley, a veteran, stayed behind long enough to go to college and law school.

In Los Angeles the Washingtons took a live-in job. "I was the maid and the cook," Mrs. Washington said, "and Jeremiah was the butler and the driver. The man we worked for was in the movies, an actor. He was nice."

By the time Stanley finished law school and moved to Northern California, the Washingtons had managed to buy a small neat white frame house with front lawn and garden. Mr. Washington said, "All our lives we wanted our own place. We'd work hard and scrimp and save, then maybe one of us'd get sick and back we'd slide a little, but we finally got this place. You know our boy went to college; he's a lawyer and when he comes down here with his family, we like for them to be comfortable."

The Washingtons themselves were not educated beyond the eighth grade. Both dark brown in coloring, their hair graying steadily, the Washingtons for the past ten years have worked for the county of Los Angeles, Washington as a school custodian and Mrs. Washington as a housekeeper in a county hospital. They are Methodists. Mrs. Washington has two hobbies: preparing lavish meals for her son's family and playing the horses. Mr. Washington likes to play poker and occasionally stops off at a pool hall for a game to keep his eyes and hands in shape. "Once during a lean period," he explains, "we lived two weeks off my pool game."

I once lived in Watts for a year. It is not a ghetto as eastern ghettoes go. It is filled with frame or stucco houses that have neat lawns, gardens, driveways and garages. Domestics live here and laborers and teachers and doctors as well. Watts is a ghetto because Negroes can live there more easily than they can live anywhere else in Los Angeles. It is a ghetto because the city does not provide the services that it provides for other sections; it is a ghetto because vice and crime are tolerated by the police more than they would be tolerated anywhere else, but this means that they must police it more, too, and this brings them directly into contact with disgruntled citizens. These black citizens see the police as jailers, not protectors. Any resident of Watts can provide a number of personal stories of police harassment. I've been stopped because I looked like someone else, a criminal, the cops said.

Watts is usually the first stop for Negroes coming from out of town to settle in Los Angeles. When they have saved some money they move to other sections of the city. The Washingtons spoke of moving to San Bernardino. "We're just tired of all the huffing and puffing here in the city," Mrs. Washington explained. "But we do like the old neighbors around here." She went on: "Beside all this rioting and talk of rioting . . . we don't understand this kind of carrying on. It isn't going to get them anything."

I asked, as if I didn't know, "What do you mean, 'them'?"

She glanced at me with some irritation. Mr. Washington ran a hand over the gray stubble on his chin and it sounded like someone stroking sandpaper. "I mean," she said, "those people on the corners, the ones standing around all day doing nothing but drinking wine. Nobody ever gave us a dime; we worked hard for every red penny we got."

What the Washingtons have got is a sturdy little home, nicely furnished, on a good plot of ground. They have two Buicks, one a 1967 and one a 1964, a color television set, a green refrigerator, an extraordinarily effective barbecue pit and a lawn sprinkler. They go to Las Vegas once or twice a year.

On the corner west of the Washingtons' home, which is Central Avenue, or on the corner east, which is Compton, the clots of men, young and old and black, still hold up the light posts. New buildings stand timidly on a few sites where their predecessors were burned to the ground during the riots; parking lots are mute testimony to still other buildings that collasped in flames in August 1965.

"I just don't understand it at all," Mrs. Washington said. "All of them need to go out and work."

Wasn't it possible, I asked, that they were no longer content to work as the Washingtons had worked years ago? Could they really be expected to share in Los Angeles' affluence on $1.25 an hour?

"I don't know anything about that," she snapped. "A job is a job."

Washington, attempting to smooth things over, remembered when he earned four dollars a week in the South. "Now," he said with pride, "we earn $11,000 a year, between us, before taxes." It is here on the barely blue-collar level that the understanding between the just-haves and have-nots appears most to have broken down. Over 11 per cent of the blue-collar workers in Los Angeles are black; less than 3 per cent are in white-collar employment.

The Washingtons spent their entire lives escaping the ghettoes of the South and Philadelphia. In Watts they've found escape, they feel. They haven't paused to consider that younger Negroes are aiming higher, much higher than they did or could. I discussed the young and the old with a Los Angeles youth, and he told me: "Some of the old folks are with us when we say we want changes. Even if they can't understand completely what we want, they go along with us. The others don't want us to raise our heads and our eyes; we'll only make trouble if we do. Okay, we're not for *that*, doing it their way, but we know what Mr. Charlie did to them. They're victims. We dig, we understand, and everything's cool. But we've got to move along; we got to hurry up!"

Robert R. Wheeler of Kansas City is a man in a hurry; everything that needs doing, he wants to do in his generation. "We have got to come to some workable conclusions about black people and education, and we've got to do it in a hurry."

Wheeler, forty-six, looks like Willie Mays, but basketball was his game when he was a student at Lincoln University at Jefferson City, Missouri. A dark, smooth-skinned Negro, Wheeler stands about six feet three inches tall. He is Assistant Superintendent of Schools, Division of Urban Education. His "Inner City" programs involve upward of 17,000 kids, most of them black. Just a few years ago, when I first met him, he was whipping from one end of the nation to the other, busy on a Ford Foundation program to secure college educations for underprivileged kids and those who had college potential but had to drop out of high school. In Wheeler's area alone some 500 youths, black and white, went through this program and graduated from college.

In his slick, modern office in the Board of Education Building on McGee Street, Wheeler peered through his glasses—one of the rare times he remembered to carry them—and said in answer to a question: "No, I do not believe that it's necessary for black kids to be in the same classroom with white kids for them to be able to learn. In the first place, school integration, after thirteen years, has been practically stymied. Everyone thought it had to do with the South! Then they discovered that the North had to be fixed up too, and what attempts to integrate the ghetto schools of the North have done, is simply to knock the bigots out of the woodwork. In the second place, if you're talking about busing kids, forget it. This is my business, right? I know too many black kids who go to so-called integrated schools, but who have been cut to ribbons psychically by white kids and racist white teachers. Who ever would have heard of that woman in Boston* if it hadn't been over the issue of open schools? I'm for integration if it works; when it doesn't, I'm ready to go on to something else."

We broke off our conversation because teachers and department heads had appointments with Wheeler; they were all white. I left him with two drama coaches and a few hours later he picked me up at my hotel. We drove through the section of Kansas City that is familiar to every jazz buff, that section which produced Count Basie, Mary Lou Williams, Charlie Parker, Bennie Moten, and many other famous musicians. Here were the great night clubs that displayed their talents, Tootsie's Mayfair, El Capitano, The Orchid Room, the High Hat. Wheeler

* Louise Day Hicks.

murmured, "This is where all the 'buckets of blood' are." He sounded wistful, as though he were being wrenched away from this ghetto against his will.

For almost half an hour every car that passed us was driven by a Negro, and the further out we drove in that city, which has a black population of 100,000, the more prosperous the homes became. Finally, we pulled into the driveway of the Wheeler home on Swope Parkway. Wheeler eased his car in next to the battered station wagon his wife, Sue, drives. A first-grade teacher, Sue Wheeler is a sturdily handsome woman of thirty-six with a light complexion. The newest addition to the Wheeler home is Robin, aged fifteen months. Wheeler has a son, sixteen, by his first marriage. He is Skipper, whose real name is Robert Russell William III, and he is a lanky six feet five inches tall.

After a dinner of fried chicken, I asked about the home the Wheelers were having built. "It's in another ghetto," Wheeler said. "Still in the ghetto." I understood that he meant only Negroes lived in the area. I wondered why he had not, as a high-ranking public servant, moved into an integrated neighborhood.

"I could have, sure," he said. "But I do a lot of traveling and quite frankly, I feel better leaving my family in a neighborhood where I have friends to watch over them, rather than leaving them somewhere where they're going to be hated and—let's face it—maybe even hurt."

Black apprehension, like a minor theme in a somber symphony, runs throughout Negro communities across the United States. This was not the first time I'd heard expressed fear of the white community; it would not be the last time either.

Wheeler is a positive man, argumentative and volatile. In education and life his course has been set and he adheres to it. His studies have never ceased. In addition to Lincoln, he has studied at Columbia, the University of Kansas, the University of Missouri and the University of California. "I can't afford to stop studying," he says. "The changes in education are too rapid, and if you don't keep up with them, you may never get a chance to come up with a program of your own." One of Wheeler's play programs is to find a way to identify the disadvantaged but talented student through new testing methods.

He believes that the key to all education is reading, and during my visit he was heading up a summer program with emphasis on improving reading skills. He said: "In order to make progress in school, children *must learn to read!* The summer months offer a valuable opportunity to increase proficiency in this crucial skill."

After dinner, Skipper, who goes to a school that is about 20 per cent Negro, excused himself and went out to the station wagon. Wheeler grinned appreciatively. "Four years ago when you were here he was really a kid. Now, he's close to being a man." For a moment I leaned back and listened to the sound of the station wagon pulling out of the driveway, and I thought that times had *really* changed. How many black teen-agers fifteen or twenty years ago had access to a family car for their dates? Not many!

Wheeler, too, excused himself and went upstairs. When he came down again, the well-dressed Assistant Superintendent of the Kansas City school system was gone. In his place stood a tall, thin man dressed in baggy shorts and an old T-shirt. Wheeler is one of the best-dressed men in his circle; it goes with his sleek Toronado.

"We're getting down to roots now," Wheeler said, uncasing a trombone. He put on a Count Basie record, then began to play accompaniment. When the record was over, Sue, in the kitchen cleaning up, cheered. "When I was a kid," Wheeler said, "I wanted to do and be everything." He pointed to a battered violin case. "I can play that thing, too."

A neighbor named Tommy came in and we listened to records, then they began to talk about their boats; they have sixteen footers that are powered with 35 horsepower motors. They haul them to the Ozarks during the summer for water skiing and fishing. Sue served coffee and Wheeler prevailed upon Tommy to drive me back to the hotel in his Thunderbird, promising that on the following night he would cook up some mustard and turnip greens. It was, as with Dr. Thomas, the getting back to the roots ritual, the growing and eating of the greens or "soul food."

Getting back to roots is important for the black middle class; but, as one man told me at a party in Kansas City a few nights later, "Getting back to roots? Man, they've never let us get *away* from them." I went to the party with the Wheelers. It was at the home of a policeman who lives in the exclusive area into which the Wheelers are moving. It is exclusive because the residents, like the Wheelers, earn upwards of twenty to twenty-five thousand dollars a year, and generally both the husband and wife work. For these people integration has no meaning; they don't trust it.

It is true that they earn good salaries. But they are keenly aware that while they are employed by the white authorities, *they work as a rule with Negroes or in the black community*. A schoolteacher at the party said, "It's the same old thing—only the money's better. You can call it high-class segregation."

I have always found the Negroes in Kansas City to be insular, turned more inward than outward. I asked Wheeler why. "For one thing," he answered, "there are people trying to do things here, black and white. We're out here in the middle of the country and nobody watching us much, and we tend to take our own time. We have a southern exposure. But this was John Brown territory, too, remember, right across the border in Kansas. What I'm trying to say is that there is both a revolutionary and a conservative atmosphere around here and in the final analysis, it's the whites who'll have to work it out. I mean the whole problem's their baby."

Here it was only a few weeks after the Detroit riots, I pointed out, but no one I'd met talked about them or about Newark, whether they were good, bad or otherwise.

Sue said, "You know I've been working with a woman's group for several years, the Panel for Americans.* We've been going

---

* Esther Brown, a panel member, died early in 1970. She brought the case, Brown vs. the Topeka Board of Education, which resulted in the Supreme Court decision of 1954. Mrs. Brown was white.

out and talking to people, telling them in effect that democracy with all kinds of people involved could work. It's been slow, hard work; I'm not as active as I was and maybe that's because I'm discouraged. But you take any of these riots, any of them. When they're over, some money goes into those ghettoes. It may not be for long, but it gets to some of the people. The authorities start examining things. And things get done."

Why, I still wanted to know, was it that outside of themselves, the Wheelers, and two or three white friends I have there, no one talked of the riots.

Wheeler sort of laughed. "Man," he said. "People aren't sure of you. You're a stranger in this town. They don't know if you're a writer or someone who could really hurt them. Does that explain it?"

It did. I met my white friends through the Wheelers a few years ago. They dine together and go out together sometimes; they visit each others' homes. Sue Wheeler tends to believe in integration more than her husband, but like him, her trust in its validity under present conditions is feeble. Further east, in Chicago, Bob Johnson has built his strength in the belief that integration is a fool's dream. Black communities, for all their shortcomings, are his reality.

Chicago has long been a bastion of the middle-class Negro. It was founded by a prosperous mulatto trader, Jean Baptiste Pointe DuSable in 1772. There was a time when Chicago ranked first as the city southern Negroes most wanted to go to. As they poured up the Mississippi River to freedom, work and opportunity, small middle-class neighborhoods sprang up on the South Side. After World War I, South Parkway, with its long row of majestic limestone and brownstone houses became not only the main black thoroughfare, but the domain of the middle class. Chicago is the home of the *Defender*, one of the great Negro newspapers. It is also the home of Provident Hospital, whose Daniel Hale Williams, a Negro, performed the first successful open heart surgery almost seventy-five years ago.

Bob Johnson, the managing editor* of *Jet* magazine of Chi-

* Now executive editor.

cago, lives in one of the newest middle-class neighborhoods, Lake Meadows, which was built fourteen years ago to accommodate the exploding well-to-do black population. "We've got the middle-class here," Johnson says. "There're about a million Negroes and maybe more in the city now, and I'd estimate that we've got a whole lot of middle-class cats. We've also got three or four millionaires."

Johnson, his wife, Naomi, and daughters, Bobby, seventeen, and Janet, twelve, moved into that tall concrete, glass and steel monument to the black middle class when it first opened up. On this trip, I found the Johnsons packing. "We are finally getting out of here," Naomi said. Carton upon carton of books from their extensive library filled the living room. Cartons in other rooms were neatly labeled. Johnson himself was not elated; he was bitter. "We just bought this condominium over on Dorchester, near the University of Chicago. It's nice and it's integrated to some extent, not that that matters any more. But I start thinking: if I could have lived where I chose to when I first came to Chicago, I'd have been a young man and my house would be paid for now. We want to move, sure; we've been here too long, and it's been too hard a struggle for me to be completely happy now. Let the kids be happy. Here I am just starting on home owning at this late date." Johnson is forty-four.

Born in Birmingham, he was a cub reporter for the *Birmingham World* before he went to Atlanta to Morehouse College, which has been called the black man's Harvard. It is a hundred years old. Musing about his college days, Johnson said, "There's a multitude of alumni, all middle-class by now, I'm sure, who, if they don't remember anything else from school, remember old Benny Mays saying: 'Let the white man enslave your body if you can't help it, but never, never let him enslave your mind.'" Benjamin Mays is President of Morehouse. World War II caught up with Johnson at the end of his second year, and he spent three years in the Navy, during which time he managed base papers in California and in the Philippines where, he says, "There never was a color problem. The first couple of years after my discharge I thought a lot about returning there." But he didn't. He returned to Morehouse to complete his studies and then went to journalism school in the North.

We were sitting in the living room of his fifth-floor apartment. We could see the steel framework of the T. K. Lawless Gardens going up a few blocks away; it is a housing development being built by wealthy Negroes and it will be comparable to Lake Meadows; its tenants will be middle-class. Janet came in from school, put on a James Brown record and danced the "Funky Broadway."

I asked Johnson if Chicago was going to remain cool for the summer; riots have a way of spreading, like forest fires. "It looks pretty cool. Now, I don't know whether that's good or bad, to tell you the truth." Johnson is a small dark man who is very voluble; he does not bite his tongue. He can drop off to sleep during a conversation and wake up and start talking where he left off. He has traveled extensively and has interviewed the great and near great.

I asked if he found the middle class making overtures to the people in the ghetto these days.

"Just like always," he said. "There's been no division. This division business is a tactic of the white man. Divide and *keep* conquered. I remember when I was in school that the Negroes had only the highest regard for cats like us who were trying to make something of themselves, because they always knew we'd be able to help them. Hell, I remember cats from the country who couldn't hardly talk English whipping up those cracker streetcar conductors who were snapping at our college instructors. You can't believe Charlie; he'll lie to you in a minute. We're united, baby, and I'm here to tell you that I'm a middle-class cat and it isn't going that great for me in many ways. Those guys in the ghetto, they're only angry; I'm *mad*. Middle-class cats like me know exactly who's been kicking us in the tail. The white landlords. The white bankers. The white industries. A few white guys sitting in skyscrapers pulling strings. We've had a peek at those cats; they let us just a little ways into that house of theirs, and if it ever really broke, it wouldn't be a random thing, throwing firebombs at just any old store. No throwing rocks at cops. That's not where it is and now we know precisely where it is: not on the street but in those offices."

Naomi came out of another room just in time to hear Johnson. She danced with Janet until he was through and she said, "You know he's not kidding, don't you?" A teacher at Mayo elementary school, Mrs. Johnson met her husband while a student at Spelman, a Baptist college in Atlanta. She belongs to the Alumni Club, the Jack and Jills—a middle-class women's organization involved with children's school activities—and the Moles, a gourmet club. She drives a Volkswagen and spends her spare time putting together puzzles, preparing Bobby for college and getting Janet away from James Brown long enough to practice her flute.

The following day, late in the afternoon, I sat with Johnson in his office; it overlooks Michigan Avenue, and we watched the five o'clock traffic barrel south. I wondered if he had been offered jobs by the white press. *Jet* is Negro-owned and mostly operated.

"I get a couple of offers every year," he said. "But those cats are something else. They'll match my salary, even better it, but they want me to be a general reporter. I mean they ignore my management capabilities altogether and this has got to mean that they still believe anything Negro isn't worth much. So I don't understand why they offer so much for a nothing position unless, as always, they want the best they can get, but won't ever let it function. Nobody's offered me a horizontal position, from managing editor of *Jet* to managing something else."

He paused to wave to a secretary who from the street had noticed us in the window. "Anyway," Johnson continued, "I don't see half the future in the white press that I see in the Negro press." He laughed. "Baby, Negroes aren't going out of style; there's more of them than ever before! And as they continue to discover that the white press isn't basically interested in them unless they're Negro 'firsts' or rioting, they'll turn more and more to the Negro press. Hey," he said suddenly. "Do you know what we call that thing (the riots) they had over in Detroit a few weeks ago?"

I said, "No, what?"

"The Detroit Urban Renewal Program."

A couple of the young reporters who'd heard us joined in our laughter. Urban Renewal, it has been said over and over again by Negroes throughout America, is really Negro removal. "Now *we're* in charge of the program," one of the reporters said. The reporters were very young, and on the trip I was taken by the youth of the Negro population in this country; the median age for Negroes is 22.5 for whites 29.8.

Because he is so well-trained himself, Johnson insists that his staff is too. When the members of Johnson's staff were going to college, roughly 125,000 other Negroes were also enrolled; that figure has now doubled. "We've got talent backed up a long way," Johnson said, "and one way or another, these youngsters are going to insist on getting the chance to use it. That's a part of the problem; they're not all going to get that big bread Mr. Charlie told them about, so, of course, they turn back to the ghetto. Where else are they going? Statistics? Why? What do they mean? Listen: for every Negro who's making ten thousand a year, there're twenty-five white cats also making it, if not more. Statistics don't mean a damned thing. The only reason there's talk of things getting better is because they are getting better for the white man; that's the only time when it's going to get just a little better for us. I can buy a $30,000 condominium at age forty-four and call myself middle-class. That's some big deal."

Two nights later we were driving home in Johnson's four-year-old Chevrolet from the Pumpkin Room deep on the South Side. It was close to three in the morning. Johnson said, "Five years ago you seldom saw any news about Negroes in the white press. Ten years ago, forget it. By the way, when was the last time you saw a Negro girl in the *Times*'s society columns? A European coming to America back then could pick up a paper and believe there wasn't a Negro in the country. Now look. If it wasn't for Vietnam, we'd be making the only news to make and maybe that, after all, is why there is a Vietnam."

When we parked in front of my hotel he said, "Look, man. My

salary, education and the way I live makes me middle-class. I wear suits and shirts and ties and all that to work. I get to Europe occasionally, but that's all tags, labels. A Negro's a Negro in this country and that's that. The thrill is gone, it's over with this integration crap. Maybe it took a few years for us to see it, maybe a few riots, but believe me when I tell you, it's over."

Bill Chiles could offer additional reasons why the thrill is gone. You do not see the bitterness in the handsome, light-tan face, and you do not hear it in the voice that is still touched with the accents of Colorado and Missouri where he was raised. But I believed the bitterness was there, maybe in the way he swung his golf club, seeing, I could imagine, the enemy in that small, pebbled white ball. The club hurtled down, the arms straightened and his body pivoted. The club met the ball and the ball sailed in a good drive over the low, green, sloping hills of the Tecumseh Golf Course at Syracuse, New York.

Chiles was shooting nine holes alone. His partners did not show up and he ventured to guess that it was because the city was under a curfew stemming from racial disorders that left the citizens tense and afraid. Chiles picked up his bag and trudged after his ball. He was lucky. He arrived at the course early and he didn't have to play through or around anyone. "I don't know if this is my morning to ask white people for favors," he said. Mist hung lightly in the valley, almost obscuring the uniformly white houses that sit along its sides. It no longer bothers Chiles that he, a Negro, could not own one of them. Or it doesn't bother him as much as it used to. He is sixty-two years old.

Chiles found his ball and drew a putter from his bag. He took his stance as a passing white youngster, a groundskeeper checking the course, paused long enough to pull the flag from the cup. "I hope," Chiles murmured, "that he isn't going to bring me bad luck." He stroked; it was a twelve-foot put. The ball broke from the club and sped toward the cup, straining against the bad lay of the grass, and dropped out of sight.

Outward-bound golfers stared at Chiles and me then spoke pleasantly and went on their way. Chiles lined up for a new drive, his stance semi-wide. "John, do you suppose it's the riots that're making everyone so—*friendly* out here today."

It was a rhetorical question; he already knew the answer: Yes.

The riots began on a hot, steaming night. Plate-glass windows were broken and there was the familiar sound of scuffling, running, cursing; the staccato, toneless voices over police radios ebbed and flowed. The cops finally managed to contain the rioters and the disorder did not spread to other sections, not yet black ghettoes, but rapidly gaining that status. At first Mayor William F. Walsh issued an order putting only the Negro areas under curfew. "But someone got to him in a hurry," Chiles said, "and told him he couldn't do that; he couldn't segregate the curfew. White folks have been friendly ever since the riots started."

"Why?" I asked. The grass felt good underfoot and the smell of it was clean and sharp. Chiles had just completed another good drive.

"They're telling themselves the riots didn't happen. If they did, they'd have to tell themselves about all the rest of it."

William McKinley Chiles knows something about the rest of it; he is the director of the Community Relocation Department of Urban Renewal and for the past six years his life has been tightly bound to the fortunes of close to 6,000 people, most of them black. The Negro population of Syracuse is about 20,000.

"We work pretty closely with similar departments around the country, checking figures and trends. The fact of the matter is that integration in housing in the U.S. just isn't working, and that's one of the reasons why old 'Boomtown Shorty' and 'Sister Sadie' who live in the ghettoes get out there, break windows and run up and down the street."

We walked to Chiles's ball, and he picked it up and put it in his pocket. "That's enough for this morning." As we drove back to his home he said, "When our staff gets out there looking for a house, we've got Negroes who can afford to rent or buy decent homes. But when we get on the phone and say 'The family we are house hunting for is a Negro family,' in most instances the answer is 'No!'"

The answers to Chiles's questions have been no a long time,

which is why he and his wife, Ruth, fifty-nine, live in Nedrow, not so much a suburb of as an extension of Syracuse. They bought their four acres and nine-room house in 1942, when Nedrow was a sleepy village of a few families, and no one cared that they were black. It has grown and most of Chiles's neighbors are white and middle-income blue-collar workers with whom the Chiles have little in common. Ruth Chiles hasn't worked since early in their marriage. They have two children, Beverly, twenty, a college sophomore and Jim, twenty-two, who works in Nedrow.

When we arrived at the Chiles's home and got settled on the closed sun porch, he said, "Ol' Bev's still in Newark. Yes, sir, she's been down there visiting her aunt. They weren't right in the middle of the riots they were on sort of the edge. She called when they were going real good, shooting and burning, and said, 'Daddy, I'm staying right in the house. We've got plenty of food and we don't have to go out for anything, so don't worry.' She's all right." Chiles lit up a cigar. The phone rang and Ruth answered it. "Is that for me, Ruth?" The answer came back: "No, relax." Chiles explained: "If 'Boomtown Shorty' and 'Sister Sadie' decide to get back in the street, John, and burn up a few houses, my department's got to find some housing, so I can't really relax until everything's quieted down."

"Boomtown Shorty" and "Sister Sadie," the black male and female who live in the ghetto, have never been far from Chiles, although he lives a good three or four miles from the nearest concentration of Negroes. "When I first came to Syracuse I worked for eleven years in the PX of Manlius Military prep school, then I went to the County Welfare Department; that was 1933, and John, I carried a segregated caseload until 1941. That was when I first realized that me, wearing a suit, shirt and tie, and old 'Boomtown Shorty,' would always have a lot in common. He was segregated and so was I. Whenever something comes up having to do with Negroes, I drive into town and find 'Boomtown Shorty' in a pool hall and we talk and I get the message loud and clear."

"What's the message?" I asked.

"The message is that the ghetto's got to be revitalized. We ought to know by now that we aren't going anywhere unless we reach back and take 'Boomtown Shorty' by the arm and lead him out of where he is, and in order to do that, we've got to get right back down there with him."

Despairing of official help in providing housing as a major step in aiding "Boomtown Shorty," Chiles, a Catholic, became the founder of the Syracuse Interfaith Committee on Religion and Race. It is composed of twenty-two religious organizations and is non-profit. "We're getting FHA financing of nearly half a million dollars to build some homes. Best thing of all, though, is that the banks, which traditionally refuse mortgages to Negroes through-out the country, not only here, will give us interim financing. This black middle class is hungry for housing, and they've got the money for it."

In revitalizing the ghetto, was Chiles turning his back on integration? "No. We want integration. We have got to have it, but we aren't going to come to that as soon as we thought we would. Back there in 1963 everyone thought it would be a snap. Some of those Negroes with the right qualifications, and I'm not calling them Uncle Toms, moved very quickly up to a certain status, but every day a lot of them are discovering that what is good for them as individuals isn't necessarily good for the masses. The siphoning off of black talent has slowed; it's now coming back to work in the ghettoes."

What about the summers' riots, good or bad?

"I believe many of the grievances are just grievances, but you know the history of this country as well as I do, and you know that the white man is going to react violently; he doesn't care for the causes. He's talking about crime in the streets and forgetting about the crimes of his own heart. If we set out to rebuild the ghettoes, we can avoid massive retaliation; we can get our own black talent together; create our own political strength, survey our own economic needs. Then we can toss this integration business around some more."

We moved from the sun porch into the dining room for dinner. After, Chiles lit another cigar and turned on the television news. When that was over, he rose with a sigh. "John, do you want to come with me? I have to go talk to a group of white people out on West Genesee Street. I have to tell them that if they rent or sell to Negroes, the real estate values in their neighborhoods are not going to fall."

"After all these years and after all the statistics to the contrary, they still believe in crashing real estate values?"

"I'm afraid so."

We went, he talked and there were no results. Chiles would speak to another group and another and another, but he would also work with the ghetto people. "We understand each other," he said.

Chiles's statement was echoed in Boston by Mr. and Mrs. Jerry Hill. She said, "We prefer to live with poor Negroes rather than with whites because we understand their aspirations better."

I had gone from Syracuse to Boston's Roxbury, the Negro section, to find the Hills. They live in the area where there had been rioting in the spring, principally a clash between Negro welfare recipients and the police. Crawford street is poorly lighted, but I found the house and pressed the Hills' bell. Mrs. Hill, a tall, brown-skinned woman called down and I hollered up the stairs, then started to climb them. She was washing clothes and putting her children to bed. She introduced me to David, three, and I could hear Denise, eleven months, making noises in another room. While I waited for Mrs. Hill to get David settled, I noticed on the table of the room where I was sitting, a group of athletic trophies, the basketball player frozen in gold plate with the ball at his fingertips, the bronze baseball player at the moment of truth in his swing. Hill, who'd been born in North Carolina, but raised in Boston, was a star athlete at English-Latin High School and also at Fisk University in Nashville. He took his M.A. at State College in Boston and now, at thirty-three, teaches eighth grade and coaches football and basketball. He was due in any moment, his wife said.

Our conversation was interrupted every few moments while

she went to change the cycle of the washing machine in the next room.

"You'll have to excuse my running back and forth," she said, "but this is the way it is with a working lady."

To another question she answered, "I came from New York. Queens. I did my undergraduate work at Queens College, graduate work at Smith."

Now Millie Hill supervises Smith students at a Veterans Administration hospital. "I also work for a private agency one night a week, and that's why I'm so busy."

When she finally sat down, I asked why they lived in Roxbury rather than in a suburb or, at least, another section of town. "Well, we live here because we feel a commitment to the area; we also feel a commitment to the kind of people we see ourselves as being." They bought their house for this reason.

Jerry Hill came in then, a dark, solidly built man, and sat down. "We hope," Mrs. Hill said, "that by the time David is ready for school, certain promised improvements in the nearby school will have been made. But nothing's happened in two years, and we're afraid now that, because the schools in Roxbury are so poor, we may have to send the kids to private school."

Jerry Hill said, "And we might have to move after all. I'd see no point in living here and paying public school taxes when my kids aren't going to public school, and then have to pay for private schooling as well. Private school doesn't excite me at all. There are bigoted teachers and parents connected with those schools too."

If things were so unsettled, I asked, wouldn't they be better off in the suburbs? Negroes were living in small numbers in them. Hill said, "I do not like nor do I want to live in the suburbs. We rarely see our friends who do live in them except at parties here in town. The wife is stuck out there; the husband pops in on the way from the office—"

Mrs. Hill cut in: "Just how many white people do you think you can get to baby-sit for black kids in a suburb? And how many Negro women can you get to go out from Roxbury?"

"That's right," Hill said.

"Another thing," his wife said. "White people have got onto this black matriarchy thing, but they really should take a good look and see who's in charge of the American suburb: women. Thank you, no. I'll stick to the city."

The black middle class is inordinately proud that in their group the family structure is intact, wih he male very much in control of his family. At this level the number of black families headed by males is almost comparable to that of whites.

"Yes," Hill said. "Living in the suburbs is not for us. Some Negroes think that's where integration is, but I'm here to tell you it isn't. I was a pretty good athlete, you know, bumping heads, teammates, buddies and all that, but I never was invited into the homes of the white guys on the team. I mean, if you can't live easy with the guy you're blocking for or who you're throwing the touchdown pass to, how're you going to make it in other ways?"

"It's all very strange," Mrs. Hill said. "You know the white people I'm friendly with treat me wonderfully all the time—"

"And you treat *them* wonderfully, too!" Hill said. Mrs. Hill laughed and went on: "But when Jerry's with me, something happens; there's a change in them, particularly in the husbands of the white girls I know. It's like he's suddenly a *threat* to them."

The Hills smiled at each other; obviously they had discussed this before. Like most of the couples I'd visited, the Hills have a great deal of respect for each other. It is as though, at long last, the black female has come to understand what the black male has had to endure in America.

What did they think of rioting in Boston, Newark, Detroit and other cities?

"Y'know, you can knock the riots, if you like, but when they're over, at least *here,* some of that poverty money came loose. Now, it's too bad, really, about the riots, and it would be better if we *could* overcome with sit-ins and love-ins, but whites behave as though they don't want to go along with that kind of program. What Negroes need to do, however, is to stop rioting in their own neighborhoods; they ought to be rioting in the downtown sections." He laughed then and said, "They're liable to burn up my house and I can understand it, but I won't have it. Sometimes it seems so crazy. They want what I've got, just like I want what Mr. Charlie's got. And I've got sense enough to be worried."

A member of the trustee board of the Ebenezer Baptist Church, Hill does a lot of volunteer community work. His wife is also a Baptist. Many middle-class Negroes shift from the fundamentalist to the less emotional churches, but Mrs. Hill was raised as a Congregationalist, then became a member of her husband's church. "It's all a part of being real," she said. She places her faith in love and hard work. "You can get by if you love people and take pride in your work, that's really the key to getting along."

The black middle class is more mobile; the Thomases and Bob Johnson travel extensively and often to Europe. The Hills on the other hand, displayed a great curiosity about Africa. "Very little about Western civilization draws us," Mrs. Hill said. "We're not interested in Europe." We talked then about two visits I'd made to Africa, and Hill said to his wife, "We ought to try and see it some day. I've been to Japan," he told me.

He had served in the 101st Airborne Division for three years. "You couldn't hardly find a Negro in the division during World War II," he said. "Now, you're hard-pressed to find white boys in them. If I'd stayed in pulling that Japanese duty, I'd have been transferred and a major by now or dead, because it's the black kids who are steady getting killed in Vietnam."

With the lateness of the hour, the prints on the walls, one of Utrillo's corners and the other of Buffet's fruits, seemed to have lost a little color. By now we were talking of local politics and how Negroes participated in them or were affected by them. The conversation led naturally to Edward Brooke, the junior senator from Massachusetts, the first Negro to be elected to the Senate since the Reconstruction. "He ran for office twice from Roxbury, but he never got the votes from here. That's got to say something about how black people see him. I mean, there's

Louise Day Hicks running for mayor and there's Brooke. We're still trying to figure what's going on."

Earlier in the evening when Hill first came in he had been cautious of me; we spoke, but we were really like boxers circling for an opening; I had to let him know that I wasn't from some local or federal agency sizing him up. He had to make sure of that without voicing those suspicions. Somehow, we managed. He offered me a drink and we sat talking until far in the night, talking that good talk.

At the door of their three-story house bought with their combined earnings of $14,000 a year, Mrs. Hill said, "You should know, Mr. Williams, that I'm about to take a gross middle-class leap; I'm looking for live-in help." She laughed merrily. "I guess that's really going to make us middle-class, isn't it?"

The Negroes of America still provide the cheapest labor. Like Mrs. Thomas, Mrs. Hill will hire a Negro maid or house helper. Whites will seldom work for Negroes. What this means then is that contact with the people in the ghettoes who provide the bulk of untrained black labor is even further increased. I think the Hills are looking forward to this newest experience.

Seven years ago Bob and Joan Waite stopped looking for the breaks to come in American race relations and went to Africa. "The exciting place in the world then was Africa," Waite said, "and we didn't plan to come back."

But they did come back in 1965. Now they live in Columbus Park Towers, a co-operative apartment building in the low Nineties of Manhattan's West Side.* Waite is thirty-nine, and he hasn't always liked New York. He likes it now, but with reservations.

"We went to Africa because of the excitement and our backgrounds, I guess. My folks were missionaries and I was born in Sierra Leone. Joan studied at Northwestern in the African Studies program." Mrs. Waite is also a graduate of Vassar and Sarah Lawrence. Once a social worker, she was in the Urban

* They now live in New Jersey. 1971.

League's Community Relations program before they left for Africa.

"America was fast going downhill," Joan said. "So we decided to leave it. But once we got there, the daily realities were different. I was totally dependent on servants; we had four of them and no privacy whatsoever. It was not that we were doing well financially. Having servants is a way of life in Nigeria."

An electronic engineer, Waite was employed by a Nigerian firm that manufactured radios for domestic consumption; it was a good enough job until the backers pulled out. Then he began to work in the United States Aid to International Development Agency, a federal overseas program.

In New York the Waites had a variety of friends with equal education and tastes and aspirations. "We couldn't really find friends like that among the Nigerians; when we did, they were generally mixed couples," Joan said.

"Some Nigerians themselves," Waite put in, "would come back to Lagos after finishing school in London, take a look around and catch the next plane back."

Mrs. Waite tried to offer her services to the Nigerians as a qualified social worker, but the authorities regarded her education and training as a threat to their own positions. She has many talents, however. An accomplished guitarist and folk singer, she appeared regularly on Nigerian television as "Auntie Joan" and received a substantial salary. "I look back now," she said, "and I believe that I contributed more to the country that way than I ever could have as a social worker."

I met the Waites in Ibadan, Nigeria, in 1964, while on a trip through Africa. They were unhappy then and upset by what had happened to them during their three years. "What's it like back home now?" they asked.

I told them about 1963 and all the things that had happened and how Birmingham with its dogs and cops and fire hoses had resulted in the March on Washington, which in turn had produced a public accommodations bill. I told them that suddenly a lot of companies were out looking for Negro talent and how things looked good.

Then Waite had nodded and said, "That's the way it looks to us. When we left New York the Negro wasn't making any waves. Now, it looks like he is."

After two years back, Waite gives this assessment of the current scene: "The Negro isn't liked much anymore, but he's respected now, and maybe this is what it's all about." Upon his return, Waite joined Mayor John V. Lindsay's Task Force for Economic Development in Harlem. "The job sounded better than it really was." Recently he moved to a position with International Telephone and Telegraph; he is a manager of sales distribution and marketing. "What it is really," Waite says, "is trouble-shooting on a world-wide level. I haven't made a trip yet, but I will."

What else seems to have changed? I asked Waite. "Years ago when a Negro got one of those rare, high-powered jobs, he just marked time. Today they get one and they hit the boards running, off and gone!"

In his spare time he still works with the Harlem group in its efforts to help Negroes start small businesses and to attract new businesses into the community. "The Negroes up there don't look at you cross-eyed anymore, the way they used to when another Negro tried to help. Now they take it for granted that even if you're black you know what you're doing. The hostility's all gone."

To visit the Waites you trod over old Irish and Puerto Rican neighborhoods that have been crushed by Urban Renewal programs. The Waites' building, like the building they lived in in Park West Village before going to Nigeria, is integrated. They have three children, Robin, the daughter, six, and Monty, four, and Robert, two. The living room of the Waite apartment is filled with Nigerian art: intricately woven cloth stretched over a board, totems, a woman carved in wood, some Hausa brass bowls and Yoruba calabash bowls. With the coming of black nationalism to the United States, many Negro women have stopped wearing their hair in "white fashions"; Joan Waite wears hers *au naturel.* None of the other Negro women I spoke to on the trip did.

Does wearing the hair this way have a special meaning beyond sympathy for the black revolution?

Mrs. Waite answered: "The question of identity is still important to me as a person and as a mother and maybe wearing my hair this way keeps me aware of my roots. Sometimes, the more mobile you become, the more the roots tend to get lost, so you fight to keep what's yours, to keep from becoming lost. Maybe it's working; Robin shows her white friends the Nigerian dances she learned without any show of self-consciousness. I couldn't have done that as a child; I had nothing to show in the first place, and in the second, we were all convinced that anything that had to do with black couldn't be much anyway."

"Maybe in line with that," Waite said, "since returning, we find that more of our friends are Negro than before, a ratio of sixty–forty, whereas once it used to be fifty–fifty."

"Our old white friends," Mrs. Waite said, "I guess you could call them liberals. The ones we still have, well, there's more frankness about things racial now, and I think that's healthy."

I told Waite that I had found many people in the middle class working to help the people in the ghetto. "Yes, I know there are," he said. "A lot of this is due to the anger and guilt many middle-class guys feel. Guilt because they seem to be doing so well, and financially, perhaps, they are. At least the people in the ghetto think they are. They're angry because the middle-class guys now realize that there's still a great deal of tokenism and perhaps they're a part of it. Where there isn't, they're not allowed to function to full capacity. Even so, you've got to realize that there are a lot of Negro cats working downtown—more than there were before we left for Nigeria."

How important did the Waites think the middle class is?

Mrs. Waite said, "It isn't in clear focus yet; its power and influence are still to be felt."

"That may be so," Waite said. "But right now the middle-class Negro, with its increasing number of scientists, has the technological capability to hurt this country if he chose to. He looked at me and his soft brown eyes twinkled. "And if a riot came, the safest place for us would be not in an integrated community but in Harlem."

Bob Waite makes $22,000 a year and there is no tokenism on his job; he expects to go all the way. Physically, he's the size of some of the linemen playing professional football today. The world of 1967 seems to be his oyster. Yet, he, like so many others, let slip his apprehension of the possibility of racial disorder; he would take his family to Harlem for safety.

I left the Waites then, disturbed once more by the air of both hope and resignation that permeates the black middle class.

Avatus Stone, thirty-five, is not torn by these feelings, although as a 1952 All-American football player and later a professional, he knows that discrimination even penetrates professional athletics. Former Director of Specialized Recruiting for the Peace Corps, Stone is now a research executive. He and his wife, Carrie, a high school teacher, live in the integrated Capitol Park District of Washington, D.C.

"Negro stars," Stone says, "cannot be benchwarmers, not in any professional sport. I played a whole season with a bad knee; I had to or they would have let me go. Jimmy Brown once played an entire season with a broken toe, because he knew if he went to the coach with it, he would have been called a coward."

Stone played with Syracuse University, Chicago and in the Canadian football league. We spoke about Carl Stokes, now mayor of Cleveland, who this spring handled the cases of a small group of Negro players on the Cleveland Browns who wanted more money. "It was a case of paying them as little as possible—just like anywhere else," Stone said. Most of the players were traded to other clubs.

"Even so, the name of the game today is involvement. Not enough of our people, particularly from the South, are willing to leave there, come to Washington and compete with the white man. And too many of us are still using the 'black crutch.' I know it's bad out here, and tough, and that these guys are slick—they'll kill you with this goddamn integration —but we've got to keep on coming, and a whole heap of guys, whether they know it or not, are already involved and it's too late to drop out of the program now. The name of the game is involvement."

At the end of my trip to find out what the black middle class thinks and feels, I concluded that four years had made a distinct difference. None of the people I spoke with had lost contact with the ghetto—Thomas' wife, Thomas through his clientele, Chiles, Bob Johnson, who also has a writing school in the ghetto, the Hills, the Waites, Stone, who is still admired in the ghetto for his professional athletic ability and for creating championship football teams out of ghetto material when he was a high school coach. Only the Washingtons appear to have turned their backs on the ghetto completely, and maybe this is because they have not been away from it long enough to turn and face it head on again. Nearly all the blacks in this nation, came from the ghettoes.

Black power as a topic in the ghetto and in the middle class is all but absent; only whites are still belaboring the point. Simply put, to blacks it meant equality through political and then economic and social means. To whites it meant the thrusting of black attitudes upon them against their will. Black power means the uniting of all Negroes of whatever class and I found that today black Americans stand on the verge of being united as never before since being brought here in 1526. It has taken over four hundred years to bring about this unification, but it is coming.

Much pressure has been brought to bear on the middle class to deny anything white, anything that smacks of a comfortable relationship in white society. The Thomases hearing of threats against "their group" is a case in point. The alleged plots of middle-class Negroes in New York and Philadelphia to murder moderate civil rights leaders is an extreme example of this kind of pressure, which is being ignored generally by the people in this class.

The schizophrenia of hope and resignation, so present in the black middle class (one person I interviewed had just bought a gun, determined that "white people would not get the chance to walk through my house and kill me") will pass in time, but much of this will depend on the speedy "education of the white man," as Dr. Thomas put it.

I became convinced while on the trip that the new Negro leaders will emerge from this group—as did the old ones—but with less an immediate desire to force a wider wedge in resisting white society than to create new political forces in the ghetto. Although their margins of victory were small, the success of Carl Stokes and Richard Hatcher of Gary in their bids to become mayors, may well herald the unification of blacks within and out of the ghetto. Michigan has three Negro mayors in Flint, Saginaw and Ypsilanti. With every election in the South, Negroes win posts.

If as Stone says, "The name of the game is involvement," and blacks, as the middle class has discovered, cannot truly be involved with whites at this moment in time, then they will surely become, as they now are, involved with the ghetto Negro. Thus, in four short years noninvolvement has become almost total involvement and all this has been spearheaded by the black middle class.

THE STRONGEST NEGRO INSTITUTION?

_____

THIS ARTICLE *was never published; this is its first publication. In 1967 my agent put me in touch with Harvey Shapiro, one of the editors of the New York* Times *Magazine. Shapiro wanted a piece on the black churches in New York, and I agreed to do it.*

I read the Magazine nearly every week; I like to read it, but I've always held reservations about writing for it. It may be prestigious, but it doesn't pay much money. Furthermore, I've never been interested in the kind of prestige that is supposed to come with writing for it. The Magazine has always seemed too precise and somewhat pompous, rather like Moses coming down from the mountain not only with his tablets, but with the entire Bible. Few publications can boast of having influence equal to the Magazine's.

But I felt two things when Shapiro asked me to do the piece. The first was that it would be a challenge, and I often respond to challenges more than anything else. Second, some editors have a way of making you feel that you owe them something, even if you don't. This is an editorial technique that works more often than not, simply because the editor is working, or rather playing, on the writer's ego.

Shapiro had set me up on the my owing him thing from a few months earlier when he asked me to do a piece on black anti-Semitism. This request had come only a few months after my wife, Lori, and I returned from a long trip abroad. I turned Shapiro down on the grounds that I'd been out of touch with things, which was true. Also I felt there was a bit too much hue and cry from the Jews about the extent of black anti-Semitism. If the Times *Magazine does nothing else, it tends to legitimize issues that are essentially frail; this was one of them.*

After my refusal, Shapiro asked several other black writers to tackle the subject. Ronald Fair, then living in Chicago, was one, and like the other writers approached, refused to accept the commission. In time an article on black anti-Semitism did appear in the Magazine; it was done by James Baldwin, then living out of the country. In the same issue, however, was another piece, a rebuttal of Baldwin's done by a rabbi, the rebuttal, of course, used Baldwin's article as a springboard. I don't know if Baldwin knew his piece was going to be handled that way; I rather think not. Ordinarily the Times is not overly concerned with presenting the two sides of a given situation. Its handling of the black anti-Semitism issue in this instance served to deepen the cynicism of black writers toward the Magazine.

Mine included, but I was already at work on the church piece before I remembered to remember what the Times was capable of. I rewrote this piece three times and even then it was not what the Times wanted. Shapiro told me it was too statistical; that was his basic reason for turning it down.

An article is not created or written in a vacuum, and a writer who sets out to analyze why his piece was rejected is wisely advised to look at considerations outside his style of writing. The best writing in the world is useless unless it also carries a message, but a message need not necessarily be conveyed by superior writing.

The message of my article was the black church as seen by whites no longer existed with its comfortable illusions. The black church, like everything else black, had changed or was in the process of change. I don't believe this was what Shapiro was looking for, the question of statistics aside. If a writer does not or cannot or will not see with his editor's eye, he has written a piece that editor will reject. Shapiro held a concept of Harlem's churches which I did not share. Editors are not in business to be persuaded to change their concepts; this I indicated in the Introduction.

The manner in which an article is rejected must of course say a great deal about the editor. One will give you reasons ad infinitum in a letter; another will slit your throat over lunch, while you're feeling little pain from the martinis; still another will hide behind your agent, letting him deliver up the rotten news. Maybe this is what Shapiro did, but I called him anyway and it was then that he mumbled something about the article being too statistical. For a poet, Shapiro is an awful mumbler. I hope when he reads his own work he is distinct and clear.

TODAY close to 200,000 people in Harlem go to approximately 346 churches. No church official in New York City knows exactly how many Negroes belong to the churches; and no one is quite sure how many churches there are. Most of the churches are Baptist. The Methodist churches run second. Others are classified from Apostolic to "miscellaneous" by the Protestant Council of Churches of the City of New York. Some worshipers went to services yesterday; they are Harlem's black Jews, Seventh Day Adventists and Seventh Day Christians.

Roughly 25 per cent of the Harlem churches are concentrated in the area defined by the Harlem River on the east and Eighth Avenue on the west, and by 135th Street on the north and 110th Street on the south. Some of the churches are impressive buildings of dark or light gray limestone and have ranging spires, while others are storefronts with simple makeshift crosses hung in the windows. For some congregations the only music will be produced by a battered piano, if that, and a tambourine; still others will vibrate with the deep-throated rumble of the bass notes of a pipe organ.

Regardless of the differences, Sunday in Harlem not only is a day of worship and rest, it also is a day of truce with Mr. Charlie and Miss Ann who reside south of 110th Street; it is a day when what has been called the oldest and "strongest Negro institution" in America most comes alive. It is the Negro church and the Negro church alone, offering as it does temporary escape from the hurts of white society plus equality in the afterworld, that for generations has served to curb the discontent of the Negro.

Over 75 per cent of Harlem's churchgoers are Protestant. Thirty-seven years ago, when the uptown church population was 67,000 persons, Protestants accounted for 61 per cent of the worshipers, Roman Catholics only seven. Today almost 20 per cent are Catholic, but the Protestants have lost only three to four percentage points. With economic gains some Negroes have moved into higher social strata and this has meant a shift from the fundamentalist to the ritualist churches of the community. The latter are considered to be the "upper-class" churches and they are Protestant Episcopal, Presbyterian and Roman Catholic.

Located as they are in the largest Negro ghetto in America, the churches have found themselves overwhelmed by two sets of problems. The first are those facing most urban churches today: mobile populations that make up the congregations but no longer live in the neighborhoods; shrinking congregations made up of middle-aged and older people; limitations (now being relaxed) on the amount of community action a church may perform set by the governing boards (this last is not true of the Baptists; government is autonomous, with authority vested in the pastor); re-evaluations of the churches' role in a society that more and more rejects their moral influence.

The second set of problems are social, stemming from the exclusion of the Negro from society. These include lack of housing, low employment, juvenile delinquency, adult crime, drug addiction and low health standards.

Although there has been considerable building in Harlem since 1960, and more planned, the occupants of the new high-risers are members of the middle class who have been the major beneficiaries of civil-rights agitation. The housing crisis among the poor continues. Seven years ago, of the 76,585 housing units in the community, only a little more than half were sound; the others were deteriorating or dilapidated.

At the same time the labor force in Harlem was just over 100,000 persons. Almost one half were women. Seven out of every ten women who live in the community work. The unemployed are about 10 per cent of the total labor force. The males who do work are usually found in the lowest categories, "operative" or "service," like the women. Harlem has the lowest percentage of white-collar workers in Manhattan.

The shadow of unemployment is public assistance. At times Harlem residents have received in Home Relief and Aid to Dependent Children 20 to 25 per cent of the total funds for these categories distributed in the borough.

Juvenile-delinquency rates have soared to as high as 141 per cent over the years, but now seems to be receding.

Drug-addiction rates have fallen slightly and this is attributed to racial pride and the fact that there no longer is any status attached to being an addict, as in the past.

The adult crime rate continues to climb and has almost replaced education as a primary community concern.

Mental health—a number of churches once offered psychiatric counseling services to their respective communities—is joining physical health as a major concern of the Harlem community.

It is the consensus of sociologists, criminologists and local, state and government leaders today that this bleak outline of Harlem is the direct result of white prejudice and discrimination directed against the Negro. Indeed, most of the American church has reached the same conclusion and is making slow and labored progress in meeting its moral obligation. However, the obvious failure of the white church to meet this obligation with all its might lies with the white members of the church.

For this reason the Negro church, still considered by many to be of inestimable strength, appears to have discovered that the issues of the present, irrevocably knotted to civil rights goals, are sprinting past its capability to adequately challenge those issues. Traditionally in the Negro communities in America, the clergyman has been the leader and spokesman. But the Protestant

Council of the City of New York study of 1962 revealed that
members of the Harlem community felt that no true leadership
in terms of the clergy existed. Two years later this feeling was
borne out during the riots that summer. Clergymen were unable
to even gain the attention of rioters. As a result a great part of the
rioting which pointed out the lack of leadership, the Ministerial
Interfaith Association was born with the purpose of projecting
the ministry back into the leadership of the community. Melvin
Bye of the MIA said the organization was incorporated in 1965
and now has 120 members from Catholic and Protestant churches.

A number of Harlem ministers speak of "carrying the ministry
into the community," and this means administering to the social
problems just as vigorously as the religious ones. This must
mean, of course, that the Negro church is now willing to attack
directly the American caste system. The original nature of the
Negro church mitigated against this, for religion was the only
institution the caste system was willing to share with the African
slave.

The Spanish and Portuguese initiated the slave trade with the
slender excuse that in the process they could bring the heathen
under the influence of the Catholic church. Protestantism overwhelmed Catholicism in the New World, and the slaves embraced its cut-and-dried formulas. Booker T. Washington, perhaps the first modern "Establishment Negro," noted, however,
that, "The white minister who was (the Negro's) guide, found it
more convenient to talk about heaven than earth."

It was through religion that the Negro came to his only position of influence in the Negro community and to some extent
outside it. The minister was the leader of the Negro community
and he dealt, hat in hand, with the white power structure
which viewed the Negro as the most religious of Americans.
There was a tacit agreement between the power structure and
the Negro minister-leader, and it was that the minister was not to
disturb the racial design of the society that in the first place
had given him his limited power.

Only Adam Clayton Powell, whose Abyssinian Baptist Church

on West 138th Street was founded in 1808, successfully used his position as the leader of his church to leap into politics on a national level. (Dr. Martin Luther King has remained a churchman and he is very much the kind of Negro leader the white American has been used to dealing with; Dr. King represents no break in the tradition of black-white relations.)

Powell also represents something of a break with his church, for Negro parishioners, like white parishioners, definitely symbolize a conservative stronghold whose philosophy on civil rights is to move slowly. One reason for this, according to sociologist Kenneth B. Clark, is that "The Negro church is a social and recreational club and a haven of comfort for the masses of Negroes. Within the church a Negro porter or maid can assume responsibilities and authority not available elsewhere . . . Here the Negro domestic exchanges her uniform for a 'high-fashion' dress and enjoys the admiration and friendship of others . . . Only in the church have many Negroes found a basis for personal worth."

White parishioners on the other hand are generally opposed to integration because of the standard American emotional reasons. In order not to cause the break-up of the Negro church in which a Negro can at least in part round out his life, the Harlem churchgoer will support to a considerable extent the civil rights activities in the Deep South, but resist supporting activities in Harlem. This was one of the reasons why Reverend Eugene S. Callender, for seven years the pastor of the Presbyterian Church of the Master in West 122 Street, left the pulpit over a year ago. Now the executive director of the Urban League of Greater New York, Mr. Callender said, "I left the pulpit, but not the church, so I could have more freedom in community affairs. I had a middle-class congregation over there that was rigid against doing anything for people less fortunate than themselves." The Church of the Master has a congregation of about five hundred persons, according to lay secretary Miss Gladys Battle. It has been in the Harlem community since 1800 and formerly was known as the North End Presbyterian Church. It was one of the first Harlem churches to offer psychiatric services in the mid-1950s. Mr. Callender is the second minister to leave that church; the first was Dr. James H. Robinson, who now heads the Crossroads African program in downtown Manhattan.

Paradoxically, the oldest of Harlem's churches were formed because of segregation. There was a point in American church history when Negroes and whites worshiped together, even in the Deep South, but Negroes were not allowed to hold offices in those churches, South or North. Thus, the Negro members of the Methodist Episcopal Church, which in 1796 was located in John Street in New York City, expressed a "desire for the privilege of holding meetings of their own." The white members readily granted that privilege and the Negroes founded Mother African Methodist Episcopal Zion Church, which is now located on West 136th Street and is the oldest church of its denomination in Harlem. Its pastor, Reverend George Weldon MacMurray says his congregation of about 6,000 persons, are "middle-class or lower middle-class, if there is such a thing."

Mother A. M. E. Zion is one block south of Abyssinian Baptist Church, which according to its assistant pastor, Reverend David N. Licorish, has perhaps the largest congregation in Harlem— 13,000 to 14,000 people. Abyssinian was founded by the Reverend Thomas Paul, a native of Exeter, New Hampshire, who preached before many white audiences and whose "color excited considerable curiosity." The current church building was erected in 1925. The autonomous control Baptist ministers hold over their churches is in part responsible for the freedom to participate in extra-religious activities by Reverend King and Reverend Powell, as foremost examples. In many cases, Baptist churches are family-owned.

St. Philip's Episcopal Church on West 134th Street is the oldest church of its designation in Harlem. The church was founded by Reverend Peter Williams who led the Negroes from Trinity Episcopal Church in lower Manhattan. Trinity is believed to be one of the oldest churches in the United States. In addition to being refused positions of responsibility in Trinity, the free Negro members rebelled against the do-nothing stand the Episcopalians took in regard to slavery. St. Philip's, first located in downtown Williams Street, was recognized as a parish in 1818 and incorporated in 1820. It has a congregation of about 4,400 persons and its pastor is Dr. M. Moran Weston, who was elected to the post by the congregation.

Dr. Weston has approximately eighteen doctors and forty registered nurses, along with a number of public school teachers in his congregation. Whenever possible, these participate in the community programs the parish house sponsors. Like Mother A. M. E. Zion Church, St. Philip's is building a new community center to service the neighborhood. St. Philip's, however, is using church funds, while Reverend MacMurray said that his new community center is not using church financing. He declined to reveal the source of the funds.

Harlem churches now own real estate whose worth is estimated at between $70,000,000 and $100,000,000. Some of it is slum; last year Friendship Baptist Church on West 131st Street was cited by the *Amsterdam News* as the owner of rooming houses which were in such poor condition that the tenants were asked to move. With the widespread funding of the Office of Economic Opportunity, the churches are expected to continue to enlarge their community programs. In 1965, twenty-three churches in the community divided almost half a million dollars in HARYOU funds. Some critics claim that government funding makes the churches too dependent on outside help. And, of course, while the overwhelming majority of the churches use poverty funds for specified programs, a few others have not. (A Negro minister in the Bronx last March was charged with the theft of nearly $8,000 and with the attempted theft of $15,000 in poverty funds allocated to his church-sponsored community projects.)

Abyssinian Baptist Church, one of the eight wealthiest (St. Philip's and Mother A. M. E. Zion are also among the eight), provides quarters for the Head Start program, a government-financed project. Like most other Harlem churches it fosters self-help programs and cultural activities. Reverend MacMurray's program includes counseling for recreation and vacation, the unwed mother, the handicapped, unemployed and the narcotics addict. Reverend MacMurray said his church supports "the civil rights movement in its major activities." Locally, his church is engaged in voter registration drives.

Dr. Weston of St. Philip's, who finds that most of his congregation has moved to Connecticut, New Jersey, Yonkers, New Rochelle and Mount Vernon, has a varied neighborhood program. One of the most effective of these is the tutorial program in which is taught remedial reading, math, French, English, Spanish and history.

A number of churches have Negro history courses and African art exhibits as well as African guest speakers from the United Nations diplomatic corps. The recent decrease in addiction in Harlem has been prompted, some observers say, by an upsurge of racial pride which may be a result of the frequent contacts between the Negroes in the churches of Harlem and the Negroes of Africa.

Some services, such as day care; nursery and addiction centers, appear on the surface to be a great duplication of effort, but the clergymen deny this. Reverend Licorish said, "there are not enough centers as it is. The young people are left to fend for themselves and that isn't good." Reverend Callender, whose former church is sponsoring his "Academy of Transition" project for dropouts and unwed mothers, said emphatically that more programs were needed.

Community residents themselves are demanding not only more services but more leadership from the clergy. Said one woman indignantly, "When you want the preacher you can't find him; he's never in the church. If he's well-off, got a rich church, then he's away in his convertible; if he's got a poor congregation, then he's moonlighting, working in the Post Office or some other place."

The clergymen are visualizing their places of leadership in the front ranks of the civil rights movement. Last year when "black power" was the rallying cry of the movement, a group of ministers representing the National Committee of Negro Churchmen issued a statement to white churchmen, national leaders, Negro citizens and the mass media calling for an understanding of the phrase:

"Powerlessness breeds a race of beggars," the statement said in part. "We are faced now with a situation where conscience-less power meets powerless conscience, threatening the very foundations of our nation."

In February of this year another group representing the same organization issued another statement criticizing the congressional move to deprive Adam Powell of his chairmanship of the Labor and Education Committee and his seat in the House of Representatives. These clergymen insisted that the contretemps was racially motivated. The subsequent expulsion of Powell may well be the goad that will drive the Negro church, leadership and membership, from its conservative position on civil rights, and if the churches in the Negro communities in America abandon their present position, the civil rights movement for the first time will be embraced actively by the majority rather than the minority of Negroes in America. Reverend Licorish, who has been at Abyssinian Baptist Church since 1944, and helped Powell campaign for his first term in Congress said, "this church has always supported the movement. This is a permanent struggle."

To be truly meaningful, the struggle would require the ultimate end of the Negro church; it would mean that the power and prestige that many Harlem ministers now possess would have to be modified with absolute integration which, as Dr. Weston put it, "is a two-way street." Negro parishioners would have to compete with white parishioners for positions of authority within the integrated church. The Negro churches in their belated moves to service the community in the street and not in the pulpit have already made the first step down that two-way street—most of them unknowingly. The current of the times is swift enough to keep them moving, for the Harlem youngsters who represent the future of the Negro church are seldom to be found in the pews on Sunday; they are in the street, believing perhaps that, while God is not dead, "He's over at the Red Rooster." For those same youngsters, "The Old Time Religion" isn't good enough anymore.

THE GREAT WHITE WHORE

MY WIFE Lori and I had checked into the Majestic Hotel in Barcelona in the mid-sixties. I didn't plan to stay in the hotel any longer than necessary, for financial reasons. We'd come over on hope, and I was going to finish The Man Who Cried I Am. We literally didn't know whether we'd have to swim back to New York or not. I was hoping I'd finish the novel, collect the balance of the advance and thus be able to return by ship or plane. I also hoped to get two or three article-writing assignments from my agent. I had one from Holiday, but as I've mentioned before, you don't get paid for articles until you finish them and they're accepted. Besides, this one couldn't really be written until we were at the end of our year's stay in Europe. That was our plan, a year.

However, if we couldn't eke out the bread, it would be another story. My son had just started his freshman year, too. So I was shaky all the way around, though Lori didn't know it. Each morning we'd have our coffee, rolls and marmalade and go out to Castelldefels, a village about 18 kilometers south of Barcelona, and look for a house to rent which would be far cheaper than staying in a hotel.

We found a cable from Byron Dobell, an editor of Esquire, when we returned from house hunting one day, asking me to call him collect about an article. I was so sure he wanted me to do something on El Cordobes, or something else that had to do with Spain, that I actually went into shock when I talked with him.

He wanted me to do an article under the title: "Why I Want to Marry Your Daughter."

I should've said no. But I didn't. I agreed to do the piece

and he gave me the deadline and I hung up. I'd wanted to get away from just that kind of cheapness, but I hadn't. I felt cheap myself for having considered all the economic reasons why I couldn't afford to turn down the article. I also felt trapped and bitter. Then my writer's ego surged forth: I was going to do that piece so goddamn well that when I told Dobell he could not use the title, Esquire would still run it, but under my title, "The Great White Whore." My agent advised me not to do it, but he didn't have to worry about swimming back to New York.

I began writing the article in the hotel, and finished the second draft of it in Castelldefels after we'd moved out there and settled in a small house nestled at the foot of mountains with a view of the sea. The article was in New York long before the deadline, and Lori and I settled back to get the house in order.

About a week later I got a message from my agent or Dobell; I don't remember which one now. The message was more important than the sender anyway, and it read: "Must have title, otherwise, no go," or words to that effect. I didn't feel too badly about it. I could submit the piece elsewhere, and there'd be some kill money coming, some small portion of the agreed upon fee to compensate for my time spent in research and writing. My confidence in my ability to earn a living away from home increased. After all, they hadn't rejected the piece; they'd rejected my demand.

I embarked on a period of nagging my agent about the guarantee, the kill money. After many letters he said that since I hadn't let Esquire use their title, they said I had no guarantee coming. I hit the roof; I was salty for months. Writers often complain about being out of New York and finding that their agents don't work as well for them. I believe this to be true; I found it to be true in my case.

When I returned to New York about a year later, I learned that Esquire very often assigns articles to be written under titles its editors supply. I'd never had this with other magazines and never with books. Titles are a sometime thing, subject to change. There exists a gentlemen's agreement that title changes will be made in consultation with the author. Esquire was

*arbitrary in this matter, but then, other black writers, like Claude
Brown and Ishmael Reed have had difficulties with that magazine, too.*

*My agent sent this piece around and around and it was re-
jected. I did see one editor, a young man who said it sounded
like LeRoi Jones had written it, and that he was tired of hearing
that old routine about white men down in the slave cabins with
black women. I pulled the article out of circulation until 1969.*

*At that time Walt Shepperd was editor of the Nickel Review,
an "underground" weekly in Syracuse. He asked if I had anything he could run in the paper, and I sent in "The Great White
Whore." So, from the time when I wrote the article until it was
published, without fee, four years elapsed. The reader response
to the article was all favorable and Shepperd was pleased, although his printers threatened to quit if he forced them to set it.
As for Esquire, its editors have never asked me to do another
piece. This may be because they know I'd refuse any commission
from them anyway.*

INCREASINGLY in the United States the eye sweeps the streets,
halts, sweeps again and stops. Another interracial couple. Another black man and a white woman, Miss Anne, Mr. Charlie's
Daughter, *Your Daughter*. And, more and more in this nation,
parents who thought they were liberal are being put to the test.
Final results have yet to come in. *Are* interracial affairs and
marriages on the increase?

If they are, and it seems to me that that is exactly the case,
then you should know the reasons why I might want to marry
Your Daughter. From the first book I ever picked up right
through this week's newsmagazines and papers, I have known
Your Daughter, and well. Not because she was wayward, you
understand, but because she was such a fantastically large segment of American culture, history, religion, economics.

When first we met, Your Daughter was Mary Magdalene or one of the whores who scouted for Joshua the night before he took Jericho. In grade school Your Daughter was Goldilocks, Rapunzel, Little Red Riding Hood, the Princess awaiting the arrival of Prince Charming. Your Daughter became a Pretty Girl, a Varga Girl; she was Little Orphan Annie, Tillie the Toiler, Winnie Winkle, Brenda Starr; she was Judy Garland, Bonita Granville, Elizabeth Taylor, Deanna Durbin, Betty Grable, Ann Sheridan. She also was Myrt and Marge, Our Gal Sunday, Helen Trent. Your Daughter sold me cars, chewing gum, cigars, cigarettes, shaving creams, hair oils, electric razors, cooperative apartments, clothes, food and suggested that I fly the airline she worked for. Your Daughter was always a left-handed kind of whore and you put her in the streets.

The presence of Your Daughter permeated my existence from the beginning. Usually, as you portrayed her, she was blond and buxom and had a firm, well filled out behind. She smiled a lot, seductively or wholesomely. Lately, she seems to have an absolute leer about her. The truth of the matter, however, was that while you were prostituting Your Daughter to sell your products, you did not intend for her to sell *me* anything for, as far as you were concerned, I didn't exist. You had even written me out of history.

But by 1963 you had discovered me. I had managed to scrape together a few dollars (starting after World War II) and in order to attract your attention I put a sign around the neck of a very intangible thing and called it The Negro Market. Also I was throwing my weight around—finally. Washington, Chicago, Cleveland, Selma. You remember. Then (was it because of desperation or demand) you started flashing in your commercials, for instants only, Negro females. But it was too little, and much too late. Negro females were symbols, not love objects, as Your Daughter.

You had already told me by word and deed that the white American female—Your Daughter—was a special creation. The Negro female was an authoritarian figure, and she was busy caring for households Negro men could not care for because of the virulence of discrimination and prejudice. Your Daughter manned the classrooms, the social agencies, the outer rooms of doctors' offices. I can even remember my father knotting his tie before a mirror and singing

> "The object of my affection
> can change my complexion
> from white to rosy red. . . ."

. . . and then, on his way out of the house he would peck my mother's lips.

Paradoxes were not for my parents' generation, at least not for them. They puzzled over how to feed four children more or less regularly. How we managed to survive the Depression with its heaviest weight upon American Negroes is totally beyond me.

But my generation is given to unraveling paradoxes, explaining them and creating others. No paradox was involved in the history of my relationship with Your Daughter. For example I understand now how long, long before you pasted Your Daughter's picture in every conceivable space, you had already done the ghastly groundwork that would leave you no alternative but to make a whore of Your Daughter. While you were placing her on a pedestal (I suspect that you were incapable of this; that was the place she wished to be and you had no choice but to put her there) you were sneaking with the cover of night into the slave cabins.

The black man who dared protest your sleeping with his wife or sweetheart died. Sometimes your heart went out to the black women and Your Little Colored Children. You could afford to let your heart go because you knew instinctively that a black woman could harm you even less than a white one. She could not harm you in the same disastrous fashion a black man could, given half the chance. Negro women, no matter how close you got to them, could not compete with you physically (except in bed), economically, intellectually or socially. If you were passing out advantages, they got them.

Of necessity, Negro men had to work the land, cultivate it and reap the harvest. That eliminated them from competition; they could not, except under unusual circumstances, become your intellectual, social, economic equal or better. America was a physical and violent land in the early days, and you thought, even if you couldn't translate into Latin as the Romans did, "so many slaves, so many foes." When the foes rose up, you slaughtered them. For you were always worried about the physical abilities of Negro men, and I don't mean in a sexual sense. I mean in the innate male-to-male competition, the atavistic animal sense.

The Spanish discovered very early in their occupation of the Caribbean and southern United States that Africans were tougher than Indians. One priest wrote to his superior, Cardinal Ximenes, that, if Africans were brought to the New World they would breed very fast and ultimately revolt against the crown. Had King Charles IV not been so young and headstrong I would not be writing this article, since he would have heeded the voice of the Church and caused the Spanish slave trade at least to be brought to an immediate halt. Instead, Charles increased the slave trade so his friends in the New World would have hands to work the lands acquired here. Somewhere, buried deep in the world psyche there must reside the instinctive knowledge that the black people who survived the slave trade, which took from 15 to 75 million lives, must be of hardy stock.

The 22 million Negroes in the United States are the descendants of three million Africans still alive in the US when the slave trade was outlawed. The white Southerner doesn't ever forget this. He knows he must deal with Negroes with guns and clubs and murder, otherwise he himself will not survive. He has said this. The presence of the likes of Cassius Clay, Jimmy Brown, and Willie Mays must rekindle ancient fears in the minds of many white Americans. And that means You.

While Negro men were holding down the land, the Negro female, if there was a break available, got it, the better education, the clean jobs. In my family, three uncles had to remain in the South until five girls, my mother and four aunts, had made their ways North and into good jobs, for that time. With the better educations, the Negro female was forced to "marry down" to a man without as much education, or forego altogether a

marriage so vulnerable to disaster. Finally, the Negro female
agreed secretly with white platitudes: a Negro man didn't make
it because he was "shiftless," just plain lazy. The black female,
like the black male, came to have the same views as the members of white society. Her idols were Skeezix, Jesus Christ,
Joshua, Prince Charming, Dick Tracy, Errol Flynn, Mickey
Rooney, Freddie Bartholomew.

A poet once noted that hate was legislated, written into the
primer and testament, shot into our blood like vaccine or vita-
mins. You legislated Your Daughter upon me. You made it
mandatory for me to be concerned for and involved with her.
You used the hard-sell and the most subliminal of approaches. I
got the message: Your Daughter equals Love, Happiness, American Achievement. Is it any wonder that I might seriously consider marrying Your Daughter?

Now, let's forget the psychological clichés of the 50's when it
was fashionable to talk of black and white affairs as being filled
with revenge on the part of the Negro and masochism on the
part of the white, although these elements may very well be a
part of *any* affair. Phrases like that were too easy; they sprang
like salt from a bad well. Besides, You must remember, they
were manufactured and stamped in *Your* communications centers. No, in the light of history and by Your continuity of per-
forming as a pimp, there is every honest reason in our society for
a black man and Your Daughter to be together. In spite of the
pure logic of it all, their being together was considered a crime
more vile than murder.

But black and white affairs continue to be the great sexual
underground in America. Some cities, like New York and San
Francisco show signs that permissiveness toward these kinds of
relationships is less an illusion than in the near past. Given the
proper situation, however, no city in America is ideal for mixed
couples. Increasingly, Europe is no longer the place to escape to
either. In Smalltown, United States, where there is a sizable
Negro population, the relationships still tend to be clandestine.
A car wheeling through a downpour of rain may reveal for a
second, a blond sitting beside a Negro driver. Then, gone. Small,

gray bars and restaurants tucked into hillsides may be the meeting places of mixed couples.

In New York, a Negro executive breaks for lunch and meets
his secretary in a midtown studio apartment he has rented. His
secretary is Your Daughter. A Negro musician visits a medium-
sized city in the Mid-West. At the very first table sits Your
Daughter; she is a Musicians' Freak and likes musicians only if
they are Negro. You must bear the responsibility for that too.
She will be in the front row of every jazz concert; she will talk
musicians' talk; she will be available any time the black musicians want her. *This* Daughter of Yours is sick—and nearly
everyone knows it. Again, she and other Daughters like her are
Your fault. They deal with black men without having shed your
propaganda; their relationships are not woman to man, they are
white to black.

I have found, however, that Your Daughter on the whole is
not at all weak, and that she does not always think of sex. The
humanistic movements in this nation, particularly civil rights,
would die on the vine were it not for Your Daughter's participation. You should make no mistake; free and equal coffee and
hamburgers over the counter are going to bring me into more
contact with Your Daughter. We are going to talk. We are going
to discover that, in this culture (and how could it be helped) we
have come to like the same books, movies, theater, people and
places; the same ideas are going to please us. We are going to
like going places together and perhaps we might enjoy making
love to each other. We are not going to be terribly concerned
with your feelings; pity perhaps, for we will be aware of the
history of things. Your Daughter has a lot of guts. More than
You. She is through with fantasy, finished with the kind of prostitution you placed her in.

What is real for Your Daughter today, *right now?* Besides
Vietnam, only the ebbing and flowing Negro Revolt, and this
applies to most young people. The fantastic explosion (or
uncovering) of news about the Negro in America has marked
the real start or collapse of this nation. It can die if it refuses
to live up to its promise. That is today's reality and that is what

Your Daughter is involved in. Unlike European women, Your Daughter refuses to deal on a temporary basis or a fanciful consideration. There is a great deal of empathy between us. I am weary of being the forgotten man; she is tired of being the neglected woman. She is not a product. In our society where there is either a direct and massive assault or a secretive guerrilla attack upon the bastions where the gold (which equals power) is hoarded, the air is thick with the sweaty smell of grasping hands. Negro hands grasp too, but they are far fewer in number than white hands. And in America the rags to riches saga is still very much a part of the fabric of our culture. The underdog is black and he tends to be attractive for that reason, just as Othello was made attractive to Desdemona by his adventures on the battlefield.

Even as Your Daughter enters this prolonged period of quiet rebellion against the past, against superficiality, however, the "Negro Mood" asserts itself. Have nothing to do with white people, it says. "Your girl is white? Later for you." Always these days in New York there is this question about the new girl: "Is she spade or paddy?" Is she black or white? Last year a Negro wife and mother told me that, if I married Your Daughter, she'd never speak to me again. And, in keeping with the mood, there is an undue haste, it seems to me, on the part of some Negro men who have married Your Daughters to be rid of them in order to "look good" before the Negro masses. Negro men who have always been married to Negro women have a smug look about them these days. Mixed couples are cursed on the streets of the Negro ghettoes across America. One friend of mine and his girl (Your Daughter) were bombarded with Navy beans a couple of years ago in Harlem. And I have not taken a white date to Harlem since 1964.

As far as Negro women are concerned, I am sure they view Your Daughter with extreme antipathy. Your Daughter, after all, is a bona fide competitor. I suppose this fact has always resided deep in the psyche of Negro women. I place far less stock in the nationalist claims of black men. Too many times the question has been put to me, if I was dating Your Daughter at

the time, "Has your girl got a friend?" And I know Negro
men whose black nationalist policies can't be broadcast often
enough during the light of day, but under the cover of night,
they can't find one of Your Daughters fast enough. This kind of
hypocrisy has always surrounded interracial sex. On the white
side because the myth of superiority could not stand up straight
if a perpetuator of it were found in a Negro woman's bed. On
the black side, because of the threat of death at white hands
and, lately, because of Negro nationalism.

One can get caught up in all these divergent currents. I suppose
for a time I was. I have been a bachelor for a dozen years,
following a divorce, and I've known as many women as any
other bachelor. They were black, white, Oriental, brown. If
there were blue women, I suppose I would've known one. Only
once during those twelve years was I involved with one of Your
Daughters who, although she would never admit it, was more
concerned with my being black than with me. I was fortunate
to know intelligent women, and I was wise enough to know
even more than they the role they had had to play in American
existence.

And of course, I went through a nationalist period, convinced
that you didn't have a Daughter good enough for me, for my
heritage, for what I meant to this nation, for what I thought of
myself. But to be a Negro writer in Negro society is a strange
thing. For one thing, Negro women *expect* the Negro writer to
have known many of Your Daughters, and they tend to put him
down for it. When they do accept the Negro writer, as a writer,
men as well as women, it is upon the most unrealistic premise,
for example, the publication of one book automatically makes
the author wealthy. Since most of the white people I know are
either in or near the arts (I know the average white person
also thinks one book makes the author a fortune) the atmosphere is more valid. In most societies there is something suspect
about a person who does not make his living the same way
other people do.

In American Negro society, moving more and more into a
dull kind of middle-class existence, this suspicion is highly

pronounced, even though, at the same time there may be faint praise. I'm sure that, coming out of the nationalist period, my white friends thought *I* thought I was becoming white. When I gave parties, beside myself there were perhaps one or two other Negroes, the rest white. It was not because I had not invited Negroes. I had in fact, worked very hard to balance out the parties with both Negroes and whites. Negro friends, some of whom I've known for fifteen years or more, consistently failed to show up. It was as if there were something between us, but I never knew what, and now I don't even care.

In the marginal existence in which I found myself—Negro, but somehow set apart from the group, not white, but somehow, among some whites, very much a part of the group—it became very easy to meet Your Daughter. It was practically automatic. I have admired many of Your Daughters; I think there were several who I might have married, had I been in love. I know my life has been enriched tremendously by knowing Your Daughter; I like to think that the feeling has been reciprocal.

I might want to marry Your Daughter as a person. I know all about history and communications and how her image has been seared into the memory of every male in America. If I did not know more, this would be reason enough for me to desire her as my mate. The average black man in America is not like me; he is somewhat like the average white man. Why should he have to think things out? Just let him obey the billboard ads and television commercials. Let him choose to marry Your Daughter because she looks good in a fellatio-like pose next to a bottle of Coca-Cola. You whetted the appetite for Your daughter, now you have to pay the check.

Younger Americans, black and white, are going to gravitate toward each other. There are signs that new freedoms may be loosed upon the land. Even if they aren't *really* loosed, communications from young boys tell us that they are. Since we've always dealt with symbols and things that seem to be, the end is going to be the same: the younger people will move toward each other. They will be growing up with new images and symbols to live by. I assume that the presence of Negroes in commercial ads is not a fleeting thing, thus the image of Your Daughter will not be quite so prominent. The choice of Your Daughter for a bride will be perhaps more honest—if just as painful for you.

But it need not be painful. Today I might marry Your Daughter, a beauty queen of roses, television, film and magazine. Tomorrow, who knows, my son might marry Your Daughter just because. The big question of the future will not be: do you want Your Daughter to marry a Negro, but, *has* Your Daughter married a Negro. In an aside, of course.

AN AFRO-AMERICAN LOOKS AT
SOUTH AFRICA

VISTA *is a specialized magazine in that it addresses itself mainly to international topics. It is a publication of the United Nations Association of the United States and the UN is the organization around which its concerns revolve. Vista is read all over the world, wherever there is a UN mission, agency or office, and it's published in New York every other month.*

I wrote this article while on St. Thomas during the summer of 1968 where I was teaching at the College of the Virgin Islands at the time. I'd known the editor of Vista, Al Farnsworth, since 1963 when he was assistant to the editor of Holiday, *Ted Patrick. After leaving* Holiday *with some other editors in 1965, Al moved over to Vista and asked me to do something for him. Exactly what neither of us knew, but by 1968 he'd come up with this idea on South Africa.*

Since Al had worked at Holiday, *where the money was pretty good, he seemed to be a little self-conscious about how little his new magazine would pay. At this particular point I was not overly concerned with money; it was summer, my two older boys were not in school. Lori, Adam and I lived rent-free in a split-level provided by the college and the summer salary was good. I give this information only to point out that it sometimes happens that writers cannot afford to practically give away articles. On the other hand, when it's economically feasible to do so, writers will, especially for people like Al, who is, at least for me, easy to work with. I suspect this is because of the old* Holiday *tradition that insists on never tampering with a writer's ideas. A* Holiday *editor may suggest structural (i.e., grammatical and paragraph placement) changes but he never touches the ideas except to sharpen them, and then only with the writer looking over his shoulder.*

Much has happened in South Africa in the four years since this article was written. Black African heads of state have been invited to visit; there are signs even of some economic accord between this bulwark of white racism and the black north above it.

Being in the Caribbean, in St. Thomas' muggy heat while writing this article helped me get a little closer to it than I would've been doing it in New York. For there are "Africanisms" still to be found on St. Thomas—women carrying pots and parcels on their heads, tropical plants, dialects, reminders of slaves and slavery in the market place and old plantations. On St. Thomas particularly, where whites own the hilltops; place the beaches off-limits in some instances to the locals; own the stores, restaurants and hotels almost completely, it was easy to visualize South Africa.

I was not more than ordinarily aware of South Africa and what was happening there until a dozen or so years ago. I have never been to the country but I am told that a Negro willing to take the pre-arranged tour, and of sufficient prestige, would be allowed in. On the other hand, I know black journalists who were not even allowed to disembark from their planes in South Africa. Books of mine, I have also been told, are banned in South Africa.

However, I do not need to see South Africa up close, since I am a black American. Who am I to cluck over Bantu reserves, while American ghettoes for the Negroes exist? Who am I to become enraged by curfews when I have seen signs in some towns in America which demanded that dogs and Negroes be off the streets at sundown? So, my studies of South Africa have been at a distance, but less of a distance than that of the great majority of Americans black or white.

In 1958 I joined the American Committee on Africa (ACOA) as information director. The executive secretary of ACOA was George M. Houser, who still holds that position. Houser, perhaps better than anyone else, can recite the record of how little South Africa interests the American people.

With ACOA I began to meet visiting South Africans, all of them white. They included Dr. Julius Lewin and Violaine Junod, both social scientists, both seeking to create interest in the growing racial problems in their homeland. The "Treason Trials" were going on then, the trials for over a hundred people accused of treason against the South African government. Among the accused were black, white, colored and Indian, and many were members of Chief Albert Luthuli's liberal opposition party. The government accused many of the defendants of being Communists. As Communists, they could be prosecuted under some of the new laws that the South African lawmakers were passing almost every week. Lewin and Junod and many, many others were afraid of what could happen if the government won its case against the accused. Archbishop Joost de Blank came to New York about this same time and stated flatly that it was "five minutes to twelve," meaning that the hour was near when the black oppressed millions in South Africa would throw off the burdens of curfews, passes, reserves, controlled jobs and sweep bloodily over the white minority.

But the South African government rolled on, oblivious to all warnings. It absolutely crushed Luthuli's liberal group, dismantling at the same time British opposition which, in order to achieve any kind of majority had to align itself with the black South Africans. ACOA, its hands bound by distance and lack of money, did manage to send to the trials as an observer Dean Erwin Griswold of the Harvard Law School.

When Griswold returned, he reported that the trials had been conducted with the greatest dignity and he could find no fault with the proceedings.

As an American Negro, I am well aware of the fact that

unjust laws can be upheld in the courts with all solemn pomp and ceremony. After all, the function of the court is to uphold the law and the letter of the law. What is at fault at the first count is the unjust law, not the court. Griswold very carefully made the distinction between the laws of South Africa and the functioning of the court.

Harassment of South African blacks and whites was stepped up at the conclusion of the trials. Into our office almost every day came letters smuggled out of that country.

The letters came from Alan Paton, the distinguished author who has chosen to remain behind in his tormented land. Paton would never have to fear the black population; he has sung of its persecutions with deep nobility in such books of his as *Cry the Beloved Country, Too Late the Phalarope, South African Tragedy, Tales from a Troubled Land,* etc. And the letters came from Chief Albert Luthuli, one of the three black men in history to win the Nobel Peace Prize. Ronald Segal, editor of *Africa South* visited New York, expecting upon his return to be exiled, and he was. He is the author of the recent book, *The Race War,* in which he states that race, not politics, will engulf the world in a devastating war. He believes that war has already begun. For a highly unsettling but extraordinarily worthwhile enlightenment, I recommend *The Race War.*

Included in the letters were some from the black athletes who urged us to carry their plea for non-discrimination in the Olympic trials to the International Olympic Committee. At the ACOA, we felt that this was just what we needed to create more interest in the problems of the black South Africans. I wrote at once to several people prominent in sport circles—Avery Brundage, Arthur Daley, Jackie Robinson—to enlist their aid. All were cautious and obviously wanted to wait to see how much of a groundswell I could build up. The Amateur Athletic Union, to which I turned next, was also lukewarm about the matter of discrimination in South African sports. It is gratifying to me now that Robinson has come out in favor of an Olympic boycott on the part of black athletes. We were far, far ahead of our time back then in 1958.

But the handwriting on the wall could already be seen for all who cared to look. By 1963 the Sharpville massacre had taken place and the pass laws had become more rigid. Reserves for black people to live outside the urban centers were growing and the South African government had committed a fantastic amount of its budget to military expenditures.

It was about this time that I met a Dutch diplomat who'd done a turn in South Africa. It was his contention that the extensive military buildup in South Africa was for the single purpose of putting down any revolt. He said there was no place in the whole of South Africa where a revolt could be carried forth more than a single mile. Planes, tanks and troops were that strategically stationed. "There will be no revolt," he said, obviously relieved to be at his new post in the United States.

A similar view was expressed by a number of American diplomats from the embassies, consulates and related agencies in other African countries, who were taking their leaves in South Africa and returning to their posts high on what they'd seen there. Black American diplomats, of course, were not welcomed in South Africa, so in the American posts where whites had gone on leave in South Africa and blacks had not, a certain tension sprang up along with a sneering attitude on the part of the American blacks who distrusted the white American presence in Africa as much as the Africans did.

Among the Dutch, who are heavy investors in South Africa, and related by blood to the Afrikaners who run South Africa, sentiment is ambivalent. The intellectuals of the Netherlands tend to be quite critical of South Africa's racial policies, sometimes at the risk of being censored, if they are writers or speakers. A case in point concerns my friend and translator, Madame Margrit de Sablonière of Leiden, a longtime critic of South African policies, Dutch and other European investments, and American power there. Madame de Sablonière, a writer as well as a translator, held in high respect in the Netherlands, had a piece of hers on South Africa boldly edited so that references to the outside influences in South Africa were not mentioned.

However, Hollanders who are not intellectuals but skilled workers consider the Netherlands a dead end, especially if they are young and have families. They consider South Africa the land of opportunity because of the extensive Dutch contacts there, and what this means is that more white immigration to South Africa must force the black further still from any equitable solution to the problem of sharing in an economy that was created on his back.

For the Afro-American, there is a hopelessness to the situation which sickens the heart. It is common knowledge that South Africa has spearheaded a "white alliance" in the southern third of Africa. It now controls South West Africa; it gave aid and more than a little comfort to Ian Smith's Unilateral Declaration of Independence in 1966 and has for some time effected a near slave-trade agreement with Mozambique in which blacks from that country are shunted south to work in South African mines. There also appears to be a tacit agreement between South Africa, Portugal and Rhodesia to pool military strengths should the Organization for African Unity finally be able to field an African army to wrest power from the white governments.

I look at South Africa and I am convinced that its cruel and exploitative system of apartheid—racial separation—can only be destroyed when South African black people, either alone or together with other black Africans, topples the South African government as it now exists along with its extensive business interests.

I do not think black people can count on help from a sufficient number of white people to do this and it is obvious that force will have to be the method used to destroy the present system.

South Africa to a far, far greater degree than Rhodesia, Mozambique and Angola, has placed upward of twelve million black people in an economic and spiritual captivity that is but a few steps from the absolute degradation of chattel slavery. To the extent that South Africa has not been brought up short by other nations in the process of building this system, which is surprisingly recent, becoming fully effective only in the years after World War II, those other nations can be said to assent with the program of apartheid.

It now seems that those of us who seek to alter the American society have to keep an eye on events abroad. Certainly if Americans cleaned house, as they must one day do, this cleansing will have its effect on South Africa, for a part of the dirtiness is what both are deeply involved in, the suppression of valid requests for a share in the societies. I am not elated that an American warship did not drop anchor at a South African port when that country could not guarantee that Negro sailors would not be discriminated against. For millions of American Negroes these highly publicized gestures are meaningless. We say, let out government boycott South Africa in all respects and to the same extent that it has boycotted Cuba. The sad fact, the final view of this American, however, is that we cannot throw stones, for our own trembling house is made of very thin glass. As some of us have indicated, our troubles extend from the streets clear around the world, and we can do little out there until we are made to do something in here.

ISRAEL

As I note in the article, I've been to Israel twice, the first time in 1964, and the second early in 1968. I was a guest of the Israeli Government Press Office the first time and my guide was Isaac Austrian, who became a very dear friend. He was the model for a character, Itzhak Hod, in my novel, Sons of Darkness, Sons of Light. A bunch of very savvy, very loose guys work out of the Press Office; they never try to sell you anything.

The second trip was different. I was a guest of the Foreign Office; those guys are something else again. For example, after an eleven-hour, 5,000-mile flight, New York to Tel Aviv nonstop, I got off the plane to be met by a retired city official, a polite little man, who told me my first appointment would be within the hour.

The Press Office people didn't wait for you to sneak off on your own and go prowling around. Many times Isaac just dropped me off and left me to do whatever my thing was. The Foreign Office people on the other hand were always with you, and I felt they were working just as hard to secure information as they were giving it out. They were particularly interested in "black anti-Semitism" in the United States.

I'd grown very fond of Israel after my first visit. When the Six-Day War broke out in 1967 I called my agent and several magazine editors, trying to get an assignment to go and cover it. This seemed to amuse a number of people. I wasn't able to get an assignment because I think my agent was one of those who was amused, and because there were a lot of editors in New York who felt that a Jewish-Arab war has to be covered by a bunch of WASPs or at least a Jew.

As it turned out, my friends were all okay. Austrian's son had *seen action, but was unharmed. Moshe Shamir, the playwright-novelist-journalist and his family were all right; the poet, Yehuda Amichi and his family were fine; Sadya Gelb and other friends who live in K'far Blum, directly under the guns on the Golan Heights, were untouched.*

The difference between my two visits was the distance from war. In 1964 the Israelis were eight years away from their war with the Arabs in 1956; in 1968, they were only seven months past the Six-Day War. There was a sense of triumph in the air then; everywhere there were signs of the war. On top of a flat building leading out of Tel Aviv was piled the wreckage of an Egyptian MIG. Areas of the Golan Heights, still filled with land mines, were roped off. Also on the Heights for miles and miles I could see trucks, transports, half-tracks, their paint still new, but their bodies filled with bullet and bomb fragment holes. I stopped counting the number of small, empty Arab towns I drove through with Shimson Inbal from the Ministry of Foreign Affairs. Somewhere on the heights I took a picture of a small, lonely detachment of Israeli soldiers frolicking with a snowman they'd built. Triumph there was but also a tangible sadness, not only for the Israeli dead, but for the future. Isaac Austrian's apartment building still had sandbags stacked at the window.

I didn't see much of Austrian on the second trip. We had dinner together one night, and some drinks. We exchanged gifts —his being a few Simon Bar Kochba coins. Bar Kochba was a leader in the second Hebrew revolt against the Romans in A.D. 133. I paid one visit to his wife and then it was time to leave Israel once more.

Austrian loved life. He was a huge man who spoke English, Polish, Hebrew and French. One night in a restaurant in Haifa I saw him doing the Twist; it was something to watch this guy, as big as an elephant, but as quick and light on his feet as a cat. He'd been born in Poland but went to Israel as a youngster. During World War II he served with Jewish units in the British Army. He'd been a member of one of the under-

ground groups operating against the British occupation of Palestine. Austrian was the man who left me alone in an Arab restaurant so I could find out and feel what it was like, who left me beside the Dead Sea to glance backward up toward Masada, who let me prowl endlessly in Ein Gedi, where David and the shepherd hid from King Saul.

In a land where the cuisine is notoriously bad, Austrian knew where the good food was. In short, I don't believe I could have come to know Israel as much as I do, or like it as much as I do, had my guide been anyone else. When Austrian died suddenly in 1970 of a heart attack, I felt Israel, as well as myself, had lost something of immeasurable value.

But Austrian was still alive when I left him the second time and returned to New York to wrestle with a problem. The problem was with a representative of the Israeli government in the New York consulate. My contact there was very eager for me to place the article I was writing with Ebony magazine; the article was on discrimination in Israel. I intended to give it to Ebony. My contact asked if he could see the piece before I sent it out to Chicago, just to check out details that he might clarify.

I was a little taken aback; this man was not an editor, after all. He represented a government. I told him I had reservations about letting him see the piece, and I'd have to think about it. As it turned, I did let him see it, out of a feeling of gratitude for sending me on the trip in the first place. Foolishly, I wanted him to agree with my points of view (which have been borne out by Amos Elon's Founders and Sons, and his summer 1971 New York Times Magazine article on Israel's Black Panthers).

My contact sent me a letter in response to seeing my article, and I answered. The following excerpts from it will tell more about the pressure of censorship than I might describe in other ways:

"I've given a great deal of thought to our last conversation and to your additional notes that came last week. . . . After this thinking, I've concluded that it would be better all around *if I did not in a rewritten form submit this article to* Ebony *as originally planned.*

"First of all, I agree that there are some areas that could be rewritten such as the lead paragraph, the paragraph about Kollek and Jerusalem and others I've checked off in my copy. But this would not alter the meat of the piece. You say that Arabs are full citizens in Israel, and perhaps by law that is quite true. But by law, Negroes here are full citizens; in practice it is something else again. Now I have spoken to Arabs and Israelis who dispute your claim and dispute it intensely. I cannot in good conscience, therefore, accept your statement.

"'As we are wishing to place emphasis on agricultural and not technological life in Israel'—a quick check of the facts indicates that today only about three per cent of the people are living on the kibbutzim.

"Our discussion about family planning and birth control—and I did talk to a social worker about this in 1964, and I cannot, as you suggest, revamp that concept. I know what I was told.

"Our discussion about 'kushi' (or cushi) sent me checking again, and I'm afraid that the interpretation I presented to you was the one I'd also understood. It doesn't matter about the genealogy of the word; it is what it now means. Double-checking with some friends who are familiar with Hebrews and blacks in Israel, I'm sorry to say that the term is derogatory, and I cannot say that it isn't."

[Privately my contact told me if the business about cushi got out it could hurt Israel very badly among nonwhites around the world.]

"In the case of Mrs. Ina Harlew you imply that I shouldn't use (her statement) because it has no support in a previous passage. I remind you that this was a direct quote made in the presence of ——.

"Once more you intrude to tell me or to imply that I am not aware of what I have heard and seen. This is on the top of page sixteen. The Israelis that I have spoken with, the Israeli man in the street, is not aware of the fundamental cases of the (Newark, Detroit, etc.) riots."

Then I addressed myself to his concern to black reaction to the article: "I think that you probably overestimated the reaction of Negro readers and have totally underestimated their ability to see things as they are honestly conceived. They appreciate any situation that is honestly admitted and have the greatest sympathy for people with human problems. They no longer will tolerate statements that do not square exactly with the facts."

I brooded over the situation for about two or three weeks. I checked back over my notes and talked with people who'd visited Israel; I reread all the material I'd been given and I concluded that I'd been supplied an ego trip. My contact at the consulate made me believe that my article would wound Israel severely, that all the years of building black good will would go for nothing upon its publication. And I believed him; I went for the okey-doke. He no doubt knew of my attachments to many Israelis.

I kicked myself and called him or wrote him, and told him I was sending the piece on to Ebony as originally planned. I'd just wakened to the fact that it was going to take a lot more than my article to tear Israel asunder. He accepted my decision with resignation. I ran the piece over to the Ebony New York office and it was sent out to Chicago where, along with some photographs of the black lieutenant from India and an Asian-African women's class studying in Haifa, it reportedly vanished. To this day no one seems to know what happened to it. Further, no one cared what happened to it. But I did, of course, have a carbon. I made no further submissions; the article is printed here for the first time.

In Sons of Darkness, Sons of Light, I drew heavily on my trips to Israel, and even suggested that the Israelis had and would use nuclear weapons, if they had to. The novel aside, this is a real consideration, not discussed nearly as much as China's possession of the bomb. World War III is most likely to start in the Middle East, not Asia.

Israel is forever in a race to come to grips with its internal problems and solve them before it is attacked once again. Those

*problems are now underlined by the birth of an Israeli Black
Panther party, composed of young people of oriental backgrounds. The presence of such a group certainly, to some degree,
vindicates the premise of this article.*

I

O NLY twenty years old, Israel, a stunning victor in the Six-
Day War of June 1967 against the combined armies of Egypt,
Jordon and Syria, may one day find that it had done to itself
what the Arabs could not do.

Since the war discrimination—*haflaya* it is called in Hebrew—
has lessened to a considerable degree. Why? Much of the army
combat personnel consisted of people who were the victims of
discrimination because they are "oriental" or Sephardic Jews,
people whose parents or themselves came from the underdeveloped countries; people who tend to be more brown than
white. But a New York Jew asks why must one die to be
accepted?

Sephardic in its true meaning means Jews whose ancestors
came from Spain or Portugal. Today Sephardic is interchange-
able with "oriental," which means any Jew who does not come
from the western countries. Jews from Europe, and lately America, are called Ashkenazim.

Many outsiders would expect discrimination to be practiced
against the Arab citizens of Israel, given the bloody history of
the two groups. The shocker is that the most grievous effects of
discrimination can be observed among the "oriental" Jews; they
are the victims of haflaya.

The Arab standard of living in Israel far outstrips that of
Arabs in other Middle East countries. The birth rate is high, the
death rate is now about 6.1 per cent per 1,000 persons. This is

an all-time low for any segment of the Arab population anywhere.

There are nine Arabs in the Knesset or parliament, and this is not a bad ratio to the population when one considers the number of Negroes in the U. S. Congress compared to the black population in the nation. Arabic is one of the two official languages of the Knesset, the other being Hebrew.

For nine years Arabs have been full-fledged members of Histadrut, the general federation of labor, where they receive training and skills and crafts and their professional and social rights are vigorously defended. One of their chief supporters is Amnon Lin, a Jew and a member of the Knesset. Amnon Lin thinks Israel should move faster to integrate the Arabs.

I was in Israel four years ago and learned then that Arabs were not subject to military conscription. The Israeli government said that it does not wish its Arab citizens to fight relatives that may be in the armies of Syria, Jordan or Egypt. But the key reason behind the government's reluctance to embrace Arabs as soldiers is that it does not want any liaison springing up between Arabs of other nations and its own that would endanger the national security. It isn't a secret that too many Israeli Arabs have remained pro-Arab and not pro-Israel. For eighteen years the Israelis maintained border security in areas mainly inhabited by the Arabs; it was abolished in December 1966.

But this is not to say that both in public and private areas work toward some kind of workable integration is not going on. I visited the Arab-Jewish center in Haifa, now five years old, which works mainly with Arab and Jewish youth under the guidance of Arab and Jewish adults. The lovely hill city with its graceful groves of trees on the summit of Mount Carmel, was an old, mixed Arab-Jewish center years ago. Some co-operation has existed between Muslims and Jews for generations.

When I sat down to talk to the leaders of the Arab community in Haifa however, I found them far readier to discuss American Negroes and their "high crime rate" than they were their own situation. This reminded me ironically that back home many black nationalist groups were fiercely pro-Arab, perhaps even to a ludicrous extent; even most of Black Africa has given up trying to have a functioning accord with the Arab states. Polite relationships, yes, but functioning, no. Disgruntled over the lack of Arab concern over unification plans, Black Africans are now recalling the role Arab slave traders played during the centuries of slavery.

I also recall seeing black Arabs in Egypt and in the Sudan a few years ago and became convinced that they are severely discriminated against. And in driving through the territories the Israelis had captured in the 1967 war, I saw the same thing: black Arabs together, always together; black Arab school children running home from school together, the lighter Arab kids in their own group. Black Arabs are called *abids,* which means slave.

To be black and an American is to know the sounds of discrimination, the look of it in the eyes of the victims, and there was that group of cultured Arab leaders talking about the "high crime rate" of Negroes.

Near Haifa, fittingly enough, is Dalyat-Al-Carmel, a Druze village, and one of the Israeli government showplaces for visitors, official and otherwise. The Druze are an Arab-like people, but are not Muslim or Christian; their religious practices remain a secret to most foreigners. They are considered to be among the best fighting men in the country and do hold positions in the Israeli army. In Dalyat I talked with Amal Naser el Adin, Histadrut secretary of the Mount Carmel region. Of discrimination he spoke for himself and the 30,000 Jews in Israel who look upon Jethro as their founding father: "We are against all forms of discrimination; we are firmly opposed to it."

I found the Jews more open and far less defensive about themselves than the Arabs back in Haifa.

Since the war the Israelis have picked up about a million Arabs in the new territories. Some Israelis believe that Israel should keep the territories and integrate the Arabs. A few cautious steps have been taken in this direction.

The mayor of Jerusalem, Teddy Kollek, has an outstanding record of co-operation with the Arab community since the Six-

Day War. Damaged buildings and crippled businesses have been and are now being restored through low-cost loans made available especially for Arabs. Educational facilities were speedily restored, and expanded and incorporated into the existing Israeli systems as unobtrusively as possible. Education is mandatory in Israel through grade school.

The Israelis like to tell the story of the oriental Jewish father who could not understand after he had moved to Israel why his son had to go to school. He needed the son at home to take care of the flock. The school officials sent many representatives to talk to the father to tell him that this was the new way of doing things in Israel, and it was the law that the son go to school. The father was adamant, and finally, a key school official went to visit the father and said, "Now look here, this is the law." And the father remarked, "But I must have someone to watch the goats." But the official said, "Your son will go to school because it is the law. You will go to jail, and there will be absolutely no one to watch the goats." So the little boy went on to school.

Teddy Kollek has even collided head on with Minister of Defense and war hero Moshe Dayan over the latter's policy of blowing up Arab homes in Jerusalem in retaliation for Arab terrorist strikes against the Israelis.

But discrimination in the final analysis cannot be considered or evaluated in degrees. The fact remains, though, that in Israel the major victims of haflaya are not the Arabs, who tend to live by themselves, particularly the Bedouin, the truly nomadic Arabs, but Jews.

II

In Israel—and an increasing number of works are being published on the subject—it is the "oriental" or Sephardic Jew who is the victim of discrimination directed by the European or Ashkenazi Jew. Israel desperately needs every Jew it can lay its hands on; that it needs warm, vigorous bodies not only to continue the development of the land and boost its rapidly growing technology and culture, but to defend it against the ever-present danger of Arab invasion.

What then is the problem?

The return to Israel sprang from the fertile mind of western European Jews, but it was the eastern European and Russian Jews who made those dreams first come true. The mosheyev and kibbutzim systems of communal farm living so prevalent in Israel today preceded the Russian Revolution of 1917, although it would appear that the Revolution came first. East European habits still influence much of the Israeli community. Even today tea, for example, is served in most places in Russian rather than in British style. The British, when they came during World War I to end the reign of the Ottoman Turks, from the beginning preferred the Arabs to the Jews.

After World War II the Jews, with the birth of Israel, almost overnight developed a technological society: it appeared that way. The fact of the matter was that many Jews who had lived in the West in the technological societies of France and Britain and Germany were well prepared to apply their learnings and techniques to this new land. And it had to be done quickly, for it was the only way they could handle large numbers of refugees from the camps of Europe and the far corners of the world. The pioneering families had always maintained close ties with the West, and they knew only a society that was technological could withstand the incursions of the Arabs, who were still in the feudal systems of the Middle Ages to large extent.

Although the British made no bones about their preferences for the Arabs, old Palestine was the only decent place the British could establish a strong military base capable of roving north, south, and throughout the Mediterranean to Gibraltar.

The technological know-how came from the Ashkenazi Jews from the western countries; rarely did the oriental Jews make a contribution in terms of the immediate technological need. But increasingly, the number of Jews from the underdeveloped countries, unskilled, very often illiterate, sometimes without knowledge of what a stove was for, or a toilet, let alone an electric drill, began to overtake the Ashkenazi population.

I've always found the Israelis in Israel to be remarkably frank about themselves, and so it was relatively easy to discover in 1964 that the government had instituted family planning and birth control clinics; I have visited some of them. This was at a time when concern over Israelis becoming an "orientalized" Jewish state was at its greatest. An orientalized state would become pretty much like any other Middle Eastern country without cohesiveness and with a great deal of debilitating clannishness. It was obvious that the government was trying to hold down the explosion of the oriental population while increasing the Ashkenazi segment. Some of the plan worked, but more of it didn't.

The Ashkenazi Jews were not arriving in Israel in large numbers, and those already there, were knowledgeable about the difficulties of life, the few luxuries that were available there, the stringent economy. They had fewer children, so they could do more for them; this was a Western trait. The Eastern or oriental Jews, on the other hand, had large numbers of children because in their previous countries the death rate for infants was high, and numbers of children were necessary to insure having enough help to earn the income needed to support the family.

Then, as always, the Arabs were rattling swords on the borders of Israel. To complicate matters, thousands of highly educated Israelis were leaving the country for the nations of the West; Israel calls them *yordim* and is constantly attempting to recruit them back home. The lack of warm bodies from the West, particularly the United States, is underlined even today. A. L. Dulzin of the Jewish agency, the section on immigration and absorption (the Israelis prefer this term to *integration*, to which American rigamarole has lent a bad name) says that "Israel can realistically expect some 20,000 immigrants from the affluent countries in 1968." Moshe Shamir, prominent journalist, novelist, and playwright, on the other hand told me in January, 1968, that Israel needed a quarter of a million American Jews.

What all this means, of course, is that in the final analysis

Israel has had to make do with the Jews it now has in the absence of others who left and still others who have no intention of giving up life in the West for life in the East. In any case, the oriental population, which in 1948 was but 9.8 per cent of the total, increased by 1960 to 29 per cent of the total and has been edging upward at a slower but more consistent rate. One of the reasons for this growth has been decreased government intervention in family planning. "Go ahead," the government seems to say to its oriental population, "make babies."

Israel, faced with no other choice, did an about-face and decided to bring the Oriental up to a functioning level of citizenship as rapidly as possible. A program was commenced which one Israeli called "a program of positive prejudice." This involved on a vast scale government allowances to large families, scholarship and technical training advantages for students who come from poor families, and top priorities in housing accommodations. This meant higher taxes for the already established citizen, but I met no one who was bitter about this arrangement; indeed, they seemed to encourage it.

Yaacov Malkin, a drama instructor and the driving force behind the Arab-Jewish center in Haifa, said, "We know that the sooner the immigrant from Morocco, for example, gets our help, the sooner he will be able to handle a responsible role. Then he will be taxed, too. Sooner or later, it all comes back. Finally, we lose nothing."

(In America a few years ago when it was suggested by a number of people that Negroes should be given advantages over whites to make up for their deprived backgrounds, the immediate reaction was that this would be un-American and unfair to whites. No consideration was given for the long-range view such as is shared in Israel.)

There appeared to be a high degree of integration among the young, and indeed, I recall on my first visit that at the parties I attended there were always present Jews from the Yemen, Morocco, Tunisia, and other underdeveloped nations. When one of my old friends asked about the purpose of my second visit in 1968, and I said, "To observe your problems of integration," he said: "Come over to my house tonight and meet my son's girl friend; she's a Yemenite." This was not an isolated case.

The army is considered by all Israelis to be "the great leveler." The fact that great numbers of the army's personnel were themselves, or their parents were, immigrants from the oriental countries, and fought so well in the Six-Day War, served to slow down haflaya and to embarrass those Israelis who might have wished it to continue. For had it not been for the immigrant army, the Israelis could have gone down to defeat.

Army service is compulsory: two and a half years for males, eighteen months for females. Since, according to the deputy director, Yehuda Dominitz, of the Absorption section of the Jewish Agency, 60 per cent of the new Israelis requiring help are oriental in origin. It became automatic that the army would have to train large numbers of oriental recruits, not only in the skill of warfare, but in history, religion, the reading and writing of Hebrew. For many Jews scattered around the world, Hebrew was practically a lost language; a language employed only in prayer. In Israel it is the official language, and many new immigrants found themselves handicapped by not knowing it.

I spent a part of one morning at the Marcus Israel Defense Forces Secondary School with Lieutenant Colonel Yitzhak Ziv, the director. The majority of students in the school are from places like Morocco and look, like many Israelis, like Arabs themselves. They are taught by other Israeli soldiers, some of them female.

One day, leaving the Galilee region on the way north, I picked up two soldiers hitchhiking home. Both were female, and one was white and one was black. The black one was a second lieutenant, and her name was Rachel. She was from Calcutta. Only a few days before, I had seen a schoolteacher from Cochin, India, leading a group of children across the street in Beersheba, and she, too, had been as black as Rachel and, like Rachel, also a Jew.

Jews from India are said to be the most reluctant to integrate, and perhaps this is because they stand out the most and therefore tend to gather together in self-protection. But Indian friends of mine in London say that many have left Israel to return to India or to London because they were discriminated against.

In 1968, neither children nor adults from the backward countries called me *kushi*. *Kushi* is a Hebrew word meaning "slave," and used broadly, it has the same meaning as "nigger." In 1964 I had heard this word several times and so had the Africans studying in the schools or in the training programs on the kibbutzim, farm settlements, complained about being called kushi. A group in a kibbutz in the north was so upset they had made an appointment to see Golda Meir. It was one of the small, but deeply felt words that seemed to make a great many Africans extremely unhappy. They were willing to forgive the Israelis almost anything except for calling them "nigger," so that perhaps it was not small at all.

For a small country, Israel has quite a large program in which not only Africans, but Asians as well, are involved in numerous study and training situations.

Not far from Beersheba, where I had seen the teacher from Cochin, is the city of Arad. In 1964 it had been a settlement of but two bungalows, a city only in the heads of the pioneer technicians who spearheaded its creation. In 1968 I found Arad had became a large city, just eighteen kilometers over the mountains from the Dead Sea.

Mrs. Ina Harlew is an attractive redhead who speaks with a slight German accent; she was one of the pioneers of the city. Haflaya does not exist in Arad, she said, but this was not true where she lived before. "There was not a good time. People were all thrown in together at once and no one knew what they hoped for; there were tensions and grumblings and sometimes fights. When we came to build Arad, we were more careful. We knew what the people wanted and we helped them to do their best. The immigrants had the first new houses; they built up the industries here themselves. They have a stake in the town. We have a good city now."

In spite of the concerted efforts of both government and private agencies to roll back haflaya, the word that it does exist has gotten out. Thus, writing in the Jerusalem *Post* of

January 24, 1968, Saul Buch noted that among the reasons why
the isolated community of Jews in Isfahan, Iran, did not im-
migrate to Israel, was that "they had heard of unfavorable
treatment meted out to Sephardic Jews."

The big difference between the Israeli and American problems
of integration or absorption is that the Israeli government is
totally involved in the problem. In America, neither separation
nor integration are matters of complete administration involvement. Size makes a difference as well. The Israeli problem is
still made manageable by the smallness of the nation and by the
comparatively small numbers of people. The 22 million American
blacks are almost a hundred times more than the Israeli population.

However, as a victim of discrimination in the United States,
I sympathize completely with those Israelis, of both eastern and
western origin, who state that no matter how rapidly the government and private citizens are making progress, discrimination
remains.

"You do not see too many oriental Jews in the government
positions or on the management level," an Israeli whose family
has lived for three generations in Israel told me in Jerusalem.

Then I remembered returning to my hotel late one evening
in the city of David. While waiting for the elevator to come
down, I saw a very dark man mopping the floor. Perhaps because I was tired, for a moment I forgot where I was; it was
like being back in New York in the small hours of the morning
and watching blacks clean hotel lobbies. I spoke to him out of
that feeling: "How goes it?"

He gave me a blank stare and then said with a shrug of his
shoulders, "Shalom." Then I realized where I was.

Israelis, some of them, whose families originated in the West,
or whose families are from the old pioneer stock in Palestine
from the late nineteenth century, admit that they have severe
reservations about their children marrying the children of Jews
from the deprived countries. My friends whose offspring were
affianced to Yemenites tend to be people who regard themselves as Israelis rather than Jews, and, therefore, culture conflicts play a small role in their attitudes.

The methods of worship between a Jew from Germany and a Jew from Cochin vary immensely; so do their daily habits and goals. Jews from Germany, for example, who live in their own sections in the large cities of Israel, are a very urban and sophisticated breed. The Jew from Cochin tends to be rural, very dark in color, and is perhaps more suited to the kibbutzim than to the city. It seems to me that having suffered as they did in Europe during the Second World War, Jews would be the last ones to discriminate against other Jews, but perhaps it is human nature to forget quickly.

It is paradoxical that with its domestic problems Israel has maintained extremely strong liaisons with several African countries. These have increased as Black African ties with Arab Africa have become unwound. "We are in touch with all the African liberation movements," an Israeli official told me in Ethiopia several years ago.* The Israelis have long and historical ties with the Ethiopians. And this paid off to a very large degree in the United Nations during the Security Council hearings on Middle East war, when Ethiopian representatives on almost every count sided with Israel.

In the Congo they talked about the Israeli army and how it trained the Congolese paratroopers. In Liberia it is known that Israeli doctors have made great progress with certain eye diseases that occur in that region of the continent.

But most of all the Israeli government, officially and otherwise, holds a great deal of concern about America and her 25 or 30 million black people. Several black people in the U. S. Congress and the state legislatures from around the country, artists and others, have been invited to visit Israel at the expense of the Israeli government.

No doubt this has built up a vast pool of good will. For Israel is a remarkable country to travel through, and its people are a remarkable breed. No one going through the country can fail to be impressed by what he sees. And of course if one is a guest of the government one does not become too closely

* These ties seem to be collapsing in recent years, as Israel's alignment with the West a fait accompli.

involved with the attitudes that the Israelis might hold about the black man visiting his country.

But as I mentioned earlier, of late Israel has come under fire from black militants and from white militants for its alleged relationship with the West in an attempt to suppress its neighboring Arab states.

American Jews have responded instantly and with full power to such attacks, often employing the leading black spokesman of the moment; for example, Martin Luther King, Jr.

Thus it seems that a little country like Israel has many pots boiling at the same time. It appears to me, however, that the pot that could boil over most rapidly and burn is the one in which racial tensions between Jews is stewing and getting thicker by the day.

The swift resolution of the problem of haflaya is mandatory for the state of Israel. It isn't large enough to absorb it and still keep functioning the way the United States does more or less, but these days, mostly less. Surely the wheels of progress already have been set in motion. That they had to be set spinning in the first place constitutes still another problem, one that lies deep in the hearts of Israelis. Delay, particularly among the young, creates successive waves of bitterness that often cannot be recalled in time to avoid harm. A nation that is a war-ready state, and has been so for almost a quarter of a century, is one capable of exploding in all kinds of directions, not merely those where the enemy sits.

Finally, one cannot help but be impressed with the attitudes of the Israelis cognizant of the problem and with the energy with which they are attacking it on all levels. It is still possible to hope for Israel.*

---

* 1972: Hope diminishes. The Israelis have run games on blacks who claimed to be Jews, making their permanent settlement in Israel an iffy thing, based on religion. However, the question of whether Israel is a religious or political state remains in doubt, but the edge goes to the latter. Furthermore, the caste system that exists between European and oriental Jews, has been more fully publicized and criticized by American Jews as well as Gentiles. Today it is only fair for me to say that Israel is in grave trouble both domestically and internationally.

SECTION II

Personalities

Is there a difference in doing an article on a person rather than a topic? I don't think so. Some writers have become specialists in doing profiles of the famous; Thomas B. Morgan, for example, who's interviewed Gary Cooper, Edward Kennedy, Nelson Rockefeller, Sammy Davis, Jr., and Bill Cosby, to name a few. I don't know what his approach was. I don't even know that he *had* an approach.

The people I've actually interviewed have been few and far between. In this section, as a matter of fact, exactly one half of the people I wrote about were dead. Thus, those four articles are basically brief biographies. People who are in the public eye, entertainers, politicians and so on, move in a world where the truth has questionable validity. You are not owed the truth, necessarily, and often you don't get it. So there's no real approach to getting the personal interview. I do the same thing I always do: look, listen and ask questions. There's something else—whenever I go out to do a piece, I imagine myself to be a sponge. I'm soaking in every glance, tone, gesture, surroundings, noises. These are all a part of the picture the writer has to paint, whether that picture be a portrait or a landscape. For me, then, there's no difference between doing a piece on a person or a subject.

SUBJECT: CHARLIE PARKER
and
DICK GREGORY: DESEGREGATED COMIC

THE FOLLOWING *two articles, "Subject: Charlie Parker" and "Dick Gregory: Desegregated Comic," are related in several ways. A single headnote for both will show why. Both articles were done for* Swank *magazine. The editor I worked with was Milt Shapiro. First, I should point out that the title for the Gregory piece was not mine, but Shapiro's; mine was something like "Dick Gregory: Safety Valve."*

If there's a single good thing about article writing, it is that occasionally you can do a piece on a person you like. I happened to have liked Charlie Parker's music. In 1959, I think it was, I got together with Bob Reisner who used to write a jazz column for the Village Voice, *and we were going to do a nonfiction book on Bird. Bob already had a lot of material, and I collected more. Then we took the idea to Sam Vaughan, an editor at Doubleday, who toyed with the idea two or three weeks, finally turning it down.*

I was still eager to do the book on Bird, but found it increasingly difficult to work with Bob. That was the first and last time I've ever tried to collaborate on a work.

Enter Swank, while all this material on Bird was bubbling around in my head. I don't recall now if I went to them or they came to me. It didn't matter, as long as they paid, and they didn't pay much. I was broke. Fortunately, I already had the material which had been collected from many people, musicians, ex-wives and the like. There was so much anecdotal material on Charlie Parker that it would easily have filled an encyclopedia. And I had had a copy of Bird's psychiatric report, some of which I used for a character in my novel Sissie. *Because Parker was so much on my mind at the time, doing the piece was quite easy. I hadn't yet realized that a novel based in part on the man and his life was germinating when the article was published in 1960. The novel was* Night Song, *and it was published the next year, 1961.*

Early in August 1961, a month or so before Night Song *was published, my economic condition a bit improved, but not much, Milt Shapiro called and told me that he'd seen a comedian named Dick Gregory in Chicago; Gregory was a black comedian. Shapiro thought Gregory's act fantastically good, and since he was coming to New York to open at the Blue Angel, would I do a piece on him. I agreed on the spot. I'd heard a few good things about this cat out of Chicago; now I could check him out for real.*

I called on Greg a couple of hours before he was due at the club in his rooms at the Beverly Hotel on the East Side. He hadn't had many interviews at the time, and I don't believe any in New York. He seemed both a little amused and stunned at his success. We drank some scotch and talked about mutual friends, how his life was changing, the animosities that were springing up between himself and other black comedians who'd been in the business much longer, but without his success.

This was my first personality interview, but that didn't occur to me at the time. I haven't changed my approach since then. You go in, talk, ask questions, watch for responses and look around, soaking in everything and evaluating it.

It always helps if you like the person you're interviewing, and he likes you, which was the case with Gregory. How could I be so sure? He told me he was going to get an apartment on Park Avenue and asked me to live in it while he was on the road. Up until that moment I had been very much impressed with Greg's hard-headedness, his rough savoir-faire. But this was sheer naïveté. I didn't tell him that Park Avenue was a hard nut for a lot of white people to crack, or that I

*suspected it was going to be a thousand times rougher for him,
even if his name was Dick Gregory.*

*I declined his offer. Why, he wanted to know. Because I
already had an apartment, I answered. He looked at me as
though I were joking, but he didn't pursue the subject. We
left the hotel to rush to the Blue Angel a few blocks away and
also on the East Side. Like a lot of other clubs, it's gone now.
I thought Greg was a smash that night. I dug everything he
said, and I just about laughed until I cried. He brought the
house down. I went backstage and we kissed each other. I felt
an immense kinship with him. That was the last time I saw
him for several years.*

In the meantime, Night Song *was published, mainly because
of an editor at Dell Books named Arlene Donovan, who'd commissioned the novel in the first place as a soft-cover original.
Luckily, it wound up at Farrar, Straus and Giroux where* Sissie
*was being considered, and it came out first as a hardbound
book.*

*A young filmmaker named Herbert Danska bought the film
rights to* Night Song *very cheaply—I could still be had for very
little money. Somehow in this game the longer you survive the
more valuable you become, and the more say-so you accrue.
You can then insist on keeping your titles (which I'd been
unable to do with several magazine articles and a couple of
books). This is infinitely more true for white than for black
authors, for whom words like "value" and "worth" often have
little real meaning in the literary world. Nevertheless, I was glad
to get Danska's money; there were occasions when, even after
publishing four books by that time, I was still having miss-meal
cramps. Danska's bread came in real handy. Danska himself had
almost no money. A painter who'd made one film,* The Gift,
he'd always liked jazz and Night Song *was something he wanted
to do because it combined both his love for music and film.*

*Herb Danska's choice to play the lead—Eagle, the character
was called in the novel, a name not far removed from Bird,
was, you guessed it, Dick Gregory. I didn't see the first version*

of the film, which was called Sweet Love Bitter. *Few people did. Danska lost control of the movie to an unscrupulous cat named Bob Furman, whom we're still trying to drag into court. The version of the film that was released early in 1967 was terrible. Furman changed the name of the film to* It Won't Rub Off, Baby *and sends it around and around the black-neighborhood theaters in America. My interest in nailing Furman is that because of the low front money from Danska, I owned a part of the film. At least on paper, and nearly everyone loses if it's only on paper.*

Which, finally, brings me back to Swank. Like most books of its kind, you never see galleys. You notice that either the copy-editing or printing has been sloppy. With the Gregory piece, I got my first inkling of white backlash. Somebody at Swank was tired of seeing Negro capitalized, and so, self-righteously capitalized white. I never wrote for Swank again.

Subject: Charles Parker

Patient *was admitted to Bellevue Hospital, Psychiatric Division, September 1, 1954. He was discharged September 10, 1954. Age given on admission was 34. Wife's name was Chan. Patient was admitted following suicidal attempt by ingestion of iodine. Admitting diagnosis was acute and chronic alcoholism and narcotic addiction. Past History: eight months in Camarillo State Hospital, California 1945 for nervous breakdown. History is . . . that when drinking patient . . . exhibits suicidal tendencies. Patient is under care of Dr. H., Psychologist. Telephone number RH---. There was one previous suicidal attempt by ingestion of sulfuric acid . . . While on Ward PQ 3 . . . patient exhibited passive dependency and proved ingratiating and friendly to all physicians. Psychometric testing indicated a high average intel-*

ligence with paranoid tendencies. Evaluation by Dr. L. and other
psychiatrists indicates a hostile, evasive personality with mani-
festations of . . . fantasies associated with hostility and gross
evidence of paranoid thinking. Psychoanalytic diagnosis: 'Latent
Schizophrenia.' Patient was discharged on Sept. 10 to care of
Dr. N. Second admission to Bellevue Hospital was September
28, 1954—discharged October 15, 1954. Patient committed himself
to Psychiatric Pavilion stating that he had been severely de-
pressed since his previous discharge, that he was drinking again
and feared for his own safety . . ."

The third time Charles Parker entered Bellevue Hospital, six
months later, he was Dead On Arrival.

Americans, rather childishly, have always expected a touch of
madness in their geniuses, and too many Americans have declined responsibility for those deviations that have been used
to entertain them. The above report on Charlie Parker is a
skeleton—most nine-day Bellevue Reports are—but it is important
because, lacking other psychiatric reports, this one, when the
tunnel of Bird's life is reviewed, brings him into full focus. His
life does not reflect the explosion of school desegregation or
sit-in violence; it is the other, less picturesque extreme: the slow
erosion of an exceptional Negro symbolic of the assonances and
dissonances that are America.

It is mere nonsense to believe that Charlie Parker existed
his life and died his death as any other person might have done
in America regardless of race or creed; it is lip-popping of the
most deluding sort, for Parker as nearly everyone must suspect
by now was a man caught between a Negro culture that had
never genuinely existed and a white culture that had little room
for him. Since Bird gave up the ghost or had it taken from him,
he has grown in stature, in legend, in music.

Bird, already on the road to the sickness bred Only in America,
lay his sometimes gross and often slender body across the chasm
of confusion that prevailed in jazz during the late 30s and early
40s, and formed the bridge from a saccharine glob of swing to
the lean, unadorned harmonies of bop. By 1950 when Parker

dominated jazz like a great, sickened Colossus, every newcomer, to jazz, whether he blew an alto-sax or not, sounded just like him. Europeans found that his haunting and exciting fragments of the classics, his structures, most nearly mirrored what they felt about post-war America.

Even today television commercials, background music for detective and cowboy shows (Bird loved cowboys) all echo Charlie Parker-like harmonic structures. Uncounted ballads and incidental music for the theatre tease with his greatness, which, though bounded by a blues framework, incorporated classical concepts. There has never been an adequate measurement of Charlie Parker's music nor sphere of influence. His greatness cannot be questioned; what made him great is open to theory, the following included:

Bird was born August 29, 1920 in Kansas City, Kansas. His parents, Charles Sr. and Adie moved soon after to K.C., Mo., across the bridge. The Parkers had some status; the mother worked and the father was a railroad man, a chef. Compared to other Negro families they were fairly well off.

Kansas City was like no other during the 20s. An old resident said it was the only city in America you could come to and do all the things you wished without feeling like a hypocrite. While northern cities were reluctantly viewing the post-war migrations of Negro *families*, K.C., Mo., saw tough loners coming up-river or in from the vast reaches of western Kansas, eastern Colorado and beyond. The city, in a sense, was the reincarnation of the old west. Crime—prostitution, bootlegging, gambling and the one hundred and one related institutions—flourished there and did not die until 1939 when the old Pendergast machine was politically dismantled. But crime made jazz permissible and it grew there; the high-school music classes were always filled with kids who wanted to be Harlan Leonard, Bennie Moten, George Lee, Chauncy Downs, Pete Johnson or Joe Turner. These were the local groups, but there was Basie, Ellington, Lunceford, Hines and two dozen others who came and went. A large can of beer cost a nickel, whisky a dime a shot and hot crawfish a dime. Bootlegging was sometimes so loosely organized that youngsters Parker's age could turn a quick coin at any time. If not that, carrying "gangster cigarettes" marijuana, could be profitable but certainly not glamorous.

This was the backdrop against which Charlie Parker came into the world. In that southern-like city where the only legitimate employment for large numbers of Negroes was in the stinking Armour and Cudahy packing houses on the outskirts of town, the various aspects of crime must have glittered.

There was a division within the Parker family. The father belonged to that glitter and music, the laughter of girls, the happy barbs which passed for the repartee of the time; but the mother was a Catholic, which in itself was out of joint with the time and place. Baptists and Methodists prevailed. Charles Parker, Sr., died in his glitter and music, stabbed, it was reported, by one of his girl-friends. There is not much to show that Bird and his father were very close, yet, nearly a quarter of a century later, Bird gave as the reason for his second known attempt at suicide the unsolved murder of his father. Parker was always closer to his mother. And she considered her son, as herself, a Catholic. About the same time Parker's father was killed Robert Simpson, a friend of the young Bird, died suddenly without explanation. The diagnosis was pneumonia, the same that was to be Bird's eighteen years later. Simpson and Bird, both fledgling musicians at the Crispus Attucks High School, used marijuana, and occasionally heroin. Later, Bird experienced the same strange recall to Simpson's death that he had to his father's.

Bird was not quite sixteen when he married a girl four years older than himself. A son Leon was born of this marriage. Mrs. Addie Parker and the junior Mrs. Parker were the only two Negro women with whom Bird had any sustained relationship; the rest were white. Parker's marriage was of short duration. Music made Bird's world, not his wife.

As an only child (somewhere in the hazy background of the Parker family lurks a half-brother, John, reported to be a Kansas City, Kansas, post office-worker, who was extremely fair in color and could have passed for white) and as a recognized great among musicians in Kansas City, Mo., Bird very early learned to take advantage of people who made themselves fair game by bleating and cow-towing to his brilliance. To put it simply, many of those who came to Bird were trapped by their own momentum into paying either economically, physically or psychically. Bird never lost the zest for taking advantage of suckers, but he never exercised it on people who didn't deserve it. It was also a method of survival Parker learned early in life. His victims often excused it as his due (as Parker knew they had to) because he was a brilliant personality and a musical genius. It is possible that this taking advantage of people—both white and black—helped leak some of the dangerous rage that suffused his being.

Parker's rage had two fuses: the first, that he was an artist unaccepted at the outset by other musicians who told him he should try to sound like Benny Carter, that he imitated Lester Young—in short, that he should be or do anything but himself and what he wanted to do. When he made it as an artist on his own terms, growling his personal theme of life like thunder on a low summer sky, there was no money, and this went back to the second fuse: his race. In addition, one can imagine his subliminal registration of the fact that Negroes expressed more shame than support of the music their musicians were playing.

Bird was cruel as an artist should be, as driving, as disciplined, as perceiving, and unfortunately as sensitive. He took his rejections doubly hard because he was sure of himself. He could play sixteen of the most fantastic bars ever heard in American music on 52nd Street to the standing ovations of those few who knew what he was saying, and then step around the corner for a drink and be refused and insulted because he was Negro. During his early years with Jay McShann and later, he with the rest of the band had to enter back doors in order to play for the house.

In those days most club owners had standing orders that the musicians were not to fraternize with the guests. Tadd Dameron, composer and pianist remembers when the whole of the new Billy Eckstine band nearly folded before it began because Bird fraternized, entered the front door, and drank water out of

glasses set on the tables and then smashed them to save the
management the trouble. The legends of Bird are replete with
fist fights in the streets, Bird threatening with guns, and even a
murder, committed by Bird.

We see from this that Bird chose the second of Norman
Mailer's two alternatives quoted in the prologue.

The choice undoubtedly shortened his life. Before his death
he more or less accused Dizzy Gillespie, a giant in his own right,
of choosing humbleness. By choosing to fight, Bird automatically
became a martyr; he is spoken of in these tones today. There is a
strong suspicion that Bird's personality helped change the role
of the Negro jazzman. The Negro no longer had to conceal the
fact that he had a mind. Musicians who can't read today are put
down in the slimiest of terms. Clowning and the happy poses of
minstrelsy "went by Bird" and so out the window.

By the time Bird was 25 he had been on for nearly ten years.
Musicians claim Bird and his addiction were maligned the way
Louis Armstrong was once blamed for all the marijuana-smok-
ing in America. Musicians usually get more spotlight than any
other group when busted for possession, but it is common knowledge or should be that doctors are and always have been the
group with the largest percentage of dope addiction.

For *some* Negro musicians the use of narcotics is to help them
maintain a middle ground between humiliation and overt hostility. There is little if any inspiration from heroin *at the moment*
it is being felt or enjoyed. Art Blakey contends that the junkie is
a neurotic who derives benefits from the effect of the heroin after the experience. Today there can be no doubt that the use of
narcotics is the result of external or internal pressure, real or
imaginary. Charlie Parker's use of heroin was no exception. If
anything his problem was magnified because he was Charlie
Parker and users with extra packets or pushers wanting to be
able to say that they knew Bird gave him stuff, pressed it on
him, even when he wasn't on. This applied to Europe as well as
to America. It was as if these "friends" were trying to destroy
him with Trojan-horse kindness.

Whether it was escape or insulation Bird wished through the

use of heroin, his problem was compounded by his second marriage—to Doris Sydnor.

For all intents and purposes, K.C., Mo., is South, and Rock Island, Illinois, where Doris came from is South also. The mores of both cities are not very different from those cities south of the Mason Dixon line. The meeting of Doris and Bird, on a social level, should never have taken place. On another it was destined to, for both were rebels of a sort. In the relationship that often prevails between the Negro jazzman and the white female who likes him, the verb "manipulate" or "use" is foremost in the unconscious mind of the musician. Nine times out of ten the Negro jazzman feels that the female is out to "use" him although she might not be consciously aware of it. In such cases the Negro "allows" himself to be used, that is, makes himself available to the female so that he might in turn derive the benefits necessary for him. Often it is money, but just as often some murky sense of revenge or attainment of a concrete position in a society that has rejected him. John Dollard notes in *Caste and Class In a Southern Town:*

". . . the superior prestige position of the white woman and her categorical inaccessibility may be a challenge to the Negro along quite American lines; from this view the proof of social advancement and mobility would be sexual contact with a white woman. There is undoubtedly the element of revenge . . . the Negro is wreaking on a symbolic member . . . rage. . . ."

It is also quite conceivable that Bird, if he did at one time plan to use Doris finally became "middle-class" about the relationship, which lasted altogether about six years. There was no attempt at suicide during this time and no discussion whatever between Bird and his wife about problems that resulted from their union or Bird's artistic or racial conflicts.

Dizzy Gillespie took a combo that included Bird to the Coast in 1945; Bird remained there and suffered a breakdown during the middle of a Dial recording for Ross Russell. The number in which something is obviously wrong is "Lover Man," the beautiful thing Jimmy Davis did for Billie Holiday during the War.

Following the breakdown, Bird was sent to California's Camarillo State Hospital for eight months.

The "official" causes for the breakdown reside in the mind of the Austrian psychiatrist who treated him, and in the hospital files. Even today one hears that acute alcoholism was a contributing cause; lack of money to buy heroin and/or marijuana another. Neither of these could have hurt as much as the utter rejection of Bird and his music by both white and colored audiences. The criticism was most severe in the pretentious Negro press of Los Angeles. Doris says today that he seemed to have assumed in the beginning of his stay at Camarillo, an unusual patience. The only thing that bothered him were his fellow patients who stood like statues staring off into space at the edge of the grounds; Bird hoped he wouldn't become like the rest of them. Doris had left New York to be near him and she made the long jaunt from Los Angeles to the hospital three times a week.

There is no known report available from Camarillo today nor is there any information forthcoming from Bird's private psychiatrist.

In passing it might be noted that 90 per cent of the West Coast jazz that came into prominence about 10 years ago came from eastern musicians who in one form or another had been influenced by Bird. (Gerry Mulligan, of these, stands head and shoulders above the rest.)

Howard McGhee, Hampton Hawes and Errol Garner, with whom he played at various times upon his discharge, concur that Bird lost nothing in the hospital. Returning to the New York scene, his style jelled. There was anger in his tone and lyricism more haunting and beautiful than before—as though what it symbolized could never be attained in life and thus had become more desirous. From 1947 to 1949 Bird played in New York, interrupting his stints here to go to California with Norman Granz' Jazz at the Philharmonic. Granz, when bop was young, had made some caustic comments about it, but wound up with the king nonetheless, thus indicating that the music was or could be a potential success. In 1949 Bird temporarily "got out"—he went to the first annual Paris Jazz Festival. Kenny Dorham said:

"Bird had all of Paris at his feet. He was playing a concert and there's this part in 'Night in Tunisia' where the break comes and Bird has to fill it. Well, he does, and the whole place cracks up. Bird in all his life never witnessed such enthusiasm. He just stood there with an expression of exuberance on his face."

The next year he went to Scandinavia. Of all Europeans the Scandinavians most appreciated Parker's music and are today ahead of most of the rest of the continent in playing jazz, in capturing the moods of Charlie Parker's America. Bird's trip was short; the return to America inevitable.

Doris and Bird parted in 1950 (they had married in 1948) and Chan Richardson, described by the New York *Daily Mirror* as "a lovely, fair-skinned brunette," became Parker's second white wife. Since Chan had been a press agent, it might have been she who urged Bird to seek the middle road of compromise; to play as artistically as possible without alienating the possibilities of commercial success.

A year later a daughter, Pree, was born to them, and when she died in 1954, Bird was plagued with the thought that he might have been responsible because of a "youthful indiscretion." This was disproved; the diagnosis was pneumonia, but Bird clung to the thought that her death might have been punishment for his bad deeds. It is possible that the child's death helped precipitate the row in Birdland which in turn led to his commitment to Bellevue. Birdland was named for Parker in the early 50s, but there were times when he could not enter as a guest or bring guests in.

Toward the end Bird was said to have had tremendous sexual powers; this from one of his last managers who emphasized the sexual profile of Bird so much that it almost has to be discounted and an examination of the manager begun. It is seldom that a junkie has the energy or desire for sex. If Parker had overcome this, the conclusion is that he had a Don Juan complex which is a classic mark of insecurity. Kardiner and Ovesey in *Mark of Oppression* also have pointed out that Negro men who are acutely embattled mentally in achieving or striking back at white (human) standards often have little energy for sex.

Bird would have liked to solve his conflicts simply, like the cowhands of the old west. He rode horses and loved western movies. Still, nihilism was inherent in his favorite picture, "The Wild One."

Greatness is seldom the end product of adversity; Parker was one exception to this rule. He survived as an artist in the American know-nothing desert; he tried to live as any other human being in that same desert; he was despised and misunderstood twice as much as a result. Lennie Tristano, who above all musicians could describe Bird's music and his place in jazz, gives an unwitting example. Tristano, while he could understand the music, did not really understand the man who had produced it. Charlie Mingus relates:

"We're in Brandeis University. Howard McGhee took Miles' place; Max Roach, Lennie Tristano, and after the concert we go down to Framingham. We're surprised to see Bird there. He's completely stoned. Lennie is hogging the conversation as usual. Bird ain't with nobody. Howard and Lennie are doing all the talking. Lennie is putting everbody down. Lennie is asking how come niggers get mad when white men call them nigger, but they don't mind each other calling them that. Bird jumped in. 'Turn out the lights and I'll kick your---,' he says to Lennie. (Tristano is blind.) I called Howard a Tom (Uncle) to allow Lennie to talk like that. I always felt Bird was with me."

Yet Tristano could say: "Almost every big name in jazz is a Charlie Parker byproduct." Dividing the music from Parker's embattled Negro personality is schizoidal and ignoring the culture that produced both is ridiculous. But it was done.

Bird was not a commercial success; in fact he was an abject money failure. He was oppressed at nearly every start, every turn. Who can say that Bird was wrong when he shrieked at one of his managers while they were aboard a plane, "Thief! Give me my money!" when money is still being made on Bird's recordings? Some were stolen, some paid for cheaply, some still unpaid for. Some sides Bird recorded for less than $50 because he needed the money. These people—managers, record company officials, club owners, and others who sought some profit (money or otherwise) were first disdainfully called "whities" by Bird, and no one can say it more vilely than a Negro jazzman.

As to his artistry, Parker became *The Artist* in jazz to an extent in death he could not have realized had he lived. And to listen to those around the circle, one would almost feel the society that both bred and branded him wished him back. But this might be a collective guilt. Guilt is the suffering of an uneasy conscience that instinctively knew the shape of Charlie Parker's time and trials.

His time came to an end in a grim and horrible psychological triumph, for if Bird all his life wished the status of a human being in America, i.e., *white*, he achieved it in death. He died in the apartment of a titled white woman in a hotel on Fifth Avenue in New York City. The weather? "Fair, continued mild. High 54, low 45." It was Saturday, March 12, 1955.

The hotel wanted his corpse out as soon as possible since it didn't want the publicity attendant upon Bird's presence there. When the doctor made his first call, he reports that Parker was in a drunken stupor, and had no temperature. At the second visit, he seemed to have sobered up. The doctor also reports that Bird "apparently was off drugs"; that he couldn't have taken a shot had he wanted to because every vein in his body had been scarred by hypodermic needles.

Bird died amid a paroxysm of laughter; he was watching the Kate Smith show with the Dorsey brothers. Jimmy had been announced as the greatest saxophone player in the world.

Dick Gregory:
Desegregated Comic

THE PLACE is New York City's Blue Angel. Dick Gregory, the Negro comic who has skyrocketed to fame in a matter of months, goes on at 10:15 after having rushed over from bed and a shower. He gives a little nod, surveys the darkened house through a pair of wide, vaguely innocent eyes, arranges his props consisting of an ashtray, a pack of Tareyton cigarettes, a lighter and a couple of "notes" which he reads aloud to the audience to gauge its fettle, and kicks off with his gags.

Standing about five-nine and clothed in a loose-fitting suit which sags about his middle and breaks flaringly over the tops of his shoes to dribble unnoticed to his heels, Gregory accepts an introduction as the Negro Mort Sahl, turning it with ". . . but in the Congo they call Mort Sahl, the white Dick Gregory." The house, about 99 per cent White, breaks up. While it does, Gregory ingratiates himself still further with: "They (Max Gordon and Don Jacoby) are so kind to me here. They've done everything to make me feel at home (rapidly). But when they put black olives in my martini they go too far!" The house breaks up again.

Without noticing it the audience is caught up in a series of jokes which are purely topical. Gregory accomplishes this smoothly, without a change of pace. And the audience is cracking up before it has realized that Gregory, standing there rocking from toe to heel, shoveling up applause with his shoulders and arms, is talking about the world of the papers and television, not merely the *in* jokes of the Negro community.

Atomic powered submarines: "They come up every eight years, just long enough to get the fellas re-enlisted."

Homosexuals: "You're in a submarine *eight years!* You'd *better* find a friend!"

Embezzlement: "I'm damned sick and tired of being robbed from the inside."

Cost of living: "I lost my rifle in the Army and it cost me eighty-five dollars. (Rapidly) And people wonder why the captain goes down with the ship."

Our leaders: "The president wanted to build a great cross on the lawn of the White House, but he was afraid the Vice President would burn it."

The audience, following him, continues cracking up. Then: "About that integrated Army—that means I can share the barracks with Puerto Ricans."

Gregory's presentation is schemed A B A, the A's representing the lines on race, the B's being the topical gags. However, only about one third of his material deals with race and racism. Regardless, Tim Boxer, his press agent, is currently slugging releases on Gregory with: *DICK GREGORY—Humor Integrated.* Not unlike many a Negro in these United States, Gregory is using the race wedge to get in (instead of out). Once there, he proves he can be just as topical as the next standee.

His most effective jokes, however, remain the ones which bring into the open the innermost thoughts of Negroes under oppression. Much of the delight and relief in the laughter must come from the fact that the secrets are human, filled with a longing for life and no worse than those voiced by the Irish comic in the Paddy and Mick era or by Jewish comics in the day of Abie and Becky. There is a waterfall of human understanding of the meager retaliatory measures a member of a minority group might take to gain human dignity: "We put Kennedy into office out there on the Southside. While you folks were voting once, we were voting six, seven times! Getting even, y'know."

There is the painful reflection of the human condition when Gregory quips: "I sat at a lunch counter down South for eleven months and when it finally integrated, they didn't have what I wanted." This joke is topical and racial, but even more it displays humanity in a search which, even ending successfully, echoes with a sickening emptiness when one calls to mind Lorraine Hansberry's words: "Who would want to live in a burning house, anyway?"

Dick Gregory has been called Hip; this is erroneous. For his humor is not that of the bitter Hipster; it is not cerebral, not vicious. His humor lies between Hip and Square. Gregory *looks* hybrid when he stands before the mike clad in that bulky suit (cuffless, double-vented). He wears it comfortably, as if he were on his way to Ebenezer Baptist Church. And though the cloth suggests a Madison Avenue influence, it is worn with such a pure abominance of fit that one is forced to place him back into a comfortable image—it is difficult to imagine an entertainer

of Gregory's present stature *not* being rakishly pressed: pants
five inches off the shoe-top, four button jackets just dangling
above the waist, and so on. Such easy-looking apparel is a
camouflage the audience soon discovers; there's nothing relax-
ing about the comic's material.

But Gregory uses another guise and that is language. When
he means The Congo he says "The Congos." When he means
there is he says "They's a." He purposely confuses the verbs
has and *have*, and these tiny, microscopic grammatical "errors"
create more comfort for the people who, while liking him, wish
to hell he were more like he "should" be.

His ability to pantomime—a stiff finger jabbed boyishly, somewhat reluctantly toward the audience, a dip of a shoulder, an
upraised arm (slightly reminiscent of: *Up yours!*), a series of
small, quick steps together with his tentative grin—also help put
over his lines. This ability to pantomime—acting or *suggesting*
out the lines is common to the man on a Harlem street or a
Southside Chicago street; jokes, tales being related are always
accompanied by gestures. Dick Gregory is this man, seen fleet-
ingly and always from a great distance. Gregory on stage is this
man close-up. And the discovery that he is not plotting revenge
is roughly charming.

Since he has been working more and more in White clubs,
Gregory has had to drop some of the material he used in the
Negro spots. In these places (Esquire and Roberts, Southside
Chicago) his targets were the compensators, the status-seekers
of the Negro community. Process jobs (the treatment of a Negro's hair to make it straight) and long, white Cadillacs carried the brunt of his jolly attack.

But he brings the weight of his humor-spiked offensive to
the White clubs. His work is not a crusade; his jokes attempt
to shape current problems into solutions, the first step being
to open up the closet and dispel the Negro bogey-men tales.
What we see then is that like all other minorities, the Negro
laughs not only at himself but at the makers of his problems.
Like the Rev. Martin Luther King's corpsmen, Gregory approaches violence (i.e., violent subjects) but rejects it, turning,

as it were, the other gag. The concept is new and striking and Gregory knows it. He's a hard-nosed man of 28 who feels intensely that his break may signal better happenings for other Negro comics like Willie Lewis and his long-time favorite ("He tells you where it is!") Pig Meat Markham. Gregory thinks a great deal about the South, and of it he says:

"Dig, baby. I could go to Germany next week, but I don't want to do Europe until I do the South. I'd want them not to segregate, but if they did that wouldn't keep me away as long as they didn't segregate any member of the press. I want to get the word out, baby, the word."

He is supported in this desire for recognition *plus* solid contact between the races in the South by letters, notes and clippings which he receives in droves from Southerners who congratulate him on his success.

All of his mail is not favorable; his success has stirred at least one Negro comic with a fair reputation to accuse Gregory of the theft of his material, a theft Gregory denies. The pen-writing Negro comic, sickened by the younger man's success and his own inevitable failure, wrote such a violent letter that Gregory, if he chose, could have had the man put away for more than a little while.

Gregory shrugs and smiles at this latest price of success which now includes a spanking new corporation, a record company with Gregory's (AG) label through which he's sold a master ("Dick Gregory in Living Black and White,") of a show to Colpix for $25,000, and his first concert, which took place May 4 in St. Louis with Dizzy Gillespie. Appearances have been scheduled in Minneapolis, Los Angeles and San Francisco.

Considered by *Variety* as "the first standup comedian of his race to crack the plush intimery circuit, and in such force," Gregory, managed by Broadcast Management (Huntley-Brinkley, Alex Dreier, Douglas Edwards and Dick Clark), seldom had it so good.

The second eldest of six children of a shattered St. Louis family, Gregory found even scuffling rough there. A brother,

Ron, is a star athlete at Notre Dame. Gregory himself excelled in the mile, half-mile and cross country competitions at Sumner High School and won an athletic scholarship to Southern Illinois University where he majored in Business Administration. The half-mile record he set there still stands. He discovered his talent as a comic while in the army, but returned to college two years later to get his degree. College finished, he turned up in that Chicago haven for Negroes with college degrees, the United States Post Office, a position from which he was summarily fired for having only a moderate interest in the affairs of the department.

Married in 1958 to Lillian Smith, a University of Chicago secretary, Gregory became father a year later of daughter Michelle. The scene became immensely rough. While John Daly (ABC), in town to cover the Republican National Convention, was indulging in some of the play that keeps Jack from being a dull boy, he caught Gregory's act at the Roberts Show Club—a spot Gregory himself had rented to showcase his talent—and decided to tape it for inclusion on ABC-TV's "Cast the First Stone," a nation-wide show on race problems in the North. Further television appearances were made on the Jack Paar Show and David Susskind's "Open End."

He was now ready for the Chicago Playboy Club, frequented often by visiting Southerners, who, as it happened, flipped over him. Soon Gregory hit a pay scale of 250 dollars a week, then went to 1,000 dollars at New York's Blue Angel.

Had it not been for the Chicago club critics, Gregory might have remained anonymous to all save predominantly Negro audiences there. Herb Lyons of the *Tribune* called him the "hottest and most unusual new talent in show biz." It was Lyons who called him the Negro Mort Sahl. Tony Weitzel of the *Daily News* (who writes: "Our Dick") named him the Negro Will Rogers. Gabriel Favoino of the *Sun-Times* asked: "Why . . . his smashing success, especially before conservative, largely white audiences?"

Favoino supplied an answer: ". . . the answer may lie in the guilt some Americans feel over the condition of the Negro, a guilt reinforced daily by newspaper headlines and Supreme Court decisions. The news from New Orleans or the Congo makes his humor all too topical."

Bentley Stegner and Will Leonard also contributed columns and notes on Gregory. One asks why. Certainly the Regal Theatre and the dozens of clubs in Chicago had spawned great, great Negro comedians who have gone ignored and whose material and delivery were almost equal to Gregory's. Why, then, a Dick Gregory?

Chicago is a great, brawlingly guilty city in terms of racism. It has had a history of race riots; it still has its Southside, though Negroes have been trickling off to the west and slightly north. Trumbull Park, which cost the local taxpayers millions of dollars, must still be in the minds of the citizens, just as Deerfield, only 20 miles northwest of the city, must fever minds with the measures of racial violence never far away in that city. (At Trumbull Park, a public housing development, racial disturbances lasted over two years and necessitated round-the-clock police vigilance which was, in the manner of Chicago police work, entirely ineffective. Deerfield is the site where a private developer planned to sell to Negroes as villas Whites' homes costing 25,000 to 30,000 dollars. The local people condemned the land for parks they never built and took over the homes already constructed. The case is pending before the Illinois courts now.)

Almost nowhere in America does the tension between races run as high so continuously as it does in Chicago. The series of recessions, effecting untold thousands who labor in the mills and foundries, hasn't helped. Gregory might therefore have become a timely safety valve, draining off that tension not only for Chicago, but for the nation as a whole. Not a great amount of laughter has surrounded the riot in the United Nations, which sprang from the untimely end of Patrice Lumumba, nor has our nation felt the sit-ins in the South a laughing matter. Granted, these are not particularly funny matters, but they might not ever be survived without humor.

The other side of the coin shows a consideration of Gregory's material; which Dick Shippy of the *Akron-Beacon-Journal* called a "novelty" and of "thin" consistency. Could Gregory, it has been asked by those disturbed by his sudden success, have hit without his material on race? There's little doubt of this once the comedian is seen in person. Of course, the question (with the answer following closely behind) is: Would Gregory be accepted as a comedian *without* his race material? The suspicion is NO. The Negro, all our communications media show, seldom *exists* in America, for he is rarely or accurately acknowledged. His contrived absence confirms his contrived invisibility. Like Gregory, he may speak out of this non-existence; he may even be felt. But as long as he is unseen—or even if he *is* seen girded within a prescribed framework (such as Gregory is with his race material) we are all safe; no waves (we tell ourselves) have been made. The boat is not rocking.

We tell ourselves this even while the likes of Dick Gregory are rapidly hacking and drilling away, filling the boat bottom with holes, unmindful that the safe label of *Negro* comic on Gregory is as hollow as the vacuum of our time. Anything *Negro*, getting down to an irrevocable fact, is topical. How can Gregory lose?

Compared to and rated far, far better than Amos 'n' Andy, Stepin Fetchit and the whole line of forced minstrel-type performers of the past, Gregory is aware of all these hustling undercurrents. But when he wakes, alive all at once in his rumpled bed, you know he's prepared to meet them head-on. In fact, one feels that he has tried on success many times before now and has accepted it not as long overdue, but as his *just* due almost on schedule. For 1961 his earnings should top 100,000 dollars.

It is not this which makes him an immodest man; he isn't. But neither is he modest. In this respect he has the Hipster's awareness; he *knows* where he is. Unencumbered by any indebtedness to older Negro comics, he knows with a calm assurance that he is just as popular with Negro audiences as with white. Why? Because he laughs at the foibles of both and these are so human that the audiences have to laugh at themselves; he reduces the ponderous sublime to the ridiculous.

There are not a few Negroes, however, who feel that Gregory is a modern-day Uncle Tom catering to the whimsies of whites, they do not see the sophistication he is said to have. They see in his movements a controlled shuffling; they hear in his lines revealing tales of their behavior, some of which they'd like very much to have remain unknown to Whites. And they feel he has mimicked the popular White comics and thus gained a success which they hope will be short-lived.

On the other hand, White audiences (the Hip ones because this man *does* require a Hip audience) follow his lines, hang on the minute, rapier-like revelations as if learning a heretofore obscure facet of history. But even the most Hip among the White audiences have reservations about Gregory, for racial problems in his hands approach the sacrilegious; they are not ponderous, not socio-economic, not Freudian theories; they become simple and biting observations. The White Hipster would prefer a more complex treatment of a rather unadorned truth.

Once off-stage Gregory himself has the Hipster's graciousness which ranges from a speedy put-down or a smooth put-on to a wild all-encompassing generosity—this last despite the fact that his success has predictably drawn to him a horde of young Negroes seeking help in their careers.

A lover of good jazz, scotch and the daily and weekly papers, he has turned the sword of prejudice into a plowshare of wealth. This is best illustrated by the way he handles hecklers whose barbs are lipped in racism. When insulted, Gregory calls out:

"According to my contract the management pays me 50 dollars every time someone calls me that. Would you mind doing it again? Would you *all* stand and repeat it in unison about a hundred times?"

SMALLS PARADISE

This Cavalier *magazine piece was assigned to me by George Dickerson in the summer of 1963. It usually happens that when an editor is pleased with your work, he'll call on you for other assignments. George and I had worked well together on "Sex in Black and White."*

In 1962 and early 1963 Smalls Paradise had regained some of the notoriety it held right after World War I and sporadically since. Harlem hadn't really closed down to whites, although Chester Himes told me that some of the residents had thrown beans as he was pointing out sights to members of a French television crew. A white crew, of course.

The real good magazine editors are often the guys with the ideas for articles. The idea of covering Smalls Paradise for a week was George's, and I thought it would be fun. But after the first couple of days it became dull as hell, hearing the same music over and over again; the same jive enthusiasm raked up by the master of ceremonies, and seeing the same types of people showing up on the scene.

Frank Dandridge, a young black photographer just coming into his own was assigned to take photographs while working with me. Unfortunately they won't appear here. Frank later went on to gain acclaim for photographing the demonstrations in Cambridge, Maryland, and the Watts and Newark rebellions.

I think George wanted a piece on Smalls because it was at that time re-emerging as one of New York's most exotic night-spots. John Dos Passos had written about Smalls in one of his novels; Carl Van Vechten, too, with other whites, seemed to see the place as one of the centers of nightlife during the twenties.

Of course, I'd entertained ideas of getting drunk every night on Cavalier's expense account, and having my pick of foxes. It didn't turn out that way. The foxes, when they came to Smalls, were with their husbands or boy friends. Also, if you've seen one nightclub floorshow, you've just about seen them all and no matter how much you may want to drink, your sanity stays with you longer if you escape the joint and go stand out on the curb.

By the third day of my week, I was drinking an average of two bottles of beer a visit, asking questions and watching the patrons and musicians more than fox hunting or drinking hard. I'd staggered my hours so I could be in the club from its opening at noon to its closing at three in the morning. Sometimes I wouldn't go until midnight, at other times very early. For the first time I understood the boredom of bartenders.

To do an article in this fashion is, of course, to unmask the publicized exoticism for the mundane, the ordinary, the boring— and I did become bored to tears.

It was for me a good thing that I was unable to interview Wilt Chamberlain until my week was up. In the article it is clear that he left a bad taste in my mouth. Rereading this article, I'm pleased to see that I didn't let my personal views get entirely out of hand, and that I was able to remain objective about Smalls as a nightclub; not a place owned by Wilt Chamberlain.

If I was able to understand the boredom of bartenders as a result of doing this article, now I could understand as well the world of the beat reporter whose life so embraces dullness and routine that he must often pray for excitement. But you learn from everything and I learned from this that boredom too often is the other side of exoticism.

DESPITE race riots and intergroup tensions, two things persist in restless, teeming Harlem, black capital of the world. One is the rumor that the city fathers secretly plan to turn 125th Street into an east-west artery linking the Triboro Bridge with the West

Side Highway and George Washington Bridge approaches. The other, more tangible, more concrete and glass, of infinitely more distinction, is Smalls Paradise.

After a succession of owners, the internationally known nightspot, now in its 38th year, has passed into the ham-like hands of Big Wilt Chamberlain, greatest basketball player ever. Big Wilt's Smalls Paradise squares its lettuce-green front between Taylor's Luncheonette and Wimple's, a diner, just south of 135th Street. One cannot pass the club without knowing it by the long, brown gold marquee reaching from door to curb. Smalls is on the ground floor of an office building, and the long, rectangular windows of the restaurant give a view of hustling Seventh Avenue traffic.

Over a quarter of a million people have visited Smalls since its latest boom began early in 1962. Sixty per cent of the annual visitors are white. Whereas Smalls, after its opening in 1925, titillated Cafe Society Downtown and the trans-Atlantic steamer set, today the average kicks-digging couple, if they can find a cab driver who will take them to Harlem, go without the black tie and gown and mix with the brownskin foxes and their studiously tailored men, the thinning jet set, the celebrities from all over the world.

The club, the last remnant of the famous, old Harlem clubs, has survived the last half of the Roaring '20s, Prohibition, the Crash, Depression, Wars, Recessions, and even the Peace; it will probably outlast the African Nationalists and the Black Muslims as well. Playgrounds have a way of surviving, and Smalls is one of the best known in the world.

Perhaps its location has helped it to survive. The rawness of 125th Street, the noise, the kaleidoscoping color, is not here. Businessmen and those in the professions seem less tense as they go to lunch at the YMCA or at Wimple's or to Jock's or the Red Rooster, where chitterling nights run back-to-back when this medieval French delicacy is in season. These clubs are small, intimate, and comparable to any downtown luncheon or dinner spot. Except in rare cases, the two-or-three-drinks-for-one bars lie south of Smalls.

The whole area seethes with a taut, new kind of prosperity: The Riverton, Lenox Terrace Apartments, and other sleek buildings rise above the shabby Lenox Avenue skyline. A new school is around the corner from Smalls; the Schomburg Collection, one of the most famous in America on Negro life and art, is only one block east. To the west (right around the corner from the nightclub) is the 32nd Precinct police station, and, rising abruptly from Manhattan Avenue, Morningside Heights forms a natural barrier between Harlem and the properties of Columbia University.

For all its notoriety as an international playground, Smalls has always been calmly considered by Negroes who live in Harlem. From time to time—not often—Smalls has had good music. It's a good place to meet someone because you have window space to watch. The help at Smalls generally agrees, with frigid righteousness, that it is the white customers who pay the freight, leave the best tips, not the Negroes. In the scheme of dollar discrimination, the most attentive courtesies are extended to the white visitor from downtown or Europe and to some Negro celebrities. Dollar or not, most Harlem Negroes refuse to be discriminated against in this fashion, especially by "their own kind." "To hell with them," one patron said, "I'd rather go to Jock's anyway."

For all of this, the bar at the front of the club is usually packed. Here the ratio is 90 per cent black and 10 per cent white, according to Big Wilt; it is in the club itself that 60 per cent of the patrons are white. The bar is a place where one could die of thirst, for the hustling, jolly bartenders and barmaids don't push; they wait with admirable restraint until they are summoned. If one is short of money, it is a remarkable bar; a beer can be nursed until it is boiling hot.

Here gather the hard drinkers, the waiters-for-action; here are the fine, brown frames and the impeccable, sun-glassed males. From one of the many sides of the bar one might hear the boyish tones of Met pitcher Al Jackson on a night off, or the eager, skipping laughter of Willie Mays, when he's in town with the Giants. From another side comes precise, curving French from a group of Paris businessmen nursing gin and tonics; from another,

Portuguese or Swedish or Spanish. But above all one hears rock-eting laughter that assures the visitor that the place, no matter who comes or goes, is solidly Negro at the core. This is just what the visitor wants.

The bandstand separates the bar and the club. Beginning Thursday nights, the traffic between the bar and the club is curtailed and a swing gate set into place. There is but one en-trance to the nightclub, and a visitor becomes two dollars lighter using it. At the time CAVALIER covered the club, the Willis Jack-son Quintet was providing music that was less special than it should have been. It was designed to please dancers and listen-ers and, even though its quality was pedestrian, the rhythm and blues line approached a neat groove.

Jackson likes to tune up with his breathy tenor à la Coleman Hawkins; he runs up and down the scales, tackles a bar of *Body and Soul*. Behind him sit Joe Hedrick, drums; Bill Jones, guitar; Frank Robinson, trumpet; and Carl Wilson, organ.

Past the crowded, little bandstand is the club itself; long, shadowed, some of its walls touched with surrealistic landscapes. Here are the white-topped tables, the stage thrusting out into the audience so that performers are surrounded on three sides by patrons.

On one wall is a montage of warping pictures. The ones with Big Wilt and Floyd Patterson are prominently displayed. Also pictured are Congressman Adam Clayton Powell, Jr., and tables filled with happy customers. There are many views of the Twist-ers who, early in the spring of 1962, launched Smalls Paradise once again to world-wide fame.

Before the Twist craze hit New York fully, Smalls had been limping along with third-rate floor shows and some good jazz. Giving up on jazz, the management moved closer to the gutti-ness of rhythm and blues, which seemed to attract more people. Perhaps this move was due to the judgment of Big Wilt who will not be pinned down to the exact kind of music he likes. ("Like jazz? No, no, I won't say that. I like music, R & B, not Rock 'n' Roll. . . . No, I like music.")

A Tuesday night Twist contest was inaugurated. After all, Twisters in Harlem had to be the best in the city, better than those who worked out at the Peppermint Lounge downtown. Hadn't Harlem given the world Trucking, Boogie-Woogie, Pecking, and the Lindy Hop? Challenges flew from Smalls to the famed Peppermint Lounge, probably at the suggestion of Major Robinson, sometime publicist for the club and *Jet* gossip alumnus. White people began arriving in droves, not only for the Tuesday night hip-tossing, but for every night.

The Peppermint Lounge never did accept the challenge, but it didn't matter; Smalls had been rediscovered. Twist combos worked down the night; the best Twisting chicks, black and white, ordered Twist dresses. Here came Patrick O'Higgins, Diahann Carroll, Baron Paolo Tallarico, Harry Belafonte, Duarte Pinto-Coelho, Mrs. Gustave Ajo, Sidney Poitier, Marianne Greenwood, Countess Nicoletta Attolico, Phil Silvers, Anthony Quinn, Van Johnson, Keely Smith, great athletes from visiting professional teams, and hundreds more—all to "Twist Again."

The publication-day party for James Baldwin's novel, *Another Country*, further spurred business by introducing New York's literary set to the nightclub. It had been a good twenty years since the book set had really invaded Harlem. Baldwin, who likes to Twist, had invited almost 200 writers, critics, literary agents, editors, and people from related fields.

Director Robert Rossen was there, and name people like Kay Boyle, Poitier, Philip Roth, Ralph Ellison, Cecil Hemley, Ruby Dee and Ossie Davis, Brian Glanville in from London, Godfrey Cambridge, and Maurice Dolbier. Millions of dollars worth of literary talent turned up their rear ends and Twisted. Viewing the crowded dance floor, one literary agent said, "You can see all the nasty, mean, vicious personalities coming out when they dance; and you can see the ones who think they're damned sexy and the ones who're shy but come on like they're real tough. This party's been a revelation!"

Baldwin's party was held at the height of the now-fading Twist craze. There no longer is a Tuesday night Twist contest at Smalls, although Tuesday night still brings visitors from down-town. The Bossa Nova, the Wobble, and the Pony are, in many quarters, replacing the Twist.

The 40-odd people who help run the nightspot (which costs $500,000 a year to operate) say that white people dance better today than did the earlier visitors to Harlem. Jackson says, "It's the younger people; they catch on fast."

A nearby waiter sneered, "It's the goddamn Twist. It's easy to do; easiest dance in the world. That's why they're still doing it instead of moving to the Bossa Nova or the Wobble. Look, look up there."

Up on the stage a white couple was doing the Twist. The girl was very good, very graceful; there was a certain poignance in her movements. But her partner was Twisting like the Little Old Winemaker.

"Are the white women better Twisters than the men?"

"Baby, you'd better know it."

Saturday and Sunday afternoons the big show room is empty; the dancers and singers and musicians who make up the show are home sleeping. The Seventh Avenue strollers pause at the bar and ask, "Throw me a little taste, baby?" The sun sends lazy rays through the windows; the juke box plays Sinatra sides as glasses tinkle, being washed out, and there is the continual hiss-ing of beer bottles being opened and the laughter and flow of soft voices.

It is the winter Saturday and Sunday afternoons that cause trouble, for then "Hawk"—biting cold weather and hard times—sends the homeless, the desperate scurrying into the warmth of the club. Very often these are the people who cause trouble any-where.

But Smalls is well equipped to handle trouble itself. Includ-ing Big Wilt's partner, Pete Douglas, there are four "floor man-agers"—the term bouncers is passé, and, indeed, only one of the four gives the raw impression of being a bouncer. He is George Austin. He goes about 240 pounds and stands about six-four. Even next to Wilt he looks more than formidable. Austin stands guard at the swing gate that separates the bar from the club. He can look very pleasant when he wants to, but he can also look as evil as hell.

"Trouble," he says, "can start anywhere in here, at the bar or in the back or downstairs. There's just no telling. It's kind of catching. One rumble breaks out, and for a few days other little rumbles break out." Mr. Austin smiles. "But we can handle 'em."

When the music tilts over and gets into a groove, Mr. Austin, light on his feet for all his weight, stands at his post and does the Twist. Pete Douglas, who usually guards the other entrance where the cover charge is paid, also dances when the mood hits him, but in the hall to the approving smiles of the two hat-check girls—and only when business is slow. One night a roaring drunk turned up at this entrance. Douglas took one look at his casual attire—shirt tail out, battered straw hat slung rakishly down over one eye—and reminded the visitor that there was a cover charge of two dollars. "Two dolla's!" the wino yelled. "What the hell you *get* f' two dolla's?"

"Man, that's just to get *in*," Douglas said, "and after that, Jack, it's up to you. You can spend all you want."

The wino stumbled away muttering, "Two dolla's! *Two* dolla's!"

Gene Tyler doesn't look as though he could handle trouble. He wears glasses and suits darker than any of the other floor managers. He walks around crowds instead of through them and he speaks softly, but firmly. He's probably the most dangerous; he doesn't dance.

Most remarkable of all is Odell Boyd, a 73-year-old gentleman who once managed the old Cotton Club. Mr. Boyd has a counterpart in every Harlem in America. Plump, cigar-smoking, he has been in the nightclub business for 50 years. He believes that had he been white he could have owned half of Las Vegas. "Even now I could go out there and run a li'l ol' casino," he says, "but who inna hell wants to be bothered with li'l ol' women and their damned nickels and dimes playin' the bandits?" There is no numbers banker, nightclub owner, gangster, cop or celebrity he doesn't know. An example of this was when a young

Negro couple came in one night, and, as Mr. Boyd was showing them to a table, he overheard the man mention the name of his home town. "You know ——?" Mr. Boyd asked.

The young man turned. "Sure, I do. He bought me my first Boy Scout uniform. You know him?"

"Yeah," Mr. Boyd said, puffing his cigar. "We're old friends." The man who was the topic of this brief conversation is an old-time, numbers man who is still operating in a city of 500,000 people.

Mr. Boyd has the quick eye and twinkling feet of a practiced maître d'. He guides the customers to their tables and summons the waiters. He loves the nightclub business; even on his night off, he shows up at the club to look over the bar and back-room.

To Mr. Boyd has fallen the task of keeping a delicate kind of order in the club. With his old, glassless eyes swinging from wall to wall, he sits at the rear on a raised platform and paternally watches out for the white couples. He, too, knows the smell of trouble. He knows that the pomaded and marcelled Negro, watching like a hawk, has received some kind of sign from a white woman sitting with her white male companion. The woman may not even be aware that she has tapped the sharp one's wave length until he is there at her table, smiling down, confident that she will be easy to have. He has paid little or no attention to her companion who, trying to be civil, smiles, laughs stiffly, suffers through a dance or two, bites his lip. By now the woman has come to her senses, the scales have fallen from her eyes, and she tries to refuse further invitations to dance. But the sharp one insists; he reeks with confidence. He holds her hand and looks longingly into her eyes.

Mr. Boyd has sized up the situation. With a flick of his finger he signals the nearest floor manager who moves in at the moment when people at other tables, embarrassed for the three involved, have turned their heads. "Mr. Boyd wants to see you, boy," the floor manager says. Reluctantly, the sharp one precedes him to where Mr. Boyd has raised his globular form from a chair to address him. His voice is harsh; he waves his cigar. "Got a table? Where's your table? Why don't you leave that couple alone? What's the matter with you? How you get in here, anyway; I say, how did you get in here? Put this boy out." The last is disdainfully said; and, before it has time to echo, the marcelled one, the lover, the sharp one, is being escorted firmly (unless he should recklessly try to pass for bad) to the sidewalk.

By and large, the white couples are man and wife, a sure sign that Smalls has gained a certain measure of respectability. What brings them to Harlem? Just the aura of Smalls? One waiter insisted, "White folks come to Harlem to do what they can't do downtown." But surely, no one would go that far out of his way just to do the Twist. During this writer's stay, there were no signs of outlandish behavior on the part of any customer.

White women seldom come alone, as Negro women do. Occasionally, they come in twos or threes or fours. White men are in the minority of lone men at the bar. Like the Negro man, he is looking for action and, if he is lucky, he may then move into the club. One weekend night, a middle-aged white man and a Negro woman of about the same age sat down at a table. The first show, featuring the dancing Tommy Johnson Trio with Arlene and Sandy, a bow-legged "song stylist" named Moondog, and singer Carl Bell, had just ended. The couple drank Martinis, a terrific expense on a weekend night when both cover and minimum are in effect.

It was obvious that the man was waiting for the woman to drink herself out and give herself over. Unfortunately, he didn't dance, and when the dancers took the floor she found herself a partner from a neighboring table. After the dance, the lady returned to her seat and had another Martini. Then she pulled her wrap around her and, patting her companion on the cheek, told him she was going to the powder room; she never returned.

Other mixed couples appear less casual in their relationships. Largely Negro men and white women (although one may here see more white men and Negro women than downtown), they mount the stage to dance without the self-consciousness that one sees in other parts of New York City. For the most part, they are young and have taken up the slack the jet set is leaving. Unless these interracial couples are well known, they will be given an intermediate table. The Negro man with his white date will almost certainly be placed in some middle area; the white man with his Negro date will get a table closer to the stage.

Of course, many patrons like to be close to the shaking bodies of the dancers. In this case, they were the vigorous, saucy Tommy Johnson and tall and handsome Arlene and Sandy. Johnson is a muscular young man with a whole bag of fearsome movements. Obviously, his oiled, half-naked body, his fantastic contortions, the fake diamond in his nose are all intended to titillate the white women in the weekend audiences. Arlene and Sandy, almost as skimpily clothed as Johnson, elicit from the white males equally evocative emotions.

In a high-light number, Johnson, clothed only in a loincloth, runs upon the stage with a torch clutched in each hand and, during a series of highly suggestive steps coupled with intermittent yelps, draws the flame slowly across his body, around his back, under his armpits and finally, head held dramatically back, thrusts one of the torches into his mouth. Each girl has her special number, too. Each has that fixed, white smile; the fine, brown frame with the long, tantalizingly curved legs. Each has the belly and buttock moves calculated to drive weak men out of their minds.

Moondog, who follows the dancers, is a stubby fellow whose disk-jockey father was involved in a suit over *his* use of the name, but won out over the original Moondog. (The original Moondog, a blind white man, was famed as the Nature Boy of the '50s. A gigantic man, the impresarios hailed his hand-drumming as the latest thing in jazz. He was exploited quickly and to the full. Disgusted, Moondog returned to the world he had left, a lonely world of standing on corners holding out a tray for the coins of passers-by. His great size and posture, the stern expression on his face belied that fact that he was a beggar in the common meaning of the term. Most recently, he has been appearing as a poet in a Greenwich Village coffeehouse.) If the original Moondog was all concrete and poise, this one is a jiggling, bent-legged, raucous shouter. A smile splits his face from ear to ear.

It is quite plain that he thinks a great deal of himself and his work. At his finale, he flings himself out of a black-and-white plaid jacket and, clutching the lobolier mike, shouts down the clamor of the quintet.

Carl Bell, who also acts as MC, grabs Moondog's coat and stands, a tight smile on his face, his hands poised to lead the applause. Then he comes forward to sing. One of his favorites is *What Kind of Fool Am I?*, in which he imitates Sammy Davis, Jr., Al Hibbler, Billy Eckstine, and "Anthony Newley after he met Joan Collins." His *pièce de résistance* is *This Land Is Mine* complete with cantorial wailings at the finish.

No part of the show attracts as much attention as Big Wilt table-hopping. His arrogance is said by many to be exceeded only by his height. He appears to be impatient and have his mind on other matters. His managers, for example, seem to know more about the functioning of his club than he does; perhaps that is why he pays them top salaries. To talk standing up to Wilt is rather like talking to a belt buckle—his. It seems to be, mockingly, on the level with one's eyes. To talk to him is also to be made aware that he makes in the neighborhood of $65,000 a year, is an internationally known athlete, and, finally, a supernatural human being. It would be difficult to mute these points; Big Wilt doesn't try.

After the show, the dancers take the floor. The best dancers knowingly pick spots at the front of the stage, the worst retire to the rear, away from the critical eyes of non-dancers. One sees a mixed couple at the front, a handsome white man and an attractive Negro woman, working out of a galloping Twist; a hefty Negro man who could pass as a double for George Austin (at least in bulk) wobbling with the concentration of a laboratory technician; an older couple hanging on to each other for dear life.

From the fast-paced music, Jackson will move his quintet into a series of ballads or standards, take each through the fox trot, rhumba, waltz—"A little something for every one, y' know," he explains with a smile. Among the numbers he most frequently plays are *After Hours, Tenderly, What Kind of Fool Am I?,* and *As Long As She Needs Me.*

The patrons keep coming despite the less than top-notch shows; it is *Smalls* that is the attraction.

Fifty Frenchmen who had heard about the club in Paris called when they were in New York to reserve tables. Before the night was over more than 250 Frenchmen on a Franco-American exchange program were in the club watching the floor show.

Jean Benoit Kesse and Kopa K. Bernard, journalists and television commentators from the Ivory Coast of Africa, heard about Smalls in the *Présence African* book store in Paris. They sat in Smalls one night drinking beer (at a rear table) and said they were in New York for six days. That was their first night in town, and they had rushed up to Smalls. Asked if they knew M. Dadier, an Ivory Coast poet who only two months ago had been in America, they replied, *"Oui,"* and added that M. Dadier was in prison.

"Pourquoi?"

Shrugging, they replied, *"Raisons politiques."*

Torun of Biot sat ringside taking a break from her exciting exhibit at Georg Jensen, Inc., on Fifth Avenue. Torun, a Swede of classic beauty, is married to American painter Walter Coleman. She is considered one of the best contemporary silversmiths and designers of costume jewelry. She has even made buttons for Picasso's work coat.

Few white patrons go downstairs or even know that another room, almost the size of the upstairs club, exists. This space is used by many of the hundreds of men's and women's clubs in Harlem. "Every week we have two or three private club affairs down here," Wilt says. "This place jumps, too, but in a quiet way." Cassius Clay held a victory celebration here. A dance floor, band, and bars set the room totally apart from the transient patronage in the upper rooms. Here one may see the Negro middle class of Harlem at play. The world above them is transitory; downstairs, away from the never-ending waves of tourists, Harlem endures.

It costs a lot to endure in Harlem. Catering to mixed patronage traditionally has cost Harlem club owners a lot of "grease." The current investigations of the State Liquor Authority and the revelation that club after club had to make the pay-off to stay in business prompted the question, "Do you have to pay off?"

"No!" snaps Wilt.

"No!" snaps Odell Boyd. "We run a good club; we close on time and take care of any trouble right away. We have nothing to do with the police."

And this is very, very probably true. Certainly, no such taint could touch Wilt without courting disaster to his career. So famous a figure would make corrupt officials think more than twice before applying any pressure. Harlem and Smalls are fortunate to have so invulnerable a personage as Big Wilt, although the invulnerability of any Negro in America is quite questionable.

One time, however, the police did rush into Smalls to the surprise of its patrons; but this was not a raid. Big Wilt explained, "We had a phone call; a bomb scare. We called the cops. No, it wasn't a raid; we have had no raids. It was a bomb scare, and they had to search the place. Some nut. No, they didn't find a bomb."

Wilt gave the impression that nothing would or could destroy his club. Perhaps he is right. Smalls, the exotic playground for all kinds of people, a miniature UN, having lasted this long, may last forever. To a great many outsiders, Smalls *is* Harlem, and there is thrill enough just sitting in the club in the middle of the biggest racial tinderbox in the world—and coming away unscathed. Certainly, diverse people find that when they get up to Twist or Wobble little diversity really exists, that this couple or that have just as much rhythm or just as little as the next.

Despite the unexciting floor shows (they're booked for two or three weeks at a time), the calculated courtesies for the dollar, the loudness of the music, Smalls does have that barely definable quality, a sense of history.

Unfortunately, Smalls Paradise probably will not work very hard to maintain or build its prestige. It will drift with its lissome floor shows and commonplace music until the next fad, or distinction, comes its way. But no matter. Smalls is an international landmark and, as such, almost commands the forbearance of its patrons. The patrons seem willing to be forbearing forever.

MARCUS GARVEY—
NEVER BEFORE OR SINCE

DAVID GARTH *is a man who stays behind the scenes producing political successes for people like Mayor John V. Lindsay. Garth, whom I first met in 1963, is extremely good at selling people. In 1965, he sold me to a friend of his, Clay Felker. Felker was then editing* New York Magazine *for the now defunct* Herald Tribune. *I was, Garth told Felker, a writer of rare talents.*

When Felker and I talked about my doing a piece for his magazine, which has since become an independent weekly, Marcus Garvey emerged as the subject. Today I don't recall whose idea it was. I researched Garvey, of course, and then wrote the article. In the course of my research I discovered a letter written to the U. S. Attorney General in which several prominent black people, including Robert S. Abbott, publisher of the Chicago Defender, complained that Garvey was skating on thin legal ice with his movement.

Garvey's life and times will be rewritten very soon. For in May 1970, more than 10,000 documents that belonged to him were found in an old building in Harlem. The historical significance of the find has yet to have its impact, and it may very well be that what was seen of Marcus Garvey was but the tip of the iceberg.

I believe I did two versions of this article, but can only find my original and the published piece. I know there were changes made in my second version, most of which was published. I did not get galley proofs from the magazine—a not unusual practice. Holiday was the only magazine I wrote for that provided writers, at least in the early stages of my association with it, with, if not galleys, a copy-edited version of their pieces.

I received complaints from two or three black people on the article. Rereading it today, I know I'd make changes, but on the whole, it'd remain pretty much the same. The changes would have to come because of new perceptions and the time in which we live. I've been to the Caribbean twice since I wrote the article, and hadn't made my second trip to Africa before writing it. Any writer capable of growth would have to take these factors into consideration; any writer worthy of the title would have to take into account also the impact blacks have made on whites in just the past five years, but also be aware of the continuum of that impact from Marcus Garvey forward.

TODAY's black nationalism, as much as ever an emotional appeal upon which to found a crusade for Negro equality, is a diffuse doctrine espoused by many shrill spokesmen. But the current tempo is mild when compared with the peaks of emotionalism reached by the black nationalist movement which surged to a climax in the Twenties under the leadership of the brilliant zealot Marcus Garvey. Never before had New York and the nation seen anything like it and certainly has seen nothing like it since.

Marcus Manasseh Aurelius Garvey was born near Kingston, Jamaica, in 1887, of a unmixed African stock, a descendant of Africans brought to the Antilles in 1509 to replace the Arawak Indians whom the Spanish had murdered or worked to death. Cardinal Ximenes had warned King Ferdinand and Queen Isabella that if Africans were taken to the New World to stock the islands, soon they would grow in numbers sufficient to overthrow the Conquistadores. Columbus' benefactors listened, but their successor, 17-year-old Charles V, did not, and Africans were transported to Jamaica, Haiti, Cuba and Puerto Rico.

The British came to the West Indies in 1670 and were faced

with constant rebellion by the Maroons, a large group of run-away slaves. Through 1831 and 1832 large slave insurrections occurred, and on August 1, 1834, they were emancipated and given six million pounds as compensation. But in 1865 still another rebellion took place, and the British lion arose astride the island with its tail twitching.

The British had already conquered. Now they divided to keep the peace. They did so by establishing a caste system based upon color. The Garveys were black, so they were at the bottom. Above them were the mulattoes or, as they are called in South Africa today, the coloreds. At the top, of course, were the whites—the colonial administrators, soldiers and businessmen. Any black on the island knew his heritage of bitterness against the British system. Garvey was no exception. But he also had another cause: he was ugly. His friends and neighbors called him "Ugly Mug," and he had to take it. He could not deny that he was a very unattractive boy.

Smarting from these hurts, Garvey took to wandering about the islands at an early age. After all, in a family of 13, favors are not always equally given. And sometimes the boy felt that his mere presence, his ugliness, only made his family aware of its problems. In his travels Garvey learned to set type and became a printer. Jamaica was predominantly a fruit-growing and cattle-raising island. Garvey had cut his ties with the past. He emerged from his teens as a squat little black man with an overlarge head and shrewd, retreating eyes.

In a special way Garvey was disarming; one look at him and the beholder was convinced that what stood before him was nothing more than an ugly black clod. Garvey surprised many people and had some success in the islands. In Costa Rica he stopped long enough to move up from printer, although he probably continued to set type, to co-publisher of a weekly paper, *The Bluefield Messenger*. In 1909 with some small reputation behind him, he returned to Kingston and led a successful strike of printers against the local press. Then, like most subjects of what was then the British Empire, he decided to go to England. Briefcase in hand, a symbol that he was going or had been to England, Garvey joined the trickle of blacks and browns.

Details of Garvey's stay in England are scant. One biographer says he worked as a printer. Others say he studied, but they are divided on what field he pursued. There are other questions: did he go on his own or did his 3,000-member organizations, The Universal Negro Improvement Association and the African Communities League, groups which he had formed after the strike in Kingston, send him? Certainly a man of Garvey's stature would not have chosen to be a printer. It seems likely he studied economics. One can imagine that he met African students, people as black as himself and also made "ugly"—in Western eyes—by tribal scars. One can imagine them an infinitesimal black group in communities which 45 years later would be rent by race rioting. One can imagine them on a monthly sojourn to Soho or taking the train to Paris for a weekend.

Garvey returned to Jamaica; but he had tasted the great outside world, had been a part of it. He was restless. Now he knew that, although he was black and ugly, there had to be a place for him on the world scene. How best to gain it? He had discarded quickly the idea of gaining success on white terms in the white world. London had been such a place. But the United States had millions of blacks, and many West Indians had chosen to settle there rather than in Britain. Casting about for a lever, Garvey wrote to Negro leader Booker T. Washington, founder of Tuskegee Institute, about educational plans for the West Indies.

Washington was dead by the time Garvey arrived in America in 1916, and the West Indian was drawn immediately to Harlem, which had a vast West Indian population. By the next year, Garvey had completed organizational plans for his Universal Negro Improvement Association in Harlem.

Garvey did not have an easy time. The schism between the Negro migrating from the South and the West Indian migrating from the islands was definite. Garvey was just another one of those loud-mouthed West Indians with a strange way of speaking. He was a monkey-chaser. And uglier than most.

One spring night in 1919, a wild-eyed man burst in on Garvey and a woman in a Harlem apartment and fired a pistol. The bullet only grazed Garvey's forehead, but with extraordinary perception of what the event could mean, Garvey tore loose from the woman and dashed into the street yelling.

The following day, Garvey's assailant, the woman's estranged lover, who had been captured by police, jumped through a cell window to his death. It is a fact that a person who makes the headlines, for whatever reason, becomes a celebrity of sorts. This is particularly true in Harlem, for the weekly press, unable to compete with the dailies, must survive on sensationalism. Garvey, ignored on Harlem streets even by the average listener to soapbox oratory, overnight became a celebrity. Garvey was ready, and the belief that he led a charmed life was quickly accepted by most Harlemites.

The war had ended and the lot of the Negro had not improved; it had worsened. Harlem boiled; ferment was everywhere, for war work in the North had increased the population of the community 108 per cent. From the Secretary of War, Newton D. Baker, came the word that even though Negroes had participated fully in the war they really could not expect any significant social changes.

Garvey had observed the hopes of the Negro—and had been cynical about them. After shooting incidents, his UNIA grew by leaps and bounds, helped by mounting disenchantment of Negroes not only in Harlem, but across the nation. Correctly gauging the Negro mood, Garvey toured 38 states and was acclaimed a leader. Amid the unrest and murder, his voice was beginning to be heard. "Back to Africa," he cried. "Africa for the Africans!" When he returned to Harlem, he had nearly a million followers, and to accommodate them he built Liberty Hall at 56 West 135th Street. He also had a newspaper.

The *Negro World* was dedicated to the African warrior chiefs who had led successful wars against European colonialists, to black achievements in culture and art, war and heroism; in short, as much of Negro history as its editors and writers could gather. So thorough was the *Negro World* staff that Attorney General A. Mitchell Palmer cited it in his 1919 report on radicalism. Garvey himself loaded the pages with opinions and essays. Skin-whitener ads were forbidden although ads of Lucky Strike cigarettes appeared occasionally. The paper was similar to *Muhammad Speaks,* official organ of the Black Muslims and distributed by them on street corners today.

The paper widened Garvey's influence. He had begun his rise with a hard core of West Indian malcontents, hopefuls and spiritual gamblers. But with times getting harder, the Southern Negro who had journeyed to Harlem also joined the movement. And Negroes all over the country who were unable to flee their poverty joined the various national branches. Marcus Garvey was rapidly becoming a Black Moses, and turned his eye to the homeland—Africa—and thus generated the first back-to-Africa movement ever started by Negroes themselves.

The back-to-Africa movements until that time had always been sponsored by whites. From the early 1700s up until Reconstruction, the movements started and collapsed. Groups of Negroes sometimes made their way back to Africa; sometimes a determined single Negro got back. Africa during those 175 or so years meant mainly the western bulge of the continent: Liberia, established by the U.S. in 1847 for returned slaves, Senegal, Ivory Coast, Guinea or Sierre Leone. But slaves had been brought from a dozen other countries, even as far east as Madagascar. They came from so many different tribes and spoke so many different languages and dialects that English was largely their common language. Many of the back-to-Africa schemes were devised by the Quakers on humanitarian grounds. All moves of this type at that time, however, were either openly or clandestinely thwarted by the combined forces of Northern manufacturers and Southern planters. If the Negroes were sent back to Africa, who would plant and harvest the cotton? Who would sweep the factories?

When Garvey spoke in Liberty Hall, he spoke to a multitude

disgusted with America; he was always promising. There would be no double talk in Africa. And in Africa they could put down roots once more. In America they only scraped along the miles of concrete and asphalt. It was hard, very hard to belong. Besides, Garvey reminded his people, the black man was better than the white man. "Honest students of history," he said, "can tell the day when Egypt, Ethiopia and Timbuctoo towered in their civilizations, towered above Europe, towered above Asia. When Europe was inhabited by a race of cannibals, a race of savages, naked men, heathens and pagans, Africa was peopled with a race of cultured black men who were masters in art, science and literature. . . ."

Garvey also planned a self-sufficient Black Economy in America. "Buy Black" was the by-word, and small stores sprang up all over the nation, and particularly in Harlem. The stores generally were poorly stocked, and prices were often at least as high as or higher than prices in white stores. In order to unite the black people of the world, Garvey formed a Negro merchant marine, The Black Star Line. And he needed white money for these ventures.

Pomp was important. "I asked," Garvey said, "where is the black man's government? Where is his president, his country, and his ambassadors, his army, his navy, and his man of big affairs? I could not find them and then I declared I will help make them."

First, a flag, red, black and green. Then the Universal African Legion, mounted, the Universal Black Cross Nurses, the Universal African Motor Corps, the Black Eagle Flying Corps. Garvey then named himself Provisional President of Africa; when he arrived there his government would be set up and ready to function at once. Behind Garvey in rank were a Potentate and a Supreme Deputy Potentate; behind them was the black nobility, which included the Knights of the Nile, Knights of the Distinguished Service, the Order of Ethiopia, the Dukes of Nigeria and Uganda.

When the Garveyites, resplendent in their uniforms, marched

through Harlem, the Provisional President of Africa himself rode in an ostentatious Packard tonneau. He favored a uniform of purple, green and black, with yards of gold braid, and a hat with plumes as long as the blades of Guinea grass.

A part of the Garvey trappings was religion. He had seen enough to know that if the black man was going to make progress, he had to rid himself of the greatest albatross—the white man's religion; therefore, Garvey created a black religion and a black god. Garvey himself was, for a time, a devout Catholic. It was almost second nature, then, that he set up the new religion along lines he knew best.

He installed George Alexander McGuire, a former Episcopal rector, as Primate of the African Orthodox Church. The liturgy, ritual and Holy Trinity were taken over and made black. In a "Special Divine Service" held in Liberty Hall, Archbishop McGuire "canonized" Jesus as "The Black Man of Sorrow" and the Virgin Mary as the "Black Madonna."

"Erase the white gods from your hearts. We must go back to the native church, to our own true God," McGuire said.

Because of his own blackness he was aware that utter blackness in American society made one an outcast even among Negroes, so Garvey declared that only pure-blooded Negroes could hold office or honors in his organization.

The "Intellectual Negro" of the period was epitomized in W. E. B. DuBois of the NAACP. From the start of Garvey's climb, DuBois had warned the Negroes that the West Indian was a fraud. This was probably advantageous to Garvey, for the NAACP was definitely a middle-class organization and rarely was it able to fully attract the man in the street to its policies, which were, compared to Garvey's, extremely conservative.

A. Philip Randolph, then editor of the *Messenger*, also railed at Garvey. "The whole scheme of a black empire, in the raging sea of imperialism," he declared, "would make it impossible to maintain power; nor would it bring liberation to Africa, for Negro exploiters and tyrants are as bad as white ones."

DuBois continued his protests. He saw black men united on

three great continents, Africa, North America and South America. His view was return but *union*. DuBois had called the first Pan-African Congress in London in 1900. Not a single African's presence there is recorded. By the time the second Congress was convened, Garvey and DuBois were locked in fierce combat. It was not until 1945, however, that the meetings attracted major African leaders.

Even as Garvey and DuBois slugged it out, the back-to-Africa movement had created another important reaction, the "Harlem Renaissance." Black American writers mingled with Caribbean writers, gathered, discussed their work, discussed Garvey, discussed black. Among them were Langston Hughes, Bud Fisher, Arna Bontemps, Claude McKay, Countee P. Cullen. "How beautiful we are," Langston Hughes wrote. Bombarded every day, from every direction, the writers plunged into black history. Haitian writers, particularly Jean Price Mars, quickly adapted the theory of black superiority. First coined by another Haitian, Aime Cesaire "negritude" soon meant something special about being black, something good, something superior. President Leopold Senghor, of Senegal, today the leading spokesman for "negritude," also credits the late Alain Locke of Howard University, another Renaissance writer, with having given the theory impetus. "Negritude" became a full-blown mystique in 1948, but oddly it is used by the French-African writers, "negritude" too often takes the arguments of Western bigots, flips them over and finds black to be superior—an old game first used by whites to justify the bondage in which they kept the Negro.

(Cesaire now says that "negritude" needs reexamination, that it has served its purpose—to instill pride in the Negro and African, especially the writers. On the other hand, Senghor, early this year, was reported considering a further refinement. He would set apart the Bantu peoples of Africa from the Hamitic-Semitic peoples—as Senegalese are classified—on the ground that the Bantus are inferior.)

Five months after DuBois convened his second Congress,

Garvey spoke in Liberty Hall to the annual August UNIA convention:

"It falls to your lot to tear off the shackles that bind Mother Africa. Can you do it? You did it in the Revolutionary War; you did it in the Civil War; you did it at Verdun; you did it in Mesopotamia: you did it in Togoland, in German East Africa, and you can do it marching up the heights of Africa," Garvey said, referring to American Negro and African participation in World War I.

The UNIA at that time had between one and three million members—enough to give Garvey the confidence to seriously negotiate with President King of Liberia for the purchase of land from which to begin operations in Africa. The negotiations were nearing an agreeable conclusion. Garvey, now approaching the crest of his popularity, threatened the white world with an invasion of 400 million black men. "Men of the Negro race, men of Ethiopia, follow me!" In Europe an undercurrent of panic followed. Leaders rose in the most undistinguished places in Africa to hail Garvey's coming. But they were summarily cut down. The *Negro World* was suppressed in British, French, Italian and Spanish colonies. Along the beaches of Calabar in eastern Nigeria, people lit huge bonfires to guide Garvey's ships safely to anchorage.

By 1923 the Garvey movement was steamrolling. Neither New York City nor the rest of the nation had ever seen anything like it. Everywhere there was a ballooning pride in being black: Negro girls had white dolls snatched out of their arms and replaced by black dolls; little Negro boys studied the histories of black heroes. But the UNIA had become top-heavy with high-salaried officials. Anti-Garvey whispers were running through Harlem. James W. H. Eason, one of Garvey's colleagues almost from the beginning, was charged with acts unbecoming a UNIA official and subsequently dismissed.

Settling in New Orleans with a few other disgruntled former Garveyites, Eason set about establishing a rival organization. But one night, as he was going to a meeting, he was surprised and assassinated. His killers were never found, but in Harlem the word was that Marcus Garvey knew all about it. The dissension in the top echelon ceased at once.

Garvey's philosophy of racial purity earned him some strange bed-fellows. He said, "It is the duty of the virtuous and morally pure of both the white and black races to thoughtfully and actively protect the future of the two peoples by vigorously opposing the destructive propaganda and vile efforts of the miscegenationists of the white race and their associates, the hybrids (mulattoes) of the Negro race." The result of this speech was that Colonel Simmons, Imperial Wizard of the Ku Klux Klan, and John Powell, of the Anglo-Saxon clubs, gave Garvey open support. Negroes outside the UNIA attacked Garvey, with A. Philip Randolph leading the charge. In the South, where every strange Negro was a chief candidate for an impromptu lynching, Garvey's recruiting forces lost not a single man.

Disaster came so gracefully its arrival was not recognizable. First, there was the assassination of Eason. Whether Garvey had been behind it is unimportant. It was laid at his door; but rather than detract from his stature, the rumors heightened it. Under strong pressure from Europe, the Liberian president was already backing out of all existing contracts between his country and the UNIA; he would sell the land to the Firestone Rubber Company.

But Garvey's prestige continued. He purchased the *Yarmouth* and rechristened it the *Frederick Douglass* for his Black Star Line. Negroes came from far and near to see the ship moored at the 125th Street pier. The *Frederick Douglass* foundered off the Virginia coast and was never in good shape afterward. Garvey had also bought the *Shadyside*, an old ferryboat, and the *Macco*. Another ship, which was to be named the *Phyllis Wheatley* after the Negro poetess of the Revolutionary War, was never seen. Garvey, at the peak of his good year, 1925, was charged with using the mails to defraud and indicted. The trial lasted about a month and he was convicted.

But Garvey was not finished. Although he was now reviled

openly—"Cunning, egotistic, boastful, intolerant, smooth, avaricious"—he quickly took in more than $100,000 from his followers for the purchase of additional ships, and formed the Black Cross Navigation Company. The first ship purchased was the *General Goethals*. It was renamed the *Booker T. Washington*. The old Black Star Line had been $700,000 in debt, it had been revealed in court, despite the fact that, from 1919 to 1921, according to Garvey's wife, Amy Jacques, UNIA had taken in $10 million from some 40,000 investors in various Garvey projects. But some of the same people rushed forward once more with money for Garvey to start his new steamship line.

In the midst of these activities, the heavily jowled Garvey seemed to have a sudden change of heart. He urged his followers to take an active interest in American politics and to become naturalized if they were foreign-born. He formed the Universal Negro Political Union, and in 1924 endorsed a slate of candidates. Calvin Coolidge was among them. Perhaps this was what had made Garvey so confident that he would win his appeal, but he did not. Sentenced to from two to five years, he entered Atlanta penitentiary in 1925—to be pardoned two years later by Coolidge, and deported as an undesirable alien.

Garvey was broken. He was back where he had started, in the islands. From Jamaica, he tried just once more to get the UNIA, which had broken into bickering little splinter groups, to reform and become a power again. That failing, he went to London, where he lived in obscurity until his death in 1940. He never went to Africa. Paradoxically, DuBois, who had worked so hard for Pan-Africanism, finally left America and went to Africa, where he died, in Ghana in 1963.

In 1928, the *Herald Tribune* noted that at the annual August convention of the sputtering UNIA, "Marcus Garvey himself, dreamer of dreams for the future of the Negro race, was not present . . . but this grip on the Negroes of Harlem, whose new and conscious race pride he was foremost in instilling, apparently has been weakened none at all by his absence."

As the UNIA tumbled, old Garveyites gravitated toward

a man named W. D. Fard or Elijah Poole, later Elijah Muhammad of the Black Muslims. Where the Garveyites had created their own religion out of Roman Catholicism, the Muslims turned to Allah, more and more the religion of the black man. As flamboyance was the mark of Garvey's forces, restraint is the trademark of the Muslim. But there are certain similarities as well: Malcom X's assassination, supposedly at the hands of Muslims, and the killing of James W. H. Eason, supposedly by Garvey people. Malcolm X's turnabout from racism to the larger principles of brotherhood and Garvey's similar turn; although it is more than likely that Garvey's was prompted by his desire to win his appeal in the fraud case.

Marcus Garvey, "Ugly Mug," squat, black, little and unattractive, shrewd, conniving, a juggler of religions and people and money, left his mark as no Negro before him. New York City will never see his like again: his scowling face the more pudgy beneath his massive hat with plumes as tall "as Guinea grass," the drums, the Universal African Motor Corps motorcycles, the prancing horses of the African Legion, the white-clad Black Cross Nurses. As the Twenties roared, so did Garvey. He was of that time, but the effect of his being in that time has not yet worn off—and almost half a century has passed.

MALCOLM X

THIS *is a long headnote to a short piece, written for and sent to* Newsweek *from Lagos, Nigeria, in 1964.*

In another headnote I mentioned having some minor difficulty with Holiday *because I wanted to travel while rewriting "This Is My Country Too" instead of staying in New York where the editors probably would've bugged me to death.* Newsweek *was interested in my travels, particularly in Africa.*

My contact with Newsweek *started with one young man who in the spring of 1963 had singlehandedly tried to open the magazine's doors to black writers and reporters. He had spent a few unfruitful days sitting in the offices of the Urban League, trying to tell someone there that he wanted black writers on the magazine. He never got past the front receptionist. He knew Godfrey Cambridge and called him; Cambridge gave him my name. He called me. We became friends, although at the time I wasn't much interested in working for* Newsweek. *There is a certain freedom a writer has even though he may work eighteen hours a day. He's working for himself; no bosses hanging over his shoulder. He's free to break and take in a movie or get stoned; he doesn't have to go the shirt and tie route five days a week, nor punch a time card. I'd become used to that kind of freedom and didn't want to give it up. Fortunately, the* Holiday *trip later that year took me out of town and away from my friend's insistence that I work in the* Newsweek *offices.*

He knew I was going to Africa. As a senior editor who worked closely with the editor of the magazine, my friend had some pull. Therefore, when my trip was all set, Newsweek *gave me some money and press and cable cards, and briefed me on who to send cables and stories to. There was a feud of some*

*sort going on between two of the senior editors, Bob Christopher
and Jim Cannon, both of whom were responsible for handling
whatever material I sent in. In addition, there was a third
party involved, a man named John Rinehart, in charge of
foreign correspondents. It seemed that, to appease all three, I'd
have to address my copy Christopher-Cannon-Rinehart so none
would be offended. It should be clear by now that this was
at best a loose arrangement, for which I was glad, although I
didn't want to be involved in any feuds.*

*At that time there weren't more than two or three black
reporters on the staffs of the mass circulation newsmagazines.
Gordon Parks, of course, with Life, was the sole legendary figure.
It has developed since, however, that the newsmagazines have
taken on a host of black researchers and more reporters than
before, while the popular, non-newsmagazines have measured
no increase whatsoever in the number of black writers on their
staffs or who work by assignment.*

*I'd never written for a newsmagazine before, although as a
free-lance, I'd produced a lot of news stories. This wasn't a
thing I worried about because all newsmagazine stories are
rewritten in the main offices, anyway, and my bread and butter
didn't depend on Newsweek. My friend and I did discuss my
availability to the magazine upon my return. My answer was
vague.*

*I don't recall now exactly how many stories I filed by courier
or cable to Newsweek. The one story I was asked to cover
—the Somalia-Ethiopian skirmishes from Addis Ababa—I couldn't
recognize when it appeared in the magazine. Only one word.
After having spent several weeks in Europe, Israel, Cyprus,
Egypt, the Sudan and Ethiopia, I went to Nigeria in May 1964.*

*This was when I met Malcolm X. A man in the United States
Information Services office in Lagos told me that Malcolm was
coming to Nigeria. I didn't bother to ask how he knew, or how
he knew which hotel he'd be staying at, but his information
turned out to be very accurate.*

On the day of Malcolm's arrival I called his hotel. I didn't know if he was using his Muslim name or slave name. In any case, I'd forgotten whether his slave name was Small or Little. I chose Small; he wasn't in and I left a message. Mr. Small returned the call, Oxford accent and all. A mistake obviously. I then left word for Malcolm X to call.

When he did I recognized his voice instantly. "Did you write a novel called Sissie?" he asked. I said yes. "Well come right over so we can talk." At the Federal Palace Hotel, we talked in his room. There were two people with him, an American black from the University of Ibadan, and a Nigerian. When we left his room to sit in the patio downstairs, we were joined by several Pakistanis, a Muslim people, and I felt that their presence put restraints on our conversation.

I wrote the story on Malcolm and mailed it to Newsweek a week after our meeting, sensing that there was no rush. It was never run. About nine months later it happened that I was back in Nigeria doing a television show when the news came of Malcolm's murder in the Audubon. In fact I was staying in the hotel where he'd stayed.

In his book, The Autobiography of Malcolm X, he states that he was interviewed by "an American Negro from Newsweek magazine—his name was Williams." That was me. He also said, "Traveling through Africa, he (me) had recently interviewed Prime Minister Nkrumah." Not true. For some reason never explained to me, I was refused a visa to Ghana.

I returned to New York late in June 1964. I'd been in Africa about five months. It didn't seem to matter that Newsweek had run almost none of my copy; they still wanted me to take a desk job. I was interested in either a desk at the United Nations or one in its New York Office. They were talking about jobs out of town, in which I had no interest.

But my friend wouldn't give up. He asked if I had any interest in becoming the book editor and I said yes. According to him, I'd have to go to the office one or two days a week. A couple of days later, however, he called back and said I'd have to come

*in maybe three or four days a week, and I told him that'd be
okay if they were not full days. He called a third time to say
I'd have to come in five days a week and it looked like I'd
have to spend a considerable amount of time in the office
every day. So, I said the hell with it.*

*Saul Maloff then became book editor for the magazine, and
not long after I learned that he only had to go into the office
one or two days a week.*

*Although I'd planned to go to Africa before I got the
Newsweek connection, the fact that I held Newsweek press
cards opened many doors for me. In fact, I could play the
foreign correspondent one day and the private citizen the next.
I believe I got as close to what makes Africa tick as anyone on
that first trip because I could switch roles if I had to.*

*For example, I met guerrillas and exiles; talked to highly
placed people and visited places where most mere tourists
wouldn't go. I was asked by a U.S. government official to tell
him what I saw in the Congo interior, for example, and I
stayed in a hotel in which there was billeted a group of
American soldiers who wore civilian clothes all the time. They
thought I was Congolese, so they didn't always care what they
said when I was near.*

*A lot of the experiences, feelings and sights of that trip went
into my novel* The Man Who Cried I Am, *which goes to prove,
as I said earlier, that journalistic writing or experiences can
be well utilized in fiction writing.*

Finally, I think I sent in good copy to Newsweek. *Rinehart
told me they didn't know what to do with it. I filed stories on
the Israeli air force, the war in the Sudan, when it was still
news (it remains news, but the press isn't terribly interested
and never has been in covering wars in which the West isn't
directly involved), and others which were later "discovered"
by other reporters. If a writer can produce out of a farce like
my association with* Newsweek *a novel like* The Man Who
Cried I Am, *then the experience is well worth it.*

Boyishly gaunt, burned from the sun, and sprouting the middle growth of a beard, Alhaji Omowale (The Child Who Has Returned Home), Malcolm X, sat on the terrace of the plush Federal Palace Hotel in Lagos and toyed with a bottle of orange soda.

Malcolm X was at the tail end of a pilgrimage to Mecca where he earned the title Alhaji; a state visit to Saudi Arabia as the guest of Prince Faisal; a three-day visit to Beirut where he was mobbed by students seeking his autograph.

"There was no riot there, as reported in the States," he said. But, after his visit to Cairo and Lagos, his jaunt to Ibadan caused some of his listeners to howl down a professor who stood to debate with the former number two man of the Black Muslims. Later, students ringed the USIS office, chatted with police who had formed an inner circle, and then returned to the University College of Ibadan.

The founder of the newly organized Muslim Mosques, Inc. was covered only by the left-verging *West African Pilot*, which, in a front-page, headlined story, filled with misinformation (Malcolm was hailed as the Black Muslim leader), carried Malcolm's denunciation of the Peace Corps as "missionaries of neo-colonialism" and spies of the American Government.

But one Peace Corps man, a part of that growing, hard-eyes new group, with idealism held at the low key, said, "What the hell have they got here that we want?" The London *Daily Telegraph* noted that there was "no indication that he has met any Nigerian leaders."

Used to the harmattan that comes ringing down, wherever he goes, Malcolm X gestured toward the luxurious gardens of the Federal Palace Hotel and said, "There is more wealth here than American Negroes ever dreamed of." Around him were one

Nigerian nationalist, two American Negroes in Nigerian national dress (one a Peace Corpsman) and a group of Pakistanis, one of them a journalist.

"I'm in Africa," Malcolm said, "to challenge the statement of Senator Douglas who said Africans were not interested in American Negroes. But I have found that Africans have an uncompromising interest in the Negro. I want to offset the influence of the American and British governments which are building a campaign to keep the African and Negro from joining hands."

He held up his cameras. "And I'm taking pictures to show the people back home."

Of his new group which works with ACT, itself composed of the more fiery elements of civil rights groups already in the field, Malcolm said, "We are no longer committed to non-violence. Anybody can belong to ACT."

"White people?" a *Newsweek* reporter asked.

"Most of the people in CORE, with whom we work, are white," he said.

"White people who are Jews?" the reporter asked.

Stoically, his gray-green eyes flashing over the fountains and lawns before him, he said, "Many of the white people in CORE are Jews." There was a pause; the Pakistanis sat quietly, the sound of the splashing fountain heightened a sudden embarrassment. "No comment on that," Malcolm said. But then, as if to soften the implications of his previous words, he told this story:

"When I was a boy, we had a horse; good old horse, worked very hard. We liked that horse. But, at the end of the day, we put the horse in the barn, and we went into the house. Now, as I say, we liked that horse, but his work was done, and we put him away."

The interview turned to summer 1964 and he sees violence in it. "The Negro is now able to see the tricks used last summer by Negro leaders. Those tricks were designed to keep the Negro from exploding. The March on Washington was a trick. This summer won't be like last summer; there's no one around as tricky as Kennedy was."

Using a Kennedyism, he called Africa a "New Frontier" and even as he was saying Negroes should return there, reporter Tony Momoh of the Lagos *Daily Times* was dissuading three members of the extremist Jamaican nationalist group, the Ras Tafari Brethren, currently soliciting to resettle in Africa. The Brethren, Momoh wrote, should, like the American Negro, "be dedicated to the cause of unfettered emancipation, MUST achieve their heart's desire someday somehow."

Malcolm denied any responsibility whatever for the Harlem gang Blood Brothers, which has been implicated in the murder of four white persons in Harlem. "I get blamed for everything," he said.

The next day he was off to Ghana, and hoped to get to Guinea and possibly Timbuktu. He was rushing to complete his journey. Reason: he is debating author Louis Lomax on May 21, "Violence or Nonviolence." With a chuckle, Omowale, the Child Who Had Returned, said that "Lomax is just as violent as anyone else." His trip began April 13.

JACK JOHNSON AND
THE GREAT WHITE HOPE

THE GREAT WHITE HOPE *is an introduction, not a magazine article. This was never published. It was written for but not included in the Dial Press edition of the Broadway hit, which was published in 1968.*

Through friends at Dial I learned that they were going to publish the play, and I asked if I could write an introduction. The response was an enthusiastic yes. I'm not so interested in boxing these days. Once I was. My father was a boxing nut and sometimes he took me to fights at the old Syracuse Arena. I could never see myself becoming a professional boxer, although when I was in the Navy I boxed some on Guadalcanal, on ships and in the Marianas Islands as a welterweight. I got bounced around enough to know that that wasn't the career for me, although for a time I followed every fight I heard about religiously. Some of this shows in my novel Captain Blackman. *In it Abraham Blackman as a teen-ager is led to believe he has the makings of a good fighter until he's pulverized by an opponent at a CYO match.*

I'd not seen The Great White Hope *on Broadway. If I had, I would not have done the introduction to the book. Nor had I seen the play by the time I left in the summer of 1968 to teach at the College of the Virgin Islands on St. Thomas. While there I got a cable from an editor at Dial asking me to do the introduction in a hurry, since the play was already in galley proofs. Someone from the Dial office was bringing a set of the galleys to me.*

I read and reread the galleys in one sitting, while I broiled on the sun deck of our house in the Tutu section of St. Thomas.

From the library at the College I got the one book on Jack Johnson, a solid work done by a Britisher named Bachelor. There was also a book of boxing records. I read Bachelor's book in one sitting, and reread it. Then I was ready to work.

Bachelor's book dealt with far more than boxing, and so did Howard Sackler's play in the reading. The newsman in the play was Jack London, of literary and Socialist fame who, I already knew, was responsible for that racist cliché "The Yellow Peril." When I sat down to write and rewrite this introduction, it was a breeze; I had it all right there, snatching it out of the air. I had no doubt whatsoever of my point of view.

A certain feeling fills a writer when he knows he's captured the very essence of a subject. No one can explain or describe the feeling; it's one of well-being, even elation, of satisfaction. That's the way I felt when I finished the piece and sent it in to the Dial Press.

After I returned to New York at the end of that summer, an editor at Dial confided that the intro was well liked by the staff, but the author, Sackler, turned it down as was his prerogative, because I hadn't dealt with the play or the merits of the production. I was more into sociology than playwriting.

Clay Felker of New York magazine expressed interest in seeing it, but it came back to me from him twice as fast as I'd sent it to him. Dial paid me a small sum for the work, which was not submitted anywhere else after New York magazine. I didn't have an agent to blame because we'd come to a parting of the ways.

Dial also got me a couple of tickets to the play. My wife and I sat so close to the stage we could see spittle flying from the mouths of the actors. I was shocked at the vast difference in the way the play was played and the way it read. James Earl Jones had very few moments as the tragic man Jack Johnson actually was, and those moments were almost completely overshadowed by the Sambo Jack Johnson the critics raved about. What made for such a huge difference? I think a black playwright and a black director would have presented a vastly changed production; on the other hand, another view of Jack Johnson, a black view, might not have become such an overwhelming success.

In any case, here's at least one black view, and it's mine.

Boxing is the nitty-gritty sport. It is eye to eye, toe to toe, knuckle to jaw, blows and blood. It is man pitted directly against man, out in the open. None of this competition against clocks or moving a ball forward with the help of four or ten other men; none of this punching out of a little white ball so nine men can catch it. Boxing is instant violence and perhaps the most satisfying kind. It is most greedily digested by the masses who made it into a popular sport. And it is from those masses that the boxers have come.

Through a single boxer the ethnic echo of *Us* vs. *Them* has sounded for almost a century through a thousand saloons, barges, barns, gyms and gardens. Given the composition of our society, whether boxers wished this or not, it could not be otherwise. The downtrodden on the bottom have always sought gladiators to represent them; the fearful guilty up at the other extreme were equally diligent, with considerably more luck. To be a champion then, was to be the best and the group he came from was uplifted. But holding a championship is risky business, especially if you are black, as Howard Sackler indicates in his *The Great White Hope.*

Nineteen sixty-eight is the year of the revolt of the black athlete in amateur (and to a lesser extent professional) American sports. For the truth is out; like any other American institution, sports has deliberately suppressed and oppressed the black man. The myth of course was that sports was the great social equalizer, especially boxing.

The obvious reason for barring Negroes from or limiting them to certain athletic competitions was to insure for whites the "truths" of the myths that they were forever to be superior to blacks across the board and in every respect. One tear in that prefabrication and the whole cloth of white supremacy could be ripped from seam to seam. On the surface, however, boxing, long before any other sport, appeared to offer the young black the best opportunity to climb up the economic and social ladder. Even today it remains so. Black and brown kids still bounce around street corners on their toes, their left hooks dazzling to see as they tease the faces of friends, their right crosses assuming the speed and power of howitzer shells, their heads bobbing and ducking cutely. Yes, they still do it, and those who make it represent the black and brown Us's, muted perhaps today, but Us all the same.

I remember the June night in 1937 when Joe Louis became the second black heavyweight champion in boxing history. There were about twenty-five radios on our block, all tuned loudly to the same station. When Louis got to Braddock in the eighth round, Negroes poured out of their homes, our family with them, and into the street. Joe Louis was Us! We were Him! There was a tear in the prefabrication.

The first black heavyweight champion was John Arthur Johnson—Jack Johnson. In setting down this play, Sackler has followed the pertinent points of Johnson's bitter life, telescoped others without losing any effectiveness—indeed, adding much that primes the play for today. A Texan, Johnson, as many other Negro boxers at that time, fairly caught hell, but in 1908 he followed the then heavyweight champion, Tommy Burns, to Australia and there in Sydney, Burns lowered his ban against fighting Negroes—for money. He said: "They want me to fight that nigger, Jack Johnson. I shall want six thousand pounds win, lose or draw." Burns got his money and Johnson, taunting him as Muhammed Ali was to taunt Ernie Terrell some fifty years later, proceeded viciously to pound Burns into a pulp, carrying him fourteen incredible rounds to do so. Unofficially, Johnson was the new heavyweight champion of the world, a fact that shook the white world, particularly America, to its very roots.

But it was the writer-journalist Jack London, four years from covering the Russo-Japanese War in which the Russians were so severely beaten, the originator of the phrase he coined in that war, "The Yellow Peril" (which intrigued Kaiser Wilhelm, spurred Teddy Roosevelt to an immediate build-up of the American navy, and set Woodrow Wilson to trembling on the eve of World War I), who first sounded the alarm from ringside where he was reporting for the New York *Herald*: ". . . one thing now remains. Jim Jeffries must now emerge from his alfalfa farm and remove that golden smile from Jack Johnson's face. Jeff, it's up to you. The White Man must be rescued."

The racist forces in America moved quickly behind Jeffries, who, like a host of the grandest white fighters in boxing history, had refused to fight Negroes. He had retired four years earlier, undefeated. Tex Ricard promoted the fight, parlaying the racist ballyhoo into a paying crowd of 42,000 in Reno on July 4, 1910. Johnson punished and taunted Jeffries ("How do you feel, Jim?") for fourteen rounds too, before he put him away and became the official heavyweight champion of the world.

Eight Negroes were lynched because Johnson won.

Having failed to dethrone Johnson in the ring, white forces, public and private, launched an attack on his personal life that drove his first wife to suicide and sent Johnson to Europe to avoid going to jail on trumped-up charges. He spent about two years in Europe. He went into show business, fought sparingly, avoiding other Negro boxers as often as he could. Tutored by Belmonte and Joselito, he also fought a bull in the Barcelona ring. On the whole his life abroad was bitter.

In the meantime, a "White Hope" was uncovered, Jess Willard, and Johnson left Europe and the war to defend his title in Havana on April 5, 1915.

Johnson took charge early in the fight but went on the defensive in the teen rounds. During the twenty-fifth round, his second wife, Lucille, left her seat. In the twenty-sixth, Willard, leading with a left, followed with a right uppercut (once Johnson's most lethal blow) and Johnson slid down on his back. As the referee counted over him, almost casually it seemed to some, the champion, whose tenure was to end in seconds, shaded his eyes from the hot Oriente Province sun. White Hope had become White Fact, finally.

Johnson returned to the States and served nine months of a one-year sentence in Leavenworth, living, many reporters claimed, as high on the hog there as he had at times in Paris or London. And Johnson spoke of a $50,000 package which was speedily denied by all parties. What good after all was a "White Hope" if it had to be bought, if Johnson had been dealt short time in jail and long count in money?

This, yes, *this*, is Howard Sackler's big point. The playwright's final stage directions send a chill to spread slowly along the spinal column with its essential truth: "The KID rides on their shoulders: . . . his smashed and reddened face is barely visible —HE resembles the lifelike wooden saints in Catholic processions . . ."

ROMARE BEARDEN

I MET *Romare Bearden through the sculptor Paul von Ringleheim in 1967. I'd known Paul a couple of years; he is a good sculptor, and, I'm told, possibly a great one.*

Until that meeting in my apartment I knew nothing about Bearden, but that wasn't amazing, since I know very little about painting anyhow. However, from that time on we called each other infrequently, had a couple of lunches and then were thrown together for the formation of the Black Academy of Arts and Letters.

In the fall of 1969, Bearden told me that a young man, a painter and poet himself, M. Bunche Washington, was designing a book which would be composed of Bearden's work. Bearden suggested to Washington that I do the introduction to the book; it would be the first on Bearden, and contain color plates. The publisher at the time was Chelsea House.

I lunched with Washington and Andy Norman of Chelsea House, and I agreed to do the introduction. Once it was set, I sat down later with Bearden in his studio-apartment, a large loft on Canal Street, and we talked. We went over his paintings. He didn't discuss them in detail; he let me see what I could see. I'd had reservations about writing about art, yet I've always been excited by good and great works. Indeed, I've seen them in many places in the world. Looking at art is like getting into an interview; you must let yourself flow into it, pores open, senses quivering. This is the way, Bearden told me, one should react to art.

After studying his paintings and reading everything about the man I could lay my hands on, I wrote the intro, checking back with Bearden and Washington to make certain of my informa-

tion. Washington liked the piece, and handed it in to Chelsea House. The Chelsea House offices are on West 40th Street, between Fifth and Sixth Avenues, overlooking Bryant Park. It got its start by publishing, with a great deal of fanfare, an old Sears, Roebuck catalogue.

In my contract with Chelsea, I was to be paid not only a flat fee for doing the introduction, but also a percentage of any European sales. Things got off on the wrong foot immediately, because Chelsea was long overdue with its first payment of the fee. When this was resolved, I had to hassle for the second part of the fee. Rarely were my calls returned. My letters went unanswered. What was it going to take? When I'd exhausted every socially accepted method to collect my money, I bopped down to the office, pulled my Black Power routine, i.e.: "I'm gonna burn this motherfucker down," and went home to await the arrival of my check by hand messenger. No such luck.

It was approaching the summer of 1970, and I was readying to leave the city with my family. Then I finally reached Andy Norman and he told me that Chelsea House was having financial problems and there'd be a delay in my getting the last check. I suspected that I might never get it. In the meantime, Washington was trying to find another publisher; Bearden was disgusted because after so many years of working without recognition, it was starting to pour in. I could understand his wanting to have out a book that firmly and permanently set forth his achievements outside the museums and galleries.

Finally, Washington got Abrams, a prominent art publisher, to do the book. I gave up the European rights to avoid additional complications, and hastily took the final check Washington secured for me. The three of us, Bearden, Washington and myself, were thoroughly soured by our dealings with Chelsea House. I didn't feel, as I have sometimes, that as a writer I was being shortchanged again. Rather, I felt very close to Washington and Bearden as a result of our experience. For in microcosm, what happened to us was what was happening every day to artists, and particularly to black artists. Here you had a first-

rate book designer, a world-famous painter and a struggling writer, all black, walking the plank together.

Since that time Bearden has had three major shows, one at the Museum of Modern Art in New York, and one in Geneva, Switzerland, 1970 and 1971, and a third in Washington about the same time.

I once knew a great photographer, who died young, who would not photograph her friends; she didn't want to know them as the camera might catch them. But I like doing articles on my friends; not any friend or every friend, of course. For the written word for me says what I cannot, will not speak, because there are some things that cannot ever be spoken; they are already understood. The article about a friend therefore becomes mainly a communication to other people about a rare friendship.

I WORK out of a response and need to redefine the image of man in the terms of the Negro experience I know best."

Romare Bearden said that a long time ago. It is exactly what thousands of black artists are saying today. If the collective human experience of the people of this nation is to be truthfully described, it can no longer be drawn as a totally white experience. It was never a completely white nation; it will never be a completely white nation.

Bearden addresses himself to this point when he says, "I have some interest in the truth—at least in presenting my view of what it is."

His truth is both personal and black. Black because he could not help it and personal because, working out of that skin, he must stamp BEARDEN across his time, rein it in and change its direction. It is most cliché to say that he desires a black truth, but the essence of that is that it must by its very presence alter the white truth that abounds not only in this land, but throughout the world. Black truth *projects* upon white consciousness another, more truthful image of man. Clichés need not be without thundering validity.

Bearden's works first and foremost give us an archetypal black man whose journey through the hell of America is pronounced in every line of his face, body and background, in every plane so subtly arranged. Looking at Bearden's work, I seem to be looking at subjects distorted by the soft movement of water in a shallow creek. In those "distortions" I see the black psyche pulsating mysteriously with contradictions of joy, defeat, victory, endurance and relationship to the whole of humankind.

There is no measuring, not by any yardstick yet devised, the amount of thought, work and experiences that brought Bearden to utilize the concepts he now displays in his paintings. But, after so many years in Harlem, in Europe, in south Greenwich Village, digging with black eyes and ears, feeling with a black heart, he has arrived with his gift to us. What is more important, as though keeping sidereal time with the events that have affected this nation in the last fifteen years, he had arrived in the proper moment when the whole crest of black awareness rushes back against the tide to break it.

What do I know about "Romy"?

I met him three years ago. He is a big man, gentle to the point of being shy. That, however, is deceptive. He does his thing so quietly that you don't know he's just gone ahead and done it. He is his own man, owing no other man anything.

We discussed at that first meeting the possibility of our working together for a large national magazine for which I had been writing for three years. Bearden would illustrate what I wrote. He had a keen interest in the Caribbean where his wife, Nannette, hails from. There was not much interest in our project at the magazine. I cite this not because I have an ax to grind, but because it may make you understand better the obstacles black artists have had to face. Not only was the magazine not interested in our project, but it was no longer interested in me.

There had been a change of editors, and this one decided he would no longer publish material by or about black people. The magazine was now going to concentrate on the "beautiful people." Blacks were not among them.

Of course, Romy needed no explanation. He simply returned to his job out on Long Island. He is a black man and such experiences are part of the daily lives of Negroes. They do not escape it because they are painters; in fact, they feel the edge of the knife even more keenly. Painters, like moviemakers, deal with the images of things, of people, and audiences and many critics do not *like* to see the images that are a reflection of a reality they have always denied.

But they fail to see in Bearden's work the triumph the painter sings that black people have survived in spite of everything.

He himself is a survivor. He was born in Charlotte, North Carolina, but, after public schools, graduated from New York University with a science degree, having majored in mathematics. He had done cartoons for the school paper and for the *Afro-American,* a weekly newspaper. At the Art Students League (for he had decided that teaching math was not for him) he studied with George Grosz and was introduced to artists like Kollwitz and Daumier, whose work was mostly social commentary.

There was much social comment then, during the Depression, and young Bearden saw that "art techniques were simply the means that enabled an artist to communicate a message—which, as I saw it then, was essentially a social, if not a political one."

Politically, it was a time of expediency. The fascists chomped up Spain, bit off Ethiopia, parts of Middle Europe and the great powers let them. Socially at home, black people were a silent, suffering, lynchable minority. We were, to be frank, content with our lot because we were unable to do anything about it. True, people were run off farms; true, the first poor people's march on Washington composed of veterans took place. No one was lynched when the banks took the houses; none of the veterans was lynched for asking a bonus for service in the First World War. Only black people, some of them veterans, were lynched.

Then came World War II and Bearden went to it, in the American pattern in a segregated army. He became a sergeant in the 372nd Infantry Regiment, a unit that had garnered hundreds of medals fighting with the French army in World War I. In the Second World War it was seen to it that the 372nd would not repeat its earlier deeds. Eleven years Romy's junior, I know of that war, and know that nothing so embitters a man, nothing turns him around quite so much as to be placed in a situation where he is the defender of a democracy that has already proved to be his most vicious enemy. To be embittered is to be involved in the process of *un*learning and, at the same time, *re*learning.

These, perhaps, are some of the experiences that produced the painter Romare Bearden, and drew forth his own quiet and forceful declaration of war:

"I cannot divorce myself from the inequities that are around me."

Every artist must make his statement. That is in fact much of what being an artist is all about. More important, every artist demands the statement from himself. He must, therefore, make himself vulnerable. He must make choices. He must say, Here I am. Know me. Hate me. Love me. I will no longer be ignored. I will be counted.

Bearden.

By 1950, now thirty-six, Bearden was studying in Paris, well on his way to drafting his statement. He was there to paint, but as a writer learns from reading, so Bearden learned more studying other painters than painting himself. Before the war he had worked almost exclusively in tempera. Then the water color influence of Grosz gave way to oils; they became thinner, almost like water color.

The montage appealed greatly to Bearden, perhaps as a reflection of life the way it had kaleidoscoped before him. He painted and glued, then "tore sections of the paper away, always attempting to tear upward and across the picture plane" until some motif appeared. After, he added more paper and color to finish the painting. Behind this method lay his in-depth studies of the compositions of Vermeer, De Hooch, Rembrandt; also the Japanese portraitists and the Renaissance works of Duccio and Pietro Lorenzetti. From the cubists Picasso, Braque and Léger he took back what was rightfully his. Cubism sprang from the precise sculpture of black Africa, examples of which had been brought to Europe by Leo Frobenius before World War I. But as far as Bearden was concerned, the cubists misunderstood the use of space. His modifications are personal and in keeping with the statement he had to make. He says: "I do want my language to be strict and classical, in the manner of the great Benin heads, for example." Thus his cubes were stretched into rectangles; he stretched out space.

Bearden in recent years has emerged as a genius of collage and projection; he has employed some aspects of the documentary film and he tries to see what the camera sees. Beyond what we see at the first glimpse of a Bearden painting is the rectangular structure, the planes of which are shifted either slightly or exaggeratedly. "Fractured" is the term the artist uses.

Ostensibly most of his works seem to feature faces, the faces that peer out of their planes as though looking right through you. There is a superficial similarity in those black faces which possess, even without the masks Bearden utilizes so deftly, masklike, stricken qualities. They seem at once to accuse and suffer from some unnamed terror. But Romy's paintings are of course more than just faces.

Once a song writer, Bearden is close to music. Time and time again we see figures holding guitars. He has chosen this instrument to depict timelessness, for the stringed instrument is perhaps the first one ever devised by man for the purpose of adding music to his life. Stringed instruments abound the world over, in the most remote islands to the most crowded cities. It is most ironic to consider that it came from the bow, also found in most ancient cultures, and it is with us today.

The guitar is an instrument loved by the most backward of American hillbillies as well as the musically sophisticated. If we think of the great Spanish guitarists, with the echoes of Africa in their strings and fingers, we naturally rate the guitar a classical instrument.

Consider the best of modern music, and the guitar becomes both a driving rhythm instrument and an instrument for fanciful solo flights. Mondrian saw modern popular music as rigid formations; Middleton sees it as being fluid. Bearden puts it where it should be: with people. *Jazz 1930's Savory* and *Jazz 1930's Chicago Grand Terrace* place us even closer to Bearden's love for music and the men who make it.

I think Romy's attachment to music relates very much to his work. I think of music and musicians when I look at a Bearden projection or painting, seeing in them the same "distortions" I heard in the music of the Forties and Fifties, which was the music of a new jazz much closer to the vibrations of black people than anything that had gone before. The assonances and dissonances. Musicians like Howard McGhee, Charlie Parker, Miles Davis, Thelonius Monk, Sonny Stitt, Sonny Rollins, John Coltrane (plus a newer, younger contingent) blew in "color," projected upon what was ordinary, acceptable, usual, mundane—white—a different sound, a changed pattern that was augmented, diminished and shaped by the personal and group experiences of the black men involved. They seemed to distort sound in order to re-create it.

Bearden is not only a lover of music, but of history, too. The worst kind, for he is a secret tippler of history (by which I mean, that which has been black-conceived as well as that which has been white-conceived). He knows his history and applies it in much the same manner as a mathematician uses his figures. With such a sense of sureness he has juxtaposed—inserted into classical postures his ordinary, broken black subjects and scapes as in *The Annunciation,* for example, or *Two Women in a Harlem Courtyard,* or *Mother and Child.* Here, as in music, he is augmenting, adding another dimension to what we have always found to be pleasant and constant. Here too Bearden lifts the much demeaned, much pitied and often feared American black to a position of the highest humanity, and the poignancy is shattering. But there is something else: the Dogon masks utilized in *Mother and Child* possess in addition to poignancy, an extremely eerie quality, a confrontation with the familiar which has suddenly become unfamiliar, even threatening.

It is possible that history lies wrapped in the cocoon of ritual; that could explain Bearden's attention to ritual. It is like an umbilical cord tying peoples together in the same performances in which they find strength. In another painter this interest in ritual would be curious; in Bearden it is simply another facet of his interests and personality.

A number of his projections and paintings are called "The Prevalence of Ritual" and they depict variously a baptism, a funeral, a conjure woman, train watching and other examples of black life. Some of that life is rural, some of it urban, but all of it has that continuity of mystery we have come to know through Bearden's use of colors, parts of photos and rectangles; they are a Bearden colophon. We know that Bearden's own life in part, and the lives of his forebears to a much larger degree, encompassed rural southern living. Does one escape completely from such memories?

No. Not Bearden. In fact, he attends to these depictions of black life and living with utmost care. But trains intrude upon some of the rural scenes; they have a twofold meaning. The trains are the new technology rushing through the cropland, numbering its days; and they are the vehicles by which many Negroes will move from the cotton to the concrete North to *The Street*, perhaps, or *The Dove*.

Bearden makes you aware of the difference. Space suggests more space in the paintings of the rural south, while the Harlem scenes burst upon you, people, faces, eyes, going in every direction, tenement windows not quite concealing still other faces, other eyes. Here the journey from the cottonfields has ended;

here are a transplanted people who barely recall their rituals, but no matter, new ones are to be found, as in *The Illusionists at 4 p.m.* and the *Two Women in a Harlem Courtyard*.

Romare Bearden has said that it was not his "aim to paint about the Negro in America in terms of propaganda." Rather, he paints his people "as passionately and dispassionately as Brueghel painted the life of Flemish people of his day."

It seems to me that Romy's dispassion lies in his years-long search for the precise manner in which to passionately render his people. Surely the men with whom he shared studios at 243 W. 125th Street and 306 W. 141st Street in New York were some of the most passionate black artists of the time: Jacob Lawrence, Richard Wright, Claude McKay, Charles Alston, Ralph Ellison and Mike Bannarn. All were in search for the tools with which to make their statements. Perhaps Bearden helped them; perhaps they helped Bearden. In any case, the tools were discovered, the statements made, but none has said what Bearden is saying today. He is indeed unique. He is the man who said, "I do not need to go looking for 'happenings,' the absurd, or the surreal, because I have seen these things out of my studio window on 125th Street."

Seeing and interpreting are two different tasks; passing on one's interpretation to others is still another. Therein lies an artist's uniqueness, his ability to share with others what he has experienced, for "painting, art, is about something," Bearden writes, and it is a something palpable and meaningful. It is, in fact, Bearden sharing Bearden.

The young black poet Don L. Lee says "each poem is the poet." If this is true it follows that each Bearden painting is Bearden. His statement. His view. His past, present and future.

And because it is Romare Bearden all this is exhilaratingly healthful. "His people" are not only black; they are all people in the final analysis, and a stronger, wiser, more vigorous people because the painter chose to "redefine the image of man" out of his own black experiences. Bearden has immeasurably enriched us with his work; we mirror what we are to him: fractures, juxtaposed planes, flat colors, masks and parts of photographs. We are then many parts, many angles. To understand that, as Bearden does, is to begin to become whole, which is what truth, forever a fraction, is really all about.

CHESTER HIMES—
MY MAN HIMES

MOST YOUNG, *newly rabid readers of black literature don't know who Chester Himes is, which is unfortunate. People who know him consider him to be a novelist, but Himes still writes articles for European papers and magazines and got his start in the United States publishing short stories and articles, many of which appeared in the now defunct* Abbot's Monthly.

As a writer identified only by a prison number, he published in Esquire *six short stories from 1934 to 1936. When he was released from the Ohio State Penitentiary and appeared at the* Esquire *offices obviously a black man, his publishing days there at least were over. But he went on to publish articles in the* Journal of the NAACP *and the* Journal of the Urban League.

This interview I did with Himes requires no headnote. I include it here, with his kind permission, because I feel that young writers, particularly young black writers, can derive much from Himes' raps about writing as it ties into everyday living. No other writer that I know of, black or white, has ever spoken so candidly about his profession.

As the interview was going to press for the first issue of Amistad *from which it is taken, I received a special delivery letter from Himes. He asked me to delete the names of certain people about whom he'd been openly and angrily critical when the interview was taped. He felt, after seeing the typed interview, that he'd been too harsh. As it developed, those same people he'd tried to protect continued their practices which had made him critical in the first place, and Himes was forced to seek legal redress—which is almost nonexistent for writers.*

The interview itself was long and we often got off the track.

My wife spent most of one summer transcribing the tapes at the same time I was editing the material into block sections and headings that would make sense in the reading. Without a doubt this was my most satisfying interview and I was grateful for the tape recorder. Sometimes I've used that instrument and come away feeling that it hadn't really captured anything.

I couldn't think of a better way to end this section than to include Himes' interview, after which nothing more can be said about the position of the black writer in the United States today.

NEW YORK was chilly that Friday, disappointing after a couple of days of hot weather. Then spring had beat a hasty retreat. London the next day was London: chilly, gray and somber at Heathrow. Then we boarded a Trident, as tight and crowded a plane as the Caravelle, and split with a full passenger list, mostly all British except us, to Spain and Chester Himes.

Lori brightened considerably when we crossed the Pyrenees. (Once we had driven through them, back and forth from the Spanish to the French borders, pausing now and again to picnic in the hot green areas between the snow-filled slopes.) Not long after, the Mediterranean flowed out beneath us as the coast of eastern Spain bent to the west, and we parpared to land in Alicante.

It was clear, bright and warm there, and going down the ramp I was conscious once more of the strange sweetness that lingers in the Spanish air, as though the entire nation had been freshly dipped in sherry or cognac. Down on the tarmac we saw Chester and Lesley waving, and I felt great relief. For Himes is sixty-one now and is not well, although he takes extremely good care of himself, mostly under Lesley's guidance. He smokes a great deal less, drinks mostly wine and adheres to a strict diet. Himes' life has been filled with so many disasters, large and small, that

I lived in dread that one of these would carry him away so that I would no longer have the chance to see or talk to him.

I suppose it is known that I admire the man and his work. This began late in 1945, when I was a boy of twenty. I was then on Guam in the Mariana Islands with my outfit, the 17th Special Naval Construction Battalion, waiting to be shipped home. There was not much to do. The war was over; we were all waiting.

I was a hospital corpsman and we held two sick calls a day; otherwise we slept, swam or read. Mostly I read and tried to write the kind of jive poetry a twenty-year-old will write. I don't remember how the novel came into my hands, but I never forgot it. It was *If He Hollers Let Him Go*. The author was Chester B. Himes. Years later, long after it was published, I read *Third Generation*. Until 1962 that was the extent of my Himes.

That year I met Himes in Carl Van Vechten's apartment in the San Remo on Central Park West. I had met "Carlo" when *Night Song* was published in 1961. Van Vechten met, photographed, knew and corresponded with every black writer who ever came down the pike; now that I look back, perhaps he anticipated their importance in and to American letters fifty years before anyone else.

If anything, Himes was even more handsome than his photographs. Not terribly big, about five-nine or ten. One remembers his eyes mostly; they sit in that incredible face upon which ravages show—but which they have been unable to destroy—and at certain angles the long-lashed eyes are soft, *soft*, as though clinging to some teen-aged dream of love and goodness and justice. The eyes have remained that way, although today, at certain other angles they clearly reveal the pain of life as a black man and artist.

Himes is perhaps the single greatest naturalistic American writer living today. Of course, no one in the literary establishment is going to admit that; they haven't and they won't. Reviews of his books generally wind up in the last half of the

Sunday New York *Times Book Review,* if they are reviewed at all. Himes will tell you that he doesn't care; that all his career he has been shuffled under the table. Perhaps this is, after all, the smallest of hurts he has suffered. He is a fiercely independent man and has been known to terminate friendships and conversations alike with two well-chosen, one-syllable words. Worse than the words is his silence. I swear I have felt him glowering at me across the Atlantic from Paris at times.

Soon after I met Himes for the first time, Van Vechten told me: "Chester doesn't like many people. He likes you."

Well, I liked him. We corresponded regularly after our meeting; we exchanged books and he gave me a quote for *Sissie;* as I recall, it wasn't used. Himes was still publishing in France in the Gallimard *Série Noire.* Although he had won the Grand Prix for detective novels for *La Reine des Pommes* (*For Love of Immabelle,* it was called here) he was still living pretty much from hand to mouth. I managed to see him once in Paris, but most often I saw him here after he arrived on the *France.* He stays at the Hotel Albert on 10th Street and University Place when he comes. In Europe I missed him often enough, for he would move frequently to avoid having his work disturbed by other expatriate Brothers. Then he would undergo periodic fits of disgust with the Parisians and go to Scandinavia or Holland. Sometimes, through Daniel Guérin ("The French expert on the Brother," Himes says), he went to La Ciotat near the Riviera to be isolated and to work. (La Ciotat, Himes says with the pride of association, is where André Schwarz-Bart wrote *The Last of the Just.*)

Chester Himes finally got a piece of what he deserves through the American publication of *Pinktoes.* He was back with an American publisher after almost a decade away from them. His detectives, Gravedigger Jones and Coffin Ed Smith, came back to America in hardcover after titillating (one of Himes' favorite words in describing the effect black people have on white people) the French for several years. The early novels of their adventures had been spirited away, more or less, by softcover publishers—often without Himes' knowing they were being published in America. He would write and ask me to confirm their presence, for word would have been brought to him by visitors to the Continent. That he was being paid little or no money for these rights only supported his contention that publishing was a brutal business and brutal businesses always take advantage of black people.

In both 1965 and 1966 we missed Himes in Europe; he had reserved a hotel for us in Paris and we were to have dinner, but he had fled France, leaving his flat to Melvin Van Peebles, the film-maker. We were to visit him in La Ciotat, but he'd packed up and taken off again. The next time we saw him was in 1967 when he and Lesley and their Siamese cat, Griot, flew to New York. That was when he started working on a film treatment of *Cotton Comes to Harlem* for Sam Goldwyn, Jr. (I read the screenplay by Ossie Davis and Arnold Perl while in Alicante and thought that if Davis as director could put on film what he has put on paper, the movie would be a very special thing.)

So, it was almost two years to the date when we saw them again in Alicante. Lesley had reserved for us around the corner from their small apartment. Lori and I unpacked, grabbed a couple hours of sleep, then went around the corner to pick them up for dinner. Chester and Lesley lived on the ninth floor of number 2 Calle Duque du Zaragoza, a step off Rambla Mendez Muñoz, four short blocks from the Promenade and the port.

With some writers you get the feeling that you are interrupting their work; that they wish you to be gone, out of their homes, out of their lives. I've never had that feeling with Himes; he has always made me feel welcome whether it was in the Albert, in the Quarter in Paris (I repaid the hospitality that time by falling asleep in front of the fire and holding up dinner) or in Alicante. Besides, Himes deserved a break away from his typewriter. He is always at it. If not books, then letters; he has always been a compulsive letter writer. (He once wrote a letter to President Roosevelt.) So I was, I think, a welcome interruption.

While Lori and Lesley shopped (Lori has a thing about Spanish eyeglasses, that never fit once we are back home) Himes and I talked endlessly in the room he uses as a study, in the living room with its balcony that overlooks the city and the port, and on walks down to and along the Promenade. There was never a time when I dared to be without the recorder, for out of Himes pours so much, at any time and at any place.

He's slower getting about than he used to be, but intellectually he is as sharp as ever and his opinions as blunt and honest as always. I am always impressed by how well he has kept up with what's going on in the United States. Most expatriate blacks I know tend not to care. Not so Chester Himes; his information is as fresh as the morning paper. Another thing: over the years he has repeated many anecdotes to me. What amazes me is that they are always the same. They are never embroidered or exaggerated. They are exactly the same. Most of us, with the passage of time, tend to embellish.

Last fall Chester and Lesley moved into their new home near Javea, still in Spain, still in the province of Alicante. We were to have seen it one day, but something came up so we were unable to make the trip.

It gave me the greatest pleasure to be able to see Himes again, to see him at a time when a kind of physical comfort was coming his way at last; to see him still producing long, articulate and sensitive works. He let me read the first volume of his autobiography, *The Quality of Hurt* (394 pages, ending in 1955). It is a fantastic, masculine work whose pages are haunted by vistas of France and Spain, of family life in the United States, of his first marriage, of Richard Wright and Robert Graves and others. American male writers don't produce manly books. Himes' autobiography is that of a man. So we talked, and the sound of bronze churchbells filled the background, and the sweet smell of Spain blocked up our nostrils and my man Himes rapped . . .

This Publishing Business

Williams: How do you feel about the double standard of payment, say, advances—this amount for black writers and that amount for white writers?

Himes: It's pitiful, you know, it's really pitiful, pitiful. You know, the double standard of advances is so pitiful. Even friends took advantage. . . . I got a thousand dollar advance for each of my last three books.

Williams: Really?

Himes: Yes. And they resold them to Dell for $15,000 reprint.

Williams: Each?

Himes: Yeah, and then in the end they didn't want *Blind Man* [*Blind Man with a Pistol*] and I thought—

Williams: Goddamn! Are you kidding me?

Himes: I'm telling you the truth. You know, I have never been paid anything in advance. I'm the lowest-paid writer on the face of the earth. So . . .

Williams: Now wait a minute, Chester, people have known you since the forties. They know everything that you produced and they offered you a thousand dollar advance for each of these three books?

Himes: Oh, yes, that's what they paid, a thousand dollar advance.

Williams: Goddamn!

Himes: You talk about double standards. I find this quite annoying. Y'know, I have been in desperate circumstances financially, which everybody has known and they've just taken advantage of this—friends and enemies and everybody alike. I remember in *The Third Generation;* I was paid a two thousand dollar advance and they resold the reprint rights to Victor Weybright of NAL for ten thousand dollars, and that's the money I came to Europe on. But then when I got broke in Europe and I had to spend a year's time helping ——, the woman I was living with at the time, write a book of her own which never made a cent . . .

Williams: That was the book you said was much better than the Caldwell-type books—*The Silver Chalice?*

Himes: *The Silver Altar.* I have it in my autobiography. You can read it if you like.

Williams: Can I take it and read it tonight?

Himes: Sure, you can read it tonight or you can take it back to

New York as far as I'm concerned. [Laughter.] I have two copies. I think if you want to do any background on me, some of the things you should know you'll find in it. But going back to the payment, you see. Now, I couldn't find a publisher for *The Primitive*. I was very broke and desperate for some money, and I finally thought that I would send it to Weybright because they had begun to publish originals. So I sent it to Weybright, and Weybright wrote me this long letter about how we'll pay you a thousand dollar advance on this because we feel it's best for the author to have a small advance and have substantial accruals [laughter]. I'll never forget that phrase. I never got any accruals, substantial or otherwise, from that book [laughter], until five or six years later they brought out a new edition for which they paid a fifteen hundred dollar advance. That's why I began writing these detective stories, as a matter of fact. Marcel Duhamel, the editor of the *Série Noire*, had translated *If He Hollers Let Him Go*. The *Série Noire* was the best-paid series in France. So they started off paying me a thousand dollar advance, which was the same as the Americans were paying, and they went up to fifteen hundred dollars, which was more.

Double standards are so pitiful. Well, as I said, the American system toward the Negro writer is to take great advantage of the fact that the black writer in America is always in a state of need, and they take great advantage of that need. They take advantage just willy-nilly. Then one or two will get through. Not one or two—I mean, the American system works like this: *Time* magazine and a few other sources and the New York *Times* and all feel that they'd like to be king-makers of a writer and they put him in a position so that he can earn some money, like Baldwin. Now Baldwin got into a position where he could command sizeable advances and royalties. But the average black writer is never paid in comparison to the white writer.

Williams: What is the most you ever made on an advance of a book?

Himes: Morrow, I suppose. Morrow paid four thousand five hundred advance, which was just for *Blind Man with a Pistol* . . . No—that's right, Putnam paid a ten thousand dollar advance for *Pinktoes*. Walter Minton was buying up Girodias' [Olympia Press] books. He had been successful with *Lolita* and *Candy* and he was anxious to get *Pinktoes*. Stein & Day had offered me seventy-five hundred, so Minton upped it twenty-five hundred. And then Stein & Day and Putnam started a lawsuit against one another, and that's why they published it jointly. They figured it'd be more expensive to go to court so they just decided that they would work out a system, a very elaborate one, so elaborate that I ran into difficulties with Stein & Day because—Putnam kept the trade book edition, they were responsible for that and for collecting my royalties—Stein & Day were responsible for the subsidiary rights and the reprint and foreign rights and so forth. And finally Stein & Day began rejecting various offers from foreign countries. The last one—the one that really made me angry—was that they had an offer from a German publisher to bring out a German edition of *Pinktoes* and Stein & Day rejected that, and I went to the Author's Guild and to the lawyers to see what I could do. And they said that that was the most complicated contract they had ever seen. Even now, even a couple of weeks ago I wrote to Walter Minton to find out what happened to my royalties because Corgi Books brought out a paperback edition in England which has seemingly been very successful. I know that they have reprinted the jacket design so I figure they must have sold quite a number in the first design to have brought out a different one.

Williams: Well, you know the younger black writers back home always say that Chester Himes has given away more books than most people have ever written.

Himes: Yeah, that's right, I must tell you the truth. You know that the younger generation of black writers are getting paid far more than I'm getting paid, even now. Even now I get paid so little. I just got disgusted with the whole business.

Actually, I have a good agent now. Rosalyn [Targ] for me is a very good agent because she will fight for whatever she can get, you know. And she tries everything she can.

Williams: How about some of the experiences, other than royalties, that you've had with publishers? You once wrote me something about an award you were supposed to get at Doubleday when Buck Moon was your editor.

Himes: Yes, well you know, *If He Hollers* sold I think it was eight thousand copies before publication. That was Doubleday. Well, then *If He Hollers* hit the best-seller list. Then I received a number of letters from all over the country. I'd been in Los Angeles and San Francisco—one brother was living in Cincinnati, one was down in Durham, North Carolina, teaching at the North Carolina College—and I received letters from all of these people and other people whom I'd forgotten, that they'd been in stores to buy copies of *If He Hollers* and they had been told that book stores had sold out, and had ordered copies, and the orders were not being filled.

Williams: That's something that happens to me all the time, too.

Himes: So I went to Doubleday and complained and said the same thing and showed them the letters, and at that time Doubleday was being run by five vice-presidents. I think about a month afterward Ken McCormick was promoted to editor-in-chief, and he was in control of Doubleday. He became the top vice-president, or maybe he was the president. So I talked to him. He said my complaint didn't make any sense because if they published a book they were going to sell it. I couldn't argue with this. But it got to be rather dirty. Doubleday was in the *Time* and *Life* building on 49th Street at that time and I was going up in the elevator with Hilda Simms and her husband and a joker who was doing free-lance promoting for Doubleday, and I was telling them that the book orders weren't being filled and this joker rushed in and told Ken McCormick that I was complaining about Doubleday. So I got in Ken's office and we had some bad words, you know. I said to Ken McCormick, "You know that you got this black corner here . . ." He said, "No, we haven't. It's not a black corner," and I said, "You got Bucklin Moon, he's the head of the black department in Doubleday." So then I didn't get any more information from Doubleday concerning anything. So, I think seven years later when I was living with Vandi [Haygood], Buck stopped by one day and Vandi was in the kitchen making some drinks, and Buck said that I was right about the whole thing, but he had felt it would do me more harm to tell me the truth than to let me remain in ignorance. That what had happened was Doubleday was giving an award called the George Washington Carver Memorial Award of twenty-five hundred dollars each year for the best book. And that year Doubleday had *If He Hollers,* the outstanding book on the black theme that they had published. But there was one white woman editor whose name was never told to me, who said that *If He Hollers* made her disgusted and it made her sick and nauseated, and if *If He Hollers* was selected for this memorial award that she would resign. They gave the award to a book called *Mrs. Palmer's Honey,* written by some white woman. It was about a Negro maid in St. Louis.

When Doubleday advertised *Mrs. Palmer's Honey* in the *Saturday Review,* they said this book has a nice story that will appeal to a lot of people and it was not like some other books that they had published, and they referred, but not by actual name, to *If He Hollers Let Him Go,* and called it a "series of epithets punctuated by spit." This was their own advertisement. I complained about this, too. But what had actually happened to *If He Hollers* was that this woman editor—Doubleday was printing their own books in Garden City—had telephoned to their printing department in Garden City and ordered them to stop the printing. So they just arbitrarily stopped the printing of *If He Hollers* for a couple of weeks or so during the time when it would have been a solid best-seller.

Williams: You were at Knopf too, for a while. *Lonely Crusade* was a Knopf book, wasn't it?

Himes: Yes, well, that's why I went to Knopf. I went to Knopf because of this. I was talking to Van Vechten, whom I had met, and . . .

Williams: You met Van Vechten after *If He Hollers* came out, which would be late '45 or '46.

Himes: That's right. Richard Wright had taken me over to meet him. Dick was going over to get his picture taken. And when Van Vechten was taking his picture he acted so pompous I got hysterical and I was sitting there laughing away and Van Vechten was peeping at me and . . . So he was intrigued with me and we became quite good friends because of that. But Dick was a real friend despite his eccentricities. He had reviewed *If He Hollers Let Him Go* in *PM*, a good review, and took me over to the Book-of-the-Month Club. Well, *If He Hollers* was being distributed by the Book-of-the-Month Club. So when I told Van Vechten that I was unhappy at Doubleday he said that he would talk to Blanche Knopf and she would buy my contract from Doubleday. So she bought the contract ultimately. It wasn't a very large sum because Doubleday had only given me a thousand dollar advance for my next book, and then I went on and wrote *Lonely Crusade*, which she liked very much indeed. I'd say she liked that book as much as any book she ever published. She gave it a very good printing, very nice—you've seen copies of the book, haven't you?

Williams: Oh, sure, sure.

Himes: Very nice book, and she lined up a lot of radio appearances for me. I don't remember all of them now—Mary Margaret McBride, CBS book shows—and I was to talk to the book department at Macy's and Bloomingdale's on the day of publication. So I sent for my father to come to New York from Cleveland and I went out early that morning to go to Macy's and this joker down at Macy's—the head of the book department —was looking guilty and said, "Well, we're going to stop this procedure of having authors speak to the book sellers because they would show favoritism since we couldn't do it for all the authors." So they canceled the whole thing. So then I went over to Bloomingdale's and at Bloomingdale's there were no books, no *Lonely Crusade* on display whatsoever. So I realized that something had happened. The director of Bloomingdale's book department didn't want to talk to me at all. So then I rushed home to get my wife and go to the Mary McBride radio program but she said she'd been trying to get in touch with me because they had received a telegram from the radio that I'd been canceled off that program. And then before the day was over, they canceled me off the CBS program. Then I learned that the Communist Party had launched a real assault on the book.

It had some of the most terrible reviews, one of the most vicious reviews I ever read. The *Daily Worker* had a picture of a black man walking across the page carrying a white flag—catch the caption: "Himes Carries a White Flag." In some of the passages they had they compared the book to the "foul words that came from the cankerous mouth of Bilbo" [Sen., D., Miss.], and so forth.

Williams: Didn't you tell me once that Jimmy Baldwin did a review too?

Himes: Jimmy Baldwin did a review for the Socialist newspaper, *New Leader* I believe, under the heading "History as a Nightmare." I don't remember the gist of the review. But all of the reviews I remember seeing were extremely critical, each for a different reason: *Atlantic Monthly, Newsweek, Commentary, New Masses*—the white press, the black press, the Jewish press, reactionary press—*all.* Willard Motley, whom I had met at a party given for the publication of *Knock on Any Door* at Carl Van Vechten's house, wrote an extremely spiteful review for the Marshall Field newspaper in Chicago.

Williams: Was that the only book that Knopf did for you?

Himes: Yes. Knopf had given me an advance for another book, but then they . . . I had trouble with Knopf too. I tried to have some kind of dialogue with Blanche to discuss some of these reactions. I said, "Now, you have all of these reviews from *Atlantic Monthly, Commentary, New Masses,* the New York *Times,* the *Herald Tribune,* and *Ebony,* the black press. All of these reviews have different complaints about this book, different ways of condemning it. Well, this doesn't make any sense, and these reviews should all be published in an advertisement showing that all of these people from the left, the right, the blacks, the whites, that if all of these people dislike the book there must be some reason. It would stimulate interest; people would want to know why. Because I never found out why everybody disliked this book."

But I know why the black people disliked the book—because they're doing the same thing now that I said at that time was necessary. I had the black protagonist, Lee Gordon, a CIO organizer, say that the black man in America needed more than just a superficial state of equality; he needed special consideration because he was so far behind. That you can't just throw him out there and say, "Give Negroes rights," because it wouldn't work that way. And so this is what most of the black writers had against it; in saying that, of course, by pleading for special privileges for the black people I was calling them inferior.

Williams: And now that's the route that everyone is going.

Himes: Yes.

Williams: Except that they're not saying it. I think a few years ago they were saying it, but now it seems to me that what the kids are saying on the campuses is . . .

Himes: Yes, that's what they're saying, that's what I'm saying. It's the same theme because it's obvious, you know, that the black man in America must have, for an interim period of time, special consideration.

Williams: What about your experiences with editors?

Himes: Well, as a rule, the whole of my experiences has been bad. Over a long period of years the editor whom I got along with best as an editor was Marcel Duhamel, the editor of *Série Noire,* because he was a friend, but more than being a friend he was an honest man, which is very rare among editors. He was honest and straightforward, although he was surrounded by a bunch of dubious people at Gallimard. But he did as much as he could. A journalist from *Combat* once said, "You know, Marcel is a good man, but Marcel is a three-legged duck as far as Gallimard is concerned." I always remembered that. They never really included him until later years. *Série Noire* became so successful that he became a capitalist.

Williams: You know, over the years in many conversations we've had I get the impression that, well, it's more than an impression now, you never found much difference between American and French publishers and editors.

Himes: No, no, I didn't, because the only difference—it goes like this: the French don't have the difficulty that Americans do because most black people that come to France realize that they are from the undeveloped countries and they keep their place.

And very few of them feel any injustice when they're not given the same accord as the French writer. They don't feel that this is unjust.

The American black man is very different from all those black men in the history of the world because the American black has even an unconscious feeling that he wants equality. Whereas most of the blacks of the world don't particularly insist on having equality in the white community. But the American black doesn't have any other community. America, which wants to be a white community, is their community, and there is not the fact that they can go home to their own community and be the chief and sons of chiefs or what not.

Williams: That old lie again, huh?

Himes: [Laughter.] Yeah. The American black man has to make it or lose it in America; he has no choice. That's why I wrote *Cotton Comes to Harlem.* In Garvey's time the "Back to Africa" movement had an appeal and probably made some sense. But it doesn't make any sense now. It probably didn't make sense even then, but it's even *less* logical now, because the black people of America aren't Africans anymore, and the Africans don't want them.

Williams: Yes, I found this to be true.

Himes: Yes, they wouldn't have him in their world, so he has to make it in America.

Williams: You were saying that New American Library once gave you a contract with sixteen pages.

Himes: Yes. Well, I was in Paris, and like George Orwell's book I was down and out in Paris and I had submitted this book, *The Primitive,* to Gallimard. But I was in a hurry and Gallimard was taking their time, so I sent it to NAL. So NAL took it and at the same time they took all of the rights, took every right worth considering, and they sent me a sixteen-page contract to sign. So Gallimard had to buy the book from NAL. What they paid for it I never discovered. I don't remember if anyone ever paid me for that. So at that time I realized that contracts were getting much more intricate than they had been previously, much more detailed. Publishers stipulated their rights. Of course, then publishing was getting to be a big business. The artists who could command a lot of money—and who could command a lot of attention, I should say, from publishers—were also getting more rights, so they could keep their subsidiary rights, even their paperback rights.

Williams: I think there's a move in the direction to recapture these rights for the writers once more. It's going kind of slowly. There're some writers whom I've heard about who manage to keep their subsidiary rights, or most of them, like the reprint rights. I understand Robbins is one of these guys.

Himes: Yes, that's right. The first one who I heard of who was able to keep his subsidiary rights (I heard about but probably a lot of them did before) was Wouk, when he wrote *Marjorie Morningstar*. Well, you see, that's a considerable amount of money. You take a writer like Jean Le Carré. I don't know what Putnam paid him for the advance for the book rights, although Putnam did very well with the book, but Putnam sold the reprint rights for I think twenty-five or thirty thousand dollars, and then Dell, on the first three months of publication of *The Spy Who Came in from the Cold* made three million dollars. So that's a considerable amount of money involved.

Williams: I recall that Lillian Ross story about Ernest Hemingway that appeared in *The New Yorker*, where he got a twenty-five thousand dollar advance from Scribner's. And now these guys are getting like a quarter of a million. What do you think about that? People like Roth and . . .

Himes: Yes, I read that piece. Well, the industry has gotten to the place where they make considerably more money out of, say, Roth's book [*Portnoy's Complaint*]. They'll make more money out of Roth's book probably than the American publishers have out of all of Hemingway, because the industry is so much bigger. The whole process of circulation of books. There's so much advance. You know, America is a very big book market, and I wonder if these people read these books. I suppose they do. But anyway, as long as they get something that will titillate them, they will read them.

I remember when the book industry was very much afraid of

television. They thought that television would do damage to the book industry. It didn't make any difference whatsoever. As a matter of fact, the book industry is very healthy now from the point of view of profit systems.

Williams: Well, I think it's healthier now than it was ten years ago.

Himes: Yes, it's healthier now than it ever was.

Williams: Who's your favorite American publisher in terms of what it does for blacks, producing good books?

Himes: Well, I couldn't say. I don't know enough about American publishers to have an opinion. As far as publishers are concerned, in talking to other people, all publishers, Morrow has a very good reputation as a publisher with other publishers. Has a better reputation I think than Putnam. But as far as publishers are concerned, that is very difficult to say.

Williams: What was the print order for *Blind Man with a Pistol?*

Himes: I don't know. Once upon a time you could get the figures. I couldn't get these from Morrow. As a matter of fact, I haven't been in close contact with them at all.

Personal Worksheet

Williams: Well, how would you place yourself in American letters? [Himes laughs.] You're sixty-one years old now, you've been writing long before *If He Hollers* came out— You've been writing now for thirty-four years.

Himes: Yes, I've been writing since 1934. Let's see, how long is that? My first story in a national magazine was published in *Esquire* in 1934. That's thirty-five years. Well, I don't know where to place myself actually on the American scene of letters because America has a highly organized system of reputation-making which I'm afraid would place me in the bottom echelon. The American communications media are very well organized about what they intend to do and how they intend to show that this person is of great importance and that person is chickenshit.

So they work this out and they make reputations. Not only do they make reputations of writers, which is insignificant, but they take people like Roosevelt and they will set out systematically to break his place in history. They'll spend millions of dollars to do so if they wish. And the same thing happens with the literary scene. That's why I never contemplate it, because I realize the Americans will sit down and they will take a white writer—he will be one that appeals to their fancy, one that has been abroad and clowned around, like Hemingway—and they will set him up and they will make him one of the most famous writers on the face of the earth. And not because of anything he has written, because his work is not that important, but because they wish to have an American up there at the top of the world literature. Anyone reading him will realize that Hemingway is a great imitator of the styles of Ford Madox Ford, James Joyce and D. H. Lawrence. As a matter of fact, if you have read the works of these four writers, you can see the lines, you can see the exact imitation. So there's nothing creative about even Hemingway's form. This was borrowed, as Gertrude Stein says.

But the Americans set out and they made him a legend. Now, it's very difficult for me to evaluate any of the people on the American scene, because if I take my information from the American white communications media then, of course, it is slanted to whatever way they wish to slant it to. So one can't form any opinion, unfortunately.

Williams: Do you foresee the time when you'll ever quit writing?
Himes: Well, no, no I don't foresee it. I mean writing is like . . . I remember I have a line in a book—I've forgotten now what book it was—where I quote [Max] Schmeling. He said a fighter fights, and I went on to say ". . . and a writer writes." That's what I do, that's all I *do*, and I don't foresee that I will quit, as long as I'm able to write. No. I do foresee the fact that age will deteriorate my writing, as it does everyone else's writing. I don't foresee the fact that because age will deteriorate my writing, and that I will realize that I can't do what I could do when I was young (I know damn well that I can't do what I could do

when I was young), that I am going to blow out my brains like Hemingway did when he discovered that.

Williams: It seemed to me when I started reading the first couple of pages of your autobiography, *The Quality of Hurt,* that you were sort of preparing yourself for the time when you wouldn't write anymore. But then I also noticed that this is Volume I, the carbon that I have. How many volumes do you foresee in this autobiography?

Himes: I imagine there will just be another volume in which I will write about the change in my writing habits or change in my attitudes toward the entire American scene, and my change from pessimism to optimism. I became much less subject to the inroads of the various attitudes of people that I didn't particularly respect. I know that I will write another volume that will concern my beginning to write detective stories, and then my beginning to write the last ten or twelve books that I have written.

Williams: In one of your letters you said—and you've mentioned it since I've been here—that you were working on the bloodiest book that you have ever worked on, that you'd ever conceived, but you didn't expect (you said in this letter) to have it published in America, that it would be difficult to have published. Do you remember that?

Himes: Well, yes, because I can see what a black revolution would be like. Now, first of all, in order for a revolution to be effective, one of the things that it has to be, is violent, it has to be massively violent; it has to be as violent as the war in Vietnam. Of course, in any form of uprising, the major objective is to kill as many people as you can, by whatever means you can kill them, because the very fact of killing them and killing them in sufficient number is supposed to help you gain your objectives. It's the only reason why you do so.

Now, when you have resorted to these means, this is the last resort. Well, then, all dialogue ceases, all forms of petitions and other goddamned things are finished. All you do then is you kill as many people as you can, the black people kill as many of the people of the white community as they can kill. That means children, women, grown men, industrialists, street sweepers or whatever they are, as long as they're white. And this is the fact that gains its objective—there's no discussion—no point in doing anything else and no reason to give it any thought.

Now a soldier, if he would have to think about the morality of going out and killing the enemy, or if he had to consider his feelings about killing people, he would be finished. To do so, he would get court-martialed or shot on the scene. A soldier just goes out and kills; no one thinks anything about it; that's his objective. The objective for a foot soldier is to kill the enemy, and that's all. It's very simple. There's nothing else to be added to it or subtracted from it.

Well, that's what a revolution by the black people in America will be; that's their only objective. Their objective is not to stand up and talk to the white man and to stand him in front of a gun and say, "Now you did so and so to me"; the only objective is to blow out his brains without a word, you see. So I am trying to show how this follows, how the violence would be if the blacks resorted to this. Even individually, if you give one black one high-powered repeating rifle and he wanted to shoot it into a mob of twenty thousand or more white people, there are a number of people he could destroy. Now, in my book all of these blacks who shoot are destroyed. They not only are destroyed, they're blown apart; even the buildings they're shooting from are destroyed, and quite often the white community suffers fifty or more deaths itself by destroying this one black man. What I'm trying to do is depict the violence that is necessary so that the white community will also give it a little thought, because you know, they're going around playing these games. They haven't given any thought to what would happen if the black people would *seriously* uprise.

The white community gets very much upset about the riots, while the black people haven't seriously undertaken in advance to commit any great amount of violence; it's just been forced on them. What little violence they have done has actually been for protection; it's been defensive, you know. So what I would hope is to call to mind what *would* happen, what *should* happen, when the black people have an armed uprising, what white people should expect. It seems that the whites don't understand this.

Because one thing is sure—I have said this and I keep on saying it over and over again—the black man can bring America down, he can destroy America. The black man can destroy the United States. Now, there are sensible people in America who realize this, regardless of what they might think about the black man. The black man can destroy America completely, destroy it as a nation of any consequence. It can just fritter away in the world. It can be destroyed completely. Now I realize of course that the black man has no money, he has very little equipment to do this, he has very little fire power, he has lots of things against him, he hasn't been trained particularly. Even a Southern white cracker colonel . . . I remember a Southern white cracker colonel in the army in the Second World War got up and he made this famous speech about the black people, saying, "You have never been taught to use violence and you have never been taught to be courageous, but war calls for these things and you must learn them." Well, he's right. That's the most right thing he ever said.

Williams: Do you think the publishers will be . . .

Himes: I don't think . . . I don't know what the American publishers will do about this book. But one thing I do know, Johnny, they will hesitate, and it will cause them a great amount of revulsion, because the scenes that I have described will be revolting scenes. There are very few war books written that have ever described actual scenes of war, 'cause in war people are killed and blown to pieces, and all. Even when they just say "blown to pieces" that doesn't describe what they *look* like blown to pieces. When a shell hits a man in a war, bits of him fly around, half of his liver is flying through the air, and his brains are dribbling off. These are actual scenes, no one states these outright.

Williams: How do you think the majority of white readers react to your books and other books by black writers?

Himes: The white readers read into a book what they wish, and in any book concerning the black people in the world, the majority of white readers are just looking for the exotic episodes. They're looking for things that will amuse or titillate them. The rest of it they skip over and pay no attention to. That was one of the remarkable things about Richard Wright's autobiography—that the white community was willing to read his suffering and poverty as a black man. But it didn't move them, didn't move them one bit. They read it and said, "Tsk, tsk, isn't it awful?"

Williams: Well, you know, I sometimes have the feeling that when they read books like that, they say to themselves, "Boy, ain't we a bitch! Look what we're doing to them people."

Himes: [Laughs.] Yeah, something like that. They're thinking along those lines; certainly they're not thinking in the ways you'd like for them to think. That's one of the saddest parts about the black man in America—that he is being used to titillate the emotions of the white community in various aspects. Now I couldn't say exactly how he titillates them, but in any case it's titillation in a way that's not serious. America is a masochistic society anyway, so they probably just like being given a little whipping, enough to get a feeling out of it, a sensation, but not enough for them to be moved. I want these people just to take me seriously. I don't care if they think I'm a barbarian, a savage, or what they think; just think I'm a serious savage.

Williams: There's a rash of books, I hear (I haven't read them)—detective books—in which there are black detectives, and of course one of these books was made into a movie with Poitier, *In the Heat of the Night.* Do you feel that these people are sort of swiping your ideas?

Himes: No, no. It's a wonder to me why they haven't written about black detectives many years ago. It's a form, you know, and it's a particularly American form. My French editor says, the Americans have a style of writing detective stories that no one has been able to imitate, and that's why he has made his *Série Noire* successful, by using American detective story writers. There's no reason why the black American, who is also an American, like all other Americans, and brought up in this sphere of violence which is the main sphere of American detective stories, there's no reason why he shouldn't write them. It's just plain and simple violence in narrative form, you know. 'Cause no one, *no one*, writes about violence the way that Americans do.

As a matter of fact, for the simple reason that no one understands violence or experiences violence like the American civilians do. The only other people in the white community who are violent enough for it are the armed forces of all the countries. But of course they don't write about it because if the atrocities were written about the armies of the English and the French in Africa, they would make among the most grisly stories in the history of the world. But they're not going to write about them. These things are secret; they'll never state them.

American violence is public life, it's a public way of life, it became a form, a detective story form. So I would think that any number of black writers should go into the detective story form. As a matter of fact, I feel that they could be very competent. Anyway, I would like to see a lot of them do so. They would not be imitating me because when I went into it, into the detective story field, I was just imitating all the other American detective story writers, other than the fact that I introduced various new angles which were my own. But on the whole, I mean the detective story originally in the plain narrative form—straightforward violence—is an American product. So I haven't created anything whatsoever; I just made the faces black, that's all. *Williams:* You know, I'm always amazed when I read your books. Here you've been out of the country for twenty years, but I'm always amazed at your memory of things and how accurate you are in details, like the guns that the cops use. In rereading the screenplay last night, there was the business of the drop slot in the car. How do you come by all this knowledge?
Himes: Well, some of it comes from memory; and then I began writing these series because I realized that I was a black American, and there's no way of escaping forty some odd years of experience, so I would put it to use in writing, which I have been doing anyway. I had always thought that the major mistake in Richard Wright's life was to become a world writer on world

events. I thought that he should have stuck to the black scene in America because he wouldn't have had to live there—he had the memory, so he was still there, but it was subconsciously, which he discovered when he went back to write *The Long Dream* and the sequel (which was never published, I don't think).

Well, then, I went back—as a matter of fact, it's like a sort of pure homesickness—I went back, I was very happy, I was living there, and it's true. I began creating also all the black scenes of my memory and my actual knowledge. I was very happy writing these detective stories, especially the first one, when I began it. I wrote those stories with more pleasure than I wrote any of the other stories. And then when I got to the end and started my detective shooting at some white people, I was the happiest.

Harlem Renaissance

Williams: Chester, how about the Harlem Renaissance? You were just arriving in New York when it was . . .

Himes: It was on the wane when I got there. I knew a lot of people involved in it. There was Bud Fisher . . .

Williams: He was a doctor or a radiologist, wasn't he?

Himes: I don't know what Bud Fisher was. I only know he was a writer. And there was a young man whose name I should know, I think he wrote *The Blacker the Berry, the Sweeter the Juice.*

Williams: Was that Braithwaite?

Himes: No, Wallace Thurman, I think. He went to Hollywood and he was one of the most successful black people writing out in Hollywood. He did very well on the Hollywood scene at that time.

Williams: How would you evaluate the Harlem Renaissance?

Himes: Well, I think it was one of the greatest movements among black writers that existed up to then.

Williams: But then Hollywood wasn't interested.

Himes: No, Hollywood had no interest in the black writer, but the black writers like Claude McKay and Countee Cullen and all, produced things of substantial consequence, and so as a group, the writers of the Black Renaissance produced works that were encouraging; it encouraged all black writers.

Now, the way I look at it, the next movement of any consequence was when Richard Wright hit the scene. Nothing happened between the end of the Renaissance and the time Richard Wright came on the scene. I always had a great respect for Richard Wright because of the fact that I believe that his first works, *Uncle Tom's Children*, *Native Son* and *Black Boy*, opened up certain fields in the publishing industry for the black writer, more so than anything else that had happened. The Black Renaissance was an inward movement; it encouraged people who were familiar with it, who knew about it and were in contact with it, but the legend of Richard Wright reached people all over.

Williams: Well, he hit it about the same time you did.

Himes: Yes, that's quite true, but his name was taken to the masses, and that is what is important.

Williams: I somehow had got the impression from something that you had said that they didn't think that much of him.

Himes: No, I didn't say they didn't think much of him. I said that Wright's works themselves did not make any great impression on the white community, although they read them. As a writer, he made an impression on the publishing world. Although the white community read his works and gave a performance of being moved and touched and so forth, it didn't mean a damn thing to them—they just shed it. It's unfortunate but it's quite true.

A few white people around were considerably shocked by some of it, but I remember in Cleveland—I think it was with *Uncle Tom's Children;* no, it was *Native Son*, which was published about 1939 or early 1940—I remember various white people expressing amazement at being told that black people hated them. But these people were people of no consequence. I'd like to talk a little bit about Langston Hughes. When I came out of prison I met Langston. He was in Cleveland; he didn't live too far from where I was; he was living with his aunt. He was writing plays for Karamou House. As a matter of fact, it was through Langston that I met the Jellifes; through the Jellifes I met Louis Bromfield, and that's how I went to Hollywood. But most of his plays were produced first at Karamou before they were produced in New York. And Langston stayed there a great deal. He lived there, as a matter of fact, and only visited New York. It was some time before he moved to New York.

Williams: Well, he's gone now. Tell me, when did you first meet Carl Van Vechten?

Himes: The year that *If He Hollers* was published. I knew very little about him, other than the legend. He was only connected in my mind (until I met him) with *Nigger Heaven,* which I think was his most successful book. Although when he published *Nigger Heaven* he was on very good terms with most of the writers of the Black Renaissance, but after he wrote it they practically never spoke to him again. He told me, "Countee Cullen never said another word to me."

George Schuyler was also in this group. I knew him, and Philippa Schuyler [killed in a helicopter crash in Vietnam in 1967] when she was a little girl. She used to go down to Van Vechten's.

Williams: But Schuyler became terribly, terribly right-wing.

Himes: Yes, well Schuyler was a man whose life was plotted like Pegler's. He is a man who wants to say strong things, individual things and all, and he makes some statements which are contradictory, which Pegler did all his life. Pegler contradicted himself so much that he wound up, I suppose in an insane asylum, or wherever he is now . . . [Editor's note: Westbrook Pegler died in June 1969.]

Hollywood

Williams: Hoyt Fuller [Editor, *Negro Digest*] mentioned your *Cotton Comes to Harlem.* How do you feel about that? With Ossie Davis directing the film and all. Are you pleased with it?

Himes: Well, I was talking with Sam Goldwyn, Jr., and he

agreed with me that he wanted Ossie Davis in it whether he directed it or not. He had this Arnold Perl, a Hollywood screenwriter, write the first version of it. First he had a young man, whose name I've forgotten, who did a version. Then I wrote a version, a quickie, about a hundred and thirty pages, which he paid me practically nothing for. Sam Goldwyn, Jr., is a nice man to talk to, but he doesn't say anything about money.

Williams: You were working on it, then, the last time we saw you in New York.

Himes: Yes, that's right. Then Goldwyn couldn't use it, which I knew would be the case, because I'm not a screenwriter. But I told him that in advance. I said, "Now listen, you need to get a professional." He said he had sounded out LeRoi Jones, for whom he had great admiration as a playwright. As a matter of fact, he had extreme admiration for him as an artist, for his sharp scenes. He said that he had taken many screen writers and producers to see LeRoi's plays when they were showing in Los Angeles, and he contacted LeRoi. LeRoi said it was a matter of money; what LeRoi wanted was for Goldwyn to pay him in advance (I don't know how much it was). Anyway, he would undertake to write the screenplay and he would do as many revisions as were required, and then he would get a second payment. And Goldwyn said it didn't work that way—which was a damned lie.

Williams: Of course it is.

Himes: Anyway, the reason he didn't get along with LeRoi was because LeRoi wanted to be paid like the Hollywood writers—

Williams: Like the white writers.

Himes: —and Goldwyn didn't want to do that, so that was that.

Williams: Are you pleased with the present screenplay of *Cotton Comes to Harlem?*

Himes: Well, no one could be pleased with that. But I don't know enough about screenplays to know what it'll be like when it's finished.

Williams: That's true. But in terms of what you see on the paper . . .

Himes: Well, it's not as bad as it was. It's much improved. Ossie

Davis improved it considerably over the Perl version . . . And he has some good things in it.

Williams: He's updated it a little, with the militants and . . .

Himes: Yes, he has a black orientation, which I like. That's what I told Sam Goldwyn, Jr. That's what I like best about Ossie Davis' treatment of it. He took the Perl treatment, which had some stuff in there that was really offensive. The treatment of the blacks in there was so offensive . . . You know, some of the Jewish writers, because of the fact that they belong to a minority too, can get more offensive than other writers do.

Williams: They mistake closeness for familiarity.

Himes: What I dislike most about the screenplay—and I told Goldwyn—it's a good story, but it's a story about Deke, and the main purpose of Goldwyn is to make a series of movies of Coffin Ed Smith and Gravedigger Jones; he wants to keep them alive. But if this is the purpose of the first movie, they are dead because they are of no consequence in the movie. He has to bring them out stronger if he wants to keep them. What you have now is a movie of a swindler, which is a good movie. But it's about Deke; Deke is the character in this movie. As a matter of fact, in Ossie Davis' treatment he comes through very fine; he comes through as a real solid character.

Williams: I started reading it. I got about a quarter of the way through just since we left you, and it recalled the book for me, which I guess is good. As you say, the difference between the printed page and what they put on the film can be—

Himes: Oh, yes, I will give them credit; they have stayed closer to the book than the usual Hollywood treatment of a book, because as a rule Hollywood lets it go altogether. It was to Hollywood's advantage to keep the story in this book because they couldn't improve on it. If they're going to depart from the story altogether, then it would deteriorate and I'm not a big enough name to carry it. Like Hollywood buys a lot of name writers and they do what they want to because the name of the writer is sufficient. The treatment of the book doesn't make any difference. But Hollywood is a strange business; don't get me talking about Hollywood.

Williams: Well, talk about it.

Himes: I went out to Hollywood because I had been working on Louis Bromfield's farm in Malabar, and he read my first version of my prison story. He became excited about it and said he'd like to see it get submitted to the movies. So Bromfield was going to Hollywood to work on a screen adaptation of Hemingway's *For Whom the Bell Tolls.* They paid him five thousand dollars a week, but finally they just threw his version away and they got a screenwriter to write the movie version. But he took my book out there and he gave it to some producers and I followed him. I was trying to get work. And then I went to the shipyards in San Francisco.

Williams: Were you aware at this time—or did you have the feeling—that your work would probably outlast Bromfield's?

Himes: No, it never occurred to me at all. But I didn't think that Bromfield's work was substantial enough to last. It didn't occur to me that Bromfield had been very successful then with *The Rains Came.* He was making quite a bit of money at that time. This was in the late thirties or 1940, and writers like Bromfield were getting that large money from the serialization in magazines. They were not so much concerned with things like book clubs or reprints and so forth. But the magazine serializations: *Cosmopolitan* was paying Bromfield seventy-five thousand dollars for the serialization of the book. Anyway, I went out to Hollywood—Los Angeles—where I met Hall Johnson and a number of other black people on the fringes of the movie industry. As a matter of fact, Langston Hughes gave me a list of names of people to see when I went out there. Most of them were connected with the Communist Party. I saw these people and then I got involved also with the communists out there. Politically I was never intrigued by communism. Communism was very strong in the States, in Hollywood particularly. —— was out there; he was the dean of the communists. Great numbers of stars and producers and directors were fellow travelers, at least. There were two young men, black men, who had been in the Abraham Lincoln Brigade in Spain. —— was the one I knew. I forgot the other's name, but his brother had been wounded and he was quite a celebrity among the Communist Party there. But anyway, the Communist Party was collecting old clothes, which they sold and then sent the proceeds to a refugee camp for Spaniards from the Spanish Civil War in Mexico. I would go around with —— in his truck to pick up these clothes and various stuff. And we would drive up to many, many big Hollywood estates, of producers and various people (I wish I could recall the names) and they'd come out and set us up a few drinks in the kitchen.

Williams: In the kitchen! But you were supposed to be a part of them, right?

Himes: Yes, but this was their home; it didn't mean we got out of the kitchen! [Laughter.] I swear to God, my material for writing *Lonely Crusade* came from these experiences. I met these people. And the CIO union there was beginning to print a newspaper. At the same time I had been considered for a place on the staff. But, you see, the communists were also playing a game. They wanted people like me to help break the color line. I was a tool; they wanted to send me to thousands of places that had no intention of employing blacks at that time because Los Angeles was a very prejudiced place and the only jobs black people had were in the kitchens in Hollywood and Beverly Hills.

Williams: But they liked them; that was a status job.

Himes: Yes, but the point of it was the Negro ghetto at that time was not Watts but Central Avenue from 12th to about 40th, I guess. And you know, they didn't open those night clubs and restaurants on Central Avenue until Thursday.

Williams: Maid's day off.

Himes: Yeah, they were closed. Because, you know, some of Raymond Chandler's crap out there, he writes in *Farewell, My Lovely,* he has this joker ride about in the Central Avenue section. Some of that's very authentic—it was like that. A black man in Los Angeles, he was a servant. So there was nothing I could do out there and that's why I went to work in the shipyards. And then someone told me to come back to Los Angeles because they were filming *Cabin in the Sky.*

Williams: Oh, yes, the great all-Negro epic. [Laughter.]

Himes: That's right. And Hall Johnson was the technical director, getting twenty-five thousand dollars. They used his music, anyway. I don't know what he was—musical consultant or something. Anyway, he was being paid quite well. And I went back to Los Angeles, to MGM, because I had been told (I don't remember who had told me) to go there and see a joker named Wheelwright, who was head of the publicity department, and I could probably get an assignment doing publicity. So I went out to get a job doing publicity for the Negro press, but they had already hired a young black man named Phil Carter. Well, when you go into MGM, just to the right of the entrance was the publicity department. And then you go in a little more and you come to what they called "Old Dressing Room Row"—a long string of old dressing rooms. Well, they had this young man named Carter to do the publicity for the black press in America. They gave him, for an office, one of the old dressing rooms, at the very end, as far as they could get from the publicity office.

I got on fairly good terms with the editors of *Collier's*. I felt I could get an assignment from them to do a *Collier's* profile on Lena Horne. But then one of *Collier's* white writers, Kyle Crichton, decided he would do the story. It was one of Lena's first big publicity breaks.

Williams: You'd said something once about the black people in the cast—no matter how high up they were—and the extras . . .

Himes: Being jim-crowed in the "commissary"—the public diner. Yes, what had happened was that I had been out to MGM several times. But first, let me tell you this: One time Marc Connelly, who wrote *Green Pastures*, had a number of screenwriters, so-called intellectuals, and various others whom he had invited to a conference to discuss a film on George Washington Carver, along with two black faces for color, me and Arna Bontemps, I think.

Williams: The story of Stepin Fetchit. [Laughter.]

Himes: Marc Connelly was sitting at the head of the table with about twenty people sitting around, and he said, "Well, now I know how we're going to start this film; I know that much about it, and then we can go on from there. Well, you see, Dr. Carver was a very humble man and he always ironed his own shirts. So when we start this film on Dr. Carver, he goes into the kitchen and irons his shirt." So at that point I left.

At that time, they had black people out there for décor. They almost always had some black face out there. I was reading something recently in the paper about black technicians and various people who are beginning to break through out there, making it seem like a real advance, when actually so few, if any, technicians are employed by studios. But to get back to my story, later I made my efforts to get work in Hollywood. I met the head of the reading department, I suppose they call it, you know, where they have people read the novels and write a one-page synopsis, which is all producers ever read; they don't have time to read a book. So I was tried out by the young man who was head of this department at Warner Brothers. It was a job of no consequence. They were only offering something like forty-seven dollars a week to start, whereas you could make eighty-seven a week as a laborer. Anyway, he offered me the job and I was going to take it. I wrote the synopsis for *The Magic Bow*, a well-known book about Paganini, and submitted it. He said it was a good job and that they would employ me. And then—this is what *he* said: he was walking across the lot one day and he ran into Jack Warner and told him, "I have a new man, Mr. Warner, and I think he's going to work out very well indeed." Warner said, "That's fine, boy," and so forth. "Who is he?" And he said, "He's a young black man." And Warner said, "I don't want no niggers on this lot." [Laughter.]

But what I was going to tell you about *Cabin in the Sky* . . . Well, in the commissary they had a sort of reserved section for people like producers and the like. Everybody ate at the commissary, and if people had a guest they would just bring them to the commissary. When they were making *Cabin in the Sky* they had this entire black personnel, and they wouldn't serve the blacks in the commissary at all. They couldn't go in there and get a piece of *bread*. And so, Lena Horne stopped Louis B. Mayer on the lot one day and told him that none of the cast of *Cabin in the Sky* were permitted to eat in the commissary; they had to bring their lunch. And then he made out like he was amazed. [Laughter.]

When you think about how things happen, then you get very discouraged about what the white community is doing.

Black on White

Williams: What about today's racial scene?

Himes: Nowadays, since twenty-five years have passed, my opinions have changed; because I don't believe the whites have any desire, any intention whatsoever, of accepting the Negro as an equal. I think the only way a Negro will ever get accepted as an equal is if he kills whites; to launch a violent uprising to the point where the people will become absolutely sickened, disgusted; to the place where they will realize that they have to do something. It's a calculated risk, you know, whether they would turn and try to exterminate the black man, which I don't think that they could do.

Williams: You don't think so?

Himes: I don't think the Americans have the capability, like the Germans, of exterminating six million. I don't think the American white man could. Morally, I don't think that he could do this; I don't think he has the capacity. Even to kill a hundred thousand blacks I think would disrupt America, actually ruin the country.

Williams: You're saying that *morally* the white man in America is unable to do what the Germans did?

Himes: Yes, he's unable to do it because it would destroy America. He doesn't want America to be destroyed, you see. I think that if he has to take the choice between giving the black man his rights or destroying the entire economic system in America, he'll give the black man equality. But that's the *only* reason he would do it now. Appeal to him—doesn't mean a thing. I think that he just has to be given a choice, because America is very vulnerable, you know. Armed uprisings by millions of blacks will destroy America. There's no question about it. There's not any question in the fact that the Americans can release enough power to destroy the blacks. Obviously the Americans could destroy North Vietnam and the whole people physically. It's not a question of whether they could destroy the blacks physically; it's the fact that they can't do it *morally*—and exist in the world. Because America exists in the world by a certain balance . . .

Williams: A sort of jive morality.

Himes: Yeah, a certain balance in more than just morality. It's just a certain balance in its relationship with other nations in the world, so that it cannot do this. It cannot destroy the black man. The black man in America doesn't realize this, or probably he doesn't act because he doesn't want to get killed; of course, life is precious. I can see why no one wants to get killed. But other countries realize the fact that the blacks have the power to destroy this necessary balance. When Israel first got its independence, you realized that Britain couldn't kill all the Jews that were in Israel, and the Jews were damn few in number compared to the blacks. Israel realized they couldn't kill them all, so Britain gave them independence.

Williams: Yes, but weren't those different times, though? Everyone was feeling guilty because of what had happened to the Jews in the camps?

Himes: Different times but the conditions now are the same—even more sensitive. Even America cannot afford to fall out, not only on account of the economic balance of the world, which is so sensitive; it cannot even afford to form any enmity with all the nations with whom it collaborates, even the small nations in South America. It's just an absolute fact that if the blacks in America were to mount a revolution in force, with organized violence to the saturation point, that the entire black problem would be solved. But that is the only way the black man can solve it. So the point is, that the white people are jiving the blacks in America by putting on this pretense of wanting the blacks to suggest how *they* can do this without submitting the white race to violence; whites want the blacks to find a solution where the blacks will keep themselves in a secondary state, which would satisfy the whites perfectly, because the whites themselves haven't been able to devise any way acceptable to the blacks.

Williams: It's quite a theory, and it's one I've not heard anyone discuss. I find that younger kids are all for insurrection and rebellion and rioting on an indiscriminate, unplanned, unorganized kind of thing. I discourage it.

Himes: Yes, well, I discourage that too because what that does —by means of the white communications media, the press and television and radio—is divide one group of the black race against the other group, and thus damage the progress the blacks are making.

Williams: How big a role do you think that book publishing has in all of this?

Himes: Well, the book publishers, first of all, are trying to exploit the black consciousness to sell books. As long as it titillates the whites, they will do so to sell books.

Williams: Except that there are some books that frighten them, like your book [*Lonely Crusade*] that they pulled off the stands.

Himes: Very few. And when they do, the white press kills them. White people in America, it seems to me, are titillated by the problem of the black people, more than taking it seriously. I want to see them take it seriously, good and goddamn seriously, and the only way that I think of to make them take it seriously is with violence. I don't think there's any other way. I see it on the faces of the whites around the world—the smirks, the sneaking grins and all this stuff; I realize they're not taking the blacks seriously. There are certain segments that are beginning to take them seriously, but they are so isolated and so unrelated to the entire problem. Like the uprisings in the colleges and the elementary schools. Of course, the white people realized the uprisings in the elementary schools [school decentralization] in New York created an extraordinary amount of resistance and enmity and animosity. But since that was in one small section they felt that they could contain it, put it down with force. But if the conflict had been enlarged to the place where every black man was out on the street popping down white people right and left, this might have achieved the black goals, as in the African countries. Africans killed the colonials and burned their flags. I remember the time in London when they thought of Kenyatta as being a black murderer of the most depraved kind. Well, then the Mau Mau killed enough of these Englishmen over there so that there was nothing else they could do but give Kenya independence.

Williams: That's kind of remarkable, because I think in total the Mau Mau killed maybe fifty-four or a hundred fifty-four whites and just hundreds of blacks, so that if you can kill a small number of whites, then the effect is . . .

Himes: Yes, now in black uprisings in America, blacks would have to kill considerable numbers of other blacks in order for it to move, because the whites will employ some of those blacks to speak up against uprisings. In addition to this, the white press will find enough blacks to publicize. When they do, they *know,* of course, that they are weakening the position of the black leaders. Take Stokely Carmichael, for instance. They give him enough publicity to realize that they are weakening his position so that in a period of time that will make him absolutely valueless.

Williams: In the black community.

Himes: Yes, in the black community. So they give him publicity to the saturation point, where his value in the black community is just dissipated. They devised that technique from handling Malcolm X. They figured that they would give Malcolm X the saturation of publicity so that eventually his effectiveness in the black community would be weakened. Of course, when you sit and look at it from a distance you realize exactly what they're doing, and I think part of the reason my relationship with the white community in America is so bad is the fact that they know that I know this. My relationship with the white community in America is as bad as a black man's could be. But what saves me is I'm not important.

Williams: Would you then agree that the amount of publicity that they gave Martin Luther King created the same reaction?

Himes: Yes, yes. Of course, absolutely.

Williams: Now, you knew Malcolm pretty well.

Himes: Well, I knew him, not very well. I met him in 1962, I guess. He told me he had read *If He Hollers Let Him Go*.

Williams: He used to visit you when you were on rue Bourbon; well, how do you feel about his death? Most people feel that the government killed him.

Himes: Yes, well, personally I believe—and I will always believe this—that the CIA organized it and black gunmen shot him. Because it would take an organization, the way it was so perfectly planned and executed with certain methods that blacks don't generally use. It's the first time that I ever read of black gunmen employing gangster techniques from Chicago of the 1920's. And we know the CIA has employed these techniques before. So the way that it was so perfectly organized—that with all of the bodyguards that he had they were able to rise up there in that place and shoot, gun him down—it had their trademark on it. And then the fact that the Black Muslims had already threatened him gave the CIA a perfect, ready-made alibi. They were doing this in many countries until lately. They were doing this in the East, in Morocco and North Africa, all over. If one studied their techniques, one would realize that this very easily could have been done by the CIA. And since I'm the type of person who believes it *was* done by them, I *do* believe it was done by them. Nothing will change that. They can say what they want to; I believe it.

Williams: How do you feel about the kind of mythology that has grown up around Malcolm? Last night we were talking about the movie that they're making now.

Himes: Yes, well, I think the reason why they became frightened about Malcolm X is, as I've always said, as long as the white press and the white community keep throwing it out that the black man hates white people, he's safe. It doesn't do a damn thing to him; he can walk around wherever he wishes to. Look at LeRoi Jones, who stands up there and tells those white people whatever he wants to tell them. Stokely Carmichael, Rap Brown, anybody—they're safe. They might find something to put them away, but most of the time they don't do a damn

thing to them. But then, you know, when the black man en-
larges this philosophy and includes a greater scope of people
in it who will understand . . .
Williams: He'd opened his own mind.
Himes: Malcolm X had developed a philosophy in which he
included all the people of the world, and people were listening
to him. And then he became dangerous. Now as long as he was
staying in America and just hating the white man he wasn't
dangerous. But then when he involved others, they figured that
if he kept on—since they themselves had brought him to the
attention of the world—that he could use this; that they had
set up for him to bring in masses of other people, masses of
whites, masses of North Africans, masses of yellow people, all
that would make him dangerous. So the only thing to do with
him was kill him. Because that's the way white Americans solve
every problem. You know, I have never even thought for a
moment that the Black Muslims organized his assassination
on their own. It never even occurred to me. First of all, there are
a few Black Muslims who are rehabilitated from prisons and
drug addiction and various things; there are a few that are
personally dangerous to each other. But when a person gets
the stature of Malcolm X at the time that he was executed, I
think that he is absolutely safe from the Black Muslims. It
would take an organization which is used to toppling kings and
heads of states and big politicians to organize his assassination.
I think he was absolutely untouchable by the Black Muslims.

Anyway, you know, there is no way that one can evaluate the
American scene and avoid violence, because any country that
was born in violence and has lived in violence always knows
about violence. Anything can be initiated, enforced, contained
or destroyed on the American scene through violence. That's
the only thing that's ever made any change, because they have
an inheritance of violence; it comes right straight from the days
of slavery, from the first colonialists who landed on the American
shores, the first slaves, through the Revolutionary War, the
Civil War, the Indian wars, and gunslingers killing one another
over fences and sheep and one goddamned thing or another;

they grew up on violence. And not only that, it's gotten to be so much a part of the country that they are at the place where they are refining the history of their violence. They don't refer to the massacres of the Chinese during the last century out on the West Coast in California.

Williams: But not until they'd helped put the railroads in.

Himes: Yeah, that's right. They got all the labor that they could out of them before they killed them. Yes, they grew up on violence, and this is the only thing that they're going to listen to, the only thing that will move them. The only people that the white community in America has tried to teach that it is Christian to turn the other cheek and to live peacefully are the black people. They're the only people they have said bounce back. They have never even suggested it to anyone else. That is why the whole legend of Martin Luther King is such a powerful legend—because his was the teaching of nonviolence.

Williams: Right. He was a godsend to the American white people.

Himes: Absolutely. There's no question about it.

Black Writers

Williams: What happens, Chester, to young black writers who go over to Europe? It seems to me they're not producing like you and Wright and Harrington and Gardner produced. You were talking about Lomax [S. P.], who started out to be a writer. William Melvin Kelley was in Paris for a while and I think he got disgusted with it and now he's in Jamaica. What's happening to these younger guys who go over there?

Himes: Well, I don't know. I never met Kelley. Some of them continue to write, you know; some of them work very hard at it. But it's just the fact that there is a great resistance among American publishers against expatriate blacks, so that they have a much better opportunity of getting their work published in America if they're living there. Because if they are living abroad the American publisher, as a rule, will just reject their works out of hand. Now this I know for a fact because I sent a

number of manuscripts, recommended them, to American publishers myself, which have been turned down flat. Now the
American publishers feel that the blacks should live in America
and they have a sort of spiteful attitude toward blacks who
escape from getting a head-beating in America.

Williams: They don't want them to get away.

Himes: Yes, that's another thing. That's part of the scene that
makes magazines like *Time* have such a great and hard and
relentless fury against Richard Wright, because Wright got away
and *Time* never forgave him for that. And they continued to
pick at him in one way or another. They thought, "Now, we
helped this black man to become famous and so forth, and here
he is escaping us." So they set out to punish him. Well, Dick
was suffering under these various things—being the black writer
who was best known in the world—he was the one that the
white communications media could pick on. He was the only
one who was vulnerable enough, being famous as he was. They
could conceivably pick on me, but there wasn't any point 'cause
nobody knew me [laughs]. When people began finding out
who I was, they did begin picking. Until then they just left me
alone entirely.

Williams: So your advice would be for them to stay in the States?

Himes: My advice to the black American writer would not be
to stay in America, but just to continue to write. Not to be
concerned about the attitudes in any place they are because
one thing is for sure: there are great segments of the world
who will be opposed to them, and this opposition, if they let
it hurt them, will destroy them. That will happen anywhere
they are. But there's no particular reason why—if they are
young, have great vitality and a great love of life—why they
just simply shouldn't stay in the States and write there. There's
nothing they can learn here, that's for sure. There's nothing they
can learn about their craft or anything else from going to places
like Paris. The only reason for going to Paris is just to have a
certain amount of freedom of movement for a limited period
of time. But they won't even get any inspiration from being
in France. *I* don't think they will.

Williams: Let me ask you kind of a cliché question. Two questions, really. What is the function of the American black writer now, and what do you think his role will be in another ten years?

Himes: Well, I think the *only* function of the black writer in America now is just to produce works of literature about whatever he wants to write about, without any form of repression or any hesitation about what he wishes to write about, without any restraint whatever. He should just produce his work as best he can, as long as it comes out, and put it on the American market to be published, and I believe now it will be (which it wouldn't have been ten years ago). All right, now, what will come out of this ten years from now? No one knows. But at least the world will be more informed about the black Americans' subconscious. And it is conceivable, since black people are creative people, that they might form on the strength of these creations an entirely new literature that will be more valuable than the output of the white community. Because we are a creative people, as everyone knows, and if we lend ourselves to the creation of literature like we did to the creation of jazz and dancing and so forth, there's no telling what the impact will be.

Williams: Can we do this? Can we make this impact without owning our own publishing companies?

Himes: I suppose so. Look, I have talked to black sharecroppers and convicts and various black people who could tell, without stopping, better stories than Faulkner could write. And they would have the same alliteration, the same wording. Some of them couldn't even read and write, but they had the same genius for telling stories that Faulkner had, and they could tell continuous stories, too. The narrative would go on and on, and they would never lose it. But then these people couldn't write, you see. So I believe that the black man certainly has a creativity that is comparable to the highest type of creativity in America because he has the same background. And probably even greater. And then the blacks of the Northern ghetto have an absolutely unlimited source to draw their material from.

Somebody else comes up—like Upton Sinclair—and draws a little from this material, and builds a great reputation. Well, look at the black man now in the slums in Chicago; look what he can do. If Richard Wright had kept writing about Chicago he could have written forever.

Williams: But isn't there a kind of censorship that goes on if you don't have your own publishing outfit?

Himes: Yes, that is very true. You say "censorship"; the American publishers have what is called a conspiracy of censorship where they don't even need to be in contact with one another to know what they are going to censor; there are certain things that they just automatically know they are going to censor, and they all will work in the same way. Yes, it's true that this automatic and unspoken conspiracy of censorship among white publishers works against the black man. He has an absolute wall against him, but in the course of time this will break down. In literature, it seems as if it's already breaking down, and it will if black writers particularly find that they need their own publishers very badly. Then white publishers, faced with competition, will have to change. That is one of the unfortunate parts of the entire American scene, that the black—well, I wouldn't say industrialists —but the black heads of firms who have sufficient money to do these things won't do them. And one doesn't know why, because it's possible for everybody else. One doesn't know why a black publisher wouldn't come up and tap this source of wealth of the black community of writers, because it seems to me it would be unlimited wealth. One wonders why one of them doesn't do so, since the white publishers realize it is rich and they are tapping it as best they can, even with their standards of censorship.

Williams: There's another young black writer on the scene. His name is James Alan McPherson. He's just published a collection of short stories called *Hue and Cry,* and most of the stories are pretty damn good. Ralph Ellison has a blurb on the back of the book in which he says that this kid is great, this is real writing. The implication is that a lot of black writers whom he considers "obscenely second-rate" use their blackness as a crutch,

as an excuse for not learning their craft. What do you say?
Himes: Well, I don't know what to say about that. If Ralph
means that the black writers are writing about their experiences
of being black in the world—what else can they write about?
Now, that reminds me of this famous conversation between
James Baldwin and Richard Wright that various people have
written about, this confrontation they had in Paris. Baldwin
said to him, "You have written my story." He meant, of course,
that when Dick wrote *Black Boy* he had written the story of all
black boys. Anyway, the point I'm trying to make is what else
can a black writer write about but being black? And it's very
difficult to hide. It's not insurmountable, but it's difficult. And
then, any beginning writer will always write about his experiences.

Well, you know, I think that Ralph is rather a little bit hipped
on the business of learning his craft. I remember when he was
imitating Richard Wright to the point where there was a confrontation and Wright accused him of it. Dick told me that
Ralph said to him, "Who else can I imitate if I don't imitate
you, Dick?" So I think he's gotten a little bit pompous in making
the statements about the craftsmanship of the young black
writers of the world. *Invisible Man* was a very good book, but
that didn't make Ralph an authority. It didn't mean to me that
Ralph was a particularly outstanding craftsman in relationship
to other black writers. I think that particular remark is uncalled
for; it's not a particularly beneficial type of criticism. It seems
that a remark like that appeals more to the white community
than the black community.
Williams: What advice do you have for all these young black
writers who are growing up and getting on the scene?
Himes: Well, I was reading that book *Yellow Back Radio
Broke-Down* by Ishmael Reed out there, and I agree that there's
no reason why every black writer shouldn't produce a style of
his own. If he has the talent. No particular purpose is served
by imitation in writing, you know. You take a writer like Joyce.
He had to produce his own narrative style, which any black
writer can—I don't say that they can produce what Joyce pro-

duced, but they can produce a style of their own whatever it might be. Like Ishmael Reed. And I think that's what they should do. And then in the course of time this will make an impact. They will have their style. I find that hard to do myself. I can give that advice, but people are creatures of habit. I would like to produce a definite style. Of course, I won't be able to do that now, that's for sure. But I have always wanted to produce an entirely different approach to the novel form.

Williams: Than what you now use?

Himes: Yes.

Williams: What do you find lacking in the form you now use?

Himes: Well, I would like to see produced a novel that just drains a person's subconscious of all his attitudes and reactions to everything. Because, obviously, if one person has a number of thoughts concerning anything, there is a cohesion. There has to be because they belong to one man. Just let it come out as it is, let it come out as the words generate in the mind, let it come out in the phrasing of the subconscious and let it become a novel in that form. Of course this has been done, but not purely; there's always been an artificial strain. Since the black American is subject to having millions of thoughts concerning everything, millions of reactions, and his reactions and thoughts will obviously be different from that of the white community, this should create an entirely different structure of the novel. Of course, that requires youth . . . I remember when I used to be able to write creatively thirty-five or forty pages a day. When I first began writing I was doing much better in introducing a story than I was doing in later years, because I would put down anything. I would be going along in a narrative form and listening to jazz and then a trumpet solo, say, would take my mind off for a second, I would follow it and write about it, and then go back to the narrative, and that would become part of the narrative. But of course this was always rejected by the editor.

Williams: You know, we once had a conversation about *The Primitive* and I told you I'd been reading it on the subway and I missed my stop. Remember? And I told you I thought it was a brutal book, I think a great book, and I remember that you apologized for its being a brutal book. But I hadn't said that it was brutal in the sense that an apology was necessary. If you're talking about attacking the sensitivites on all levels, this is what I mean; this is what *The Primitive* did.

Himes: Yes, but that was what I was able to achieve in Mallorca because I didn't have any distractions with *The Primitive*. I wrote that out of a completely free state of mind from beginning to end; where I saw all the nuances of every word I put down, so *The Primitive* is my favorite book.

Williams: Yeah, that's a fantastic book. It's my favorite, too. But you once said *The Third Generation* was your most dishonest book. Do you remember?

Himes: Yes, yes. I had read a number of pages of a manuscript that my mother had written about her family. Her family was one of these slave families that had been interbred into the Southern white slaveowners until the time of the Civil War. My mother's grandfather (I think it was) was the half-brother of his master; they were about the same age and they looked a great deal alike. When his master went away to the war, this half-white slave of his went with him as his body servant.

Well, she had produced this novel in detail and I thought that that should have been part of the book. The reason I didn't use it was that—I needed for it to be published and I thought that would be offensive to the publishers and would make it difficult for publication at that time. That was some time ago. Nowadays, the black man has got over that thinking. They do have the freedom to write, more or less, what they want. Many books I read now by black writers would not have been published fifteen years ago under any circumstances. And there are a number of themes that won't be published now, and that's why I want to write a book and break through a certain reticence on the part of the publishers.

I read *The Godfather* [Mario Puzo] and the author has experienced a certain hesitation on the part of the publishers to publish a book that relates all the gruesomeness and the power of assassination, of ruling by this power; that relates the effect that a group of people can have by controlling—by simply shooting other people in the head. Shooting people in the head generates power. This is what I think black writers should write about. I remember Sartre made a statement which was recorded in the French press (I never had any use for Sartre since) that in writing his play *The Respectful Prostitute* he recognized the fact that a black man could not assault a white person in America. That's one of the reasons I began writing the detective stories. I wanted to introduce the idea of violence. After all, Americans live by violence, and violence achieves—regardless of what anyone says, regardless of the distaste of the white community—its own ends. *The Godfather* is not only a successful book, but it's a successful book about a successful organization that rules by violence. And not only do they rule by violence, but the American community has never been able to do anything about them.

Williams: Well, I think this is largely because people who control the American community are in cahoots either directly or indirectly with the Mafia.

Himes: Yes, that was the same thing during all the days of prohibition, when everybody realized that the gangsters and the politicians worked side by side, close together. As a matter of fact, the gangsters were only servants of the politicians, the servants of the rich. That's why the gangsters in America were almost an untouchable breed during that time.

White Writers

Williams: What about your experiences with white expatriate writers?

Himes: I don't have any experiences with white expatriate writers.

Williams: Remember once you told me a story about how James Jones used to hold this soirée every Sunday at his place, and he said he'd like to meet you and you should come over, and you said, "What the hell do I want to see James Jones for?"

Himes: Yeah, that's probably true. I never met James Jones all the time I was in Paris. I actually don't know if I'd know him if I saw him. Lesley's pointed him out once or twice, but I don't remember what he looks like. I have nothing to say to James Jones, absolutely nothing to say to him whatsoever. And from what I've heard about his career and so forth, I don't *want* to know anything about him.

The thing about white writers . . . it's very pitiful you know. Take white writers like Hemingway, for instance. Now Hemingway became one of the great writers of the world, but as far as I know Hemingway never, one time, in one book or one story, had any message or statement to make about anything other than what he called courage or bravery and so forth, which I think is simpleminded. And that is all. But then, you see, to a black writer they say, "Well, what statement is he making?" He could write a book, one of the most fabulous stories in the world, and they'll say, "That's a good book, but what is the statement? What is he saying about the conditions of the black people in America?" Well, most black writers have something to say about this because most black writers from America— what else can they say, what else can they write about, what else do they think about? So that is why it becomes an absolute part of their writing, because it's part of their thinking. But I don't think that it's all done deliberately—just to sit down and make a statement; it's subconscious. Of course, most writers of any consequence are against various forms of social injustice. Take them all—even go back to old Russian writers like Dostoyevsky, old English writers, Dickens and so forth, and the new English writers, Joyce and all. Because this is part of the human emotion, you know, to protest against various forms of social injustice. And all the rest of them who are famous throughout the world. So the black writer does so because as a writer this is part of his trade. But to sit down and deliberately do so, results in a tract which quite often gets away from the author.

Williams: Are there any white writers that you admire? Not necessarily contemporary. You mentioned Dostoyevsky . . .

Himes: Yes, I mention Dostoyevsky so much because I've always admired him to a great degree because by reading him I understand his process of writing. There was a man who wrote very rapidly and very brilliantly all the time, and the reason that he did so was that he needed money all the time. He'd need it all the time, and as soon as he'd get money he'd throw it away. Also, being epileptic he had this extraordinary perception that most epileptics have.

But then I also like Faulkner because when Faulkner was writing his stories, his imaginative stories about the South, he was inventing the situations on sound ground—but still inventive. He was inventing them so fast that if you breeze through Faulkner you can find any number of mistakes. Faulkner would forget characters. You can read certain books, especially *Light in August,* and Faulkner has forgotten the names that he attaches to certain characters, then he goes on and he gives them other names.

Williams: I've noticed this, but I always figured it was something I had misread.

Himes: No, no, he was writing so fast he forgot. I do that myself. I remember years ago when I was starting to write short stories I had a joker shot in the arm but later I forgot he was shot in the arm. [Laughter.] Yes, you know this happens quite often, especially in the movies. Not that they forget it; they just pass it over.

Williams: You know, Chester, there seem to be more white guys who are writing about black people today than ever before. There have always been some, but now they seem to be crawling out of the woodwork.

Himes: Oh, yes, everywhere, everywhere. This has been happening about the past five or six or seven years. And you know why this is? Because at the beginning of the black uprisings in America, when the blacks were seemingly going to use violence to the point where it would have some meaning, well then they had world coverage. They had the greatest coverage of any story—more than even the assassination of Kennedy or the politics in Russia. Total saturation in the world press made the white writers eager to cash in on what they figure will have the greatest appeal, so as you said before they came up with the idea. On the whole, the white writers are better trained than the black writers, because they've had more facilities for education in many of the techniques and crafts of the trade. So a white writer can sit down and he can write some of the goddamnedest, most extraordinary bullshit about the blacks, but he will successfully project his story since he's not interested in having any authenticity. All he's concerned about is reaching the largest audience and what he can do with it. Like this joker who wrote the book, *The Man*.

Williams: Oh, Irving Wallace, yeah.

Himes: He didn't give a damn about whether this story was possible or whether it had plausibility; the main thing was to write a story that would titillate the greatest number of whites and make them buy the book. It wouldn't even make them think; it would be a diversion. It is true that the white writers of the world have a much better chance of learning their craft.

Then, the white writers in America conduct writing as a major business, which it is. Harold Robbins has more writers working for him than Shakespeare had. All he has to do is just sketch out the plot and put his writers to work and knock out his books.

Williams: I didn't know he used other writers.

Himes: The way I found out, I was in New York talking to Bucklin Moon, who had become, after some hard times, the editor-in-chief of Pocket Books. And I found that in addition to working as editor-in-chief, he was also working on Harold Robbins' *The Adventurers*. Yes, he was a competent writer, so he was writing some of the passages. Harold Robbins didn't have time to write. [Laughter.] After all, it was a million-dollar project. He could afford to pay Bucklin Moon probably better than Pocket Books was paying him as editor-in-chief.

Williams: Did you read the Styron book, *The Confessions of Nat Turner?* You know the big stink about it.

Himes: I didn't read very much of it, just off and on. I read in an English paper that Styron was employing a gimmick there.

He figured that he could write about Nat Turner as long as he made him a homosexual, lusting after white women. That was the only way the story of Nat Turner could be acceptable, because Nat Turner was one of the only black slaves who had the right idea: the only thing to do with a white slave-owner was to kill them. But Styron couldn't have him just kill him outright because he wanted to be free; he had to make him a homicidal homosexual lusting after white women. Which I find very . . . [laughter] funny. It was a cute gimmick, you know, and it went down very well.

Williams: Yes, it was an immediate best-seller.

Himes: Yeah, obviously. Black homosexuals and black eunuchs have always been profitable in white literature. The profit incentive has corrupted American writing, but that's what writers write for anyway—white writers as well as black writers; they write for profit. The only thing is black writers get such very little profit. In the last ten or fifteen years it's become very big business. Now, whether this is true or not, I heard that when Martin Luther King was assassinated, no serious money-making publisher was particularly interested until they realized the world was not only incensed but extremely interested in the life of a black Christian who had been assassinated, and that it was a very big story, a tremendous story. So the publishers began bidding for the biography of Martin Luther King which was to be written by his widow. I don't know who told me this, but probably my editor, that the publishers bid for this book, unwritten of course, but it didn't make any difference whether she could write or not because they would supply any number of writers to write it. But anyway, McGraw-Hill won it on a bid of a contract to pay her $500,000 advance.

Williams: I heard it was $450,000, but who the hell is going to quibble about $50,000 when you're talking about that kind of money.

Himes: Yeah, well, there you are—half a million dollars.

Williams: That's a lot of money involved in that book.

Himes: Yes, because anything which will hold the public interest, for the next ten years anyway, will be popular. King was a much greater man in the world and a much more significant personality in the world and touched more people in the world after he was killed than before. That's when most of the people in the world even got to know who he was. But everybody knows who he is now—even the people walking down the street here, and most of the people who live in Spain.

Williams: So you say that for the next ten years he'll be a viable subject?

Himes: Yes, that's the way I feel. It might be longer than that, but I think certainly ten years.

Williams: The piece that you have in here [*Beyond the Angry Black,* 1966] I see quoted pretty frequently: "Chester Himes says . . ." And you told me that you did that piece in nineteen-forty . . .

Himes: I guess I must have done that when I was at Yaddo [a writer's colony] and that was in 1948. Horace Cayton, who was the director of the South Parkway Community Center, and the woman who was teaching creative writing out at the University of Chicago got together and decided that they would bring me to Chicago to read a paper on The Dilemma of the Negro Writer. When I finished reading that paper nobody moved, nobody applauded, nobody ever said anything else to me. I was shocked. I stayed in Chicago a few days drinking, and then I was half-drunk all the rest of the time I was in Yaddo. That was the time I started getting blackouts, I was drinking so much. I would get up in the morning and go into town, which you weren't supposed to do, and by eleven o'clock, I was dead drunk.

Williams: Into Saratoga . . .

Himes: Yes. I lived across the hall from Patricia Haysmiths who wrote *Strangers on a Train* which Hitchcock bought for practically nothing but made a classic out of. He bought the full movie rights for five thousand dollars. Hitchcock doesn't believe in paying writers either, you know.

Williams: Who else was up there in Yaddo when you were there?

Himes: Well, part of the time, there was Truman Capote. I think he had already published *Other Voices, Other Rooms.*

Williams: He's done very well.

Himes: Yeah. I don't remember any other people who were there. I think Katherine Anne Porter, who wrote *Ship of Fools* was also there most of the time, but I didn't see her. She spent almost all her days when she was in America up at Yaddo. She had a special room up there in the big house in a tower.

Williams: What did you think of *Ship of Fools* as an example of an American book that's supposed to be long-awaited, with the great writer?

Himes: I found it innocent enough but I didn't think it was a serious book that had any particular meaning other than the fact that I could see her up there typing away. It wasn't worth waiting twenty years for it. I would think that the book that — and I wrote, called *The Silver Altar*, was certainly as good as *Ship of Fools*.

"Black Anti-Semitism"

Williams: What does the "B" in your name stand for?

Himes: That was my mother's family name, Bomar.

Williams: Because when I first read *If He Hollers* . . .

Himes: Yes, I was using the "B" then.

Williams: Chester, let me ask you, do you know what your name "Himes" is derived from? Is it English or . . .

Himes: It's Jewish, like "Chaim," "Jaime" . . .

Williams: Spanish Jewish?

Himes: I don't know. It came down from "Heinz." Anyway, my father's grandfather's owner was "Himes." I don't know, maybe it was his father's—my grandfather's—owner. He was a slave blacksmith, that's how my father got into that. It was a trade that came down from father to son. My father was able to go to college and learn a few other things, like wheelwrighting and various skills. But the trade of blacksmithing was a hereditary business. It came out of slavery and the owner of our family was named in a certain variety of "Heinz," but it was a Jewish name. My forebears just took the name "Himes"—that's the way it was pronounced by the slaves. It was a literal translation, whether it was "Chaim" or "Jaime" or "Heinz." I don't know. But the "Bomar" of my mother's family's slave name is Irish, of course. I should call myself Chester X.

Williams: That's interesting. That's interesting. Let me ask you one final question and we'll quit for the day. I see you sitting there getting kind of wilted. I'm getting pretty tired myself. I don't know whether you've been reading about it or not, but there appears to be growing animosity, at least in New York City, between blacks and Jews (though one can't really trust the press). Do you think this is a result of the closeness, as I said earlier, whereby familiarity breeds contempt?

Himes: No. You know, I have a very long discussion of this in *Lonely Crusade.* That whole business between the black people and the Jews in America is part of the book, and that's the part the Jews disliked so much. As a matter of fact, I have a copy of the French Jewish magazine which has a photo of me on the cover. They ran an eighteen-page interview on my discussion of the relationship of blacks and Jews in *Lonely Crusade.* It was obvious, even when I was a little boy in the South that the only stores black people could go to, like hardware and department stores, were owned by Jews. When you went to non-Jewish stores you couldn't get in the door. So, where the black man and the Jew are concerned, the Jew has always taken the black man as a customer. Because the Jew has always been in business, and he found out that in a basically anti-Semitic country like America the most available market for a poor Jew on the lower rung of business was the black man. That was his market. He could rent them houses and he could sell them food.

Well, because the blacks were ignorant and the descendants of slaves, the Jewish merchants and landlords misused them. Where blacks might have been creative in other ways, in the ways of the commercial world they were babes in the woods. They were pigeons; anyone could take advantage of them who wanted to, so the Jewish merchants did—and the Jewish landowners (the ghettos were owned by Jews). It's very seldom any other name than a Jewish one appears as a landlord or proprietor in any ghetto in any city of America. All businesses in the ghettos were owned by Jews, and then a few of the blacks were eventually able to buy some of them. Then, of course, the black majority developed an unspoken anti-Semitism, even though they were doing business every day with the Jew around the corner. The black had an ingrown suspicion and resentment of the Jew. He realized that he was being used in certain ways by all Jewish landlords and merchants. Even today a Jew will make a fortune out of the race problem, and this builds up a subconscious resentment—although most of the white people I do business with, who help me, whom I love and respect, are Jews. But that doesn't negate the fact that the Jews are the ones who had contact with the blacks and took advantage of them. Now the gentiles had enslaved the blacks and worked them as beasts, but when they were freed, the gentiles didn't want to have a damn thing to do with them. They left the blacks without food or shelter. They worked them for a pittance and that was all. Whereas the Jew realized that to house and feed the freed black man was a business, a business that paid off. This paid off better than any other business because where else could Jews, who were in a ghetto themselves, open up any kind of a business and have customers, other than in the black ghetto?

Williams: Well then, why is there such a great reaction—as in New York—to the fact that, particularly in the school system, the black teachers want their thing, the black people in the community want their thing? The Jews are saying this is anti-Semitism—which to a large degree it is—but it's also, as you seem to imply, an awakening to the fact that they have been used.

Himes: Yes, that's right. You see, the way it is in the city school system in New York, a quarter of a century ago the only white teachers who would teach in black communities were Jews.

Williams: That's where the Irish sent them.

Himes: Yes, they're the only ones who would go there. So, over a period of time they got entrenched, and now that the black people are rising up, they're resentful of the kind of un-

committed teachers, more so than the fact that they're Jewish
teachers. It just so happens that most of them are Jewish teachers
and that they are guilty. The blacks claim they're guilty of:
giving kids bad education, ignoring them on certain points.
These teachers on the whole are Jewish, but they have been
entrenched in the school system because this is where the gentiles sent them. It's an unfortunate situation but it's inevitable,
because as the blacks begin to have any kind of protest, it's a
spontaneous protest against the first individuals whom they have
had direct contact with—who they know are guilty. They have
not looked back far enough to realize that the Jewish school-
teachers are no more guilty of actually misusing black students
than the white gentiles who exiled them there in the first place.
No one is looking at it that way, because no one ever does. The
younger Jews, I read, seriously are trying to get the older Jews,
who are people of great habit too, to see that there is a different
side . . .

Williams: Yeah, this is something that I've noticed too.

Himes: Well, this whole problem in America, as I see it, developed from the fact that the slaves were freed and that there
was no legislation of any sort to make it possible for them to live.
So this is what has built up to such a tremendous problem that
now . . .

Williams: Right. They felt that freedom was enough by itself.

Himes: Yeah, what is it that they have in heaven—milk and
honey? That some poor nigger could go and live on nothing.
Just to proclaim emancipation was not enough. You can't eat it;
it doesn't keep the cold weather out.

Wright

Williams: What was Paris like, with you and Wright, Harrington, William Gardner Smith and Melvin Van Peebles? It must
have been a pretty great scene.

Himes: Well, we always met at the Café Tournon. In fact Dick
Wright wasn't in it as much as Ollie Harrington, who was actu-

ally the center; and Melvin wasn't there then. Ollie was the center of the American community on the Left Bank in Paris, white and black, and he was the greatest Lothario in the history of the whole Latin Quarter. And he was a fabulous raconteur, too. He used to keep people spellbound for hours. So they collected there because of Ollie. Then the rest of us came. Dick was a good friend of Ollie's; as a matter of fact, he used to telephone Ollie every morning. Dick was a compulsive conversationalist in the early hours of the morning. When he woke up he had to telephone somebody and have a long conversation. When Ollie wasn't there he had to find someone else—Daniel Guérin or even Jean-Paul Sartre. But they got tired of these conversations, so he chose Ollie. As long as Ollie was in town Dick would telephone him as soon as he woke up in the morning, whether Ollie was awake or not (it didn't make any difference) and have long conversations about the CIA and the race problem and all. You know, that kind of conversation doesn't go down too well at seven-thirty in the morning.

Williams: What did you decide about the CIA in Paris? I know that Wright had some pretty positive ideas about what they were doing.

Himes: I don't know really. You see, I can't make any definite statement about the CIA in Paris because I didn't have any knowledge or even any thoughts about their operation. I realized that the FBI had a dossier on me going back to my childhood anyway, so it didn't make any difference to me one way or the other. And when I got my passport from the State Department I had to go and send my certificate for the restoration of my citizenship.

Williams: What's the restoration certificate?

Himes: Well, you know, when you've been to prison they take your citizenship away. And then the governor of the state returns your citizenship after a period of time. And my citizenship had been returned to me by a governor named Burton, who later became a Supreme Court Justice. He was a Supreme Court Justice at the time I applied for my passport. So I realized that the CIA knew everything they wanted to know about me already. They weren't interested in me anyway. The CIA was only interested in Richard Wright, and only because of the fact that they thought that he might have had information concerning the communist affiliations of people in high places in government, and that he might conceivably be having a dialogue, not a conspiracy or anything, but just a dialogue with people that they considered dangerous such as Nkrumah or Frantz Fanon. The only other person I know they were seriously interested in was Malcolm X. And of course everyone knows the CIA was interested in Fanon. They went to Fanon's assistance in the last years of his life to show that they had good will. Took him over to America and put him under medical treatment. By the way, he wrote a long article on my "Treatment of Violence" which his wife still has, and which I've thought I might get and have published. Because he had the same feeling, of course, that I have.

Williams: How long is the piece?

Himes: I don't know. Julia Wright told me that she had read it and that his wife has it.

Williams: You know, Julia is in New York. No . . . it's Rachel.

Himes: Yes, Rachel. Well, Rachel never got along with her mother. Rachel was Papa's daughter all her life. 'Cause she was a little blonde daughter, you know, and Dick was devoted to her. But Julia looks just like her father.

When Dick died Ellen was in London and then she didn't know what to do. When she came back she wanted to have a private funeral. Ellen and I personally had a furious argument about this. I told her she couldn't do that. When Dick died Lesley and I were spending the winter in St. Tropez and our landlady asked us if we knew a man named Richard Wright. And she said he had died; it had just come over the radio. So we got into our little car and rushed up to Paris and when we got up there we found that Ellen had said that she was going to have a closed funeral, and that no one was going to be admitted, and that Dick's body was going to be cremated.

Well, we were staying with Ollie Harrington. As a matter of fact, he had just moved into this apartment, so we were sleep-

ing on a mattress on the floor. So Ollie didn't say anything—
he didn't want to cross Ellen. Ollie was a great diplomat. But
anyway, I telephoned Ellen and told her she couldn't possibly
have a closed funeral for Dick. So she decided after Dick had
been dead three or four days and the funeral was rapidly approaching that she would open it. Which meant that a great
number of people were not there who would have been if they
had known earlier that it was to be an open funeral. But as it
was, Dick had been on the outs with great numbers of people
by that time. The head of *Présence Africaine,* Alioune Diop,
was one of the people who gave the funeral oration. But at that
time, before Dick's death, Dick and Diop weren't speaking. It
was a relatively small funeral and he was suddenly cremated.
After his cremation a very strong rumor started in Paris that he
had been poisoned.

Williams: I remember hearing about it at the time.

Himes: Yes. Now, Ollie was supposed to have more testimony;
he had more evidence than anyone because Dick had sent Ollie
a telegram, which I saw when I was in Ollie's house, which said
something like "Come to see me right away." And Ollie hadn't
gone because, as I said, Dick was always telephoning him early
every morning and he was sort of pissed off with him, so he
didn't go. Well, the next Ollie heard of Dick, he was dead.
He *did* die suddenly. Everyone knows the circumstances of his
death—the fact that he was being released and was in supposedly good health. And then supposedly a mysterious woman
had come to see him. Whether this is true or not, I couldn't say;
this is the essence of the rumor. And the rumor still persists.
Personally, that is one death I do not connect with the CIA,
although of course with these things one never knows because
the CIA was interested in many, many things . . . And Dick
realized that he was a sick man and he might have had some
revelation to make and decided to make it, and people might
have decided he was better off dead. This is all guesswork on
my part.

Williams: Had he made a public talk in the American Church
two or three weeks before this, in which he was running down

the CIA activities of people connected with the arts? Connie mentions it in her book.

Himes: Yes, well, everyone was doing that too, you know. And whether that has any relation to his death or not I couldn't say. I wasn't there anyway. I had been away from Paris for some time, moving around. I wasn't close enough to the scene to have any definite information until I arrived back and talked to Ellen, mostly just about the funeral.

Ellen and I never got along, as you already know. We got along very well once upon a time, but then we fell out just around the time Richard Wright was writing *The Long Dream,* because she didn't want him to write it. She didn't want him to go back into his Mississippi childhood and write about the black oppression in America, because he had written a number of books on the world scene. And I felt just the opposite. I felt that he should go back to the roots, the sources of his information, and write about the American scene. As a matter of fact, I was doing the same thing myself at the time. And Dick had come and talked to me at great lengths before he began writing this book.

Then Ellen stopped me on the street one day and said that I shouldn't encourage Dick. And I said, "Well, you know, I can't encourage Dick to do anything." And she said, "Yes, you're encouraging him to go back and write this book, and he's a big man now and he should not do this." So that made me so angry that I said some very impolite things, and we were shouting at one another on the Boulevard St. Germain. After that Ellen and I never got along. I see her now, I kiss her and embrace her because we've known one another many years. But it's just the fact that I know without a doubt that she wants certain information about Richard Wright's life not to be revealed. If Dick hadn't had his sexual relationships, if he hadn't seen the people that he had, if he hadn't had that certain type of curiosity that he had, he wouldn't have been Richard Wright. So there's no point in trying to hide the character of a man. But Richard Wright also reached a point, after he had been in France for four or five years, where he was well entrenched, had a really splendid apartment equipped in the American fashion, was a real celebrity to the press and everybody else. As my translator said, he was such a celebrity that if he had called a press conference at the foot of the stairs leading up to the Sacré Coeur and said, "Gentlemen, I want you to run up these stairs," they would have done so. But anyway, after a time, Dick became ashamed of his own image. The French continued to think of Dick as "Black Boy," and Dick was beginning to think of himself as a world figure, which he was. But at the same time, he was still Black Boy. The French were subject to thinking of him as Black Boy exclusively and excluded the fact that he was a world personality. Also, the French liked to believe that he belonged to them.

Williams: Why did they turn on him?

Himes: Well, they turned on him primarily because just that— the fact that he began writing on the world political scene. The French are very sensitive to any world figure in France who writes on the world political scene, especially if he's a black man. They are very sensitive about it. And then what the French do, they just take him out of the press. And to take Dick out of the press, since he had been such an extraordinary celebrity . . . He was plagued by it—this sort of comedown bothered him. So eventually this sort of corroded him and he decided he was going to move from France and go and live in England. But then he discovered England wouldn't give him the—racism in England had tightened up to the point where they wouldn't even consider having Dick living there.

Williams: I remember Ollie's description about when Wright went in to see about his passport, his permanent visa. He wanted an explanation from this official, who threw his passport at his feet and said, "I don't have to explain a goddamned thing to you."

Himes: Horace [Cayton] actually knew quite a bit about Richard Wright from the time of the publication of *Native Son* until Dick left for France. He was quite close to him. He'd have Dick up to the South Side Community House in Chicago, where he was director. Dick was very naive, you know, and Horace used to get embarrassed because he was such a slick cat himself, and he'd have some of these white chicks over from the University of Chicago, and Dick would get excited and wouldn't know how to behave. Dick was a strange man anyway. He was not only a genius but an astute political tactician—but in some ways he was very naive, too.

SECTION III

Personals

The Personal Essay has its place in Letters. Expanded, less concentrated, it becomes the Autobiography and, depending on who you are, its value is increased a thousandfold.

The Personal Essay and the Autobiography are supposed to be accurate recapitulations, short and long, of the author's often uneasy relationship with his world. With these the writer sets straight the record. One should approach these forms not because of demand or a commission, but out of free will. He should want to do them because he wants to, and in such a mood his work, either Personal Essay or Autobiography, will be stalked luxuriously, perhaps even reverently and, certainly, it is to be hoped, truthfully.

The Personal Essays that follow are a mixed bag. I was paid for most of them. Three of them are intensely personal, one of which relates an ugliness that took place a decade ago. I didn't enjoy writing most of them, but I suppose even if I approached my life through free will and not because of a paycheck, there'd still be things I'd write about that would make me unhappy.

It's easy enough to tell how I write a Personal Essay, generally, but the specific points remain even to me a mysterious mix of individual chemistry. I do two things. I climb inside myself and check how I feel, what I see and what I think, given certain defined situations. And second, I climb out and watch myself from a distance as it were, as objectively as I can. Finally, I edit the two views into alternating tight and long shots. In the end I have what I've called the Personal Essay.

WE REGRET TO INFORM YOU THAT

THIS ARTICLE *pretty much speaks for itself. I don't think I'd have written it had not my friend Sy Krim, editor of* Nugget *at the time, a girlie magazine, asked me to do it. No one else had asked me to write my version of the debacle with the American Academy in Rome and the American Academy of Arts and Letters. There are of course many versions of what happened, and some I've heard have been amusing while others have not. A decade has passed and the stories continue to come, with more embroidery than ever, which I suppose is the way it is with time.*

The truth of the matter is that if I had any illusions about the literary scene in New York, when I came out of this mess they were all gone. The bitterness remains. A bunch of creeps in a castle tried to rip me off, finish me, while wearing silk gloves. Working out of that bitterness, I paid a visit to the American Academy while I was in Rome about seven years ago. I went to have words with Mr. Kimball, who was then far from the support of the New York crowd. I was told that he was very ill and in the hospital. I borrowed a typewriter in his secretary's office and wrote him a note. As far as I can remember it said: "How does it feel to have almost finished my career?" It wasn't the kind of note you send to a man supposedly lying at death's door, but I didn't care and, as it happened, he didn't die anyway.

There were many people in New York who could not or would not believe Kimball had been instrumental in rejecting me from the Academy in Rome, some of them with large names as writers. One of the judges, however, John Hersey, insisted that the American Academy of Arts and Letters literary fellow-

ship to the Rome Academy be canceled because of this situation. And as far as I know now there still is no literary fellowship to the American Academy in Rome. I could be wrong. Another judge on the other hand wrote to urge me to accept the consolation prize. A petition was got up by several people in the arts, to protest what'd been done. It had no effect on the matter.

Of course I used this business with the AAAL and the American Academy in Rome in The Man Who Cried I Am, *so in the final analysis it was grist for my novelist's mill. It was therefore strange to hear some people say of the fictional aspect of this real incident, "That could never happen in real life."**

BEING a writer has very often seemed unreal to me. During the unreal times it was as if I had been afflicted with the *Alice in Wonderland* syndrome—outside myself watching myself move, listening to myself speak, sensing myself think. This springs from my background; there were no writers in my family, only hard-muscled day laborers.

But I accepted what I thought I was when I was recognized by certain constituted authorities as being what I always desired to be. A good writer.

For me this recognition came with a telephone call on January 23rd of this year. The call was to ask if I would be able to accept the American Academy of Arts and Letters Fellowship to Rome for a year. I had made plans which included an associate editorship on a new magazine. In 15 minutes, after having made some calls of my own, one of which assured me of my job with a year's leave of absence, I was able to return the call and accept what is more commonly known as the Prix

---

* Nineteen seventy-two: The Prix de Rome episode has been researched and written by a doctoral candidate, and the possibilities of publication in an expanded form appear to be good.

de Rome, an award which cannot be solicited. My worth as a writer became a reality for me with this recognition, perhaps foolishly so.

On January 31st, a week after the call, I was notified by Douglas Moore, President of the American Academy of Arts and Letters that the AAAL "has chosen you as the recipient of a Fellowship to the American Academy in Rome for the year October, 1962–October, 1963, subject to the approval of the American Academy in Rome."

Mr. Moore's letter outlined the disbursement of the $3,500 award ($600 transportation, free residence at the Academy, $150 for books and supplies, $500 for European travel, $500 for services performed by the Academy, and the balance of $1,750 to be paid in monthly installments), and ended with, "May I offer you my warm personal congratulations upon the action of the Academy."

When I wrote to Mr. Moore, asking for more information, I included a wow! in my letter. Undignified, sure, but honest; it was the way I felt. In answer to my letter, I received one from AAAL dated February 7th, in which Mr. Moore's assistant said, "I hope that by now you have had an interview with the Director of the Academy in order to make this appointment definite."

I had not been told that I had to have an interview. I called the AAAL and the personnel there set up an interview in the Manhattan office of the Academy in Rome. I looked with suspicion upon certain phrases in the correspondence—"pending approval of Rome," and "to make this appointment definite," but I was advised by those who should know that these were mere formalities. After all, no one wanted an absolute nut running about, Fellow or not. I was further told that no one who'd been awarded the Prix de Rome had ever had it withdrawn.

I had my appointment with Mr. Richard A. Kimball, Director of the Academy in Rome, on February 15th. I want to go into the following details before getting into the interview because they may have been important:

I do not like hats, because they always strike me as being too goddamn formal, but I have some slight sinus trouble during

bad weather. That is when I wear caps. I have a rather Mephis-
tophelean beard which I wear because I have a grossly receding chin. The image of a guy walking into a Park Ave. office
wearing a rakish cap and satyr-like beard should not be dismissed.

I found Kimball a ruddy man with a mustache, I think, and
glasses, and good strong teeth which may or may not have been
his own. My first impression was that he was dapper because
beneath his tweeds he was wearing a gold-colored waistcoat.
We shook hands.

Kimball said he'd started reading *Night Song,* my novel
which came to the attention of the AAAL and won me the
award. I said I hoped he'd enjoy it. He asked if I'd ever done
social work, and I admitted that I'd done some. His question
made me wonder if he were trying to square what he'd read
so far about narcotics-addiction, jazz, interracial love, with a
nice, clean-cut colored American boy who had absorbed the
material in the book legitimately. I truly think he was trying to
see me as this in spite of my cap and beard. With us during the
interview was Miss Mary T. Williams, the gray-haired Executive
Secretary of the American Academy in Rome.

Kimball asked about my life, my writing. I told him I'd been
conceived in Syracuse, born in Mississippi and raised in Syracuse, which is true, but in retrospect perhaps I should not
have said so. He did not laugh. My health, mental and physical?
Good. The Academy, he told me, was a rather small place. The
Fellows lived in rooms, took their meals together, etc. It was
very necessary to fit in. I told him I had had a two-week scholarship to the Bread Loaf Writer's Conference in Vermont and had
some idea of what it was like. I also indicated that three years
in the Navy had taught me the knack of getting along. Most of
the Fellows, he went on, were a great deal younger than I, but
knowing that Fellows much older than myself had been at
Rome, I said nothing. Kimball gave the impression that Fellows
were like lesser American ambassadors; the Academy liked for
them to get about among the Europeans. This was to my liking:
I have a strong distaste for confinement.

When we discussed writing, I let Kimball know that I'd begun work on a novel which dealt with the Roman Empire and ancient Palestine. Not only, I thought, could I look up material on Augustus and Tiberius in Rome itself, but the Academy would serve as a jumping-off place for Israel, for this novel will move in the shadow of the Christ story. Toward the end of the interview, which lasted about 15 minutes, Miss Williams and I talked of the best ships to take to Italy—those of the Italian Line or the American Export Line.

The interview ended rather abruptly, I thought. And I had detected what seems in retrospect to have been some uneasiness on Kimball's part during my talk with Miss Williams about the ships.

My next letter was not from the American Academy in Rome (an institution chartered in 1905 by Congress), nor from the American Academy of Arts and Letters, but from the National Institute of Arts and Letters. This was the lead paragraph: "You will shortly hear from the American Academy in Rome stating why the recommendation of the American Academy of Arts and Letters that you be elected a Fellow was not approved."

The letter went on to point out that I now, however, would receive a grant of $2,000 from the NIAL, parent body, for my contribution to American literature. After that, a letter of March 2nd from Miss Williams of the Academy in Rome said in part: "We regret to inform you that another candidate also recommended by the American Academy of Arts and Letters was awarded the Fellowship in creative writing."

There was no explanation.

Mr. Roger Straus, President of Farrar, Straus & Cudahy, publishers of *Night Song*, then wrote the NIAL:

"It should be noted that the letter (of March 2) gives no explanation of why Mr. Williams was rejected, but seeks to give the impression that there was no rejection, but rather a choice between two possible candidates. Both your earlier letters, however, make it clear that Miss Williams' letter is an evasion of the facts. We recognize that the NIAL wishes to make clear to Mr. Williams through its recent grant of $2,000 that it does not share the opinion of the Academy in Rome (whatever that is). And though we appreciate this sign of confidence, it by no means alleviates the injury that has been done him . . . We insist that some explanation is owed him, and us as his publishers, as to why this honor which was to be conferred upon him was so suddenly withdrawn."

Straus was on very solid ground. Of three final candidates for the Fellowship, I was unanimously chosen first. The jury included such distinguished writers as John Hersey, Dudley Fitts, Louise Bogan, Phyllis McGinley, S. J. Perelman, Robert Coates and John Cheever. There was not, as I understand the material which has come into my hands, a choice for the Academy in Rome to make; it could only make a rejection and it did.

Douglas Moore, President of NIAL, partially confirmed this when he answered Roger Straus' letter on March 14th: "My notification to Mr. Williams was premature, and I apologize to him although he was first on our list as originally submitted."

It is my belief that if Farrar, Straus & Cudahy—from receptionist to boss—had not stepped in to register complaint, the deed would have remained underground with similar others that must be perpetrated in this foundation-and-fellowship area every year.

Now, let's hang out the wash.

If a rejection rather than political juggling took place, it could only have been on two counts—racial or political or both.

There is a very real possibility that the rejection was based on political considerations. We all should know by now that there are lists upon lists in the power palaces, of people who are, who might be, and who have been, you-know-what. There are also lists (Dirty Lists, they're called) of persons who have been associated with the people in all these categories, knowingly or not, willingly or not.

Now, of all white institutions I detest politics the most. Politics has made an Augean mess of the few basically good concepts that brought this nation into being. There are too many men who, with too little equipment, have come to this place of power simply because millions of people—black people

—have had no voice in the matter. And this is a condition these little men with little equipment fear to see altered.

But to move on, in 1960 I was hired to put on a rally as a fund-raiser by the New York Chapter of the National Committee for a Sane Nuclear Policy. The Rally was a success even though the Dodd Committee was on the prowl for Communists before, during and after it. There were a good many volunteers and I worked with most of them. I talked to people from *Tass* and the *Daily Worker;* I talked with people from the *Times* and the *Tribune* as well. In the course of putting together what was then the largest concerted protest against nuclear testing and assembling the largest delegation for peace, I talked to many people. My name went out on letters and press releases, checks and so on. Proudly. I don't know if the phones were tapped, but I wouldn't have been surprised; very little surprises me about America, and a great deal angers me. Yes, I believed then and still do, in a moratorium on nuclear testing; yes, I believe in peace.

I was not among those people subpoenaed by the Dodd Committee after the Rally. But I had certainly been associated with some who had been called before the Committee. Who was what politically, I didn't know, didn't ask, didn't care. When the Rally was over I went looking for work among the very types of institutions where one's politics were not supposed to matter. I learned then that I was not supposed to be "a good risk" because of my participation in the Rally.

If the rejection by the American Academy in Rome was based on these political associations, the wrong was no less than if I had been rejected on racial grounds.

So here I am face to face with that other possibility. We first must admit that it is no longer fashionable to be publicly anti-Negro, which may explain the lack of communication between myself and Rome. It is said that even the better, moderate people of the South feel it is bad taste to be anti-Negro out loud, and that it is the rabble who do not care for fashion or taste who are raising all the hell. Perhaps. But I for one am weary of hearing about the good, moderate white people North and South, who stand in the shadows waiting to be interviewed by the New York *Times*. I don't think they exist. If they did or do, surely they have had time enough and room enough to make their stand if indeed they wanted to make one.

Which brings me to Mr. Kimball who, as far as I know, is not a Southerner, but a product of the liberal North. It is my considered opinion that this entire affair pivoted around his acts. I do not mean to give the impression that Negroes have never gone to the American Academy in Rome, they have. Ralph Ellison, the novelist, and Ulysses Kay, the composer, are two who readily spring to mind; and there have been two others. Kimball has been at Rome two years. Negroes have not been there under his tenure.

Earlier I mentioned that I wore a cap going to the crucial interview. This, together with the beard, the authorship of *Night Song* and being a Negro in the bargain, might have broken it. While race I am now positive was the largest contributing factor in the rejection, there were other things, such as a lack of "proper background." (I did not go to an Ivy League School.)

The vast silence—the awful, condoning silence which has surrounded this affair fits a groove well worn. Though the NIAL and the AAAL and many of their members might have suffered some embarrassment, I remain the single person most affected. I spoke of the affair fitting a groove well worn. I mean that the rejection confirms suspicions not really ever dead, confirms an inherent distrust and makes my "paranoia" real and therefore not paranoia at all. That is the sad thing, for I always work to lose it. It is costly and sometimes crippling to have about. But I would be an ass, wouldn't I, to toss my armor into the moat while the enemy continues his charge?

In my new novel, *Sissie*, I say something about whites expecting black to absorb blow after blow and go off to Harlem or Bedford Stuyvesant (Brooklyn's black belt) and nurse their wounds or die, but not to complain about them. I believe my experience with the award gives more truth to that statement than I dared think possible. Having thought and thought, having seen the program for the joint ceremonial of the NIAL and the AAAL, which listed my name as one of the recipients for the $2,000 "consolation prize," I changed my mind. Although my financial need was great and I flirted with the idea of coming away from this mess with *something*, my ultimate decision was to turn down the $2,000.

On May 7th, in a letter to Douglas Moore, I said: "I feel now that were I to accept the award it would be tacit agreement that no explanation (for my rejection) was due me. I regret to inform you, therefore, that I must decline the award." Mr. Moore, in answering my letter, merely said that the Grant would be "in effect and available until the end of the year," and expressed his disappointment that I wouldn't cop the bread. Moore noted that he was requesting the President of the Rome Academy, not Director Kimball, to write me. Further, Mr. Moore told me in his letter that my name would be removed from the Ceremonial program if I did not reconsider within a few days. I responded to this last by asking him not only to leave my name on the program of the Ceremonial, but to read aloud my letter declining the award as well. I felt for a time that I was about to be made invisible, non-existent. And I am very much alive.

Meanwhile, back at the ranch, I got a letter from the President of the Rome Academy, Michael Rapuano, who assured me that any racial charge against the Academy was unfounded. Rapuano admitted that I *had* been the first choice, but that the second candidate, poet Alan Dugan, "would profit more from the year in Rome than would you." This apparently was the long-awaited explanation.

But it explained nothing.

By declining the Grant in Literature I had suddenly become a bad boy; I was making waves and that embarrassed The Establishment. What Allan Morrison of *Ebony* has called "the silken curtain" descended. There was some newspaper coverage about the incident, but in most places the stony silence continued. Reporters Barrett and Asbury of the influential New York *Times* were on the story, but it was never filed. Farrar, Straus & Cudahy were told that the *Times* definitely would not be running the story. And all my life I had wanted to make the New York *Times!*

That was the picture on the day of the Ceremonial. Malcolm Cowley, President of NIAL, told the fashionable gathering that I had declined the Grant because of some "misapprehension" concerning the Prix de Rome. He did not elaborate and I leave it to you to decipher what he meant. My letter declining the award was not read. The affair seemed to have been successfully glossed over. And it would have been had it not been for Alan Dugan.

Now, much to the dismay of the officials of the Ceremonial, he rose to his feet and explained that I had declined the Grant in Literature because I had been rejected as the Rome Fellow. He told his audience that he had been the second choice. Dugan said that in the confusion created by the situation he would "take the money from the AAAL and go to Rome in the hope that the AAAL would behave better in the future."

Dugan said that if the panel of judges had been firm in its choice of myself, the "painful mess" could not have happened. Dugan, winner of the National Book Award and the Pulitzer Prize—both for poetry, brought the issue into the open. He was offered many congratulations for his act. Had it not been for this calm, rather lean gray-haired man, the issue would have remained behind the closed doors of the officials of the Institute and Academy. And if it had not been for Dugan the press might have continued to hang about on its haunches. Even the noble *Times* had to do something. Further, Dugan's statement, which startled more than one honored guest, forced Malcolm Cowley to state publicly that the contractual relationship between the American Academy of Arts and Letters and the Rome Academy would be "reviewed."

Those involved in the behind-the-scenes transactions did such a good job of concealment that Dugan did not come into possession of the facts about the Farce de Rome until about 24 hours before the Ceremonial. I sincerely hope that Dugan will not incur any of the hostility of which many of the Literary Powers are capable. I hoped from the start that he would not be involved. But as he told me, he was involved and intended to act. It seems to me a damned shame that of all the people somehow involved, only Dugan was capable of acting when it counted.

However, it's all over; the awards have been presented and the furor has died. I am glad, for the experience left me drained and cautious. But I found many new friends—men cut out from the boys and women cut out from the girls. There was a gain after all. And I learned a valuable lesson; self-recognition, that thin line between arrogance and self-confidence, is infinitely more important than public recognition. This was a difficult and painful lesson to learn. But while I have forgiven those responsible for the experience, I can't forget.

BLACK MAN IN EUROPE

AFTER *you've been hanging around a magazine awhile, you get an assignment like this, simply because you're going to Europe. And some editors feel that it's important to keep the writers they work with happy so they won't run off and write for other publications on too regular a basis.*

In my notes on "The Great White Whore" I mentioned that I had an assignment from Holiday, *but that it couldn't be written until I was at the end of a year's stay in Europe. This, "Black Man in Europe," was that piece.*

I was at this article for about a year, asking questions of people all around Europe, comparing personal notes with other blacks living there and just letting things happen. The pace was easy, the material all over. And these travels and experiences, like many others, provided information I incorporated into The Man Who Cried I Am. *In others words, this piece simply had to do with me being in Europe, a personal kind of journalism with me looking out most of the time, and then measuring my reactions to what I was seeing and experiencing.*

The response to the article was immense. Excerpts were printed in the Paris Herald-Tribune. *A number of readers wrote in to complain that I didn't know Europe at all, including one black journalist who'd spent about fifteen years there. A black minister and his wife accused me of stirring up trouble. But other blacks talked about it at gatherings in Paris, London and Amsterdam and agreed with what I said. A black student in Germany wrote to the editor of* Holiday, *Don Schanche, and declared I'd been right on the button.*

"Black Man in Europe" was published in Holiday *in January 1967; I'd sent it in from Europe in the fall of 1966. Even then*

many blacks I'd known from previous trips were asking me about "things" back in the States. Obviously they meant the racial situation. They were becoming disenchanted with their lives on the Continent. By 1969, when I had occasion to return to Europe twice, more than half of the men and women I knew personally, had returned to America—painters, writers, photographers, journalists.

As I mentioned in an earlier headnote, I wasn't sure just how my wife, Lori, and I were going to get back to New York or if we'd be able financially to remain in Europe for the year. Before leaving New York, I'd tried to scrounge up all the assignments I could get. This was the only one that came through. I was, after all, Holiday's race relations expert. (Or as the plantation help at Ebony-Jet called me, Holiday's nigger.)

After this piece was published, I learned that the then travel editor (later editor of Holiday), Caskie Stinnett, tried to kill it but was overruled by Schanche, the editor. Both men are Southerners. Stinnett, now editor of Travel & Leisure magazine, is pretty much unreconstructed, I think, when it gets down to black people. Therefore, I was all the more pleased that "Black Man in Europe" was run way up front in the magazine, in the "Party of One" pages of Holiday's "Issue Devoted to Europe."

> The last time I saw Paris . . .
> I was running like hell.
> —From a new Negro folk song

I am rarely surprised any more when my white friends return from Europe and describe places I too have visited or lived in. With great assurance many of them utter reverently the names of streets and villages, rattle off the names of restaurants and museums, quaint old sections of London, Paris, Athens, Stockholm or Rome.

Very often the places do not sound like the ones I know, but I am not shocked; I am black, and they are white, and I have learned in America that white Americans rarely see the country my eyes have so painfully beheld. Why, then, should I see the same Europe they see? Why should I expect them to see the same Europe I see?

The circumstances under which I view things make the difference. For example, I can enjoy the Prado more if I am not disturbed by gawking, giggling, pointing Spaniards, to whom the sight of a black man can be the most comical event of a lifetime. No white American has to suffer this, and there lies the tip-off on the way that many Europeans really view the racial situation in the United States today.

Passing through Europe's air, bus and rail terminals, ship docks and highways, I've seen thousands of white Americans (and, more and more, a scattering of black ones) traveling with their cameras and guidebooks, absorbing European culture. But Europe is more than museums and restaurants and people in delightful costumes. First the shifting patterns of war, and then of peace, have disrupted the historically rigid social structure on the Continent. Now there are more than 5,000,000 people from the poorer European nations seeking social and economic opportunity in the richer ones. Spaniards, Portuguese, Greeks, Italians, Yugoslavs, Turks and Algerians have moved to the north countries in such numbers that some countries have begun to restrict immigration. (It is said that the costliest trip in Europe today is the one the Portuguese make from their villages to the French Bidonvilles, or slums; they have to buy food, passports and bootleg work permits—at impossible prices.) These people are the "niggers" of Europe. Their precarious position is made somewhat safe by the presence of a comparatively few additional strangers who are black—students, visitors, G.I.'s, diplomats and expatriates. Whenever I talked with Europeans about the racial impasse at home, they in turn talked about the Italians, Spaniards, Greeks, who had come to their lands. For many Europeans the American race problem and the European immigration problem of "guest workers" (as the Germans call them) are the same. That, however, is patently untrue.

Given suitable employment, a knowledge of the new country's language, and a home in a decent part of his city, the "guest worker" melts easily into the majority—just as the immigrant does in America. But no black man, no matter how well he lives or knows the language, can ever be anything but a Negro. Even the most naïve black man living in Europe—African or American—soon comes to know this. If he has not forgotten his conditioning at home, the real Europe, still shot through with nationalism that often includes racism, can be stark indeed. His racial experiences in the United States have trained him to see beyond the Europe of the tourist.

Therefore, when my friends sing the praises of Rome, I too can recall pleasant times there, but I remember most of all the night a mob surrounded me while I was walking to a delicatessen with Ignazio Silone's white secretary. When my friends speak of Greece, I think only briefly of the great, rugged mountains, their necks beaded with clouds, their feet washed by indigo waters. Mostly I think of Carnival three years ago, when I was jeered and hooted at on the main street of Athens by celebrators in blackface. The Athenian friend with me became incensed, but he would not tell me what I had been called. A young Nigerian student, a girl, told me with great sadness that, unable to stand being laughed at or hearing people point at her and shout, *Mávri!*" (black woman)—as though it were either a crime or the funniest joke imaginable—sat down on a curb and cried.

There is always talk of Paris, but for nonwhites (and the French place the Algerians in this category) the lights of Paris have been dimming steadily. I have had some very good times in Paris, but my Negro and white friends there tell me that it is becoming increasingly difficult for nonwhites to find decent places to live, because the landlords are not so eager to rent to them. Thousands of Algerians, black Africans and Portuguese live in tumbledown slums. And the situation is not getting better. There are now half a million Algerians in all of France, and it is estimated that by 1980 the black population will hit a million. In the words of a musician living in Paris, "The French are getting shaky." A generation ago Paris was the haven for American

Negroes putting the United States behind them; today it appears to be just a stop on the way to some other European city. In the old days, Negroes plunged into the French language, tried to draw the essence from it. Today they don't try so hard; no Negro wants to know exactly what the French innuendo or idiom is saying about him. "*Sales nègres*" is as common in France today as its translation, "dirty nigger," is in the States. No Negro who has quit America, cutting ties with family, friends and even precarious position in American culture, wishes to discover that he has not, after all, escaped racism.

I have friends, black and white, who are Anglophiles and swear by everything British, but England is now a place where the hot sun of racial hatred is rising with ungodly haste. My Negro and "coloured" (in England this often means mulatto) friends in London are generally restricted to renting in slums or in neighborhoods that are becoming slums. Lodging places and hotels increasingly turn away nonwhites, with the spoken word and with signs. Last year a white friend found a hotel room for me where there would be no problems; it cost twenty dollars a day. Three years ago, rather than waste my time or risk becoming angry, I had my British agent book a room for me. But what about the nonwhite who doesn't have twenty dollars or an agent to tell the hotel people he's all right?

The bluff of the British has been called; they are just as bigoted as anyone else and probably even more. It is no secret to nonwhites in England, says an American Negro painter living in London, that if Ian Smith of Rhodesia were a black man, his regime would have been crushed within a week of his unilateral declaration of independence. This painter must pay a higher rate of auto insurance because of a "temperament liability" clause in the contracts of most nonwhite drivers. Philip Mason and Nicholas Deakins, of the Institute of Race Relations, and Anthony Lester of CARD—Committee Against Race Discrimination—are fighting an uphill battle. Government financial aid is slow, private contributions are slow; public opinion seems to contain deep-seated hostilities against blacks. Ironically, Mason, Deakins and Lester are pressing for legislation of the kind passed in the United States. Unfortunately, racial rioting in American cities tends to confirm the British bigot's belief that immigration restrictions on nonwhites should be made even more stringent than they are now. The nonwhite population of England, with the majority gathered in London, is less than 2 percent—but it is quite enough to have touched off riots in the Notting Hill sector. Most of the nonwhites are Indian and Pakistani, and about 500 of these a year, on the average, are allowed in to become doctors, who are sorely needed in England. It is the West Indian, who contributed so much to Britain's World War II effort, who seeks most to integrate into the English mainstream; but that mainstream has always been reserved for whites. The Englishman has always believed his own cliché about being "insular," even with the empire to enrich and educate him. He believes that "the niggers begin at Calais"; that is, he has basic reservations, leading to intense dislike, toward anything or anyone not British and not white.

Despite these stinging evidences of racism in Europe, a peculiar kind of schizophrenia exists there. I've noticed that with each outbreak of racial violence in the United States, the European press sets up a tremendous hue and cry, castigating white America. Representatives of the European press hop aboard the first jets to Washington, New York, Los Angeles, Selma, Chicago, Milwaukee, Cleveland, Omaha (how the list grows!) or Oxford, Mississippi. Paul Guihard, a reporter for Agence France Presse, was killed while covering the riots that broke out when James Meredith was enrolled at the University of Mississippi. After each explosion—when they did not come so often—private citizens, and in the past even governments, gathered funds to aid the most publicized disadvantaged Negro of the moment. Some Negroes prominent in the civil-rights movement, notably the Reverend Dr. Martin Luther King, have carried their campaigns abroad to Holland, France, Germany and Switzerland—with negligible success.

But in 1961, during the Congo eruptions in which many white

people (and thousands of Africans) were killed, including some Italian nuns, Roman mobs attacked African and American Negroes in the streets. Two years later, when the news of Kennedy's murder reached them, Neapolitans seized a group of American Negro sailors, hoisted them to their shoulders and bore them silently and respectfully through the streets.

Most Europeans have no understanding of what it means to be an American Negro. Black to them means African. They cannot grasp the historical process through which the African became an Afro-American. It would only confuse them to point out that, although there are about 22,000,000 identifiable Afro-Americans in the United States, there are just as many who are fair enough to pass for white, and who do so.

Actually, most Europeans, although they recognize that it is not polite to say so, have a low opinion of the black man. They feel not one iota of guilt for their own role in the slave trade, which helped to create the present American dilemma. There are exceptions, but the black man in Europe is an object of levity. The folk tales about him are all derogatory, all low comedy. In store windows one comes suddenly upon black dolls with the most grotesque Sambo expressions on their faces. Little pickaninnies decorate a multitude of cans, jars and candy bars. At Christmas thousands of European shop windows and store fronts are decorated with vicious caricatures of black people. Such an unrelieved willingness to make comedy of a human situation must have a deep and devious root in the past.

In some way that history has not yet explained, black people have left an indelible mark on the European mind. Before modern times, the last great contact between Europe and Africa occurred from the 8th to the 15th Century, during the Moorish invasions and occupations of Europe. The Almohades, who came to Spain in the last wave, in the 12th Century, were more African than Arab in color; the Moslem conquest had penetrated the northern parts of black Africa, and the Almohades came from there. It is not very likely that the racial myths Europeans live by today were formulated at that time; we can assume they were born only when Europeans became the invaders instead of the invaded.

Once created, a myth dies hard, as the American racial experience is proving. The European has had no real exposure to black people as Americans have had—in literature, press and television. It is not probable that he will have this exposure in the immediate future, because he does not have an indigenous nonwhite population. The French and the British are getting one, and not liking it at all. The Germans, who in the wake of World War II discovered a flock of babies fathered by Negro G.I.'s, refused to accept them as German. But the babies were placed in homes in Denmark with little or no difficulty.

By and large, when there has been the possibility of exposure, the European has turned his back. He is not interested. He wants to keep his myths; they are comforting. In Eastern Europe, where there has been some exposure to African students, the result has been disastrous; often race riots have occurred. Journalist Joel Blocker visited Russia recently, and as he was being driven past Lumumba University, on the outskirts of Moscow, where African students take their classes, his driver turned and said, "We keep them as far away from us as possible."

There persists among many Americans and Europeans the belief that of all Europeans, the Swedes are most interested in and best understand our racial turmoil. But the fact that expatriate Negroes have not gone to live and work in Stockholm, as they have gone to Amsterdam and Copenhagen, indicates something else. Jørgen Schleimann, a Dane, gave me his opinion of this view: "For the Swedish intellectual in Stockholm or Uppsala, to be involved in the problems of other people is a mark of status. That involvement, however, is too often very superficial." Big, red-bearded Björn Kumm, a Swedish journalist who has lived in America and gone on Freedom Rides—with one arrest by the Greenwood, Mississippi, police—remarked, "Genuine Swedish interest in your problems can be measured by the fact that Gunnar Myrdal [author of the monumental *American Dilemma*] has never been translated into Swedish." Martin Luther King and Chief Albert Luthuli of South Africa, two black men who have been awarded the Nobel Peace Prize, are seldom read in Sweden. The Swedes, however, are genuinely shocked at the treatment Doctor King receives at the hands of hoodlums during his marches. They feel that a winner of the Peace Prize should not be treated in such a disgraceful manner; they also feel that such treatment is a slap at Swedish efforts to bring peace to the world.

According to Kumm, the Swedish-American who returns for a visit reveals a bigotry not unlike that of a Southern white. I found a great deal of hostility in Stockholm and the other Swedish cities I visited. In retrospect, it seems that the Swedes I've known and liked have been away from Sweden a long time— including one woman artist who married an American Negro and then left the country with him, because she could no longer tolerate being called a whore. In many ways, Sweden was like Spain.

Spain is another place where few expatriate Negroes have gone or stayed long. Of all the Europeans, the Spaniard is most isolated from all foreign problems, including the racial one in America. The rare Spaniard who is aware tends to be very definite in his opinion—no true Spaniard will admit to not understanding anything. As a result, he is either violently prosegregation or vociferously opposed to it.

Del Arco, a columnist for the leading Barcelona paper, *La Vanguardia*, seems to favor segregation. His *Mano a Mano* column, I discovered too late, and his caricatures, are very much feared. Señor Del Arco, a small, dark, hawk-faced man, interviewed me one day. He was brisk, quite to the point and untrusting of the interpreter who was present to help us both. "In general," he said (after we had dispensed with which of my forebears had been slaves), "isn't the Negro less cultivated than the white?" This theory is taught in the Spanish schools. I reminded Señor Del Arco that there are more Negro college graduates today in the United States than Spain *and* Great Britain have produced throughout their histories.

Another Spaniard, a radio interviewer, asked me, "Just how many Negro intellectuals are there in the United States?" The

ignorance from which the question sprang rendered me so helpless that I could not answer it. I could not imagine keeping count
of the number of intellectuals in a nation.

Throughout Europe I asked the question: "What would happen in your city if 25,000 Negroes came to it tomorrow?" I received three interesting answers in Spain. "It would be all
right," one student answered, "if they were cultured." A diplomat said wryly, "There would be a lot of mulatto babies." The
third Spaniard responded glumly, "Probably the same things
that are happening in America would happen here."

A Catalan *caballero* and I briefly discussed the situation one
afternoon as we were walking in Montjuich Park, which overlooks Barcelona. "You will not have any trouble in Spain because you are black," he said. "You have culture. Not like the
Andalusians, who come here to the north and want to dance the
flamenco all the time. They are lazy and do not want to work."
He added with some heat, "We don't want them in our neighborhoods. They have absolutely no culture." The Spaniard is en-
amored of culture; his pursuit of what he thinks it is has made
him shallow. For all this, racism has not yet entered his land,
but United States Ambassador Angier Biddle Duke believes
that increased tourism, which will bring with it many more Negroes, could turn the nonracist attitude of the Spaniard into quite
something else.

The European leader of the "whip America" campaign is
France, but the French, faced with a growing racial problem of
their own, lean heavily on Viet Nam, forgetting their own mis-
adventures there. The influx of thousands of nonwhites into a
city is a reality for the French. If the Spanish are shallow, the
French, according to French book editor Jean Rosenthal, are
hypocritical. "We've always said we were interested in the American race problem, but we seldom buy books about it." Now the
Frenchman will be able to produce his own books on the subject.

Novelist Alain Albert, author of *The Crossing*, a small, Alge-
rian-looking Frenchman who, for reasons best known to himself,
sometimes passes as a Negro, concedes that the situation is

worsening in France, partly because of the Frenchmen who have had to give up their holdings in Algeria and return home, and partly because of French affluence. "The French now need people to clean their streets and sewers—someone to designate the bottom of society—and the Africans and Algerians do that for them very well."

Swedes say that if 25,000 Negroes came to Stockholm, "Well, look, we are already having problems with the Italians. And we have Gypsies here—they are Swedish—and we don't seem to be able to absorb them into the community very well."

German columnist Wolfgang Ebert says he doesn't know "how people would react to 25,000 Negroes; the reaction to a million foreign workers here even now evokes not very hopeful feelings." I do not think there is much danger of an invasion of Germany by black men on peaceful pursuits. A lesson was learned before and during World War II; the German doctrine of racial superiority would have meant death for Negroes. Although there are African and American Negro students and Negro G.I.'s there, Germany does not attract expatriate Negroes.

My first day in Germany left me with a bad taste in my mouth. In Munich my wife and I were refused rooms in three hotels. Tired, hungry and angry, we drove on the Autobahn and managed to find a room at a motel not far from Dachau. An interracial couple we know told us they had similar difficulties traveling through the "Fourth Reich," a land that seems forever active with the movement of troop convoys. The couple said hotel managements would only rent them separate rooms, for which they paid, though they used only one room. These incidents support Ebert's statement that "black students find it difficult to obtain rooms, especially in the country."

With racism in Europe growing like a weed, the expatriate—to save face, perhaps—will say that his years abroad have been the most fruitful in his life, even when he has little to show for it in the way of creative work (he is usually an artist; employment opportunities for aliens in Europe are tightly controlled). The difference between United States and European racism is in the degree, and the expatriates know this very well. A Negro singer in Amsterdam says: "If the rest of the brothers knew just how cool Amsterdam is compared to the rest of Europe, they'd really pile in here, and there would be hell to pay." Thus the degree of racial tolerance in Europe is inversely related to the number of black strangers present. I do not know how many black men or Asians are in Amsterdam, but there are not yet enough to make the citizens react violently to them.

To a man, the expatriates agree that the European doesn't understand what is happening in America for one simple reason: he doesn't want to. Black expatriates, American Negroes particularly, have adopted a wide range of names for Europeans that reveal more than anything else their feelings about being guests in foreign lands. Mr. Charlie, of American origin, becomes Monsieur Charles or Señor Carlos or de Heer Karl. The European man in the street—who in too many ways is the black man's foremost antagonist, because his position in his own society tends to be precarious, and this makes him look on strangers with suspicion and hostility—has also gained some names. The Frenchman has become Pierre, the Italian Tony, the German Herman, the Spaniard Juanito, and the Dutchman Hans Brinker.

Given the choice, and increasingly he has it, the European would rather deal with black Americans than with Africans. I've seen black Americans, after wearing their hair long in order to look more like Africans, return to the short haircut. Maybe Europeans believe that in spite of everything Afro-Americans have money. It is possible, too, that in some way they believe the whiteness of America has rubbed off on them. For this reason, many Negroes who speak European languages fluently choose to speak English when seeking hotel rooms. There is less chance of being refused, especially in France.

For great numbers of Europeans, the black man is still the exotic stranger. Some Negroes who have lived in Europe for decades, starting as entertainers in the 1920's, have passed through this period of greatest "pre-Negro" exoticism and now live quietly in large homes they bought with money they made;

they are no longer victims of racism in reverse. But how often have even the most intelligent Europeans interjected remarks about Louis Armstrong into our conversations! The man is an institution abroad, and I think this is because he fits the image of what a black man should act and look like. Jazz impresarios have been known to cater to this image under the guise of bringing the best jazz to Europe. They will bring the worst musicians to their countries because they are black, and because they know that no local group, no matter how good, can fill auditoriums as black musicians do. To my knowledge, Amsterdam is the one exception when it comes to big bands. Barcelona residents last year paid ten dollars a seat for a Duke Ellington concert—and filled the house for three shows. It is a myth that the European knows and appreciates jazz better than Americans do; it is the black stranger he is interested in. Witness the continuing success of the Delta Rhythm Boys and the Mills Brothers; one gets the idea in the States that they have long since retired, but they haven't—they play only in Europe. Sometimes the Afro-American takes advantage of this European penchant for black performers. One prominent musician tours the Continent because the money is good and he doesn't have to work hard. "They don't know the difference over there," he says.

Classically, reverse racism—where whites are overly fond of blacks—is usually tied to the mixed couple in Europe—the black man and the white woman: there is some truth to this observation, but it does not represent the entire picture. To be sure, some black-white, male-female relationships are based merely on color. However, a multitude of Negroes have gained an economic foothold in Europe by pretending ignorance of this situation. My Danish friend Jørgen Schleimann said, "Many Danish women find you Negroes very exotic, and feel that they must . . . get to know you better."

Novelist Chester Himes, always a hard-nosed realist, said in his dry, humor-filled drawl, "There are any number of chicks in Denmark, not all beautiful, trying to give away you know what. They don't even know the slave has been freed, and seriously believe that those soul brothers on whom they lavish so much sympathy and you know what are still in fact slaves. And one can hardly exonerate the soul brother either; he acts like one."

The liaisons between black men and European women first gained notice in France during World War I, when no less an American authority than the United States War Department, in a secret memo to the French, cautioned them not to allow black doughboys to associate with white women. Then, almost fifty years ago, "Pierre" thought that memo ridiculous. Today he is not so sure. The influx of single Algerian, African and Portuguese men is resulting in an intense competition for women on the lower levels. It is not uncommon now for a Frenchwoman to be howled at in the street for having a black escort. "Pierre," the observant black expatriates say, "is losing his cool."

The European male, on the other hand, considers the black woman the most exotic of females. I had just passed a group of hostile Italians near the Trevi fountain one day in Rome, when I heard applause. I turned and saw the Italians on their feet, whistling, clapping and shouting at the passing of a Negro woman. I have an Italian friend in northern Italy who is married to an American Negro woman. He reports that "people are always turning completely around to stare at her when we're on the tram. They stop dumfounded in the street and call out to each other. Men make so many propositions to her that she no longer goes out alone. Mad, these Italians."

In Germany, columnist Ebert tells me, "Mixed couples are not frowned on in public, even when dancing," but it has been my experience in Germany, where the Nazi salute is secretly back in vogue, that mixed couples *are* frowned upon. In Madrid I once saw an old Spanish lady shriek out *"Puta!"*—whore—to a white woman walking with a Negro man. And once I caused an auto wreck by walking hand in hand down a Barcelona street with the blond, eight-year-old son of poet Philip Levine. The average Spaniard is stupefied by the mixed couple, because he has not invested the black man with sexual capabilities—though the black woman, oddly, has been overinvested with them. But there is probably less resistance to interracial marriage in Spain than anywhere else, at least for the time being, as long as the Negro partner has "culture."

My impression is that Holland—and to many Holland means only Amsterdam—is perhaps the most libertarian capital in Europe, and this is not only because mixed couples flood the streets. Tolerance seems to exist among all classes of Hollanders, and this may explain the presence of so many black expatriates who previously lived in other European capitals. Though brothers to the racist Afrikaners of South Africa, the Dutch deplore bigotry and violence. A variety of nonwhite peoples move freely through Amsterdam streets, many from the former Netherlands empire. If the city has a ghetto in the American sense, I have yet to see it.

As always, the individual who takes exception to the trend to evil labors almost unnoticed. I know a man in Florence who spends a great part of his very valuable time prying fascist stickers loose from walls and lampposts. This man has also raised funds for American civil-rights groups from his fellow citizens. "They don't understand what the words are all about," he said, "but they understand the pictures of police with clubs, guns, dogs and fire hoses. So they give what they can."

For about a decade a Swedish housewife who works in a department store in the model town of Farsta, not far from Stockholm, has been writing friendly letters to an American Negro confined to the death cell in a prison in the American South, continuously appealing his conviction. "That is about all I can give," she explained, "writing the letters." Last fall the woman received an anonymous letter from Philadelphia, threatening her with death if she ever set foot in the United States.

In the men's room of an isolated gas station in northern Germany, near the Danish border, I met a man who told me that during the War American Negro troops had spared his life. He wanted to buy me a drink as "part repayment."

These are some of the good people I've met in Europe, and there are more—hundreds, thousands, perhaps millions. But the problem with good people, as we know from the American experience, is that they are seldom capable of getting together to form solid opposition to what threatens them. And good people never want to employ the tactics with which the bad people are defeating them.

The Congress for Cultural Freedom held a Seminar on Race and Color in Copenhagen in 1965, in which Africans, Negroes, Indians, Japanese and others participated. The seminar was probably brought to a standstill when it was disclosed by a report from a delegate that the Japanese are becoming more and more color conscious, preferring lighter to darker skins among themselves. In July, 1966, a National Seminar on Emigration was held in Algeria, with heavy emphasis on the problem of racial discrimination in France. So it goes; the good guys hold seminars and the bad guys plunge ahead, just as at home.

The hard truth about European racism, however, is that it has always been a part of the European scene, a close and constant relative of nationalism. Only one or two nations can boast of being relatively free of that old European disease, anti-Semitism.

An important factor in what is happening in Europe is America's unwillingness or inability to solve its race problem. Most Europeans expect to witness additional violence in the United States and even national emergencies. Europeans may not like the idea that a brash new nation has taken over as world leader, they may laugh at the American standards of comfort and cleanliness; but they would much rather have America the leader than Russia or China, and they are laughing less at the idea of being comfortable. But if the United States, with its massive prestige and power, cannot solve the racial dilemma, it must then be permitting it to remain unsolved. Surely new laws or even speedy enforcement of the old ones would have brought success. Europeans cannot understand the delay of some states in complying with the Supreme Court's desegregation ruling of twelve years ago. The lesson has come home to Europeans: if the world leader can play games, why, they can, too. And they do.

A PESSIMISTIC POSTSCRIPT

THIS *turned out to be my last article for* Holiday *magazine. Caskie Stinnett had become editor-in-chief by now, and the word I got, not from him, but from other editors on the book, was that he wasn't going to run any more "race stuff." That was fair enough because I too wanted to do other things in the way of travel or personalities. But it became clear soon enough that Stinnett was not only through with my writing he was through with* me.

An editor of course is free to choose his writers and I know of none who doesn't; every editor has his "stable" of favorite writers, and he goes to them for material. But, somehow, I could take this better if I did not feel that Stinnett's decisions were perhaps racially motivated.

Anyhow, "Postscript" took me full circle with Holiday *from 1963 with Harry Sions and Ted Patrick, the editor at the time, and "This Is My Country Too," to 1967 and Caskie Stinnett. The years had been rough for many of the people on the staff of the magazine: Sions, Farnsworth, Schanche and others I've not mentioned in the headnotes, but they were good years for me in my relationship with the magazine.*

Despite those four years, I've not been approached by a single magazine of Holiday's *stature, or any magazine trying to become what* Holiday *was for writing assignments. To be sure there could never be another* Holiday, *but writers always hope against hope.*

Because this was 1967, the year of Newark and Detroit, and police murders of black people, it seemed to me that not only Holiday, *but most magazines, if they ever had, were backing away from Negroes. Like* Good Housekeeping *and* Redbook *and many others, magazines were hiring blacks for staff positions, but were not running articles written by blacks. The year 1967 now appears to have been my peak in magazine journalism; not many commissions have come since then, nor have I sought them out. I've had one or two rejected since then, but on the whole my magazine writing days, such as they were, seem over. I can't say I'm sorry. For me, finally, writing for Holiday made writing exciting, pleasurable and fulfilling.*

ONE NIGHT a few weeks ago I watched a television report called *A Time for Burning*. This moving program was about the efforts of a young white Lutheran minister to integrate his church in Omaha, Nebraska. He did not succeed, and he resigned.

The older Negroes involved in the efforts seemed sympathetic to the problems the minister faced. But it was the young Negroes who caught my eye, as they have been doing for a couple of years now. Their eyes are hot and hostile. Their smiles are thin and meaningless, almost cruel. Their laughter is loud, hard and hollow. In the Omaha case, the young Negroes had told the white minister exactly what to expect from his congregation if he tried to integrate it. The predictions of the kids became fact. Theirs was a grim I-told-you-so attitude.

My interest in *A Time for Burning* was heightened by the arrival in the mail that morning of a note from a woman in Rochester, New York. She wrote some kind words for my article, *Black Man in Europe* (HOLIDAY, January, 1967). The woman's husband had been a minister. He too had tried to integrate his church, Rochester's First Baptist. But, she wrote, "We were harassed, threatened . . . until he could take no more." The minister took his own life. His widow continued in her note: "I pray *more* for the church—or The Church—than I do even for myself.

. . . I know that there are those 'good guys' around who are try-ing—however feebly—to find answers somewhere, somehow, be-fore it is 'too late' for the world."

Examples like these, to be found in the news almost every week, point to a terrifying fact: that the church in America is unwilling or unable to halt the spread of the moral decay that has come to the surface as a result of the civil-rights movement. The kids in Omaha, in cool, almost detached voices, told the young white minister in effect that religion had played a great part in what had happened to the Negro over the centuries. For most Negroes, the white church joined the battle too late and with much too little. I can still see the minister's hurt and troubled face as he listened to a young Negro recite without passion what white America had done to his people.

The kids know so much these days. If there really is a gap be-tween generations, a part of the reason must be that all kids see those of us who are forty and over as hypocrites, weaklings, nothings and worse. Negro kids, at least, do not seem at all will-ing to accept the world we apparently are leaving to them. They are through with the delays, evasions, untruths, half-truths and immorality of race relations. If the civil-rights movement has done one thing well, it has been to teach and clarify the history of the Negro and his position in this society.

They say they are unwilling to go to Viet Nam or fight in any other war; they say, rightfully, that the Viet Cong have done nothing to them, while white America has degraded them every single day of their lives. They listen to discussions about the evil of communism and smirk. As a workable political philosophy, democracy isn't so hot either. Besides, both systems are the products of the minds of white men. It has come down to this: I may be one of the last American Negroes to *ask* for an im-mediate and peaceful solution to our problems; those who come after will be in no mood to ask for anything.

Consider that Stokely Carmichael was once a disciple of Bayard Rustin. Rustin still believes that black and white must work together in order to secure integration in all areas of American society. And so, by the way, do I. Carmichael, on the other hand, seems to believe that white America is faking it, that it does not intend to share with black America what must be shared, and there is a mountain of evidence to support this belief. Carmichael, therefore, has called for black power, and the reaction of white America is still definitely measurable, as the 1966 elections proved.

If the Negro voice has evolved from Rustin to Carmichael, it follows that the next voice you hear will not be as gentle as Carmichael's, and I've yet to talk to a white person who did not believe Carmichael stood for anything but wanton violence. The leadership of the movement appears to be on the verge of change. Where change already has occurred, it has been toward less rather than more willingness to continue old dialogues. John Lewis of the Student Nonviolent Coordinating Committee (SNCC or "Snick") was so outspoken that leaders from the more established organizations were hard put to quiet him. The 1963 march on Washington was nearly called off because Lewis's address to the marchers was considered too strong, and he refused at first to mute it. He did, however, and the rally went on. John Lewis was replaced by Carmichael, who has said he will not run for office this year.

At CORE—the Congress for Racial Equality—James Farmer was replaced by the fiery Floyd McKissick, who, although not an orator in the tradition of Farmer, excites listeners to a greater extent. The wear and tear on the Negro leadership cannot be measured. As a result, the validity of the nonviolence philosophy, which until now has been mainly a form of protection for Negroes, is being challenged. The kids today are saying: "If they had used nonviolence on Christ, He wouldn't be a hero. But they used force, and look what happened."

Nonviolence is intended to appeal to a moral society. The signs seem to be growing that the nation is weary of pretending to follow a Christian code of morals. This evidence must be depressing to the leadership. Furthermore, age is catching up with them. Martin Luther King (the kids call him "Martin Loser") came to the movement a dozen years ago; A. Philip

Randolph, Bayard Rustin, Roy Wilkins and many others have been around twice as long. In the scheme of any revolution, be it peaceful or not, there are going to be several changes of leadership. If the opposition won't deal with the mildest leaders, who tend to be the first, then it must deal with the hardest, who come later. And the ages of the new leaders—political, revolutionary and otherwise—are becoming younger, as is that of the overall population.

People of my age have had to promise to their children what we do not actually possess. Younger Negroes will have none of this; what they want, they want now, and if they don't get it, they don't mind being catalysts for a moral and economic disruption in a nation to which they belong only nominally anyway. It isn't any good telling these youngsters about your efforts to halt racial injustice; they become impatient with you. "What about *now?*" they want to know.

They are fed up with the kind of jobs they are offered. While it may seem that in some areas "things are getting better," in others they have become worse. Negro unemployment remains as a result of discrimination, and these youths who take training in job skills are too often being taught tasks that are already being phased out by automation. The kids don't want to start at the bottom and work up; they want to start in the middle, which is where the white kids begin. Too many of them are the sons of fathers who started on the bottom and today are still there.

A few months ago I spoke to some Negro teen-agers in a Chicago high school. The first question they asked me was, "Do you make a lot of money?" This was getting to the heart of the matter. No value in America is as great as the value of money, and they know it. The paradox is that if the young Negroes think you have "made it," automatically you become an "Uncle Tom." If you do not live in their neighborhood, you're a "white man's Negro." There are plenty of those around. Every day on television and in newspaper ads, magazine and news stories, the kids glimpse the only Negro who has really gained from the agitation of the movement, the one already in the middle class. On the record, it is the upper- and middle-class Negro who does the most talking about civil rights, voicing his protests in genteel places, such as the church. But it is the ghetto man who, without benefit of police protection, gets out into the streets and does something about his condition—even if it means burning his surroundings to the ground. For if he doesn't go ahead and destroy his prison, who will?

As I see it, the Negro leadership has faltered in the pursuit of its main objectives: education, housing and employment. The kids are crowded behind them, clamoring. The Supreme Court decision of 1954, now about to be uniformly enforced without more delays, is a case in point. Thirteen years have passed since the Court ruled against segregation in the schools. Stokely Carmichael was a child then. His voice, which now seems to raise the hackles of many whites, might not have been heard if the law had been implemented. The angry black youth of America is of a generation—*another* generation—that was given a promise that wasn't kept. White America has only its own duplicity to blame for the angry young black America. The kids who make up this generation could have been less bitter, less threatening.

Ghettoes still exist, for the simple reason that they are lucrative to some people; if they had no value, they would have been discarded long ago. Negro kids know this from the first time they see white cops engaged in criminal activities in the ghetto, see white merchants making money in the ghettoes and spending it somewhere else. The American ghetto is the American pork barrel; everyone takes, but few people give. It is more expensive to maintain an apartment in a ghetto than outside it. Food chains have been known to charge more for their products in ghettoes than elsewhere. Buildings are not well-maintained, because few people care how the ghetto man lives. Sure, Negroes have bought homes or rented apartments outside the ghetto, but they are the ones who have managed to accumulate the necessary funds. The others, the great majority, have not. And restricted communities and real-estate combines make it even harder for the Negro to get himself out of this community.

In employment, one Negro being an assistant manager for a savings-and-loan association does not mean that the way is clear for all other Negroes to secure similar positions. That Sidney Poitier won an Academy award doesn't mean Hollywood has gone wild over Negro actors. The poverty programs founder, and many, in fact, will die. America is determined to win the war in Viet Nam instead of the one at home. Poverty carries a stigma, and so does any program with which it is associated. The only people I know who speak highly of the poverty programs are those who are making money from them.

In the face of delays, failures and defeats, what is the answer for Negro youth? There is political power, but so many of them can't vote yet. Besides, it takes time for political power to come to fruition. The kids look, too, at the contretemps surrounding the unseating of Congressman Adam Powell. Sure, they say, he was a hippie; sure, maybe he beat them for $40,000, but it was *our* $40,000. Look, they say, what about this cat Dodd, in the Senate? They were investigating that man for a year. Adam blows in, lallygaggin' as usual, and *wham*—right away they got him. Dodd? Baby, you know; they give him a censure. Powell's situation could have been predicted. The kids know almost from birth all the machinations of America's double standard.

If there are no jobs, if education is nonexistent or inferior, if a man cannot raise his family without rats, and acquiring political power is a slow and sometimes unrewarding task, what is left? White America must ask itself this question, because Negroes are doing so. Generation upon generation of Negro Americans have grown to adulthood reaching for some of the dream, as a greyhound lunges forward to get hold of the mechanical rabbit that is always in sight but never caught. How long can they be expected to go on?

Much of this has been said before and more eloquently by other writers. But the last time I wrote of such things in this magazine was three years ago, and although I wrote of some humiliating incidents that had happened to me in this nation, I was nevertheless hopeful that we could meet and best the crisis of racial equality. Today, however, I believe that if such a time comes, it will first have seen this nation in a degradation perhaps comparable to Germany's at the peak of World War II. Violence will clear our eyes.

I began the present essay with a reflection on the morals of the country, citing what happened to two white ministers. In just three years a great many white people who wanted to make the change have discovered that their fellows did not and do not want to. It seems to me that formerly the writing and talking about civil rights were left mostly to Negroes. This is not so today. More and more white people are discovering, some of them at great cost and pain, that civil rights is a valid, indeed necessary issue, so it has taken on new urgency. But the widow in Rochester mentions in her note that it may be too late. When General Eisenhower was President he said that men's hearts could not be changed by legislation. Those hearts are not being changed by moral persuasion, either, but there is a chance that both may work if they are relentlessly pursued.

Even as I write, I am told that the Federal Civil Rights Commission has issued a statement saying that the educational plight of the Negro child is worse today than it was when the Supreme Court decision was made. Neither moral force nor law, then, has worked as most of us knew all along they wouldn't. But perhaps they might have worked if the other guy had done something about the situation.

The other guy, however, was wishing the same from us. Or perhaps we are all waiting for the kids.

It is the nature of man to strike out when he is hurt. This not only is natural; it is dignified. I do not wish to sound like a Negro leader. I am a writer, and my responsibility is to set down and interpret what I see. Even doing this tends to threaten some, as Negro leaders seem to threaten white America with their frequent appearances on television and radio and in newspapers. How could a Negro leader, issuing even the most innocuous statement, fail to threaten?

It has been 192 years since the Negro Peter Salem, just as frightened as the other militiamen at Concord and Lexington, took up the defense against the British. That is a very long time to dream. No other ethnic group in America has had to wait so long for a share, and I can tell you that waiting among Negroes is no longer In. It is Out. Paradoxically, Viet Nam has had a great deal to do with this view. For the umpteenth time the United States has got into a war to ensure democracy for other people. But at home, democracy moves slowly, if at all; and this is exactly the way most white Americans, regardless of the moral and legal implications, want it to be. Even in Viet Nam the infant-mortality rate is 35 per 1,000; in the United States the mortality rate for Negro babies is 45 per 1,000. I, personally, do not know how most white Americans dare look at themselves in the mirror.

We have a restless and immensely bitter Negro youth—and some of us who are no longer kids can match the intensity of their emotions. We also have a war in which, according to all reports, Negro servicemen top the casualty lists. If you have a war, you have veterans. Charles C. Moskos, Jr., a Northwestern University sociologist, notes that Negro ex-servicemen may be less willing to tolerate second-class citizenship than before. Negroes and whites today remark, "They had better have some jobs for these fellows when they get back."

Moskos also points out that the men who organized the Deacons for Defense and Justice to combat the Ku Klux Klan in Louisiana, in 1964, were veterans of World War II or Korea. Little need be said of James Meredith, who spent nine years in the Air Force before entering, over great obstacles, the University of Mississippi.

I see the future of the civil-rights movement shifting very quickly from nonviolent to violent; nonviolence has worked only around the edges. I see leaders who are younger and younger, and less patient. There will be further fragmentation of the various groups, and the extremists of today may well be the conservatives of next month, so extreme will groups become.

None of this is new; it has all happened before in history. But it seems that white America, which has dodged so much history, must now face it head on.

Youth, history tells us, will be served, and if we are now almost overwhelmed by the music and fashion of youth, the philosophy of the young, with all its recklessness, must follow.

CAREER BY ACCIDENT

THIS ARTICLE *was never published, although it was commissioned by Ted Solataroff of* New American Review. *It's remained in my files. Like "Time and Tide: The Roots of Black Awareness" this was one of those very personal pieces editors often ask black writers to put together. And the more you bleed, the more they seem to like them.*

My agent got us together; the theme: what it's like to be a black writer. I did two rewrites on the article, but Solataroff and I never came close. Like many white editors, he had a model in mind. I should, he suggested, write like Ralph Ellison and eliminate what he called the "gossip." People who are prominently involved in New York's literary circle seem unable to stand criticism of it, something I certainly should've known by 1967 when I wrote this.

I've never published in New American Review. *Few black writers have. The NAR fee was small to begin with, so the kill fee was but a fraction of that. I've not approached Solataroff since then and neither has he approached me.*

To BE a writer who is Negro in America today is to be variously a figure of tragedy, satire and comedy. The situation hurts, it is bittersweet and is funny as hell for writing after all is a very stupid compulsion.

Yet writing by Negroes seems to be growing in volume, if not like weeds, then like the slow burgeoning of spring grass.

Some editors have even managed to put together large, heavy books containing the writing of only Negroes. Imagine it.

I became a writer by accident; I became a writer because I couldn't find a job. When I began the process of becoming a writer, it wasn't for the money and it wasn't for fame; it was to keep my sanity and to find some purpose in my life. And dignity, for the bigots of California had been ripping that out of my hide for almost a year in 1954. Had I remained in Los Angeles, I would have automatically become one of the leaders of the Watts riots. Until that year I had earned most of my way at a variety of tasks. In California "they" would let me do nothing to earn a livelihood.

I began a novel that year and finished it in 1956 for the same reasons I began it. There was a slight difference; I was now in New York City.

If the world away from writing was filled with prejudice and racial hatred, the publishing and literary worlds didn't want to offend it because that's where the books were sold. It was perhaps this reason why that first novel, published as a soft-cover original under the title *The Angry Ones,* did not come out until 1960, six years after it was begun, four years after it was completed. It was not a great book; first novels rarely are. But I've never been ashamed of it; it said what I wanted to say at the time and this should be the first consideration of any writer.

Becoming a writer took a great deal more than putting together that first book. Like an old-time baseball player in the Negro leagues before Jackie Robinson and integration in the majors, I played all the positions, writing for monthlies, dailies and weeklies; I wrote advertising and radio advertising copy, publicity copy. I cranked out speeches and I've written screenplays, short fiction, novels and long nonfiction. Once I even put out my own weekly newsletter. I think of myself as a writer only because I've done nearly all kinds of it—and I hope to do much more.

While I studied creative writing under Daniel Curley, the novelist, playwright and short-story writer at Syracuse University, the only thing I learned was discipline. I don't really think a person starting out can learn much more than that. Looking back on the time I spent in Curley's classes, I think it must have been amusing. A Negro sitting there not knowing that so many doors were closed to him. Yet, I don't know that any other people in that class were as fortunate as me.

Yes, I think making a living as a writer takes luck. Talent counts, I think, only if you have it when luck comes down the pike; otherwise, it counts for nothing. In my case, because my luck was so bad for so long, I began to wonder whether or not I had talent; the system does that. I tried to help push the luck late in the 50's by getting an agent, but she could not sell what no one wanted to buy, and I left her for that reason, not because I thought she was anti-Negro, as rumors in New York have put it. Some of her other clients at that time have come into their own, like Bruce Jay Friedman and Joe Heller.

The search for another agent would have been funny if it were not so sad. Two agents left my works in progress in the halls to their office, as if they were garbage. Times have changed, though, and one of those agents now handles my friend Claude Brown, author of *Manchild in the Promised Land.* That's how the sweetening goes sometimes. My next agent had as a client James Baldwin. I went to him in desperation, which I am sure was the main reason why he agreed to "give me a whirl." Now, these words do not inspire confidence, but I was pleased then and relieved to be with an agent who had fought his way through the barriers with a Negro writer.

But, of course, having Baldwin as a client meant that he had a top talent *and* his Negro writer and did not need or really want me. To be quite fair, he probably felt very sorry for me. Twice when Baldwin could not fill speaking engagements he asked me to substitute. Naturally, I refused. By this time I could see precisely where our liaison was going, and I left him. I cite these agent vignettes only to show a bit more of what many Negro writers have to contend with besides writing. I have been with my current agent four years now.

In addition to the situations with agents, editors of both

magazines and books displayed an alarming tendency to send me harsh notes after reading my material. For some reason, a lot of my work is taken at a very personal level. But, as I've said before, time does not stand still and some editors who assailed me for carrying a chip on my shoulder (not at all original; my grade school teachers used to say the same thing to Negro pupils) are now working with Negro writers "angrier" than I could ever be. That, too, is sweet.

I struggled through the first part of 1960, just barely getting by, but somehow you always do. *The Angry Ones* came out and got two reviews. I had rewritten it three times for publishers. One option was taken on it and dropped. If it hadn't been published when it was, and at that point the cover could have been of toilet paper, I would have quit as a writer. The advance was gone long before the book came out, but another project had kept my head above water. Even so, in the early part of 1960, I borrowed fifty dollars from a friend and I didn't know how I would pay it back.

Then, in the space of a week, I contracted for three books, two novels and a nonfiction work.

The last came through two friends who run a Fourth Avenue book store; they asked if I would do a book on Africa for them. They publish a small number of books each year; one of these was Henry Roth's *Call It Sleep* in a second edition, some thirty years after it first came out. It was through Cooper Square Publishers, and its owners, Sid Solomon and Henry Chafetz, that some years later I met Roth.

Farrar, Straus & Cudahy (now Farrar, Straus and Giroux) took *Night Song*, which went into three American and three foreign editions and was made into a not very good film, *Sweet Love, Bitter*. I have been writing about luck. To me it is an accident or a series of accidents, and the best example I can give will explain how I came to Farrar, Straus.

After *The Angry Ones* was published, Arlene Donovan, then an editor at Dell, called and asked if I would write a novel for her. It seemed to me then that my writing would be confined to producing softcover books. I agreed for two reasons. First was the money and second was that Arlene was one of the nicest people I've ever met in publishing. The novel I wrote for her was *Night Song*. In the meantime I was working on a third novel. I had, in addition, sent to *Noonday* a short story which was returned with a note saying that the magazine was overstocked, but they wanted to see the story at a later time. A few months passed and I called to see what the situation was. I learned that *Noonday* was now a part of Farrar, Straus and that the editors were looking for novels and not short stories.

I was far enough along on the third novel, *Sissie*, to show it, and I carried it to Farrar, Straus. The week I contracted to do *Africa: Her History, Lands and People*, for Chafetz and Solomon of Cooper Square, Cecil Hemley, himself a novelist and poet and editor, called and said he wanted *Sissie* for Farrar, Straus. He wanted to know what else I'd done and I told him about *Night Song*, which Farrar, Straus then bought from Dell, who kept the reprint rights.

It was all a matter of luck.

The second Farrar, Straus novel, *Sissie*, was published in March 1963 during the New York newspaper strike. My luck, now running all bad, somehow seemed more normal. The same year, *Africa: Her History, Lands and People* came out. The publisher of the book, Cooper Square, is small; not many people have even heard the name. But that book is the only one of several that brings me royalties twice a year.

The year 1963 was also the year I gave up trying to explain that because I am Negro and my characters for the most part were Negro, I wasn't necessarily writing about things that have no relationship to the whole of the human race.

One of my friends, the late Edward Lewis Wallant, was faced with a similar problem. He was Jewish and wrote about Jews to a large extent, but he felt that his work had application to all people. His sudden death prevented his plan to write novels about Negroes, Puerto Ricans and Italians. He remains a "Jewish writer." Writers who are Negro are universally called "Negro writers."

The astute critic, however, will have to agree with the late Richard Wright, in his view that Negro writers were really writing about the white man, even if there is not a single white character in a given book. In one form or another, Wright contended, Negro writers are recording oppression and if they are talking about oppression, they are then talking about the white man. Wright, by the way, produced *Savage Holiday* and *Pagan Spain*, neither of them concerned with the Negro.

I think the label has been applied so that, unthinkingly in many cases, limitations can be drawn for writers who are Negro. For example, Negro writers may be invited to lecture on civil rights, but rarely on American history. Both publishers and the reading public are guilty of having manufactured the category.

Paradoxically, no other art form allows those so restricted so much freedom to protest. In the novel or "nonfiction novel" the Negro writer can voice exactly what he wants to, once he has a publisher. Film does not allow this. From an economic point of view, the theater can't afford to. Poetry is limiting; the dance only suggestive of deeper meaning; painting freezes an idea or group of ideas.

Further, the economics of the pigeonhole are not always unattractive. By way of explanation let me say that my only employment, if I may be crass, is writing. Therefore, I do all kinds of it. Ninety-eight per cent of this work has been about the Negro in America, and I support a family with these earnings.

I've hit periods when I've been bored silly with writing of this kind, for I have additional interests in history, geology, archaeology and sports. And one day I'd like to make films. But I can be in the deepest pit of boredom when I realize that the more I write about Negroes and Negro life, the more I discover about Negroes—and other Americans as well. Then I find myself putting off the departure from the pigeonhole.

In other words, there is an excitement about writing of black life in America that I would never have found as a white writer. And as a Negro writer I can measure the mounds of sand upon which the glass house of this nation is built. A Negro writer knows, as few white writers do, for they have no roots that need to be found, precisely how every American endeavor, political, military, economic, religious, have been tied irrevocably to the Negro.

When I came to understand that completely, the label "Negro writer" was unimportant. A Negro writer? *Yes!* While that designation was meant to restrict, it has opened up a vast, breathlessly appalling view of America and Americans.

Occasionally I've been asked who my influences were and I've had to answer that to my conscious knowledge there were none. That is, I've never tried to write like someone else. I had read Wright's *Native Son* when I was fourteen or fifteen and some of Langston Hughes's poetry, but I also read Twain and Melville and Whitman. I read so much and without discrimination that I can't remember all the books. There were a few books in our home, but they were uneasy guests. Most of the books I read came from the libraries. My first writing was poetry; I started it while I was in the Pacific during World War II. As an exercise in imagery, rhythm and sparseness, I liked poetry. One day I hope to get back to it.

I think the combination of writing news and poetry is at the core of whatever writing style I may have. I sometimes find my sentences altogether too tight, and at other times they are overstated, running on like a line of poetry trying to seek the rhythm of its predecessor.

If I have been influenced at all in attempts to *shape* a novel, it is through Malcolm Lowry's *Under the Volcano. Volcano* is one novel I still read every few years. The author took a single bit of time and breathed into it the lives and tragedies of each character, moving effortlessly back and forth in time. I tried to do this with *Sissie,* but I believe I did it better in my

latest novel, *The Man Who Cried I Am*. The actual time span
of the novel is twenty-four hours, but within that framework
thirty years are unfolded. I think the novel has become a very
stodgy genre, generally possessing a calm, orderly progression
of events from A to Z. What needs to happen to the novel,
I think, is what has happened to much classical and jazz
music, i.e., improvisation and then improvisation upon the improvisation.

If poetry and news writing have formed the base for style,
and Lowry's book the base for form in two of my novels
anyway, then what influenced content?

It seems to me that what happens to a man during his life
influences the content of his work. Like most Negro writers
my age and over, I was born in the South, but I lived there
only briefly as an infant. My home town became Syracuse,
New York, a city incorporated in the early nineteenth century.
It was a rather genteel community; racial discrimination was
not a sledge hammer the way it is in large cities. There was
always a Negro section, but there were always white people
living in it too. The neighborhoods merged, did not break off
sharply. If more Negroes had lived there discrimination would
have been more overt. This is not to say that the Syracuse
system was not effective, but I didn't really know what the full
ramifications of being Negro were until I went into the Navy.
Then, by leaps and bounds, I caught up with the facts of life
that I'd missed in Syracuse.

But Navy service gave me a chance to go to college and my
growth continued. Outside I was grown; inside I had some
distance to go. Some Negro writers I've met seem to have
grown up all at once and at very early ages. If I had grown up
in the South or had to meet the constant challenge of a big
city ghetto, I'd have grown up in a hurry too.

Travel has opened up a new universe for me, and I don't
mean just scenery; I mean people, how they think, live and
work. I've been to twenty-eight countries and each stop has
added immensely to my experience. My new novel, drawn a
great deal from travel situations, is set in Europe, Africa and

the United States. All writers need to get out into a world that is shrinking too rapidly.

In America, Negro writers share only one common experience, and that is being black. But the degree to which we share this experience is infinitely varied. How has one reacted to the condition, how is one *prepared* to react? Some of us spring from middle-class backgrounds; others from the lower class bringing with us a hard view of the world. Many of us were educated in the South, which is very different in some ways than being educated in the North. At least it used to be. Some of us went to college and some of us didn't, but this isn't a big thing when you consider the state of the world which is being run by college graduates. Some of us are from the West Indies where living conditions differed sharply from those in the U.S. Some of us are capable of great satire, like Chester Himes or, at times, William Melvin Kelley. Many are realists like Wright. Not many have, like Frank Yerby, escaped the restrictions imposed on Negro writers. Like other writers, some of us came to the field to take all the marbles, but leave very little of ourselves behind. Therefore, each Negro writer, riding the crest of his personal experiences, brings to the scene his own view, comment and solution. I believe that the primary obligation of Negro writers is to tell it like it is. All great writers create out of their own time. If a Negro writer chooses to write a Russian novel, that is his business, but it is a phony business.

Unfortunately, or perhaps they just can't help it, many critics and publishers see the works of Negro writers as being identical. Now, this is pretty silly. How can the work of LeRoi Jones and Bill Kelley—they are about the same age, I believe—be compared? Still, editors grumble about being inundated by "Jones-isms," an indication that they believe we are all producing the same kind of work that contains the same kind of message. The equation too many responsible people use on the literary scene is Negro writers=like experience, and like experience="protest work."

However, no group of writers at any previous time in contemporary history has demonstrated so concentrated a concern for a given people, and through that people expressed concern for all people.

One hears the frequent complaint that the crop of Negro writers is reaping a poor harvest. The writers are said to be a result of the times, the "Negro Revolution," and it is said that in the rush to get Negro writing talent, publishers have not been selective. The Negro writers I've talked to about the question of permanence in American letters seem to feel little trust for the capriciousness of publishing, but they are determined to remain a genuine part of American literature rather than the commodity their writing has become in recent years. When I say "commodity" I mean that writing by Negroes rarely moves on its writing merits. It now moves on demand, by the racial situation, and it moves first in white America. The Negro writer is accepted by the Negro community only if he has made it in the white community. Because of his tremendous success in the white community (which does, after all, own the radio, television and press outlets) James Baldwin must be the single Negro writer read most widely in the Negro community. It is worth noting that Wright came along before television; when Ellison's *Invisible Man* came out in 1952, television was an awkward infant and almost the only Negroes seen on it were boxers. But when *Another Country* was published, television, plus the racial unrest, created a natural situation for exploiting Baldwin and his work.

Economics play a great part in the Negro community's failure to raise up its own heroes. The price of books continues to climb and there are hundreds of statistics to prove that the Negro's buying power hasn't increased greatly in ten or fifteen years. Negro publishers of magazines cannot match the prices paid by white periodicals, so they seldom offer assignments to Negro writers who would be reluctant to take them anyway. The obvious result is that the Negro writer is thrown into direct competition with white writers, restricted as he is by label, for space, price and sometimes subject matter, with white writers often being better paid.

Some studies have been made that show how very few novels Negro writers have produced. Well, I think, first of all, that breaking into publishing has been a heart-shattering affair for most Negro writers. There must be casualties by the hundred, for discrimination has existed in publishing, too. And Negro novelists do not command anywhere near the money white writers do, which has led to a great amount of nonfiction writing and which, in recent years, has paid better than fiction. Nonfiction work has always been strong in most literatures and, in fact, that was what literature was in the beginning.

In addition, one cannot help but ponder the inequities rampant in literary recognition. For example, Richard Wright and Chester Himes, although some five or six years older than Ellison, nevertheless were his contemporaries. Between Wright and Himes, they've produced in the neighborhood of two dozen books, a vast number of them novels. Ellison has produced one novel thus far, and in my estimation a great one, and one nonfiction work. Wright and Himes, for personal reasons along with disappointments in their writing careers, left the country to labor in the next thing to obscurity. To Ellison, whose creative works are so thin in number, came the awards, the comfortable life and, in the minds of many young writers, the position of Establishment Negro Writer.

To be sure, however, younger Negroes look upon any Negro who seems to have made it as a turncoat. But even in their most forgiving moments they must ask, Why this kind of inequity and who makes it possible? What makes it possible?

Because success must be gained on white terms, the pathway to it for a Negro writer is narrow and he must pass over it in single file, one at a time. Thirty-seven years ago, Wright was the darling of the Left; much of his success at that time was directly due to that association. It ended, though, when the Left discovered that it was not *his* darling. The association ended, but Wright's work lasted. Ralph Ellison's is compared to it; James Baldwin's is compared to the work of both; Clarence Cooper's is compared to the writings of all three. Thus, we

Negro writers are forced to measure our individual advances by those of our contemporaries, and not writers generally. We jealously guard or meager attainments and are quick to run down other Negro writers. "He's a Tom." "He hasn't said anything in twenty years." "He isn't writing about this as much as he's writing about *that*." And so on. It is of some concern to see which of us is writing for what magazine or writing what kind of books for what publishers. *We want very much to know just exactly what the other cats are putting down.*

When I came to New York the writers I knew were white and what they were writing about didn't seem important to me, and I hungered to talk endlessly with another Negro who was writing. Since then I've come to know some writers.

I never knew Richard Wright, but I've talked to his widow on a couple of occasions and noticed how amused she is by the Negro writers of today. Chester Himes and I used to exchange letters frequently or visit when he was in New York or I was in Paris. It is Himes, more than anyone else, who can recite endlessly the relentless cruelty Negro writers are capable of venting on other Negro writers. His tales about publishing are not much happier. I've had one brief conversation over the phone with Ellison and three with Baldwin. John Killens makes a great martini; we have been having a running skirmish over Africa.* Our views differ, and healthily, I think. There are a number of Negro writers I've never met, but hope to one day. My most recent acquaintance has been with Claude Brown, who appears to be heading toward politics rather than full-time writing.

I would venture to guess that, like me, most Negro writers know a number of white writers. One of the most impressive of these I've met is Henry Roth and this is because he does not exude, as so many white writers do, the attitude that if there were not a racial situation there would be no Negro writers. Many white writers have this condescending view and I find it irritating and unfair. After all, white writers write about *their* lives and institutions; I reserve the same right for myself

* Today we are at peace.

along with the right to criticize his life and institutions for barring me from participation in them. Further, as I've pointed out before, many of these same writers earn more money writing about the racial situation than two or three Negro writers put together.

It is Ralph Ellison who has said that we Negro writers ought to stop listening to and believing in the sociologists who tell us how bad our plight is as Negroes. The sociologists really haven't clicked, as anyone should know, and they've been in the business for a long time. And the first sociologists who pointed out the Negro condition were not white, they were Negro. Cayton and Drake's *Black Metropolis* was one example. Gunnar Myrdal's *American Dilemma* is a fine work, but no one really acted on it. It has not even been translated into Swedish, the author's native tongue. The Moynihan Report is now well known. One cannot do a report on an abyss; one can only report on the facts already present and this, I believe, is what the sociologists do. But more to the point is that novelists can do infinitely more with the information than can sociologists. A Negro novelist who does use his eyes and ears cannot help but see and hear anguish. And racial anguish continues to spread around the world. It is not that sociologists are distorting the view; rather, it is that the view is so big they cannot perceive it completely. Proust said, "We all come to the novelist as slaves stand before an emperor. He can free us with a word." In the case of racism, a Negro writer or a Jewish writer has the words and we need them. This is not to say that other writers are without the words. Tom Berger, for example, for me, has all of them.

For all my talk of economics and restrictions, the Negro has brought to writing a new vitality that centers around his experience and is conveyed through his language. So rich is the "Negro idiom" that white writers cannot leave it alone. Everyone is "making it" these days; everyone is "baby." All men are "cats" or "dudes," and white Americans no longer leave a place, they "split." Few people understand any more, but everyone "digs." There is a paradox here, for how can the idiom be so widely adopted and put into general use unless the ideas, the *feelings* which these words and phrases are used to convey also are admitted to the general consciousness?

All about us we seek rock 'n' roll groups made up of white kids trying to sound like what they think Negroes sound like. A white person isn't at all hip unless during the course of an evening he can turn a phrase like a Negro. Now all this has meaning and I think the meaning is that the Negro in the U.S. suddenly has become visible in more ways than could have been imagined fifteen years ago. I think Negro writing has made much of this possible and because of it, the white American can never go home again, baby.

TIME AND TIDE:
THE ROOTS OF BLACK AWARENESS

IT OFTEN *happens that a writer may like individual people at different publishing houses, and he will therefore write a book or an article not so much for the house itself, but for the person he likes who works there. This is how I came to write this article. My friend was E. L. Doctorow, himself a novelist. He was an editor at the Dial Press then, and later, for a brief period, its publisher.*

Some years before I'd met Tom Wheeler, when he was an editor at still another publishing house, Holt, Rinehart and Winston. After leaving them, Wheeler decided to put together an anthology of the immigrant experience and took the idea to Dial, where Doctorow was one of the editors who liked it. Wheeler first spoke to me about the anthology early in 1965. The collection was to come out in about two years from then. I said I'd do a piece. I finished it in Amsterdam in 1966. From that time up until about a year before the collection was published in 1971, Wheeler kept bugging me to redo certain parts of it. I'm not certain whether Tom Wheeler is a nitpicker or a damned good editor. I tend to think the former.

But he made me dig deeper and say a little more than I wanted to say, simply because I'd said much of it before in other articles. The fee for this piece was under three hundred dollars, although Wheeler often behaved as though it was three thousand. One of the reasons why I didn't quit altogether was Doctorow, although he wasn't directly involved. Wheeler angered me a few times with his demands for rewrites, which I felt were totally uncalled for. We had hot words on the phone and in an exchange of letters, and I believe that once, I did declare

myself out of the collection, with the result that Wheeler's de-
mands melted away. Almost.

Delayed in coming out over four years, The Immigrant Ex-
perience, Wheeler's title for the anthology, finally was published
in the middle of 1971, but without many of the contributors
Wheeler led me to believe would be included. My contribution,
while beginning the section called "Personals," was actually the
last article I've done on myself and my experiences. Frankly,
I'm tired of writing about myself, but editors have often asked
for that kind of article, nothing else. So, I did them. Often for
money, but occasionally to present my side of controversial
matters. While I can see the possibility of writing of my ex-
periences in the future, it is highly improbable that I will be
writing about my personal life. Tom Wheeler absolutely mur-
dered any desire I might have had left to do that again.
Furthermore, if you complete this section, you'll agree that
there's not much more to say anyway. I don't believe, rereading
this piece, that Wheeler's nitpicking improved it, but without a
doubt he certainly got from me a hell of a lot more than I
wanted to give him at first.

O f ALL the immigrant Americans, the blacks represent the
only ethnic group still migrating in large numbers, and what
they are leaving when they can, as other immigrants left, is
oppression and economic and spiritual poverty. Their movements
from South to North, from farms to city, express the unfaltering
hope of all men that a better life exists in regions where they
did not grow up.

As with most American Negroes of my age, my roots lie in
the Deep South. My mother's family lived for generations in
that most obscene, most vicious, most ridiculous and murderous
state in the Union, Mississippi. When you are oppressed, as

any immigrant can tell you, you fight back if you can or dare;
if you cannot and you have the means, you leave. If that is
impossible, you stay and accommodate yourself to it, and hope
for a break in the near future.

My mother was the eldest girl in a family of three boys
and five girls. Her name is Ola, a name found also in West
Africa. She went from Mississippi to Syracuse, New York,
joining after World War I that restless wave of humanity
shuffling from old home to new. Descended from a family
five generations in America, she traveled within the boundaries
of her country and was untouched by the immigration laws
of 1882, 1917, and 1924. But she was a stranger who was quickly
recognized by and restricted because of her color.

She met my father in Syracuse, a city that counted blacks
among its residents in 1769. My father's family had lived in
the city for many generations. They married, these two, and as
my birth neared, they journeyed to Mississippi for the event.
It was some kind of custom.

That journey to Mississippi in 1925 and the return to Syracuse
still represent the longest trip my father has ever made. That
trip, plus the memory of the trains that rolled down the street
near our house, must have triggered something in me; I've
crossed America five times and visited twenty-eight countries,
some of them two or three times. The lust for travel could have
started in the womb.

Blacks existed in the backwashes of the Syracuse community.
The war had raised the economic level of the city. In fact, my
mother had come North to work for a white family. She thought
the North was salvation; while the streets were not paved with
gold, she sensed opportunity. In Syracuse white people did not
ride down upon you at night, and they did not lynch you. But
she did not know that in Syracuse the white population simply
left the black population to molder in the narrow alleys along
E. Washington Street, where the Negro section was.

There were few complaints of segregation or discrimination;
the immigrant population the world over expects to start at the
bottom and work to the top. I sometimes think that the blacks

of my parents' generation were the last to believe, at least
partially, that hard and honest work brought good reward.
We moved about the city, within well-defined areas, most of
them close to the New York Central rails that went through
the heart of the city. Our moves, of course, were made hand
in hand with our fortunes and these were tied to my father's
work. He was a day laborer; the label "nonskilled" bears a stigma
today, but it didn't then. I live in New York City now and I
don't often see men dressed in the clothes of a laborer—gray
trousers, bulky, colorless sweaters, dust-lined faces and crumpled
caps or felt hats bent out of shape; nor do I smell honest sweat
any more, strong and acrid, as I used to smell it on my father,
and later on myself. I remember him—a chunky little man a
bit over five feet tall, all muscle, and with the sharp face, high
cheekbones and prominent nose of an Indian—walking briskly
down the street in the mornings, trailing his handtruck behind
him. He supported us on his back and muscle, his sheer strength,
which was considerable.

Death visited our home twice, taking two girls in infancy.
Not satisfied, it hovered about. My mother suffered a severe
case of spinal meningitis, but recovered completely. My younger
brother, Joe, fell ill with pneumonia, but my grandfather, Joseph
Will Jones, visiting us from Mississippi, rushed to the hospital
and gave Joe some of his blood and Joe pulled through. We
like to remember that story; it somehow adds strength to the
family.

Besides Joe, I had two sisters, Ruth and Helen. We had a
host of minor illnesses: earaches, sore throats and toothaches. We
learned very early that one of the side-effects of being poor is
that you become used to pain. Medicine and doctors cost money.
There were free clinics, to be sure, vast halls smelling mysteriously of medicines, nurses in starched dresses rustling by,
and from some far away room sometimes you could hear a
scream or a groan. But to go to the clinic could cost a parent
a half day away from work and this in turn would cost in food
and rent. Therefore, if you woke up ill, you concealed it as
long as you could for fear that the moment when you revealed

the illness, the light of accusation would spring to your parents' eyes. We tried not to get sick.

I should not have survived childhood. Once I electrocuted myself (at least, that's what the folks said) by pounding a nail through the cord of a radio that was plugged in. Once I set fire to some flypaper and it fell flaming to the dining room table, which caught fire. Once I stumbled into a deep shaft and was just barely caught by the wrist by a stranger with red hair. Twice I almost drowned. When I was not in that kind of trouble, it was something else. I swiped the grape juice used in the church communion; I darted between the legs of passing women and looked upward; I snarled at strangers, was rude to elderly people and regularly played house with the neighbors' daughters.

Then, peace, I discovered books.

The Syracuse Public Library on the corner of Montgomery and Jefferson Streets, a gray limestone building of some mongrel design, smelled of books from downstairs, and clay from the craft rooms upstairs. I was allowed to take out four books a week instead of two, the only kid in my class allowed this privilege. I began to change, I think, when I discovered books and began to devour them. My chores seldom got done. The books were always being confiscated. "Those damned books" was a phrase I heard for a long, long time.

Of course, if I had read the Bible with as much diligence, it would have been all right. My mother was a Methodist. My father wasn't much of anything, as far as religion went. I did not like church, perhaps because we had too much of it. We went to Sunday school, stayed for church and then either returned in the early afternoon or went to a local mission. I was usually given the longest "speech" to learn and recite for Christmas, Easter, Mother's Day, and soon I did these in a secondhand black Buster Brown suit with a celluloid collar and tie which someone had given to me. The suit was the most durable piece of cloth goods I've ever worn; I spent the better part of my childhood Sundays in it.

The first Sunday of every month was communion. I don't

remember at what age I stopped taking it, but it was early. I recall deciding that I was no angel and I wasn't going to pretend I was, or would be, so I didn't go up to the altar and kneel for my grape juice and matzoth. The church was already filled with people who raised hell all week and became Christians on Sunday; I was not going to be one of them. I did not know then that that was the way things were; that that was the way they had to be if you were a black adult living in Syracuse. For, if you thought honestly about your life there, and did not bring in a deity to help see you through, you'd have to kill yourself. Church helped.

In the worst way, my mother wanted me to stand, as is the habit in the African Methodist Episcopal Zion Church, and acknowledge God. The occasion for this opportunity was every Sunday when a part of the services was dedicated to saving sinners. I was not aware that I was a sinner. I had some knowledge that I wasn't a good boy at all times, but I was damned if I was a sinner. "Won't you come to God?" the pastor would intone, holding out his arms while the women wailed and men closed their eyes so they could not see which one of them would this time be the victim. The choir would sing chorus after chorus of its most gently menacing hymn; tears would flow and from time to time a muffled voice would cry out in a mixture of joy and anguish, "Oh, Lord God Jesus!" My father, who at my mother's behest had joined the choir, would sit up there looking straight ahead, seeing nothing. My mother would look at me, her eyes filled with tears.

My first Sunday in church after three years away in the Navy during World War II, my mother and I sat in a front pew. I was in uniform. The pastor looked down at me during the "Save the Sinner" portion of the services and held out his arm. *He* cried, my mother cried, everybody cried, and the choir sang as if it was really out to get me this time. My mother was pinching me and pleading with her eyes. "Go to Jesus, Johnny." I had to refuse her because I didn't have it in me. She gave up that day. It had been a long struggle; the clash of our wills had exhausted her. I don't think she thought that her God had brought me back and therefore, in her eyes, I shouldn't have needed saving anymore.

But the church was more than a worshipping place; it was the place where the immigrant renewed himself as a member of the group, where the traditions of the group were reinforced, where shelter was found from the storm. The person who veered away from church was liable to get hurt. More important, by his acts, he could bring hurt to the group.

I had no clash of will with my father, for he left the running of the house and the disciplining to my mother. He was a soft-hearted man; not a coward, just soft. The world was running right up his back with all those mouths to feed and he discovered he could not fill them. For a man who thought of himself as a man, he realized that he was failing in that most basic of manly tasks, to provide for his family. He was not privy to all the sociological and psychological information about why he could not; he might have blamed it on being black, and that was indeed correct. But there was also the Depression and he could not handle both. And so he left, repeating an old, old black immigrant pattern. He didn't leave because he wanted to; he left because, being a man who for some reason was not able to perform as one, he was too filled with shame to remain with us.

Long before he left, however, my father and I had good times. He was a sports fan from his chitlins out; they don't put them together that way anymore. I don't know how many Sundays we spent walking or riding the streetcar to some far section of the city to watch a baseball or football game. Even today my father will not tolerate being disturbed on Saturday or Sunday afternoons when the football games are on television.

It took me some time to realize it, but both my parents were strong people; they had no choice, they had to be. But then, most blacks have had to be strong and were. Oh, they worked the most menial jobs, performed the toughest labor, but I remember laughter and parties and singing and dancing; remember picnics and loud voices; suits and dresses carrying the odor of just coming out of the cleaners that afternoon. All was not totally grim; life bubbled, or forever sought to, beneath the hard grind

of everyday life. However, for me something of a pall settled
when my father left.

But there had always been school to keep a kid busy. Sometimes I enjoyed it. Washington Irving school was in a mixed but
predominantly white neighborhood when I attended it. I got
along well with most teachers, but there were some who did not
like Negro children.

It now seems that my generation that lived in cities like
Syracuse went through what the black kids are going through
now by entering neighborhoods and schools where they are not
totally accepted. A child feels but does not always retain the
feeling; life is too filled to bursting with new experiences, why
cling to the bad ones? So, I'd almost forgotten about Miss Wooley,
whose name and image now comes raging back without hesitation. She taught arithmetic. If you *looked* like you were going
to make an error, she'd let you have it with anything handy,
fists, an eraser, a ruler. Because of Miss Wooley, I make my
eights from the wrong side. I know that it's easy to place
psychological blame on the past, but the truth of the matter
is that Miss Wooley scared me and ruined my capacity forever
to deal effectively with numbers. That I *do* remember her and
have written about her speaks for itself; Miss Wooley was one
of those experiences I could not outgrow.

I can recall reading *Little Black Sambo* and feeling warm because the eyes of the white pupils were on me and the two
or three other black kids in class. He was black, we were black,
and black back then was neither an adjective nor a noun that
Negroes spoke with pride. Little Black Sambo was grotesque-
looking; we were grotesque-looking. *Little Black Sambo* hurt; it
hurt very much. The story made me aware that I was different
from the white kids I played with, and from *Little Black Sambo*
on I was likely to be more evil than pleasant or merely competi-
tive when we played our games in the school yard. I had to
prove, man, that *I* was not like that little clown in the book.

As a child I was more readily accepted in the homes of poor
whites than in those on a somewhat better economic level. I can
recall waiting on more than one porch or in more than one

hallway while white friends ran into their homes for a moment, their parents standing guard across the door or watching me on the porch through curtains.

This was in the 15th Ward, the nicest section we'd ever lived in. It was heavily populated with Jews, mostly from Russia or Poland, and a scattering of Poles and Irish. I did most of my growing up in the 15th Ward and had as many white friends as black for a time. I didn't have any feeling one way or another when, upon reaching the sixth grade, the Jewish kids began to draw together, walked home in clots and after school went to the YMHA; nor did I feel anything when the Italian and Irish kids began going to the Catholic Youth Organization. We went to Dunbar Center. Of course, we had our little battles with the Irish and Jewish guys; our snowball fights on the way home from school, which were continued after dinner and on into the night, degenerating into free-for-alls. We had our thing, they had theirs. Wasn't that the way it was supposed to be?

The Center, named for the black poet Paul Lawrence Dunbar, was our home away from home. It was located on South McBride Street across the street from the building that served as the Syracuse University Medical School at that time. I was a bugler in the Center's Drum and Bugle Corps. We were good enough to be asked to parade several times a year and on one of those occasions a group of white businessmen gave us a plaque. It read: *Dunbar Center Fife and Drum Corps*. For years that plaque hung on a wall of the Center and no one spoke of the error. I don't think anyone dared. That plaque always signified to me the futility of black existence in Syracuse.

After my father had gone, to be seen no more on Sunday afternoons dressed in a suit, vest, spats and cocked felt hat, set off with a brilliant tie, my mother worked every day. Sometimes I went with her to take care of the heavy work. I came to hate the back doors of white people's homes, hate the sight of my mother laboring in kitchens—eyes sparkling, however, because she had a job. At home she was the figure of authority, but in someone else's house, she might just as well have been as young as me and without any authority at all.

How unconsciously has white society undermined the relationships between blacks, even blacks in the same family.

My father was in the city, but we didn't see too much of him
following a rather stupid agreement made by the Children's
Court where we lived with my mother for one month and with
my father the next. Finally, we settled with my mother and had
to listen to her unending commentary on my father's shiftless-
ness."

But he had not been a lazy man. Work as he knew it, as he
had always known it, had run out for him. Poles and Italians
who could not even speak English were given the few jobs
available. There had been times when I went with my father
in search of a job to those public places where jobs were sometimes available. The faces of the applicants were crushed, beaten;
the men wore dirty, crumpled caps and the stink of poverty,
black and white, hung thickly in the air. I remember the embarrassed greetings, the reek of stale cigarette smoke, the spit-
toon disinfectant. My father was not lazy.

At home we went on the dole. A great amount of illogical
thinking went on in the public assistance programs. If you were
on the dole you weren't supposed to work, even if you wanted
to, or your dole would be cut down. Many people desperately
wanted to keep their self-respect and would work at anything.
Recipients cheated, but the cheating had little to do with money.
It had everything to do with self-respect. My mother lied to the
inspectors and told them she wasn't working when she was; she
told us how to lie to them. A matter of self-esteem and survival.
We survived and the wounds healed; a sleeve could be pulled
down over the scars.

I could not, of course, depend on my folks for pin money.
Sometimes I went out on Tuesday nights alone or with some
kids from the neighborhood and collected magazines, newspapers
and metals and sold them to the junk man. If I knew of an
empty house, I would strip it of its lead and brass plumbing
to sell. When there was nothing else, I climbed over the fence
of the junkyard at night, stole a bag of rags, put them into another
bag and sold them right back the next day. During the high

Jewish holidays, I'd linger in the street and wait for the orthodox Jews to call me in to light the gas on their stoves or turn the lights on for them. I became self-sufficient at a very early age.

Long, long before my father left home I had become a runner-away. If I'd had a whipping coming, a real bad one, I simply cut out. If I believed the whipping unjust, I also ran, but for a kid who had wings on his feet, I only ran so far because I didn't even know the roads out of the city and I didn't know which relative to run to. I usually spent my nights in a pine grove on the Syracuse University campus. I swiped Christmas trees from this same grove whenever it began to look like a sorry Christmas was coming on, which meant no tree and no gifts. I'd take my sled and pull it to that grove planted by the College of Forestry, select a tree, whip out a saw and cut it down. Things always looked better to my brother and sisters when I came home with the old Yule tree. We never had a Christmas without gifts, though, never. As for the whippings, whenever I returned from one of my little trips, the whipping was ten times worse than it would have been had I stayed. It took me a long time to learn that by my behavior I was threatening the black immigrant group. Had I not returned, the police would have had to be called; there would have been notoriety. Mrs. Williams can't handle her son; he's a terrible boy. There was a tremendous amount of pride in that poor, black, pathetic in some ways, society, and there were values of the highest humanistic quality. Crime was not tolerated; neither was disobedience. One way or another the kids had to measure up and those who couldn't or wouldn't placed their parents in awkward positions. And there was sympathy for the parents.

The immigrant poor are always torn between two poles: the immediate needs and the long-range satisfactions. For many the immediate needs were money, and money could only be obtained by working. Thus, parents watched their children grow and considered that at sixteen they could, according to law, drop out of school and take jobs to help support the family. On the other hand, the parents also realized that only with education could the vicious circle of poverty handed down through the generations be broken. In my family we too had to face these considerations.

I don't really know how I viewed school at that point. I was just starting to get into literature, and I liked sports. I ran track, played football, baseball and basketball. I never realized until I was an adult that I was just a bit undersized for some of these things, which was a blessing; I grew an ego more than twice my size.

At first, staving off the inevitable, I worked mornings before school in a pet shop, and afternoons when classes were over as a delivery boy. It seemed then that just about every other elevator operator in Syracuse was queer. They came at you with jowly smiles and stiff forefingers; you were forever forced to keep your back to the wall in deliveries. Later I worked the four to twelve shift in a factory that made rifle stocks, for World War II was already on. Eventually, I started to work full time and as a result I didn't graduate from high school until after I was discharged from the Navy, at the age of twenty-one.

If I had thought that discrimination affected my life before the Navy, I was overwhelmed by it after I was in. From start to finish it was segregated. The Navy was one great club for Southern bigots and I hear it still is. Strange when you consider that once the American Navy was heavily black. From Great Lakes, Illinois, to the Solomon Islands, the Marshall Islands, the Palau Islands to the Mariana Islands, Jim Crow walked the planks of the Navy, on ship and shore. I had a little trouble with it.

And I had that trouble alone. No fellow marchers, no reluctant police protection, no newsmen to report the black side of it. My letters went Stateside with only the salutation and closing surviving the scissors, and many a censor ordered me to his tent, gave me beer and explained why I shouldn't write what I was writing. But my personal war had to go on.

While I know that much of the popularity of writing by Negroes today rests on what we black writers call the "black crucifixion syndrome" (Look what you done to me, Charlie!),

I don't set down the following for any other reason than to chart, to some degree, what goes into the makeup of a black immigrant.

It was inevitable that I would get into "trouble" in the Navy, and I did. On Guam I was brigged within sight of Admiral Nimitz's headquarters for "disobeying an order"—one of those racial orders which I did not obey. My sentence was five days' bread and water and hard labor. It was a Marine brig and therefore considered to be much tougher than a Navy brig. I had to walk two miles for the half loaf of bread and pitcher of water that I got three times a day. I was lucky. Four other black sailors had to go it in chains. They had killed a white officer who deserted during an action down in New Guinea. The trusty for my barracks was a cracker who'd put his .45 at the head of a Negro and made him go down on him. Most of the people in the brig were black.

On the way home I was brigged in the fire control room of an LST for washing my socks in fresh water, like the white sailors did. As I was led into the small room, two white marines tossed in packs of cigarettes and matches. There is no place to lie down in the fire control room of an LST. It's used only for the fire control officer to press the buttons that permit the guns on the ship to fire. I did three days there, bread and water and utter darkness. The marines dry shave you when you become a guest in their brig. I was shaved often.

Once while *not* in a brig, *I* walked shaking into the mouth of a cracker's .45 and walked away without holes in me. Of course, I'd never do that now; I'd have me a .45 too.

In short, I was glad to get out of the Navy where I had started to write what I considered poetry. I don't really remember how or why I started. But I was drawing more and more within myself.

When I was discharged I returned to high school and finished the semester. I met my first wife during that time and we married the next year when I entered Syracuse University. I applied to Howard University, but they turned me down, so it was Syracuse, and like generations of black young men before me, I wondered how I would do in competition against white

students. Of course, in the public schools I had met this challenge,
and in athletic events as well. The Navy, too, had prepared
me for this. Still, to a small extent, I was apprehensive. I need
not have been.

No one can point to my breaking any scholastic records
while a student, because I certainly didn't. I was working part-
time and raising a family as well. It did seem to me that the
white students were a great deal more casual about the college
experience than I was, and this went for the ex-GI's as well.
Perhaps they understood that, being white, a college education
was merely frosting on the cake they already had. I looked at
college as though it was the handtruck with which to secure
work. My father had to take his with him when he was looking
for jobs; a man who didn't own his own handtruck was seldom
hired. College, I thought, was to be my tool. There was a big
difference between its being the frosting and the handtruck.

I was writing poetry now, not still convinced that I would become a writer, and publishing some as well. I went through the
regular and summer sessions and the summer I graduated, my
second son was born; the first had come three years before.

To be married is strain enough for there are always two urges,
one male, one female. Infinitely more so than white females,
the black female cries for security because it has been so lacking
in black marriages for external reasons. The Negro wife directly
or indirectly makes it known to her mate that she doesn't appreciate any divergence from the normal; security is the
goal and all else—until very recent times—is virtually unimportant. (Much of this has changed, at least on the surface, with
the advent of Black Awareness. Black women are just as outspoken, if not more so, than black men.) It is all right to want
to be secure, to raise children in security; it is a fair and an
utterly human desire. What is more fair, and we have now
come to that time, is for the black woman to be able to share
the dangers, with her mate, that lie outside what has been normal
in past black existence. My wife and I simply grew apart. Once
she had not the slightest desire to meet white classmates or
co-workers. I thought this was a fear of competition, and if it

was, she later overcame it and, indeed, far outstripped her white contemporaries in her career.

As for my sons, their lives will be vastly different than mine was. The world may be the same rotten place, but their approaches to it are more deliberate; they are vastly more sure of themselves than I was. They are far less intense about how and where they will fit in. Gregory graduated from Syracuse in 1969. He is now teaching and pursuing a Master's degree in education. Dennis entered Cornell in 1968 and shows considerable talent as a writer. Adam, from the second marriage, is only three. Greg has married and their mother's house seems empty with them away. There they had their own rooms; they drove their mother's car. They moved then and now, at ages twenty-two and nineteen, with a sureness I envy with all my heart, but I am grateful and proud that they are better able to handle the problems of today than I was when I had them yesterday.

But I often sense that they must prove themselves to be at least equal, if not better than me in all things, and I fear they may have built a trap for themselves. It is a human trap, but for black families where fathers traditionally have rammed the wall of failure (and I have not, just yet), the drives to outdo Dad can become all-consuming, excluding goals that are more important to them. We have discussed this and we're all aware of the risks, and of the reasons why this feeling exists at all. This, of course, was something my parents never could have done with me because the situation was never present.

To speak of failing is to recall my own as a writer; I had just about failed on my terms. My first book was written when I was thirty, and published when I was thirty-five. I came by writing accidentally; if there had been opportunities with white companies in a number of fields in which I trained, I'd have wound up in the nine to five routine, gladly. But I've found discrimination and prejudice in publishing and writing. I've not been freed from these things because I'm a writer, but, indeed, have just come in touch with an entirely new facet of race relations. I think I've grown accustomed to the fact that in America a black man, wherever he is and whatever he is, cannot escape racial considerations, an experience untrue with other immigrants. In publishing I've found just an extension of the old life, whether conscious or unconscious. The end is the same.

My family now has accepted my being a writer; it did not at first. They seemed to feel that writing was like a bad cold and soon would pass. In a family where everyone for generations had earned their bread with muscle and sweat, as I once earned mine, I felt I had become a freak. I was like a brain-damaged child born into the bosom of a hearty, muscular clan, and I felt guilty for a long time.

Young black writers will go through the same thing until we have established as a race, here in America, a tradition of books, literature, and writing. Once in this nation, it meant death for a black man to even learn to read; but we are freeing ourselves of this fear.

Like most American blacks, with the coming of what has been called the "Black revolution" I thought more and more about where my family came from. Other immigrants had roots in Europe or Asia; they could return to those homes and feel a sense of continuity. Not so with the Negro immigrant.

My father's family was a mess. He had the sharp features and prominent nose of the New York State Indians. There was an Uncle Bernie in the family, as white as this page, with blue eyes. A couple of cousins have freckles and, in the correct sunlight, red hair. Still, my father's name was John Henry and some part of the South must have touched one of his ancestors at one time.

Ola, my mother's name, always struck me as odd, and Mississippi was a great state in numbers of slaves. It happened then that I went to Africa twice and in Nigeria found my mother's name. It has two meanings: in the Eastern Region, Biafra, the land of the Ibo who make up the dominant tribe, it means "courageous one" and "keeper of the beautiful house." In the Western Region where the Yoruba live it means "he who wants to be chief." All three fit very well.

I told this to my mother and showed her slides of buses with her name on them, but she remained unimpressed. She has always been concerned with the here and now; the problem of finding roots was an intellectual one for which she had little time in her life. She only knew that her parents had given her the name; she did not recall any grandparents or great aunts having it, and yet through the curious routes of the mind she was given it, an African name.

Because Negroes were excluded from American society, many of us turned with a vengeance to Africa and African "culture" with the coming of the "Revolution" in the late fifties and early sixties. We didn't seem to feel or notice that the independence sweeping Africa was at best tenuous, filled with economic considerations that were still very much tied to Europe; nor did we pay attention to the sudden rising of the "black elite" on that continent who were just as officious and cruel and greedy as the Europeans had been. We were so eager for a small sign of black self-assertion in this great white-dominated world that we accepted African independence without reservation.

I had met a number of African students and they always seemed to me somewhat distant; and I had worked for a time with an organization concerned with the politics of the African countries. Like many organizations with like interests in this country, we were always backing the wrong man to become premier. So it happened that I became one of the few, very few American Negroes, compared to the black population in the United States, to visit Africa, and I went twice, in 1964 and in 1965.

I met American blacks who had fled the United States and its segregated social systems who were anxious to return to New York, Chicago, Detroit—wherever they came from, for they had discovered that Africa, after all, was not a place of refuge for them. Many African communities in the western part of the continent set aside a small portion of their villages for people who did not have family or tribal ties; in Nigeria this part of the village is called the Sabongari and a man may live in it all his life and not ever really belong to the community. The American blacks did not live in these areas, but they were just as effectively cut off. As a result, American blacks and whites in Africa tended to be closer there than at home. Single Negro women from the States tended to fare better; these usually were with the foreign service or the Peace Corps.

One of the saddest cases involved a young Negro man who had worked at the U.S. satellite tracking center in Kano, Nigeria. He resigned from what obviously was a challenging and lucrative position as an engineer to help the Nigerians; he planned to teach electrical engineering. The Nigerians did not accept his offer and he had to move into the Sabongari, where he did odd jobs in order to survive. I hear that he finally left the north and went down to Lagos to sell American-bred chickens in a super-market.

I traveled through ten countries trying to see reflections of my family, but what was most obvious was that the white man had done as effective a job on the Africans in his own land as he had done with blacks in America, for everywhere those Africans who could, appeared to be living by or trying to live by the standards of the European. In the Congo and in Nigeria many of the young women wore wigs; I even saw a couple of young men with the processed hair one used to see occasionally on young "hip" Negroes here.

Much of this piece has been given over to reviewing the past, but a black immigrant must also look to the future. It is a future in which all the other immigrant groups have been absorbed into the American system; so absorbed in fact that Afro-Americans stand alone as an outgroup, with those who came along after him barring his entrance to the supermarket of the nation.

I see this as a most dangerous time for the black immigrant. After eight generations his patience has run out. What nonsense is it that he cannot have as much as those who have been here but one generation and contributed far, far less? It is dangerous because the black man can no longer be turned away with faulty education, the dregs of a technological system already outmoded, and the clichés of the past. But the system is not now geared to even care more than adequately for the white population, which in any case regards what it has as being too much for the black. The clash appears to be inevitable, which is fitting because the system was established on nearly free black labor in the first place.

Blacks held in slavery, in fact, could be said, as Ralph Ellison has said, to have subsidized immigration. They were the backbone of an agricultural society, provided the wealth therefrom to kick off the industrial revolutions, which in turn required more labor, cheap, of course, from Europe.

The most unlikely white coalitions have been formed; white immigrant neighborhoods have spawned the likes of Daley of Chicago, Louise Day Hicks of Boston, and Spiro Agnew of Maryland.

The one thing that can deflect the disaster is the back-to-the-ghetto movement by educated blacks who are taking the time to help train Negroes who haven't had their opportunities. And what we say at the conclusion of meetings or seminars with the man in the street is that when we do come out, we're coming out bad. That means with all the skills, education and tools this society demands—plus whatever else is necessary to secure a place and function in it as a black human being.

In America the black immigrant looks around the world and sees that it is the nonwhites who have the poorest educations, and he asks, "Is that an accident?" He sees that it is the nonwhites who are always starving, and he asks, "Is that an accident?" He sees that it is the nonwhites who have the highest death rates and he asks, "Is that an accident?" More and more by circumstances, by awareness, he is being drawn outside his nation to other nonwhites because he is weary of the global "accidents." He is coming to know that his salvation lies with these liaisons because white America has demonstrated time and again that it doesn't mean what it says.

The black immigrant has settled, I think, into a pattern of cynicism out of which he has begun desperately to cope with his problems. He can't count on anyone else. Not anymore. I share this view; in fact, I help to promulgate it.

In that respect my views and the views of many children of

other immigrants are the same. The lid has been lifted off the can; America, man, do you stink.

But in my time I've also been a garbage man and as such I handled the stinking cans, turned them up and emptied them, banged their edges on curbstones until the last white maggot fell out to cook on the hot asphalt roadway. And sometimes with lye and brush and steel wool and boiling hot water, I scrubbed those garbage cans until they glistened, could never stink again as before, and maybe, never stink at all.

GRENADA—
THEIR COUNTRY TOO

EARLY *in 1971 my wife and I were contemplating an escape
from work and the rotten New York weather. This would be
our first winter vacation. The cost of it might be offset by some
writing I could hustle up.*

*I wound up on the phone with the New York Times' Travel
Editor, Bill Honan, who once worked at* Newsweek. *The travel
section paid very little, and offered no kill fee whatsoever.
But once again my conceit didn't allow room for the possibility
that "Grenada" would be rejected, for we were bound for that
Caribbean island.*

*The travel section under Honan had run a couple of large
pieces on "black power" in the Caribbean. They were done by
white writers. He didn't want, therefore, any other material that
might be similar. And later, when in Grenada I wrote to him
for clippings of the "black power" articles, he warned me once
again, to steer clear of it.*

*Black power as viewed by whites and as seen by blacks has
always been two different things. Whites see it as black violence
directed against them and blacks see it as getting the white
man's hands off their throats by whatever means possible, and
violence has to be the very last consideration given the logistics.*

*The travel business is a lucrative one for hotel people, air-
lines, agents, newspapers and perhaps a hundred other businesses. Black power does not belong in the same breath with
money, and Honan's selections of the "black power" dispute in
the Caribbean were most superficial. My first draft of the
article on Grenada dealt with scenery, travel tips and the like.
But I also included some views of the Grenadians about white*

tourists and how racist many of them were. Honan didn't like
the first draft, but I agreed to do another.

We had returned from our three-week trip by now, and it
was early in April 1971 when I moved on to the second version.
As usual, with this department of the Times I was given editorial
direction:

I would begin the article stating that I went to the islands not
just for a vacation, but to look at the Caribbean as a kind of halfway house between Africa and the United States for American
blacks. I'd write about black consciousness as expressed by the
Grenadians, then deal with the racism of white tourists, giving il-
lustrations, and move on to Black Power.

I took this to mean that I was pretty well back to doing what
he'd not wanted me to do in the first place, so I did it. The
version that follows is the second draft, and that was rejected
by letter May 3 the same year. I thought many of his reasons
for rejecting the article were silly. I'll give a couple of examples.

I said in the article that Caribbean touring has always been
known for the promiscuity of many white women. Honan wondered what the evidence was for this statement. The evidence is
abundant on nearly all of the Caribbean islands. In Barbados, for
example, I've been told by the relative of a doctor practicing
there, that a new strain of gonorrhea has been introduced to the
island. He lays that introduction at the doorstep of Canadian and
American women. I also said that the U. S. Fifth Fleet keeps the
Virgin Islands a colony. He claimed there was no evidence to support this statement, either. But anyone who lives in the U. S.
Virgins knows it to be true. When the Fleet's in St. Thomas, even
the hotels switch from glass glasses to plastic ones, and the marines are proud to tell you that, in case of trouble, they can land
in force in the Virgins in a matter of five hours from wherever
they are.

Anyone who knows anything at all about the Caribbean knows
that one of its larger, although quieter aspects is the hustle
between black and white flesh, and had I given examples they
might have made Honan reject the piece even faster. They're
too numerous to remain instances; the examples have become

patterns that are accepted behavior, even with the advent of black consciousness, at least in the Islands which is why it goes on there.

Eastern Airlines, as a matter of fact, in late fall 1971, began running television commercials using a black male model, his body well greased to show the ripple of his muscles, sitting in swim trunks on a beach in the U. S. Virgin Islands. The model was handsome, his voice soothing. The camera opened on his face then pulled back slowly to find him in a languid position, Magens Bay in the background. When big business starts selling flesh all the pretense goes out the window.

The Virgin Islands are a U. S. Territory and it is patrolled by the U.S. Fifth Fleet. White people dominate the politics and business of St. Thomas, St. Croix and St. John to such an extent that the black people are virtually powerless to do anything about it, even if they could, and today they can't.

On May 5, the same day I got Honan's letter of rejection, he called me and said he'd had second thoughts about sending the article back to me. Would I discuss or redo it again? I said no.

MY FIRST TRIP to the Caribbean was almost ten years ago—two years before I made my initial trip to Africa. In 1968 I want back to St. Thomas, to the College of the Virgin Islands, to teach black literature and history to the students in the Upward Bound program. Of black writers the students knew nothing. They didn't know about Marcus Garvey, Stokely Carmichael or Roy Innis, Islanders all. Nor did they seem to care. When I began teaching the old African states and empires, I was all but denounced as a liar. In short, the black light that was shining over many parts of the world had not been permitted to shine in the U. S. Virgin Islands.

So I was surprised to read recently, and all of a sudden,

that what most white people call Black Power was spreading through the former British and French islands and to the American Virgins as well.

The news was timely, for I was due a vacation. White friends recommended Grenada, an island state that'd been cropping up in the news, the subject of "bad press" in these columns, the Toronto *Telegram* and *Look*. It was accused of being (1) primitive and (2) ready to explode with Black Power.

I was not surprised to discover that all the articles written about Grenada, a former British colony and still a member of the Commonwealth, were written by white journalists. I was sure black journalists hadn't even been invited to write about the Caribbean at all, though there are a number who not only come from the Islands, but return to them with far greater frequency than most journalists because of friends and family.

Over the years I'd become intrigued with the Carribbean as an important halfway house between black America and Africa, a place where a person desiring a return either physically or psychically to blackness can get his feet wet, so to speak; Africa is a long way off. It is expensive getting there with your family and household goods, and should you decide Africa is not the place you want to be just yet, then your expenses for returning doubles the cost of your investigation. The Caribbean is much closer, and Africa is far more pervasive there than most black people have been led to believe.

It is there, as on Grenada, in the claims of membership in the Yorubas or Ibos of Nigeria; there in boatbuilding skills, homemaking, and to some degree in farming. Rural dialects are spoken with the same lilt you hear in West Africa. Black novelist William Melvin Kelley left Paris for Jamaica almost three years ago and is still there in the Caribbean halfway house.

I suspect that he is or will be followed for there is presently an increased resentment and reluctance on the part of American blacks who have them, to spend their dollars in a foreign white nation where they can be used somewhere along the line to humiliate and oppress them. England, where immigration is publicly based on color, and where nonwhites are closely questioned at customs, is the main case in point.

Grenada is an impressive island. At its highest point it looms more than two thousand feet up out of an indigo sea; the place is vibrantly green, its forests spilling down to white beaches or stark volcanic inlets. It is at the health and customs desks at Pearls Airport that so many white tourists begin to reveal the kind of visitors they'll be, loudly protesting the necessity of having their passports and health cards examined. "They think because we're a black country," an angry Grenadian official later told me, "that they needn't be bothered by the formalities they suffer without a word in Europe or America."

The customs jams at Pearls, which tend to intensify the ill-mannered behavior of so many tourists, may soon be over. Air Grenada, a black-and-white company, will begin operations late this year or early next, flying big jets directly from American, Canadian and European ports on the lengthened runway. Work begins on that in June and the terminal will also be refurbished.

We were driven—myself, my wife, Lori, and our three-year-old, Adam—through the mountains toward St. George's, the capital. In the cool, mountain air, I smelled burning charcoal, the same odor that permeates the air around dinnertime in so many places in Africa, a lovely, comforting smell. We arrived at our cottage, exhausted, but tingling with the ride and the distant sounds of Carnival approaching its night-time phases. We were next door to several Grenadian families, nearly all with children. These were Adam's playmates for the next three weeks.

It was clear from the outset that there is a difference between the black American's version of Black Consciousness, and the Grenadian's. The black American is concerned with the overall historical view of his place in the American community, what he's contributed to it, and how little he's received in return. The Grenadian's concept of Black Consciousness seems to begin at the time when his island gained political independence from Great Britain. He speaks of his black government, of always being aware of his blackness; and he speaks proudly of what black Grenadians own and what he hopes to achieve in the future.

I asked a Grenadian friend, "What's taught in the schools about African and American blacks? Is there any attempt to draw a relationship between yourselves and other blacks in the world?"

We were sitting in his office on the colorful Carénage. A cruise ship was in and taxis and private cars were jammed bumper to bumper in the downtown streets. Ladies with plastic-filled bags of spices on trays balanced on their heads hawked their wares.

The Grenadian answered that there wasn't much being taught in the schools now, but it was on the way. Although Black Consciousness in Grenada appears to be but a thin shadow of what it is in the States, it's coming. Not so much in the dashikis or Afro-cuts, and not even so much at the moment in the new Third World Bookshop on John Street (next door to the home of Ida McCray, perhaps the only black woman glass-blower ever to come out of Brooklyn), not even in the requests of young Grenadians for books from America. Black Consciousness will grow because of the unrelenting pressure of the White Presence on the island.

"We are not jealous of the whites," a young waiter in a hotel on Grand Anse beach told me. One writer had written of hostility in the eyes of the Grenadians. "They make us wonder, think perhaps for the first time since the British left, why it is that they have the money and we don't, why they have educations, and we don't, and slowly it comes to us that this was planned of course by the British; we still use their textbooks in our schools."

Once the island of Grenada provided, during slavery, it is estimated by black Caribbean scholars, more wealth for the coffers of the British Empire than did all of British Canada.

And once many of the Caribbean islands, together with a few black Americans, provided the only effective thrust toward W. E. B. DuBois's dream of Pan-Africanism. At one point DuBois gave up on the Africans altogether. Today there are still dreams of Pan-Africanism, a link, a very powerful one in Black

Consciousness. Young men travel around the Islands, talking, seeking out other dreamers. I met one at the airport, and after a conversation with him, I could only conclude that he was about five years behind the philosophy of American blacks, but at least he was on the way.

Of course, three weeks on an island didn't make me an expert on its problems, but the problems were of interest to me and I'd been to the Caribbean before. You work harder when your lacks are obvious. Through the painter Romare Bearden, we met American blacks like Miss McCray, Jim Rudin, owner of the Yellow Poui Art Gallery (and also from Brooklyn), George and Helen Gregory from New York, who are repeaters to the island. I talked to Grenadian officials, white repeaters from the U.S. and Canada and England, and to the average Grenadian in the towns and in the countryside. And to hoteliers. Driving is also a part of the work, so you get out of the city, brave the traffic of the banana trucks that hurtle down from the northern hills on Tuesdays; you get out in front of the fire station on the Carénage at four in the afternoon and stand with the locals while the fresh fish is brought in and cut with machetes; you talk to the parents of the kids who play with your son and with the kids themselves, bribing them with ice cream and cookies.

Grenadian officials claim that tourism is the number two industry of the island, but it probably is number one. It occurred to some of them that the concerted "bad press" recently might've been designed to kill off tourism. Why? Oil has been found offshore of Trinidad. A British engineer-writer told me that the Trinidadian shelf is contiguous with Grenada's and that he knew oil people had been "snooping" around the island. If tourism collapses, oil rights could then go for a song; since the industry would be badly needed to offset the approximately twenty million dollars that tourists pour into the economy.

Collective paranoia on the part of the officials? "No. We just won't let them put anything more over on us." One man cited how Grenadians had been stung by whites taking advantage of

the ten-year tax-free incentive program. "They come down here
and start businesses. In the ninth year, they sell them. We get
stuck."

I spoke to such a man. He owns and rents his yacht. I spent
a day aboard with my family and the family of Ann McGovern,
the children's book writer. Tom (not his real name) once owned
a famous restaurant on the Carénage. He believed Grenada's
"bad press" unfortunate and exaggerated. He'd found Grenadians to be "clean, nice people." Wealthy whites like himself did
everything they could to aid the government in its project and
often initiated their own. Tom owned a home in St. George's and
one on Musquetta Bay, complete with docking facilities for his
yacht in l'Ans aux Épines. He allows Grenadians to drive down
the road to this home "if they behave themselves."

I mentioned Tom, complete with his remarks to another
Grenadian official. His eyes blazed and he smacked his fist on
the table.

"Help us?" he shouted. "The man is a thief and he'd better
mend his ways. They come down here and take advantage of
our kindness. He's no better than some of the whites you find
on the beach."

A major hotel on that beach last year was the place where the
entire island could've ignited into bitter racial conflict. A young
hotel owner, a Grenadian, told me that the white guests had
started to draw up a petition for presentation to the hotel manager to prevent blacks from sharing the dance floor with them.
"Can you imagine their nerve? On this black island, trying to
force blacks out."

I asked what'd really prompted the petition. The answer was
expected. Caribbean touring has always been known for the
promiscuity of many white women who unashamedly—perhaps
because of the racial factors of the islands—seek out the island
"boys." Predictably, white males, whether they know the white
females or not, cast their mantles of "protection" over them, or
try to. In this case, Premier Eric C. Gairy was called and appeared at the hotel and promptly declared the petition out of
order. The incident faded, only to be whispered about, with,

for those who were interested, Gairy's intercession the high point of the story.

The white repeaters I spoke to dislike the Premier; they consider him a strong man, a Grenadian Duvalier. Members of the Opposition Grenada National Party may be disenchanted with him too, but the average Grenadian swears by Mr. Gairy because of episodes like the one at the hotel. "He stands up to the whites," a local told me proudly.

His view is echoed by others, if cautiously.

But grumbling about white tourist racism continues. It is particularly pronounced among the car-hire people. Royston Hopkins, who has such a service, told me that car rental service people are "concerned with the many attempts of the tourists to bounce our cars. I'd say about 85 per cent."

"Bouncing" means that a tourist will reluctantly pay a deposit on a car for a day or two, then call in and say he's decided to keep it for the duration of his stay and will settle up at the end of it.

"But you never hear from them," Hopkins said. "You get a call from the airport where the police've found your car. They've gone off—doctors, lawyers—all kinds of professional people, without paying.

"One day I happened to see a man driving one of my cars. He had his bags in his back seat. I asked him where he was going and he said he was just driving around. 'With bags?' I asked him. His wife was ashamed that he was trying to sneak off without paying. I put them both in the street. And that wasn't the only time, either."

Grenadian cab drivers complain that tourists often will not pay what they agreed to pay. More than one tourist has walked away from such a hassle not only paying, but with a swollen mouth as well. But with each incoming cruise ship or plane, the patterns of tourist racism are repeated. Grenadians have responded so far by crying out "Honkey!" to tourists in passing cars. There's not much more they can do. The Grenada Tourist Board watches over tourists like a benign uncle in most cases, though it deals fairly in disputes that occur between locals and visitors. And as our vacation approached its close, we learned through the cocktail hour grapevine, and from a more reliable source as well, that the Parliament had issued an "edict" to fine up to one thousand dollars anyone whose speech or actions contribute to racial discord. If true, this is an attempt by the Gairy administration to insure the well-being of tourists visiting Grenada. It remains to be seen if this protection extends to Grenadians as well.

Whatever problems Grenada has, and a member of the Opposition outlined them for me one night, they are not nearly as explosive as those on St. Thomas. Grenada doesn't have the slums you see in Charlotte Amalie, crouched among the beach hotels. Nor has Grenada had its beaches and mountaintops bought by whites and sealed off from blacks. The U. S. Virgins are a colony and the frequent presence of the U.S. 5th Fleet underlines that fact. Grenada is politically independent and whatever else its faults, its people possess the dignity of the free, and often I found them friendly to a fault.

The situation then, as I see it, is that white tourists in the main haven't yet learned to respect people who don't look, live, talk or behave like themselves. Their fears of bloody, black uprisings are their own, and they seem to be impatient for the dream to become reality.

Fortunately, Grenadians are concerned with other things, such as making their islands the most desirable vacation place in the Caribbean. Indeed, the outer islands of Petit Martinique and Carriacou, fifteen minutes away by air, four hours by boat, have yet to complete their facilities for tourists. Both are practically virginal and easily as picturesque and exciting as Grenada itself.

I liked Grenada immensely, and I believe I detected the great humanity of its people, particularly in the rural areas. The problems I examined in the three weeks there are not only the age-old problems of black and white, there muted by the island's all-encompassing beauty, but of a small, newly independent black nation to make itself viable. The process to achieve this goal has to be one of trial and error, for when the British returned home, they left only textbooks, school uniforms and accents, not much else. The Grenadians then, like so many of these island states in the "Eighth Continent," are struggling up out of a vacuum.

I met two white people who told me they'd been called "honkies." One was a repeater, and this year was the first time he'd heard it. The other was a college student, a coed. Neither seemed to be unduly upset, and although I didn't ask them why not, I sensed that they were willing through this time of trial and error to bear the name in much the same way blacks have always had to bear "nigger."

SHEPARD AND A NEGRO*

In 1970 the New York Times began a new one-page section just opposite the editorial page; it was called the "Op-Ed" page and seemed to be for the purpose of providing a platform on which citizens could express themselves on a variety of subjects.

Although one of my contributions to this page was published shortly after it was introduced, a member of the Times editorial board asked if I would do another, utilizing any theme I wished, which is the way the Op-Ed page was conceived.

On April 29, 1971, there appeared a story in the Times headlined on the inside pages, "Shepard and a Negro." Alan Shepard, the astronaut, and Samuel L. Gravely, Jr., had just been promoted to Rear Admiral. Not only was I incensed at the headline, I was really boiling over the self-praise both the Times and the Nixon Administration appeared to be heaping upon themselves. I was in the last stages of the final draft of my novel Captain Blackman, so I was well informed as to how badly this nation has always treated black servicemen and officers.

A couple of weeks later, after I'd written this piece and sent it in, I got a note from the member of the editorial board to whom I'd sent it. He thanked me for it, said it was nice and that they'd try to work it in as a short. I called him to make a correction about a week later. His secretary told me the piece was in galleys and she could make the correction, which was minor. Days later, two more promotions to flag rank were made, both black, so in a way my article required some updating, but, for some reason, I never heard from the Times again.

* "Shepard and a Negro Named Admirals," New York Times, April 29, 1971.

SAMUEL L. GRAVELY, JR., a new Rear Admiral of the United States Navy, must feel a great sense of personal achievement with his recent promotion to flag status.

But his promotion heavily underlines the fact that for nearly two hundred years the Navy has been without a single black flag officer, although black sailors have long served in the Navy and in larger proportionate numbers than they are today, and with distinction. (There were eight Congressional Medal of Honor winners from 1863 to 1898, for example.)

One of the superficial causes of the War of 1812—the impressment of American seamen—involved black sailors. When the British seamen from the *Leopard* stopped the *Chesapeake* and forcibly removed four sailors, we started to fight, not so much against impressment, but to gain Canadian land while the British and French fought each other in Europe. The black seamen were Ware, Martin and Strachan. During the same war, Commodore Perry's command in the Lakes Campaign was over twenty per cent black. A segregated naval camp was named after Perry at Great Lakes where Robert Smalls, a black naval pilot of Civil War fame, is likewise honored.

The Navy aside, the Armed Forces as a whole mirror, and have always done so, the racism so deeply woven into the fiber of American life. It is incredible that there have been, including Rear Admiral Gravely, only five black flag officers in the entire military history of the United States, or one about every forty years, less than one per generation. Only three are active, Gravely, Major General Frederick Davidson of the Army and Brigadier General David C. James of the Air Force. The other two generals were the late Benjamin O. Davis, Sr., a Brigadier, and his son, Benjamin O. Davis, Jr., a Lieutenant General of the Air Force, now retired. These statistics do not even approach being absurd tokenism; they prove racism.

For the nearly two million black servicemen throughout our history, these figures are an insult and Admiral Gravely has come much too late to be a vehicle of apology; the actions of today's black servicemen indicate this. The dues have been paid at the Battle of Rhode Island, during the Civil War from 1863 forward, during the disgraceful Spanish-American War which, had it not been for the black troops there, might have deprived America of Theodore Roosevelt (who later kicked out of the Army elements of three companies of the 25th Infantry); in World War I, when Pershing vainly pleaded with Foche to return the black Americans who fought with the French because the A.E.F. didn't want them; in World War II when Eisenhower called upon blacks to help stem the German breakthrough in the Ardennes in the winter of 1944, although he had to rescind the order, not make it a naked appeal to "Ethiopia"; in Korea at Yech'on; and in Vietnam. The dues are paid in full and with interest, and it is clear that membership in the military establishment was only an illusion, as it was elsewhere.

I congratulate Admiral Gravely, but condemn a system that takes pride in announcing his promotion as a triumph for blacks.